SOCIAL STUDIES
THROUGH
PROBLEM SOLVING

MAXINE DUNFEE / HELEN SAGL

HOLT, RINEHART AND WINSTON, INC.

SOCIAL STUDIES
THROUGH
PROBLEM SOLVING

a challenge to
elementary school teachers

Indiana University

New York · Chicago · San Francisco · Toronto · London

Preface

Teaching social studies through problem solving is not a new approach to learning in this area of the curriculum. Indeed, if any single element has remained constant in a curriculum that is always peculiarly in flux, it is the problem-solving approach to learning. Yet, for reasons that are both fundamental and incidental, it has not been widely implemented in social studies programs.

To begin with, the teaching of social studies through problem solving is a marked departure from traditional teaching in this area of the curriculum. To implement it requires change in the perspective with which goals are conceived, as well as in the means for achieving them. Change is often a slow process, however, and curriculum changes are no exception.

What is more, resources that facilitate the change-over from traditional teaching of social studies to a problem-solving approach are limited in variety and number. Why they are limited is anybody's guess. The fact remains, however, that problem solving as a way to learn has not been explored in depth by professional writers. Consequently, even those teachers disposed to incorporate the problem-solving approach into their instructional procedures have been handicapped by a dearth of enlightening information about it.

On the other hand, the need for illuminating information about problem solving has increased in recent years. For the trend in social studies instruction is clearly in the direction of more emphasis on learning how to learn—on the process of learning by inquiry, problem solving, and discovery. In short, it is increasingly apparent that today's social studies teachers must be as knowledgeable about the processes by which children

v

acquire desired learnings in social studies as they are about the content they teach.

The motivating force behind this book, therefore, is a desire to provide teachers with insights into the problems and processes of teaching social studies through problem solving. It has as its particular cornerstone the unique needs of the inexperienced teacher—his untested frame of reference for teaching social studies, his lack of operational models, and his limited repertoire of resources that facilitate learning in this area. In a word, this is a book designed to teach as well as to inform.

In it the writers have sought to clarify certain fundamental ideas about social studies: that the ideas, concepts, and generalizations making up the content of social studies are drawn from many social science disciplines; and that learnings in social studies are reinforced and enhanced by integration with other areas of the curriculum. But it is the desire to illumine the problem-solving approach in the context of the goals and purposes of social studies instruction that underlies the orientation and organization of the book.

The dialogue that introduces each chapter serves as a frame of reference for the ideas presented in the chapter that follows it. It serves, in lieu of firsthand observation, to induct the reader into the context of the chapter through a classroom situation and thus to provide him with a meaningful experience for use in interpreting what is said in the chapter. Questions for discussion of each episode appear at the end of the chapter. In addition, each dialogue serves as a unique link in a chain of episodes that collectively illustrate how a teacher and his children identify a social studies problem of significance to them and engage in experiences that yield information about it or that enhance its solution. To read these dialogues from beginning to end, in sequence, independently of the chapters to which they relate, is thus to glean some insight into the problem-solving approach in operation in a classroom.

Included in the text is a resource unit the writers have designed to illustrate important relationships that must exist among the purposes, methods, and learnings incorporated into this teaching aid. Readers who are following the suggestions at the end of each chapter for constructing a resource unit should find this example a useful reference. A selective bibliography, organized according to topics of concern to teachers of social studies, is also included in the text.

It has seemed important also to establish certain similarities among chapters, especially among those chapters that identify and explore kinds of experiences that develop social studies learnings. The purpose in doing so, of course, has been to facilitate the reader's grasp of the relationships that exist among these experiences as well as to provide an orderly approach to learning about them. Hence, the function of these experiences, the type, and the criteria for implementing them receive attention in each chapter. Readers looking for criteria for implementing experiences in social studies, for example, should thus find their task facilitated by a parallel organization among chapters.

Also, to further understandings of the ideas and concepts discussed, the book contains more than the usual number of examples. Long experience with the needs of preservice teachers has convinced the writers that ideas, to be understood, must be illustrated. And since their primary concern is that this book shall be a teachable book, they have used examples and illustrations as a means of introducing, clarifying, and reinforcing ideas to be assimilated.

To write this book, the writers have drawn on their backgrounds of broad and varied experiences, their personal experiences with elementary school children of all ages, their firsthand observations of the evolution of the problem-solving approach to learning in social studies, their long-time experience with prospective and experienced teachers of social studies, and their knowledge of research in the area of social studies. In preliminary form, the book has been read by students in classes taught by the writers. Much of it has been used as instructional material in these classes. Thus, both the inexperienced teacher's ability to grasp its subject matter and its challenge to the mature teacher have been confirmed.

To sum up, the writers have designed this book to present a particular philosophy of teaching social studies—the problem-solving approach to learning. It is designed for optimum flexibility so that it may be equally useful as a textbook or as a reference from which excerpts may be abstracted. In preparing it the writers have been cognizant of the current ferment that exists in the field of social studies and have taken account of this ferment in their treatment of the subject. In short, in this book the writers have sought to provide answers to these questions: Why is social studies taught in the elementary grades? What is taught in social studies? How is social studies taught?

M. D.

H. S.

Bloomington, Indiana
January 1966

Contents

SOCIAL STUDIES
THROUGH
PROBLEM SOLVING

1

Exploring
the Foundations
of Social Studies

The telephone in the waterworks night office jangled sharply. Mr. Ross roused slowly from his chair to answer as an excited voice shouted, "Get on your feet, Ross! Third Street looks like a river!"

Mr. Ross snapped to attention. "Water-main break, you say? Looks serious? Yes, yes, right away. Sure will knock out this end of town tomorrow. Yes, I'll get things going right away."

Mr. Ross alerted his crew quickly by phone. In a short while the extent of the damage was confirmed. The north side of town would have no water service for at least twenty-four hours. There was nothing that could be done except to give the homeowners a few hours warning. Even McKinley School would have to close for the day.

When everything was done that could be done so early in the morning, Mr. Ross called his wife to tell her the news, hoping she would have time to draw some extra water before the repair crew went to work. Mrs. Ross at once called her neighbors and advised them to save all the water they could.

In the meantime the local radio and television stations began hourly announcements of the news, giving directions for filling emergency water needs, and informing the public that McKinley School would be closed. The television studio supplemented its news with a map showing the exact area affected by the water shutoff. By school time, the word was fairly well distributed.

The Ross children decided to use the unexpected holiday to tidy up the yard to earn a little extra spending money. As they were busy raking leaves, other children passed by on their way to school. Their insistence that school would indeed open as usual—and why not?—sent the boys into the house to check with their mother. A telephone call to the schoolhouse confirmed the announcement that there would be no classes that day.

"There's nobody there except the janitor, kids," the Ross children reported. "Might as well go on home."

"Not us," replied the still-doubting classmates. "We'll find out for ourselves. You'll see who's right."

At school on the day following the emergency there were many questions and some lively discussion.

"Were we surprised when we got to school and nobody else was there!"

"You should've had your radio on. Then you'd have heard all about it."

"We saw the water-main break on TV when we tuned in to hear the news. Boy, was the water shooting out. There was a map, too, showing just where the water would be turned off."

"TV's easier to understand than radio. You can see, too."

"All we had was the newspaper. It didn't say anything about school being closed. My dad always reads the paper at breakfast, but he didn't see a word about it."

"My mom talked to Jack's mother on the phone. Mrs. Ross knew it straight from the waterworks. We knew about no school before anyone else did!"

"Yah, but my dad knows the patrolman who found Third Street full of water. His two-way radio spread the word around. He radioed the police station and they called the waterworks plenty fast."

"Some excitement, huh!"

Mrs. Johnson, the teacher in this classroom, listened with interest to her children's conversation.

"Whether they realize it or not," she thought, "the water-main break has opened up problems about communication in our community that the children can't answer without some serious investigation.

"And this, of course, is what I've hoped for—a real-life situation that will give meaning and purpose to social studies."

The essence of social studies is human relationships. The natural context of social studies is real-life situations, the commonplace happenings of everyday living. Real-life situations are embryos of understandings about the problems and goodnesses of human relationships. In miniature and in a contemporary setting, they are examples of man interacting with other men as he seeks to meet his basic needs in the environment in which he lives. They are laboratories in which to learn, at firsthand, the meaning of such social studies concepts as interaction, cooperation, and interdependence, in which to study the problems and processes man faces as he carries on his basic activities. They are, in short, concrete, realistic demonstrations of the meanings and values of human relationships.

Thus, to repeat, there is power in real-life situations for learning in social studies. They give it reality. They give it purpose. Their very nature makes them natural pragmatic approaches to learning: something about human relationships to explore, to analyze, and on which to generalize; something concrete to use in training children in the orderly process of inductive thinking; something to perceive in establishing cause-and-effect relationships; something that sheds light on human relations.

Yet, using real-life situations as a means of helping children pass progressively from concrete experiences with human relationships to more abstract ways of thinking about them will not, of itself, assure the desired learnings in social studies. Rather, the use of these situations as a springboard to learnings is but one of many considerations in the complex process of teaching social studies, a process that, paradoxically enough, is both fluid and structured.

Without question, the content and the experiences a social studies teacher selects and the procedures and materials he uses must center on the goals of social studies. Ways of stating these goals are legion. At the heart of all statements of goals in this area, however, is the basic goal of democratic citizenship, the development of responsible citizens capable of thinking rationally and creatively. Inherent in all social studies goals, also, is a degree of understanding that not only reflects knowledges about people but elicits empathic behaviors that reveal these knowledges.

What many teachers fail to realize, however, is that the achievement of these goals is an edge that cuts four ways. Social studies instruction, to be effective, must inextricably be linked to four basic concerns—the child, the society, society's educational demands, and social studies as an area of the curriculum (see Figure 1). Without recognition of these concerns, indeed, without deliberate effort to weave them into the warp and woof of his social studies instruction, no teacher can adequately develop the understandings, attitudes, skills, and behaviors children must have if they are to survive and progress in an ever-changing, shrinking world.

Fundamental to the task of teaching social studies, then, are the answers to these four questions:

1. What is the nature of today's child?
2. What is the nature of the American society?
3. What does the American society expect of children growing into its culture?
4. What is the nature of social studies as an area of the curriculum?

To shed light on the answers to these questions is thus the purpose of the discussion that follows.

Today's Child

Of paramount importance is the answer to the first question: *What is the nature of today's child?* Certainly the teacher who desires to create the democratic citizen must look first at the material he hopes to mold in this image. How does today's child act and feel and learn? What are his needs —his biological needs and his psychological needs? What are his interests and his experiential background? What are his special problems? How does the child of today differ from children of the past? And, conversely, how is he like children of all times?

The child of these times stands directly in the shadow of adulthood and designs his behavior to conform to this shadow. No longer restricted by traditions, he moves often now in a wide range of adult activities, perhaps only in the small realm of his own family or community, perhaps in a national field. Although the once restricted role of childhood that society thought essential to the young is past, he has established a new idea of individuality in the quickened life of the present. In this new light and motion his look and outlook have changed. Changed, too, is society's view

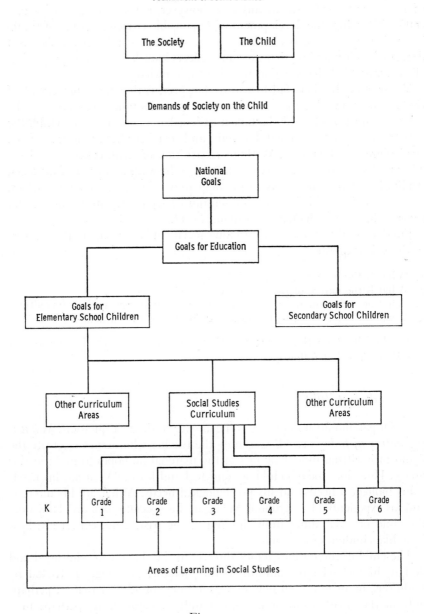

Figure 1

Decisions about social studies instruction are based on forces and goals basic to the culture.

of this new individuality. But at the same time that society has freed to-day's child from many of the hidebound traditions of the past, it has ensnared him in the problems of the present. As a result, he lives with uncertainty, a captive participant in the frequent crises that are the hallmark of modern society. He feels their pressures. He knows their demands. And he reacts to them by acquiring a kind of pseudo sophistication that is often mistaken for maturity.

Today's child is a mobile child. He is an automobile traveler. He is an airplane traveler. He may even, in time, be a space traveler. Where once he satisfied his need for activity in free play in the neighborhood, he now uses many community facilities, most of which are organized for his special benefit. His orientation into the adult world is accelerated and varied. His understandings, his attitudes, and his behaviors reflect the scientific revolution in ferment around him. He is, in short, more scientifically oriented than any child in the past. What is more, he will become more, not less, so as he grows to adulthood.

Yet, although today's child bears the stamp of modern times, he is essentially a child of all times. For his growth patterns, his basic needs, and his maturity characteristics are the characteristics of human beings throughout time. He grows and he matures in stages, with each stage marked by unique and distinct patterns of behavior. He grows in sequences, and, unless something is done to alter these sequences, they occur spontaneously. At the same time his growth pattern is unlike that of any other human being. So-called norms of behavior rarely hold true in operation. Rather, every child is his own best norm.

But as the modern child is basically a child of all times, so the unique child is a child like all other children. Every child is an organism living in a natural world seeking to meet his biological needs in appropriate ways. He is also a human being who lives in a cultural world. And unconsciously, more often than not, he alters his behavior to conform to the demands of the people with whom he desires status. Most important, every child is an individual who lives in his own private world of meanings, seeking to assimilate experiences and making his own responses to the demands that are made of him. How the child feels about himself and other people is largely determined by the successes and failures he experiences in establishing himself as a person in his own right and in building secure relationships with other human beings.

He seeks self-realization through learning. His seeing, pushing, and probing are carried on for the purpose of learning that which he considers important to his needs and goals. He determines and rules out what he will learn, functioning as a dynamic, active agent in the selection process. And he is highly individual in the way in which he interprets, chooses, and determines what he will permit to become a part of him. Moreover, it is increasingly apparent that the child not only conceptualizes his experiences in greater depth than has been generally realized, but he also seeks to understand cause-and-effect relationships that explain them. And he formulates generalizations about these cause-and-effect relationships. Although these generalizations are more often than not erroneous, they clearly indicate his readiness for this type of intellectual stimulation. Most of his questions are "how" and "why" questions, questions that indicate a desire for reasons and explanations deeper than the "what" or informational-level questions that have led to "knowledge about" the physical and social environment.

Today's child derives his information about peoples, places, and events from many sources. Whereas in the past his primary sources of information were word of mouth and reading, he now draws on a variety of communication media that are not only diverse but readily available. His scope of available information has been expanded by such developments as international television. By the simple act of turning on a switch he opens doors into the lives of people everywhere. And as a consequence his curiosities are expansive and his interests fed by the facts he sees and hears.

In other words, today's child is an overt seeker of knowledge. His early childhood years are literally years of learning by searching. Thus, by the time he enters school, he takes with him a body of information that astounds adults who have not kept pace with the phenomenon that is today's child. Most astounding, perhaps, is the ability of today's child to verbalize his information. Not only is he a collector of information; he is also a ready dispenser of information who delights in sharing his knowledge with anyone who will listen to him. Having information and using it in a variety of ways is an immensely satisfying, motivating experience.

Nor does the child confine his testing of knowledge to trying it out on adults. Much of it he tests through play acting. As he play-acts he tests his ideas for validity and extends their meaning, using his information as raw materials, classifying it and organizing it and expressing it. And in so doing he reaches conclusions that are, in effect, generalizations. In a word, not only is today's child far more capable of associating ideas, reasoning, and generalizing than has been generally thought to be true in the past, but he does so voluntarily and satisfyingly.

Today's child, therefore, has a degree of readiness for learning in social studies that teachers in the past have considered to be improbable if not impossible. He is ready to come to grips with reasons, with causes and effects. He is ready to search for answers to problems and to sweep widely in exploring the world of man. But, for all his readiness for cognitive thinking about human relationships, he is still a child who learns through concrete, firsthand experiences. Direct, nonsymbolic experiences that build meanings and vocabulary and concepts and generalizations are the natural channels that lead to higher, more abstract levels of learning.

The American Society

To prepare a child to live fully in his society is to know what that society is like. The social studies teacher's second concern, therefore, is the answer to the question: *What is the nature of the American society?* What are the basic tenets that influence the thoughts and feelings of American people? What is the composition of the American society, its ideals, its stresses, and its strains? How do the people in the American society carry on the basic activities of life? Important also is knowledge of the configuration of the American society's cultural patterns and the dynamics that influence this configuration. Obviously, it is not possible in this context to provide truly illuminating answers to these questions. Still it is important here to shed some light on them, however inadequate this light may be.

The American society is a complex, dynamic society. Change is its life-blood. Indeed, change is the constant that motivates many of the behaviors that pattern the mosaics of the American culture. Change may be slow and imperceptible or swift and mercurial. But whatever its rate, it is a force that exerts a powerful influence on American life. It is a force that keeps the wheels of American economy, government, and education operating progressively. And the compelling desire for change moves the American restlessly over the face of the land. A nomad, he moves for business reasons and for pleasure—by airplane, by train, by bus, and by automobile. Yet, although change is an active, ever-present force that affects lives of Americans, many have not learned to use it to their advantage. Nor have they learned to distinguish between desirable change and change for the sake of change only. Hence, change for many people in the American society acts to disintegrate as well as integrate human endeavors and ultimately creates misery, anxiety, and even despair.

Change has brought many facets of the American society to the threshold of complete automation. In fact, the old concept of a robot doing a man's work is now a reality. Implicit in this fact are two very real truths: the worth of the individual and the dignity of man are seriously threatened by automation; automation of man's daily activities has diminished the circle of his face-to-face relationships. Moreover, automation, born of the American's cult of efficiency, as well as his passion for the mechanical and ingenious, will burrow more—not less—deeply into his daily activities. In the decade and the quarter century that lie ahead, the electronic brain will supply information and services in minutes that in the past have required weeks and the work of many men. Thus, increasingly the American man is forced to turn to sources other than his work for the human relationships he needs to survive.

It is not easy for the American to give up his conviction that work is a primary Christian virtue. Still, with machines doing work more efficiently than he can do it, there is no choice. He can, however, decide how he will spend the time released from work. The challenge to spend it in creating not only exists but is catching fire. Witness the national upsurge of interest in music, the grass-roots dramatics, and the multiple art exhibitions that cities and even villages sponsor and that attract hundreds of people.

Because machines produce the necessities of life and do most of the routine work, Americans are free to use their minds and hands in crafts-manship and to turn their interests and talents to creative efforts. Through creating, the worth of the individual may be restored; through activities that man shares in creating, the face-to-face relationships he loses in auto-mation may be regained in new patterns of human relationships.

But automation is not the only threat to the American's individuality. Another comes from what is often regarded as characteristic American be-havior—huddling homogeneously. At the time of this country's settlement there was strength in such groupings. Without them no individual could long survive. Today there is another kind of security in them, a kind of safeguard in the knowledge that group membership cloaks the individual with a degree of protection from the elements he cannot cope with alone. The labor union's fight against job displacement is a case in point. The vast network of organizations of all types with which Americans align them-selves is another. In exchange for wearing their cloak of protection and the security of belongingness, however, groups demand conformity to the en-vironment they have created. Consequently, the individual becomes a little less free, a little less autonomous in such situations. Yet individual freedom is one of the taproots of the American society.

The American way of life is a testimonial to the fact that individual freedom is a basic tenet of the American society. Despite serious conflicts and contradictions, Americans are a people deeply committed to individual freedom. Every man is free to think what he pleases, say what he pleases, and read what he pleases, so long as what he does neither harms nor men-aces nor interferes with the rights of others. But along with America's gift of freedom to the individual is a charge of individual responsibility to his government.

Government in the American society is set up to protect all minorities against the majority, including the government itself. Justice is man's right, and every man is judged innocent in the eyes of the law until authorities prove him to be guilty. Americans think apart but act together. Thus, there is great diversity of ideas expressed among the people of America. At one extreme are the radicals; at the other, the reactionaries. Yet their rights to free expression are strongly defended and in times of crises Americans close ranks and act together for the common good.

Even so, the voice of the common man in America influences the acts of his government less and less. In fact, not only is his voice not heard; the common man finds it more and more difficult to understand his government's multiple, complex actions. Because knowledge of world affairs is exploding so rapidly, because the world scene is like a chameleon that changes in a moment's time, the common man is hard pressed to maintain a feeling of responsibility for his government's actions. To relinquish this responsibility, however, is to surrender the American heritage of self-government.

Many Americans take their privileges and freedoms for granted. Having enjoyed them in the past, they expect to continue to enjoy them in the future. This is not a truism to be acted on, however. The United States is now engaged in a struggle for survival unlike any she has experienced in the past. What its outcome will be no one can foresee. It is a struggle that has been called a battle for the minds of men. The ramifications of this struggle and their meaning are truly incomprehensible—appropriations of vast sums of money for space research, for foreign aid, and for the support of world organizations like the United Nations; the almost unbroken chain of crises to be met and resolved day in and day out; the domestic conflict over civil rights; and the problems created by revolution abroad—all touch the life of the American citizen. But, perhaps because he does not understand, he is all too often a passive bystander who watches the drama but sees no way to participate in it. Too, his primary concerns are his basic needs. Being an American, he meets these needs with the highest standard of living man has ever known, earning more money and owning more things than man anywhere. Because of his material possessions, the American man has been accused of having a materialistic approach to living. But, like men everywhere, his family is the pivot of his life. He dreams of a better life for his children than the life he has experienced. And many of his dreams will come to fruition. The barriers of language that now inhibit his understanding of men of other cultures will not exist for his children. Although his life span will probably be longer than that of his parents, his children's will be even longer. Family relations are more democratic than those of the past or than those in most other cultures. Because in many instances the American woman is employed outside her home, maintenance of the home is a cooperative enterprise. As a consequence the roles of the male and female in the American society are changing. But the exact nature of these roles is yet to be defined.

In sum, from these observations it is obvious that the American society is a society of contradiction and conflict. But it is also a society of proud heritage that only a population of rational, creative citizens can protect and perpetuate.

Educational Demands
of the American Society

Because of education's role in perpetuating a culture, the third question is perhaps the most fundamental of all questions a social studies teacher must answer. *What does the American society expect of children growing into its culture?* What should children growing into the American culture know about their heritage, the ideals and values of the society, and the nature and meaning of democracy as a way of life? What should they know about the contemporary scene? Specifically, what understandings, attitudes, behaviors, and skills should a child acquire and assimiliate in order to live compatibly and productively in the American society?

A nation moves forward on its children's feet. They etch its history. They chart its future. The imprint of these feet is the mold that shapes a nation's destiny. Education plays a vital role in determining the direction of this imprint. In the most fundamental sense, education casts the child's mind, fashions his values, and influences his motivations. Education is the matrix that sets the course a child takes as he seeks self-realization, as he strives to fulfill his dreams and his visions, and as he searches for the possibility and meaning of the full life.

In primitive societies the education of the child is achieved through generation grids, a kind of apprentice system in which the child learns, at firsthand, the knowledge, the values, and the skills he needs to survive and to perpetuate the society's way of life. In advanced industrial nations the education of the child is delegated to the school as the institution created for and charged with the task of shaping the plastic child into the image the nation envisages as desirable.

Every advanced nation teaches the three R's to all its children. There are dramatic differences in the way these three R's are taught. And there is increasing evidence that the educational systems of some nations produce more of the skilled people the nation needs than others do. But nations do not survive or progress on the quality of their children's nonpolitical education. Rather, the critical question all nations face is how well the political education of their children prepares them to meet the demands of public life in that nation.

In the American democracy the critical question is how well do schools nurture in the child the qualities of the democratic citizen. In short, do they lay the intellectual foundations for an understanding of what democracy means and what it demands of its citizens? Do they develop the attitudes and behaviors that will perpetuate the American way of life? Equally important, do the schools produce creative thinkers whose knowledge and skills will further the progress of the American democratic way of life? Are they producing human beings who not only will retain their birthright of freedom but will also acquire freedom in its more personal forms, psychological and philosophical?

Certainly totalitarian societies do not leave their children's philosophical and political education to chance. Not only do they indoctrinate children in the basic tenets of their society, but they also systematically and persistently train all students from grades one through graduate school to defend their way of life. In contrast, how many Americans can counterargue as logically and persuasively the values of the democratic way of life? But the relevance of totalitarian education for American education should not be interpreted to mean that the two systems are analogous.

Totalitarian education is regimented education in which the child is a captive recipient of a designated role in life. Opportunities to alter this role are rigidly controlled. In contrast, in a democratic society, which accords every individual the right to liberty, freedom, and the pursuit of happiness and which looks upon the individual as the essense of strength, the child's education is a fluid process. It allows for freedom of choice. It offers alternate choices. It opens up many directions to follow and many ways to go. But the ever-blowing winds of change make a course of direction difficult to follow. Old bench marks are replaced by new ones, some of which conflict with those that have served as guides in the past. Also, the American child has fewer traditional aids to follow, fewer ancestral habits, fewer preconceptions than most any other group of children in the world today. In short, the American child growing to maturity is a child largely on his own.

Out of these facts must come a deep sense of unease among those who are concerned with education of American children. Teachers must recognize the breakdown between the purposes of American education and the results really achieved. Today's facts may be tomorrow's fallacies. The axioms of the past no longer apply. Mere coverage of subject matter is no longer, if it ever was, an assurance of an educated citizenry. In fact, the whole concept of political education cries out for analysis and reinterpretation.

Objectives, content, and method are in need of imaginative effort if children are to be prepared for life in a world that changes geographically, politically, and historically, not in a decade, not in a year, but literally overnight. Clearly there are critical questions to be faced about the political education of America's children. Just as clearly there must be answers to these questions if schools are to succeed in setting the course of their children's feet toward the goals for Americans living in a changing, shrinking world.

In the past, however, teachers who have sought to develop plans of action that implement and meet the educational demands of the American society have been handicapped for lack of tangible guidelines. To be sure there are America's historic documents—the Constitution, the Bill of Rights, Abraham Lincoln's Gettysburg Address, Franklin D. Roosevelt's famous declaration of the Four Freedoms, and the *Primer for Americans,* written after World War II and widely published by the nation's newspapers each Fourth of July—all of which provide much content for a program of instruction that will nurture democratic citizenship. Yet, despite the availability of these documents, all too few teachers have translated them into operational learnings for children.

Perhaps the reason they have not done so in the past is that they have needed more clearly defined guidelines for translating the uniqueness of democracy, its meaning and values, into functional learning for children. If so, *Goals for Americans,* the 1960 report of the President's Commission on National Goals, may be an answer to this need.[1] A compilation of ideas and beliefs pertinent to democracy, *Goals for Americans* is a series of generalizations that, in effect, are goals to be achieved by Americans. Following are the key ideas and beliefs that *Goals for Americans* embraces: The Individual, Equality, The Democratic Process, Education, The Arts and Sciences, The Democratic Economy, Economic Growth, Technological Change, Agriculture, Living Conditions, Health and Welfare, Helping to Build an Open and Peaceful World, The Defense of the Free World, and Disarmament and the United Nations.

Although not intended as a mandate for educational change, *Goals for Americans* has strong implications for the education of today's children. For it opens the way to curriculum planning that focuses children's attention on the American society as it is and as it should be. Note for example, as illustrated below, that it is possible to translate certain of the goals defined in *Goals for Americans* into desirable understandings, attitudes, and behaviors appropriate for both primary and intermediate-grade social studies instruction.

GOAL 1—THE INDIVIDUAL

The status of the individual must remain our primary concern. All our institutions—political, social, and economic—must further enhance the dignity of the citizen, promote the maximum development of his capabilities, stimulate their responsible exercise, and widen the range and effectiveness of opportunities for individual choice.[2]

Primary Level
Understanding: Everyone is important to the community in some way.
Attitude: Interest in the role of each person in the community.
Behavior: [The child] treats every person with respect and consideration.

Intermediate Level
Understanding: In a democracy it is important for every individual to be free to develop his own abilities and skills.

---

[1] *Goals for Americans, The Report of the President's Commission on National Goals,* by *The American Assembly.* © 1960. Prentice-Hall, Inc., Englewood Cliffs, N.J. Excerpts reprinted by permission.
[2] *Goals for Americans,* p. 3.

Attitude: Desire to help others realize their goals.
Behavior: [The child] encourages others to develop their talents and to use them wisely.

GOAL 3—THE DEMOCRATIC PROCESS

The degree of effective liberty available to its people should be the ultimate test for any nation. Democracy is the only means so far devised by which a nation can meet this test. To preserve and perfect the democratic process in the United States is therefore a primary goal in this as in every decade. . . .[3]

Primary Level
Understanding: When people work well together, they often accomplish more than persons who work alone.
Attitude: Desire to participate in cooperative projects that have real purpose.
Behavior: [The child] works well with others in home and school activities.

Intermediate Level
Understanding: The democratic process is the best way we now know for people to live and work together.
Attitude: Desire to make democracy a reality for everyone.
Behavior: [The child] practices democracy in activities at home, at school, and in the community.

GOAL 4—EDUCATION

The development of the individual and [that of] the nation demand that education at every level and in every discipline be strengthened and its effectiveness enhanced. . . .[4]

Primary Level
Understanding: Good schools and good education help people live happy and successful lives.
Attitude: Desire to learn and to help others learn.
Behavior: [The child] works to make his school a better place in which to learn.

Intermediate Level
Understanding: Effective democracy demands that all citizens be properly educated.
Attitude: Awareness of the importance of education in democracy.
Behavior: [The child] takes advantage of his own educational opportunities.

GOAL 10—LIVING CONDITIONS

We must remedy slum conditions, reverse the process of decay in the larger cities, and relieve the necessity for low-income and minority groups to concentrate there. . . .[5]

[3] *Ibid.*, p. 4.
[4] *Ibid.*, p. 6.
[5] *Ibid.*, p. 13.

Primary Level

Understanding: Keeping the community clean and attractive is the responsibility of everyone.

Attitude: Interest in improving the appearance of his neighborhood.

Behavior: [The child] does his part in keeping his home and school neighborhood clean.

Intermediate Level

Understanding: People can improve living conditions by solving problems of civic development.

Attitude: Desire to make living conditions better for those in need.

Behavior: [The child] participates in projects to improve living conditions in the community.

GOAL 15—THE UNITED NATIONS

A key goal in the pursuit of a vigorous and effective United States foreign policy is the preservation and strengthening of the United Nations. Over the next decade, it will be under tremendous strain. However, it remains the chief instrument available for building a genuine community of nations.[6]

Primary Level

Understanding: When people know each other well, it is easier to understand and to solve problems.

Attitude: Interest in the problems of other peoples and groups.

Behavior: [The child] takes advantage of opportunities to know well persons from other countries.

Intermediate Level

Understanding: Friendly relationships among nations are important in maintaining a peaceful world.

Attitude: Awareness of the importance of each nation in the world family.

Behavior: [The child] builds lasting friendships with persons from other countries.

Further thoughtful consideration of all the goals set forth in *Goals for Americans* will reveal other equally significant understandings, attitudes, and behaviors toward which elementary school children can make progress. Using these goals as guidelines, teachers can thus plan and implement dynamic social studies programs that will help children identify problems that have meaning for them and that provide for experiences that further these goals. In short, with these goals to guide them, teachers can plan and implement a social studies program that makes a unique contribution to the preservation of all that is good in the American society and to the improvement of that which does not measure up to the American ideal.

[6] *Ibid.*, p. 20.

Social Studies
as an Area of the Curriculum

The fourth question is an obvious one. *What is the nature of social studies as an area of the curriculum?* The teacher of social studies—of any curriculum area, for that matter—must know the nature of the subject he teaches. What are its characteristic features? What is its genesis, its subject matter? How is social studies content selected? How is it structured for optimum learning? What methodology most effectively develops the understandings, attitudes, behaviors, and skills that children must have if they are to live as productive, democratic citizens?

Not only is social studies one of the newest areas of the curriculum; it is also one of the least understood, most misinterpreted areas. Since the National Education Association sanctioned the term in the early part of this century, the gamut of definitions of social studies has ranged from those concepts or experiences that are social in nature to formalized recitations focused on information in geography and history textbooks. It is not surprising, therefore, that the teaching of social studies has suffered appreciably from such a range of interpretations.

Much of the confusion that exists brings to a focus the differences between social sciences and social studies. This confusion is not without reason, however, for the social sciences and social studies are not only related generically; they also share a common body of content. The social sciences are the genesis of social studies, the parent disciplines, the soil and roots of its content, its ideas, and its generalizations. In both the social sciences and social studies the center of focus is man's relationship to man and to his environment. Both focus on man engaging in a variety of activities for the purpose of meeting his basic needs, man communicating his ideas and feelings, transporting goods and people, producing and consuming the necessities of life—food, clothing, and shelter; protecting and conserving human and natural resources; providing education and recreation; organizing and governing; and expressing esthetic and spiritual impulses. In other words, human relationships are the common denominator of the social sciences and social studies (see Figure 2).

At the same time, however, the social sciences and social studies are markedly dissimilar. The social sciences are scholarly disciplines—anthropology, economics, geography, history, political science, sociology, and social psychology. Each discipline is a body of subject matter pertaining to some particular aspect of man's activities, subject matter that is useful for its own sake. The social scientist sees his task as one of finding out more and more about a body of subject matter. His interest is concentrated on research that will deepen and extend knowledge about this subject matter.

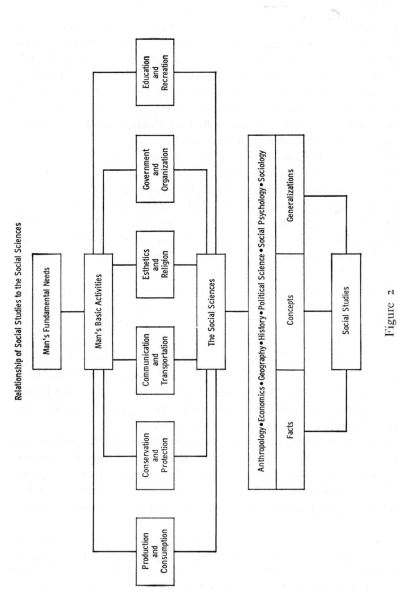

Figure 2

Social studies derives from the social sciences a body of content focused upon the activities man undertakes as he meets his fundamental needs.

His approach is an academic one with little if any concern for the concomitants of his efforts.

To be sure, some social science scholars look at their disciplines from the point of view of children's learning. The following noteworthy cases are examples: Lawrence Senesh, of Purdue University, who has introduced a program of economic education into the public school social studies curriculum;[7] a group of social scientists, composed largely of scholars from Harvard University and Massachusetts Institute of Technology, who are designing and testing experimental units for Educational Services Incoporated, an organization engaged in rebuilding school programs;[8] and a committee of geography specialists that has prepared a curriculum guide setting forth a sequence of geographic concepts to be acquired by children from kindergarten through secondary school.[9]

Whether or not such interest in teaching their disciplines to children will become widespread among social scientists only they can answer. Should such interest spread and should it seep into the grass roots of the elementary school social studies curriculum, teaching in this area will undoubtedly be affected by it. The degree of its impact and its outcomes are yet to be assessed, however. And for the time being, at least, it must be said that social scientists who concern themselves with children's learning of their disciplines are relatively few in number.

On the other hand, children's learning is the focal point of concern among those who plan and implement the social studies curriculum. In contrast to the concentrated, careful research orientation that is the hallmark of the social sciences, the central purpose of social studies is the development of personal sociocivic behavior that is compatible with the goals of democracy.[10] In social studies, knowledge about subject matter is not an ultimate goal. Rather, knowledge is the means by which the understandings, attitudes, and behaviors needed for responsible citizenship are achieved.

As noted earlier, social studies draws on the social sciences for its content. Obviously, however, much social science content is beyond the grasp of elementary school children. Moreover, its volume is too great for assimilation at any level. Determining the content of social studies is thus a matter of selection; the usefulness of the content in developing the goals of respon-

---

[7] For descriptive details of the way in which Senesh's program functions in the elementary classroom see Martin Mayer, *Where, When, and Why* (New York: Harper & Row, Publishers, 1962), pp. 78–84.

[8] Further details about the work of this group appear in publications released by Educational Services Inc., Cambridge, Mass.

[9] National Council for Geographic Education, *Curriculum Guide for Geographic Education* (Normal: Publications Center, Illinois State Normal University, 1963).

[10] Shirley H. Engle, "Decision Making: The Heart of Social Studies Instruction," in Byron C. Massialas and Andreas M. Kazamias (Eds.), *Crucial Issues in the Teaching of Social Studies* (Englewood Cliffs, N. J.: Prentice-Hall, Inc., 1964), pp. 28–34.

sible citizenship is the selective factor. Social studies, in other words, is a synthesis, a composite of important generalizations about human relationships and allied problems and institutions drawn from the social sciences, together with the facts needed to make these generalizations meaningful to children.

To be more specific, each one of the social sciences offers its own setting for ideas presented. Each of the social sciences is a discrete, distinctive body of knowledge made up of its own set of facts, concepts, and generalizations. For example, the subject matter of political science pertains to man's efforts to govern himself; economics, to his producing and consuming activities; geography, to his adapting to and using his environment. But because all social science disciplines focus on man, many concepts and generalizations, like a musical theme, recur in all the disciplines. When extracted and synthesized these form a core of generalizations that are suitable for instructional purposes—generalizations that children can comprehend and that serve the purposes of social studies.

Indeed, various suggestions regarding the generalizations to be drawn from the social sciences for use in structuring social studies programs is one of the more tangible outcomes of the current ferment in this area. Among these suggestions are Hanna's nine basic human activities and their attendant sets of generalizations.[11] The fourteen basic themes proposed by a committee of the National Council for the Social Studies are another.[12] Still another is Engle's minimal list of nine basic concepts that explain human experiences, concepts that should recur regularly in a social studies course of study.[13] And the following high-order generalizations prepared under the direction of the California State Department of Education are the result of another effort to amalgamate social science content into social studies generalizations that can be developed in elementary and secondary schools.

> 1. Man's comprehension of the present and his wisdom in planning for the future depend upon his understanding of the events of the past and of the various forces and agencies in society that influence the present.
> 2. Change is a condition of human society; societies rise and fall; value systems improve or deteriorate; the tempo of change varies with cultures and periods of history.
> 3. Through all time and in all regions of the world, man has worked to meet common basic human needs and to satisfy common human desires and aspirations.

---

[11] Paul R. Hanna and John R. Lee, "Content in the Social Studies," in John U. Michaelis (Ed.), *Social Studies in Elementary Schools* (Thirty-second Yearbook of the National Council for the Social Studies; Washington, D.C.: National Education Association, 1962), pp. 62–89.
[12] National Council for the Social Studies, Committee on Concepts and Values, *A Guide to Content in the Social Studies* (Washington, D.C.: National Education Association, 1957).
[13] Shirley H. Engle, "Thoughts in Regard to Revision," *Social Education* (April, 1963), pp. 182–184, 196.

Clearly in these generalizations, or in their counterparts, exists a partial answer, at least, to the dilemma about what to teach in social studies. Not only do they provide a structure around which to build a sequential program for acquiring desired learnings—a structure that many social studies programs now lack—but, even more important, they also hold the key to increased efficiency in learning in this area.

Few will deny that the traditional lock-step approach to learning the subject matter of social studies has been less productive than desired. Bruner and others believe that discrete facts making up a body of subject matter hold little meaning in themselves.[15] Rather, the way to desired learnings is to bring into focus the act of discovering relationships. Underlying this theory of learning through the discovery of relationships are several basic assumptions:

1. The elements of structure of a discipline are the relationships that exist among the inherent facts of the discipline. The explaining power of a discipline lies in these relationships or generalizations.
2. The way to help children gain a mastery of social studies subject matter is to help them discover and learn the relationships to be found among the facts that make up the subject matter of the discipline.
3. The way to build power in discovering relationships is through ideas, concepts, and generalizations that are introduced in simple forms that children can understand and are presented spirally again and again in successive grades with increasing depth and preciseness.
4. The way to the discovery and mastery of social studies generalizations is through a method of inquiry in which a child starts by taking part in the processes, by getting involved in them through experiences, and then arriving at conclusions or generalizations.

Consider the broadened dimension that emphasis upon inquiry gives to the goals of social studies. Consider also the change in direction it indicates for social studies instruction. Although the acquisition of knowledge continues to be an important focus of attention, it is not the only goal to be achieved. In this frame of reference how a child learns social studies subject matter is as important as what subject matter he learns. Consequently, mastery of the methods of inquiry—ability to solve problems, to think critically, and to use the scientific method—assumes paramount importance in the social studies curriculum.

Can children acquire mastery in the methods of inquiry? The children in the El Paso, Texas, schools are an answer to this question. Since 1957 these children have been engaged in learning the process of problem solving.

---

[15] Jerome Bruner, *The Process of Education* (Cambridge, Mass.: Harvard University Press, 1960); Dorothy M. Fraser, *Deciding What to Teach* (Washington, D.C.: National Education Association, 1963), pp. 225–226; Bruce R. Joyce, "Content for Elementary Social Studies," *Social Education* (February, 1964), pp. 84–87, 103; and John Cord Lagemann, "A New Way for Children to Learn," *Redbook Magazine* (February, 1964), pp. 105–110.

4. People of all races, religions, and cultures have contributed to th
cultural heritage. Modern society owes a debt to cultural inventors o
other places and times.

5. Interdependence is a constant factor in human relationships. Th
realization of self develops through contact with others. Social grouping
of all kinds develop as a means of group cooperation in meeting individua
and societal needs.

6. The culture under which an individual is reared and the socia
groups to which he belongs exert great influence on his ways of perceiving
thinking, feeling, and acting.

7. In the United States democracy is dependent on the process of free
inquiry; this process provides for defining the problem, seeking data, using
the scientific method in collecting evidence, restating the problem in terms
of its interrelationships, arriving at a principle that is applicable, and
applying the principle in the solution of the problem.

8. The basic substance of a society is rooted in its values; assessing the
nature of its values is the most persistent and important problem faced by
human beings.

9. Man must make choices based on economic knowledge, scientific
comparisons, analytic judgment, and his value system concerning how he
will use the resources of the world.

10. The work of society is carried out through organized groups; group
membership involves opportunities, responsibilities, and the development
of leadership.

11. Organized group life of all types must act in accordance with
established rules of social relationships and a system of social controls.

12. All nations of the modern world are part of a global interdependent
system of economic, social, cultural, and political life.

13. Democracy is based on such beliefs as the integrity of man, the
dignity of the individual, equality of opportunity, man's rationality, man's
morality, man's ability to govern himself and to solve his problems
co-operatively.

14. Many people believe that physically man is the product of the
same biological evolution as the rest of the animal kingdom. Man is in
many ways similar to other animals, but a most important difference exists
as a result of man's rationality and in the body of knowledge, beliefs, and
values that constitute man's culture.

15. All human beings are of one biological species within which occur
negligible variations.

16. Environment affects man's way of living, and man, in turn, modifies his environment.

17. One of the factors affecting man's mode of life is his natural
environment. Weather and climate and regional differences in land forms,
soils, drainage, and natural vegetation largely influence the relative density
of population in the various regions of the world.

18. Because man must use natural resources to survive, the distribution
and use of these resources affect where he lives on the earth's surface and
to some extent how well he lives. The level of his technology affects how
he produces, exchanges, transports, and consumes his goods.[14]

[14] *Report of the State Central Committee on Social Studies to the California State
Curriculum Commission* (Sacramento: California State Department of Education, 1961),
pp. 40–42. Reproduced by permission.

They learn to track down information quickly and efficiently, to evaluate it, and to reorganize it for reports and problem solving. They learn to think, to deduce the truth from different viewpoints, to tell what is real and what is propaganda, to organize ideas and draw conclusions. In other words, El Paso's sixty schools have discarded traditional textbook teaching for problem solving as a way of learning.[16]

The Educational Policies Commission, in its latest statement of the purposes of education, underscores the importance of developing the inquiring spirit and of helping the pupil grasp the strategies of inquiry by which man has sought to extend his knowledge and understanding of the world.[17] Theodore O. Yntema, vice-president of the Ford Motor Company, identifies abilities in the scientific method—the process of seeing and solving problems—as man's most durable skills and those that are transferable from one field of endeavor to another. He urges training in the perception of the problem and the discovery of hypotheses, pointing out that the student needs to be involved in a complex of problems so that he can develop, by practice, the needed skills.[18] Others elicit support for training in the processes of problem solving and inquiry through articles that reach a wide range of non-professional readers.[19]

Commonly the vehicle for problem solving in the elementary school is the unit of study. The "unit," as defined in the *Dictionary of Education*, is "an organization of various activities, experiences, and types of learning around a central problem, or purpose, developed cooperatively by a group of pupils under teacher leadership; involves planning, execution of plans, and evaluation of results."[20]

A single definition of the unit may be misleading, however, for the precise meaning of the term is conditioned by usage. Categorized according to use, there are two general types of units, each of which has many variations. One, the *resource unit*, is a teacher's guide to planning and action. In effect, it is a blueprint of suggestions and resources for developing a theme, problem, or topic. All *resource units*, regardless of form or structure, include the following elements: statements of objectives related to a theme, problem, or topic; an approach or initiation; content or subject matter basic to the area of study; direct and related experiences; organizing and sum-

[16] Ruth Dunbar, "How El Paso Teaches Its Children to Think," *Chicago Sun-Times* (March 9, 1962), p. 20.
[17] Educational Policies Commission, The Central Policies Commission, *The Central Purpose of American Education* (Washington, D.C.: National Education Association, 1961).
[18] Theodore O. Yntema, "We Must Also Teach Reality," *Chicago Daily News Panorama* (May 2, 1964), p. 2.
[19] Lagemann, "A New Way for Children to Learn."
[20] From *Dictionary of Education*, by Carter B. Good (Ed.). Copyright © 1959. McGraw-Hill, Inc. Used by permission. P. 587.

marizing experiences; evaluation of learnings; and a collection of instructional resources.

A second type of unit is the *teaching unit*, a term used to describe the development of a unit of work in the classroom. Also referred to as the unit in action, the *teaching unit* focuses on implementation, on the learning activities and processes that take place as the unit develops. In the *teaching unit*, the areas of learning and the sequence in which they are presented may or may not be prescribed. Always, however, the needs, the maturity level, and the background experiences of a particular group of children set the boundaries of the *teaching unit* and determine its direction.

Yet, despite the preciseness of its meanings—or perhaps because of it—there are many misconceptions, even stereotypes, about the unit concept. To avoid confusion, therefore, and to emphasize the dynamic, flexible nature of the problems approach to learning in social studies, the term *area of learning*, rather than *unit*, is used throughout this book.

The area of learning is born of problems. They are its reason for being, the core around which it unfolds. Ideally the roots of an area of learning are real-life situations in which a teacher perceives opportunities to realize social studies goals and in which children sense problems to be solved. From these situations, an area of learning develops as a cooperative enterprise carried on for the purpose of solving problems vital to children and developing desired understandings, attitudes, behaviors, and skills.

The heart of the area of learning is cooperative planning. Acting as a catalyst, cooperative planning keeps the area of learning moving in the desired direction. It controls the pace of experiences; it directs them into channels of fruitful learning. Cooperative planning also binds and unifies the evolving experiences, threading them together and relating them. Most important, cooperative planning acts as a check and balance that inhibits teacher dominance of the learning experiences. Cooperative planning, in a word, keeps the area of learning democratic, flexible, and dynamic.

The beginning of an area of learning is an initiation that sensitizes children to an awareness of problems and sharpens their need to solve them. To solve these problems, children engage in a series of transitional experiences progressing toward their solution in an orderly yet flexible manner, accumulating information, making choices and decisions, and evaluating the results of their efforts.

Working at their individual maturity levels, children engage in a variety of direct experiences to find information that sheds light on their problems. They utilize a wide range of audio-visual materials in their search for information, draw on the community for firsthand knowledge, construct and process materials to give ideas structure and form, read widely to illumine ideas and to discover new knowledges, and carry on discussion and group activities to further their efforts to solve problems.

Searching for solutions to their problems, children turn to other areas of the curriculum for needed skills and enrichment. To carry out their purposes, they acquire and reinforce abilities in the skill subjects—research, arithmetic, reading, writing, and spelling. And they enrich social studies learnings through the arts—through music, through literature, through dramatization, and through arts and crafts. The area of learning is thus not only a vehicle for social studies learnings; it is also an integrating experience that gives purpose and meaning to learning in other areas of the curriculum.

To organize the information they acquire in an area of learning and to summarize their knowledge, children engage in various kinds of culminating experiences. Drawing on a variety of activities designed for this purpose, they reach conclusions and formulate generalizations about the information they accumulated as the area of learning evolved and thus reap the rewards of learning by searching. In addition, through culminating experiences, children open up new vistas for learning, new experiences, and new purposes.

Evaluation in an area of learning goes on continually as the area of learning progresses toward its goals. From its early stages to its close, teacher and children engage in evaluation experiences to discover weaknesses and needs. They look critically at the results of learning activities, they analyze the results objectively, and they judge them in terms of the original goals to be achieved. Specifically, they use evaluation experiences as safeguards to assure solutions to the problems they sought to solve by engaging in the area of learning.

Thus, from its inception to its termination, the focus in an area of learning is on the problems approach. And the needs and interests of individual children are the sextant that sets the direction of its course.

How do teachers identify and select problems that are significant enough for study? In other words, how can teachers identify problems to be solved through areas of learning? The answer to this question is necessarily relative to the conditions under which teacher and children work. But the following criteria should provide direction for such selection:

1. Is the problem intellectually challenging to children? Will it stimulate critical thinking and evoke a desire to seek cause-and-effect relationships, and to discover reasons as well as information? Will it open up opportunities for formulating and testing generalizations?
2. Does the problem touch the lives of all the children? Is it within the realm of their past experiences? What is the extent of their present contact with the problem? What is the impact of the problem upon the children?
3. Does the problem center on a basic human activity? Will the problem illumine man's efforts to meet his needs through basic activities? Will it shed light on the role of basic human activities in community life?
4. Is the problem a practical one? Is there an adequate number of opportunities available in the community to assure meaningful development of the problem? Is the range of instructional resources sufficient to meet the varying abilities of children?

5. Will the problem lead to new and expanding interests among the children not only in the development of the problem itself but also in a variety of the side interests it stimulates?

Identifying and Selecting Areas of Learning in Social Studies

Critical to the problem-solving approach to learning in social studies is the design of the curriculum. A curriculum plan that specifies a number of required topics and that sets the sequence and time limits for their completion restricts problem-solving opportunities. On the other hand, an unstructured, fluid curriculum offers little direction for implementing problem solving.

A curriculum design that facilitates problem solving probably lies between these extremes. It provides a carefully structured framework within which desired goals and content are defined for each level of instruction; but is sufficiently flexible to allow teachers to develop specific areas of instruction related to the needs of children and the current scene.[21]

It should be clear, then, that the task of identifying and selecting significant areas of learning is one of decision making. It should also be clear that knowledges about children, society, and social studies facilitate this decision making. Knowledge is most useful, however, when it is structured as working principles that serve as guidelines for action. To that end then, here is such a list of principles:

1. Because children are by nature problem solvers, areas of learning should precipitate problems that stimulate inquiry and critical thinking and that lead to insights into cause-and-effect relationships.
2. When areas of learning are related to real-life situations, the transition from concrete knowledge about human relationships to abstract thinking about them is enhanced.
3. Areas of learning at all levels of maturity should hold the potential for organizing and structuring factual knowledge into significant generalizations about human relationships.
4. Since the senses operate functionally in children's learning, an area of learning should provide for a variety of sensory materials and experience.
5. Although an area of learning should provide for common learnings to be developed among all children, it should at the same time open up many channels that will lead to divergent behaviors among individual children.
6. Not only should an area of learning focus on desired understandings about various aspects of human relationships; it should also include unique oppor-

[21] For detailed treatment of the subject of problem solving as a method of learning see Alma Bingham, *Improving Children's Facility in Problem Solving* (New York: Bureau of Publications, Teachers College, Columbia University, 1958; also, Richard E. Gross, Raymond H. Muessig, and George I. Fersh (Eds.), *The Problems Approach and the Social Studies* (Washington, D.C.: National Council for the Social Studies, 1960).

tunities for developing democratic ideals and skills needed for responsible citizenship.

7. To assure a balance in the development of the major generalizations of social studies at all grade levels, areas of learning in every grade level should focus on basic social studies concerns: the American heritage; man's essential needs; the interdependence of people and nations; and empathy with other cultures, peoples, races, and religions.

QUESTIONS FOR DISCUSSION

Consider once more the real-life situation described at the beginning of this chapter.

1. Why did the teacher decide to utilize this situation in her classroom?
2. What areas of learning in social studies might grow out of such an incident?
3. What does pupil involvement in this situation suggest in terms of pupil interest?

SUGGESTIONS FOR CONSTRUCTING A RESOURCE UNIT

A resource unit is the blueprint of ideas and resources for an area of learning. The preparation of a resource unit is an experience in planning worthwhile for all teachers who desire to improve the teaching of social studies. There are many formats for such units; the appendix includes one such form. Each chapter of this text suggests steps to be taken in constructing the resource unit.

Using this chapter as background information, select a significant area of learning for a group of children. Justify your selection, using these questions as criteria.

1. Is the area of learning a natural outgrowth of a real-life situation?
2. Will it reveal significant problems to be solved?
3. Does it have potential for helping children move toward one or more of the goals referred to in this chapter?
4. What present needs and interests of children can be satisfied through this study?
5. What previous contacts have children had with this area of learning?
6. What new interests may be developed?
7. Is the area appropriate for the developmental level of the children?
8. Is the choice a practical one?

Survey instructional resources and compile an annotated bibliography related to the area of learning you have selected. Include materials for both teacher and children.

2

Initiating
an Area of Learning

DONALD: Mrs. Johnson, the water-main break was in the paper this morning.

MRS. JOHNSON: Yes, and I've been thinking what an interesting experience it would be to act out everything that happened when the water main broke. Could we do that during the social studies period this afternoon?

ANNE: You mean just make it up as we go along? Without writing it first?

ROBERT: I'd like to do that. Can I be a policeman?

DONALD: I want to be on television.

SUSAN: I'll be Mrs. Ross. I already know what to say.

MRS. JOHNSON: Perhaps other boys and girls have ideas, too. We can plan together this afternoon.

. . . .

WAYNE: We're ready for our play, Mrs. Johnson.

MRS. JOHNSON: So am I. What do we need to do first?

JACK: Decide on the parts.

PATRICIA: And arrange the furniture.

MRS. JOHNSON: Don't we need to plan a starting place and decide on what happenings we want to act out?

FRANK: Well, things started happening when the policeman found the water-main break.

ANDY: Then he called the water office on his intercom.

ANNE: And Mr. Ross telephoned some of his repairmen.

PATRICIA: He called his wife to tell her about the water.

DONALD: And she telephoned some neighbors.

SUSAN: The radio and television stations got the news, too. They told everybody what to do.

MRS. JOHNSON: That covers the events of the night. What about the next morning?

FRANK: Some people knew about it, but not everybody. Some of us didn't know that school was closed.

ANNE: The janitor had to tell them.

MRS. JOHNSON: Who are the characters? The policeman? Oh, you, Robert. And Susan wants to be Mrs. Ross. Donald, the television announcer. Who else?

. . . .

MRS. JOHNSON: The rest of us will be the audience. We'll watch closely. Perhaps we'll want to talk about the play later. Are you ready, policeman?

POLICEMAN (*drives up in cruise car. Locates the water-main break. Picks up his two-way radio*): Ross? Patrolman Stone speaking. Third Street's half under water. Better get a crew out here to Third and Jordan fast!

ROSS: That bad? Okay, I'll get action right away. (*Dials the telephone.*) Frank, this is Ross. Water-main break at Third and Jordan. Round up half a dozen men and get at it.

FRANK: Will do, boss. We're on the way.

ROSS (*dials telephone again*):   Mrs. Ross, the water's going to be cut off until sometime tomorrow. Fill up everything. Better call the neighbors.

POLICEMAN (*waits at the water-main break until the repair crew arrives*): How long will the water be shut off?

CREW MEMBER: Don't know yet. Probably until tomorrow.

POLICEMAN: Guess the radio and TV stations should have the news. (*Speaks into his two-way radio.*) Have someone there at headquarters notify WTTS and WTTV-TV that the water will be off out here until tomorrow.

TELEVISION ANNOUNCER: We'll put the news on right away. I'll mark the spot on a city map and put it on the screen.

RADIO ANNOUNCER: I'll spot-announce the break for the rest of the night.

SCHOOL SUPERINTENDENT (*hears the radio announcer report the water-main break*):   That means no school tomorrow. They'll have to announce that, too. (*Dials waterworks office.*) This is School Superintendent Marsh. I caught the radio's announcement about the water-main break at Third and Jordan. All the water in that area to be shut off? How long? Tomorrow afternoon? That means McKinley School will have to be closed. All right. Thanks. (*Dials radio station.*) School Superintendent Marsh. There'll be no school tomorrow at McKinley because of the water-main break. Will you get the word out? Fine. Thanks. (*Dials television station.*) School Superintendent Marsh speaking. McKinley School will be closed tomorrow. The water'll be shut off out there. We need to notify people. Good. That and the radio announcement ought to get everybody.

· · · · · · ·

MRS. JOHNSON: That was quite a performance; wasn't it? I've been jotting down some notes. Let's talk about your acting.

DONALD: This wasn't in the play, but I can't understand why the newspaper didn't report the break the way the radio and TV did.

SUSAN: I thought it was funny the way Mr. Ross called his wife "Mrs. Ross." Daddy doesn't talk to my mother that way.

MRS. JOHNSON: Do you remember that Mr. Ross spoke to his crew in a different way?

ROBERT: I don't know about that, but I wasn't sure how my two-way radio worked.

MRS. JOHNSON: Yes, I noticed once you talked to Mr. Ross and later you spoke directly to police headquarters. How did you manage that?

ROBERT: All I know is that it worked.

MRS. JOHNSON: You made it sound like magic, but we really ought to know how these communication systems work.

ANDY: What I want to know is why the newspaper didn't have the news. I had to walk all the way to school just because it didn't.

MRS. JOHNSON: We are getting so many questions. Let's write them on the board so that we'll have a record. Two of you asked, "Why didn't the news-papers have the news?" What are some others?

ROBERT: Mine about how the two-way radio works.

MRS. JOHNSON: And questions about putting TV and radio programs on the air.

PATRICIA: Don't forget about how the telephone system works.

SUSAN: I'm going to be a news reporter. I'd like to know what to do.

ANNE: How would people long ago have found out about the water-main break? They didn't have telephones or radios or television.

MRS. JOHNSON: Do we have enough questions for now? We can add others later as we work on these.

There is much to be said for a social studies curriculum in which pur-poses and learnings are clearly defined. Yet, paradoxically perhaps, a struc-tured curriculum creates more, not fewer, problems for the teachers who implement it. Consider, for one, the problems of assuring children's readi-ness to engage in predetermined areas of learning.

Children's interest in an area of learning cannot be left to chance. Inter-est is the propellant that activates the area of learning and starts it moving in the desired direction. Readiness for response, tenacity of purpose, incen-tives, choice of activities—all depend on it. It is a child's reason to learn, the source of his curiosity, the force that impels him to seek the answers to his questions.[1] Indeed, of all factors that influence the activation of an area of learning, none is as potent as interest. It must be present at the outset of the experience, strong and evident.

Many areas of learning generate interest by character or circumstance, but others, equally significant, do not. Reasons are both practical and psy-chological. For one thing, children's interests are so closely bound to the present that values of experiences outside this orbit are not readily appar-ent to them. For another, children's interests tend to be short-lived and frequently wane before a teacher can capitalize on them. Still another, their interests are diffuse and fluid and seldom bring into focus at the same time the same interest in a single classroom.

Thus, whenever a teacher decides to implement a desired area of learn-ing, he must face the central task of stimulating interest in the area and creating a need for it.

[1] Horace B. English and Ava Champney English, A *Comprehensive Dictionary of Psychological and Psychoanalytical Terms* (New York: David McKay Company, Inc., 1958), p. 271.

Functions
of the Initiation

Interest grows on what it feeds upon. This is a fact tested and proved. It is also a fact that interest results from a desire to obtain certain values. Stimulating interest in an area of learning and incentive to engage in it, then, is essentially a matter of regulating a classroom environment so that children attain foresight into the consequences of the learning experience, its effects and its results—in short, the personal gains to be obtained from the learning experience.[2] Certainly this principle offers teachers many possibilities for meeting the challenge of assuring children's readiness for specific areas of learning. In fact, the vista of possibility is limited only by a teacher's understanding of the principle and his ability to utilize it. Two examples of the initiation—a term that has been applied to the implementation of this principle—are a start in this direction. One, the initiation presented at the beginning of this chapter; the other, the initiation described below.

Preliminary to the study of the nation's largest cities, a fifth-grade teacher has hung a very large map of the United States on the classroom wall. For several days, small groups of children have clustered about this map, sharing their knowledge of it.

"That's where my dad was during the war," says one boy, pointing to the dot that marks San Antonio, Texas.

"We took a trip to my uncle's in Kansas last summer," says another, as he runs his finger across the map.

"There's Cincinnati. That's my favorite baseball team."

"Mine's the Twins. Look how far the team has to go to play in New York."

But today a new interest has caught the children's attention. They are crowded together at the map exclaiming excitedly, "Here's one!" "I got one." "Me, too." "They're all over the country." "How come?" "Look, Miss King. See what we've found!"

The teacher, crossing the room to join the children, remarks to herself, "It must be something especially interesting to excite them so much."

"See," the children exclaim, "we've just found out that nearly every big city in the United States is on a river or a lake or an ocean. Just a few aren't."

"Cincinnati, Pittsburgh, and Louisville are all on the Ohio River."

"Minneapolis, St. Louis, and New Orleans are on the Mississippi."

"Chicago's on Lake Michigan. San Francisco's on a bay."

"Why is that?" they ask.

[2] Herbert F. Wright, "How the Psychology of Motivation Is Related to Curriculum Development," in Arthur P. Coladarci (Ed.), *Educational Psychology: A Book of Readings* (New York: Holt, Rinehart and Winston, Inc., 1955), pp. 351–354.

A grinning boy answers, "Maybe so people can have a place to fish and sail their boats."

"Could be," someone acknowledges. "But that doesn't seem like a very good reason for the great big cities being near water."

"No, there are better reasons than that," Miss King replies. "I can help you find the answer. Is this your problem: Why are large cities located on water?

"Let's see first if we can find out why Pittsburgh, Cincinnati, and Louisville are located on the Ohio River since this is the river nearest us. A good starting place would be our geography book, wouldn't it? Can anyone suggest other ways to find the answer to the question?"

Actually the initiation does more than stimulate general interest in an area of learning. Its special functions are, first, to preserve or revive expressed interests as well as to stimulate new ones; second, to create opportunities to identify and ferret out significant problems; third, to give children an exploratory contact with facts and information about a subject that is, in effect, a preview of the area of learning; fourth, to provide a common experience for children that will unify their interests and purposes (see Figure 3).

But as is true of any formalized procedure, the initiation is subject to misinterpretation and misuse. It can become a kind of superficial activity that stirs up momentary interest without establishing a real need for the experience. It can distort a simple interest or need by extending it beyond the limits of its significance. It can camouflage a teacher-prepared unit of work as a child-centered experience. It can become so patterned that it degenerates into a stereotype that no longer fulfills its original purpose. Yet, despite these pitfalls, the planned initiation, used wisely and with integrity, can be a dynamic force in the nurture of children's interests and needs.

Ways of Initiating Areas of Learning

At stake in any initiation is a teacher's interpretation of the two basic principles that underlie it. One, already identified: All initiations are, to some degree, regulated situations. The other: All initiations involve teacher planning, pupil activity, discussion, analysis of value judgments, critical thinking, and identification of problems to be solved. Unfortunately, it is a common error to equate regulation with uniformity just as similarity is falsely identified with uniformity. They are not the same things. Regulation and similarity in themselves do not propagate uniformity. Changing needs of children, differences in areas of learning, the settings in which experiences develop—these all make for variety among initiations, not for uniformity. To initiate all areas of learning in the same way, to stereotype initiations, is to ignore this fact. The effective initiation is the unique initiation—unique in type, unique in the way it fulfills its function of stimulat-

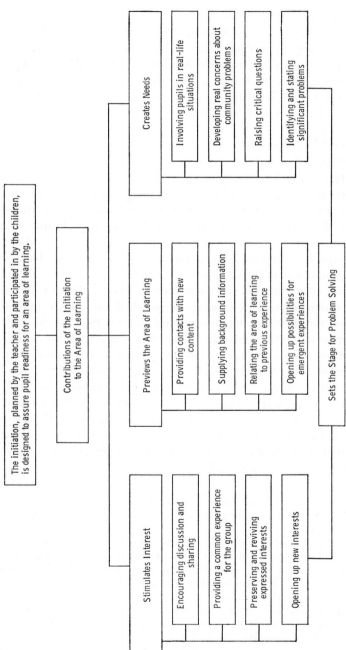

Figure 3

The initiation sets the stage for the development of the area of learning and serves as a springboard from which to launch it.

ing interest in a particular area of learning and creating a need for learning about it.

The answer, of course, lies in functional knowledge of many types of initiations. In other words, it is knowing which initiations are unique in the number and variety of problems they yield, which are especially effective in uncovering children's virgin understandings about a subject, which provide strong incentives for learning, and which are rich in elements that arouse curiosity. It is knowing, also, effective ways of achieving the optimum values of each type of initiation.

DRAMATIC PLAY

Few types of initiations are as revealing of children's needs as the *dramatic play initiation*. Dramatic play, the core of this initiation, is a spontaneous, unrehearsed enactment of a human experience in which children relive and interpret, in their own way, activities and relationships involved in these experiences. Used as a technique for initiating an area of learning, it enables children to identify themselves with a situation and describe, through words and actions, the ideas and feelings they have about the people and things in the situation.

A dramatic play initiation is a continuous experience that usually begins with a discussion of a real-life situation or episode during which children decide to enact the situation. The teacher and children then set the stage for the enactment—identify and select characters, consider ideas to be presented, arrange the environment, and obtain or improvise props. The enactment follows. Children not directly involved in it act as critical observers while the teacher notes misinterpretations and misconceptions that the enactment reveals. At its close he brings the children together to discuss their feelings about the experience and their reactions to it. He questions their interpretations and points out any misconceptions. Thus, he provokes a critical analysis of the enactment during which he helps children identify significant problems to be solved.

> A sixth-grade teacher, after considering the merits of several ways to initiate an area of learning on Russia, decided to use dramatic play to introduce it.
>
> "Certainly," he reasoned, "most sixth-grade children today have many ideas and feelings about the peoples of Russia, their government, their way of life. They have seen pictures of life in Russia; they hear about it continually; they have formed their own generalizations about it."
>
> To introduce the area of learning, the teacher created a simple story. (He might also have used a published story, an environment of displays and realia of Russia, or an incident currently in the news.) The story that he created was a narrative of an American family's travels through Russia, a travelogue rather than an adventure story, factual in content without interpretations or elaborations.
>
> During the time set aside for initiating the area of learning he read the

story. After he read it, he asked, "As I read this story, were you imagining what the family did as they went from place to place in Russia? Perhaps you even imagined yourself traveling with them. What did you see? With whom did you talk? How did you travel? Could you act out the actions and conversations that took place during the family's travels?"

With this introduction as background, the teacher and children set the stage for the enactment and carried it out. The following excerpts from some of the episodes in the enactment are truly revealing of the children's understandings and misunderstandings about Russia.

Episode One

While wandering through the streets of Moscow, the family stops to listen to a man standing on a box in a park. He is waving his arms wildly and he is shouting, "You wanta support the Russian government. Buy bonds. Bonds give us the money we need to keep ahead of the Americans who threaten us with war. Be patriotic. Buy bonds."

Episode Two

It is nearly supper time and the children are hungry. The father suggests that they stop at a market where they can buy some fruit. The mother asks, "Do you think we can find one of the fruit markets where the rich people buy their fruit? Only the best fruit is sold there. The poor people of Russia have to eat spoiled fruit that's sold at markets just for them."

Episode Three

One of the boys in the family becomes separated from the others and is picked up by the police because he is caught taking pictures. The father goes to the police station in search of his son and discovers that he has been arrested. Angrily, he shouts, "Release my son at once! What do you think you are doing arresting an American citizen? I'll get a lawyer. I'll bail my son out. Here's my money. How much?"

Following the enactment, using these clues to the children's knowledge about Russia and many others like them as guides, the teacher discussed the enactment with the children. He challenged their portrayals with these critical questions.

"Does Russia raise money for its government by selling bonds as we do in America?"

"How does an American citizen who is traveling in another country get help when he is in trouble?"

"Are there rich people with special privileges in Russia?"

The questions were not answered during the initiation. Rather, they were designed to stimulate the children's thinking about the normative judgments they revealed in their portrayals. They served to point out to the children their need for further study of the subject and to guide them in identifying questions and problems for further study.

The initiation terminated when all the questions were recorded and the teacher and children were ready to begin cooperative planning of ways to solve them.[3]

---

[3] H. L. Sagl, "Dramatic Play: A Tool of Learning in Social Studies," in John U. Michaelis (Ed.), *Social Studies in Elementary Schools* (Thirty-second Yearbook of the National Council for the Social Studies; Washington, D.C.: National Education Association, 1962), pp. 208–209.

Because play is the natural behavior of all children, the dramatic play initiation appeals to primary- and intermediate-grade children alike. Basically a dramatic play initiation is the same at both levels. However, it is often elaborate, even complicated, in the intermediate grades, whereas in the primary grades, it is short in duration and simple in form. Necessarily, the dramatic play initiation at the primary level is influenced by the size of these children's vocabulary and the variety and extensiveness of their experiences. Consequently, firsthand experiences are excellent raw material for this initiation in these grades. The morning milk lunch in a second grade, for example, was the stimulus for a dramatic play initiation that opened the way to a brief, intensive study of the problem: Why do we need dairies?

One morning a severe snow storm prevented the milkman from delivering the day's milk to school. Yet milk was delivered to many of the children's homes. Hearing the children puzzle over the reason for this, the teacher asked, "Does all of our milk come from the same place?"

One boy was certain that it did.

"No, it doesn't," another disagreed. "Our milkman drives a truck that's different from some I've seen on our street."

"Where does the milkman get the milk?"

"The dairy."

"No, the farmer first."

"Perhaps if we acted out our ideas about how we get our milk, we can straighten out our thinking about it," the teacher suggested.

"We can make a list of all the different people we think handle our milk before it gets to us and act out what each one does. That will help us decide what we need to find out about the way we get our milk."

Whether the stimulus for dramatic play initiations is a real-life situation, a story from literature, or a story that a teacher writes, depends on several factors. For one thing, the more actively children are involved in the situation to be enacted, the more ideas and feelings they have about it. From this point of view, therefore, a real-life situation is the most desirable of all types of stimuli for dramatic play initiations. But the time when a real-life situation occurs and the time when an area of learning can be developed do not always coincide. For this reason, a story from literature may be a satisfactory substitute for a real-life situation. Yardsticks to use in selecting such stories are these questions: Is the context of the story related to the area of learning to be developed? Is the plot of the story one that children can image in their expression? Does it have strong emotional appeal—much action, strong conflicts, or problem situations? Is the story a simple one, free of complex subplots or subtle characterizations?[4]

[4] Winifred Ward, *Playmaking with Children* (New York: Appleton-Century-Crofts, Inc., 1957), pp. 86–115.

Obviously, teachers may find it difficult at times to meet these criteria. Another alternative is to tailor a story to fit the purposes and needs of the area of learning. The story of the family traveling in Russia, referred to earlier, illustrates this point. A teacher-written account of a real-life situation that has touched the lives of children is another example of a tailor-made story.[5] Such a story, of which the following is one example, has the advantage of capturing some of the emotional involvement of a real-life situation while it also meets the practical problem of timing.

A warm autumn wind blew through the forest, dropping dry leaves to the ground below. Across the highway, in a nearby farmhouse, Mr. Adams and his wife lay sleeping, their young daughter curled up on a bed near a window in an adjoining room. The animals in the farmyard were quiet and still. Only a dog stirred restlessly. Suddenly he barked excitedly, startling the little girl into wakefulness.

"Skippy, what's the matter with you? Quiet down! Quiet now! Skippy, what's scared you?" The girl hunched herself nearer the window, peering into the darkness.

"Oh-o-o!" She was off the bed in a bound running to her parents' room. "Mother, Daddy, wake up! The forest is on fire!"

"What?" her father mumbled. "You're dreaming. Go back to bed."

"Daddy, no. Come. Look."

Protesting loudly, Mr. Adams fumbled through the dark to the window by his daughter's bed.

"See, there in the sky; it's getting redder."

Fully awake now, the farmer hurried to the kitchen switching on lights along the way. "Scoot out of the way, honey; I've got to use the phone."

Dropping the receiver back on its cradle, Mr. Adams turned to his daughter. "Honey, get Skip in here and then go back to bed. I'm getting dressed."

At the switchboard, the operator worked swiftly.

By daylight a heavy gray smoke hung over the burning forest. High in the sky an airplane circled the area. The pilot was speaking to a ranger in the fire tower. "It's spreading fast. We can't go it alone. Call National Guard Headquarters; then send out an alert for civilian volunteers."

Less than fifteen minutes later Jim Clark, announcer at radio station WTTS, broke in on a broadcast of Sunday morning church services.

"Radio audience, we are interrupting this program to report that the fire at the state forest is spreading fast. Volunteers are needed immediately. We repeat, volunteers are needed immediately. The fire is out of control."

As usual on warm autumn Sundays, the highway north was crowded with automobiles filled with pleasure seekers, picnickers, joy riders, and people looking for excitement. By afternoon a steady stream of automobiles lined both sides of the road. Traffic was held up more than an hour when two cars collided on a curve. No one was injured seriously, but volunteers, responding to the call for firefighters, were delayed several hours.

Toward dawn the next morning, hundreds of men, battling the fire, brought it

---

[5] George Shaftel and Fannie R. Shaftel, *Role Playing the Problem Story* (New York: The National Conference of Christians and Jews, 1952), pp. 37–38.

under control. Acres of charred trees stood smoldering and black. Little spirals of smoke floated over the devastated area.

Monday morning in homes, on street corners, in the stores, in restaurants— everywhere that people congregated—the fire was the topic of conversation, and the comments were always the same.

"How'd it start?" "A cigarette?" "Picnickers?" "The park will never be the same." "Thousands of trees gone."

Carol Adams, riding on the school bus, talked excitedly of discovering the fire. Later she described the experience to her teacher and third-grade classmates.

"Miss Moore, it was like the movies. Daddy says it's lucky there wasn't more wind with everything so dry."

A boy sitting near Carol interrupted, "My father was a volunteer. He said the same thing."

"Does anyone know what started the fire?" Miss Moore asked.

"Cigarette maybe. Who knows?" quipped a girl in the back of the room. "What are we going to do today?"

ARRANGED ENVIRONMENT

Another type of initiation, the *arranged environment initiation*, capitalizes on children's need for sensory experiences and on their desire to explore things about them. As its name implies, this initiation centers on a classroom environment that is especially designed to arouse curiosity and to stimulate interest in a specific subject or problem. Children are encouraged to explore the environment and examine materials displayed in it —look at them, feel them, ask questions, speculate, and express their ideas about them. The teacher, meanwhile, circulates among children, listens to their comments, and notes the misunderstandings and needs they reveal. The teacher and children then discuss individual reactions to the environment and raise critical questions about it. Subsequently, they identify and record significant questions for further exploration and study.

In its initial stages the arranged environment initiation is undirected and leisurely, with the children moving about the classroom much as they do when visiting a museum. The exploration of the environment, unlike the enactment in dramatic play, may or may not be a continuous experience. Quite frequently several days of intermittent explorations may be necessary to stimulate children's interests and uncover their needs. Some teachers set aside the beginning of the school day for this purpose. Others provide time for it during the day's scheduled activities. Still others encourage children to browse among the materials during their free time.

The success of the arranged environment initiation depends, in a large measure, on the character of the environment itself—its potential for arousing curiosity and stimulating interest, its presentation of important facets and aspects of the area to be developed. The effective arranged environment displays many and varied materials, but is not so saturated that it confuses rather than stimulates children. It provides information about an area of learning but does not stifle opportunities for questions about the content. Adequate space encourages free, unhurried exploration of materials. Books, maps, pictures to look at, realia, artifacts, and models are grouped to permit children to cluster about them, handle them, and explore them. Materials are especially selected and arranged to fit the developmental level of the children who will use them.

But an effective arranged environment is not necessarily an elaborate environment. On the contrary, even the simplest everyday materials, skillfully selected and attractively arranged, can challenge children's interest. Consider, for example, the materials that a third-grade teacher used to arouse interest in the problem, How do we get our bread? Among these materials were bulletin boards of pictures pertaining to bread—children eating slices of bread, bread as a part of a meal, a bakery truck, a wheatfield, a stone mill, granaries, and other similar pictures—all captioned with questions such as these: Why should we eat bread? How is bread made? A map of the states studded with pins raised the question: Can you locate the places that produce our bread? Kinds of bread—white, whole wheat, corn, and rye—and samples of grain focused attention on the question: Why is some bread dark, some white, and some yellow? A farm-implement catalogue was marked with the question: Which of these machines is used in harvesting the grains that make our bread? On the reading table were many and varied books and pamphlets.

COMMUNITY EXPERIENCE INITIATION

The *community experience initiation* serves as a springboard for areas of learning that foster interaction between a child and his community. Centered on the ever-fluctuating, constantly changing forces and events of community life, its activities and its problems, the community experience initiation is one of the most, if not the most, dynamic of all types of initiations. Conforming to children's natural interests, their interest in the "how and why" of everyday living, their ranging inquisitiveness, it is exceptionally lifelike and realistic in operation. A mobile initiation, it has the advantage of being as flexible and adaptable as the situation demands.

Often this initiation begins with a direct community experience. Children, for example, visit a local kiln to observe the manufacture of bricks, then return to their classroom stimulated to find out about markets for the bricks produced in their community and to discover what, if any, contributions the industry makes to the community. They watch the erection of a prefabricated house in the neighborhood and as a result identify for study such questions as these: Why does it take so many people to build a house? Why do some houses have sloping roofs but others do not? Why are the houses on some streets built in a straight line? Or they observe the soil erosion of a newly seeded lawn near their school or along a highway and later decide to investigate the causes and prevention of erosion.

Often, too, the stimulus for the community experience initiation is a community problem or event—a community campaign, a drive to reduce fire hazards, a movement to beautify the community, a community celebration, or a centennial. In this case a community seeks children's help with its problems and events by direct appeals to the school and through newspapers, radio, and television. If a teacher considers the problem or event significant, he discusses it with his children, guides them in thinking critically about it, and assists them in identifying aspects of the problem that are personal and tangible enough for them to solve. In other words, as in the following initiation, he helps them adapt broad, remote community problems to their interest level and to the level of their problem-solving abilities.

Periodically, a local newspaper featured news items, editorials, and news stories about stray animals that scrounge about the city menacing the health and safety of its people. When a child was bitten by an unlicensed dog, the newspaper launched a campaign to raise money to build an animal shelter. Service organizations were asked to contribute to the campaign; collection stations were set up on street corners; contributions were solicited from various church groups. Schools were urged to participate actively in the drive.

Shortly after the newspaper began its campaign to build an animal shelter, a first-grade boy planted himself in front of his teacher and exclaimed, "Guess what! Mabel's babies came last night. Three of them. One's black; one's white; and one's black and white all over."

"Mabel? Mabel who?"

"Mabel, my dog, you know! You've heard me talk about Mabel. We fixed her a nice warm place to stay. Just like Mary's dog, close to the radiator."

"I don't have a dog any more. Daddy said we couldn't keep him. He wouldn't tell us where he took him."

"Maybe he's just running around like my dog," another boy said. "He ran away. We looked and looked and couldn't find him. He didn't have his dog tag on so I guess he's lost."

"If our community had an animal shelter he might be there," the teacher suggested. "You all know about the campaign to raise money for an animal shelter; don't you?"

"But if people took good care of their dogs, we wouldn't need to spend money for an animal shelter," Mary argued.

"But they don't, Mary. If they did, there wouldn't be so many dogs running in packs, biting mailmen, and turning over garbage cans. I'm certain that many people who own pets don't fully understand how to take care of them.

"What were the first things that you did for Mabel, Johnny? Did you take her to a veterinarian regularly to be sure that she is all right? I've heard that a good veterinarian can do the same things for animals that doctors do for us. Do you think that dogs in an animal shelter get the same careful attention that you give your dog?

"Actually there must be a great deal to learn about caring for pets. Their food. Training them to be good pets. Our community wants us to take care of our pets properly. Where can we start?"

TRANSITIONAL EXPERIENCES

Commonly, as children concentrate on an area of learning, they encounter problems and questions that relate to it but do not bear directly on the area of learning under consideration. They also uncover intriguing bits of information that capture their interest but that in themselves are not pertinent to the area of learning that is the current focus of attention. When a teacher and his children pursue these emergent problems and interests for the purpose of initiating a new area of learning, they are, in effect, engaging in transitional experiences that build readiness for the next area of learning.

As is true of most experiences that are productive of learning, these transitional experiences are the result of a planned, rather obvious strategy. To begin with, a teacher is constantly on the lookout for emerging problems and interests. He records, for future reference, those that seem to be significant. He nurtures these interests and problems by encouraging individual children to search for information that will spark an interest in another area of learning. For example, note the following account of the way in which one teacher helped his children move from a study of the relationship between waterways and cities to a study of their community.

In the beginning the children seemed unaware of the fact that Lake City, their own community, was also on a waterway. Obviously it was important that they not only recognize this fact but discover the relationship between the lake and the growth of their community. So, while we continued to concentrate on large cities located on waterways, I laid a foundation for a firsthand study of the history and development of Lake City.

Among our library materials was a pamphlet which was published in 1930 to commemorate the community's fiftieth anniversary. The pamphlet was interesting, and I recommended it as enjoyable reading material.

Later, in talking about the pamphlet, a child recalled that there were pictures of early Lake City hanging on the courthouse walls. A picture of the old lighthouse that now sits far back from the shoreline on a dry, grassy slope had aroused his curiosity.

"Was it ever used as a lighthouse? Did anyone know anything about it."

Opening the way to the answer to this question I asked, "Isn't there an old man or woman in the community who remembers what Lake City was like in 1880?"

One of the boys found an old settler, and from him learned that, as a boy, he had seen the lighthouse beacon sweep through the sky, warning ships of storms and dangers. He had watched ships anchor offshore and had even been in a rowboat that carried sacks of a farmer's wheat from shore to ship. There was little doubt that the lake was important in the lives of the early settlers of our community.

Inevitably someone asked, "Why is Lake City still small? If waterways help cities grow, why didn't Lake City grow into a city like the others?"

I didn't answer the question. Instead, I said, "There is an explanation, I'm sure, but it will take time and a great deal of searching to discover it. Shortly we can all work on the problem together. Meanwhile, if anyone is interested, he might look for the answer on his own."

Not long afterward we began, in earnest, a study of the historical development of our community. I think the children were scarcely aware of the shift from one area of learning to another.

Transitional experiences are particularly effective in areas of learning that are related in content. An area of learning concerned with problems of communication, for example, may raise problems and questions about transportation. Indeed, many areas of learning mentioned in this chapter have the potential for stimulating interest in other areas of learning. The children who wanted to know why cities are located on waterways might become interested in the immigration pattern of the United States and its effect on the development of the nation. The historical development of their own community or the romance of an important river is another possible area of interest. The area of learning on conservation may lead to a study of national parks; or the children may decide they want to know more about the government's protection of natural resources. The problem about why we need dairies may develop into a study of other kinds of food. Contributing to a community animal shelter may encourage children to participate in other community experiences, such as a Junior Red Cross drive, a safety campaign on a community-wide basis, or a Christmas celebration.

INCIDENTS AS INITIATIONS

Incidents are natural, useful springboards to areas of learning. Yet there is need for caution in using them for this purpose.

Many kinds of incidents elicit immediate, intense reactions from children. They may be major catastrophes or tragedies, they may be playground skirmishes, or they may even be classroom incidents like the following:

One group of children, in their search for information about scientific expeditions to the North and South Poles, discovered that their public library offered little information on the subject. Disappointed, the children complained, "What's a library for anyway if you can't find what you need. There's no up-to-date information at all. This isn't the first time we couldn't find what we wanted. Aren't we ever going to have a good library?"

As a consequence of such an incident a teacher may conclude that his children possess the essential readiness for studying the community's information services and the problems associated with maintaining them. In reality, however, what a teacher interprets as interest may be little more than short-lived frustration or a similar emotion. In other words, teachers cannot rely on children's spontaneous reactions to incidents as wholly reliable indicators of readiness for engaging in areas of learnings. To do so not only leads to impulsive, hasty decisions but also inhibits the critical thinking activities that act as safeguards in the launching of areas of learning.

The decision to use an incident as a springboard to an area of learning should rest not on the singular qualities of incidents but on the soundness of the judgments made in implementing them. Certain evaluative judgments must be made; certain measures must be taken—the significance of the incident established, total pupil involvement assured, normative judgments analyzed, decisions weighed, and opportunities for fruitful learning identified. Thus, to repeat, using incidents to initiate areas of learning demands both judgment and caution.

OTHER WAYS TO INITIATE AREAS OF LEARNING

Each of the foregoing initiations is unique and, in a number of respects, unlike all other types of initiations. Each has its special contribution to make to the successful development of the area of learning. Together they constitute the principal ways to stimulate interest in an area of learning and to create a need for learning about it. Their ramifications are many.

It is common, for instance, to combine types of initiations for one or several of the following purposes—to prolong the overview of the area of learning, to ensure a thorough exploration of the problems to be solved, to broaden interaction among pupils, and to increase the time spent in nurturing their interest. Readiness for an area of learning on pioneer life, for example, is strengthened when a teacher collects and arranges pioneer realia and artifacts for his children to examine, discuss, and use later in a dramatic-play enactment of pioneer life. To the point, also, is the advantage of combining the incident initiation described above with a community experience in which children visit the community library to establish the value of the area of learning before identifying problems to solve.

There are instances, too, when a supplementary initiation is used to reinforce one that has elicited only moderate interest in an area of learning, or that has not produced enough significant problems to develop the experience. This approach to stimulating interest in an area of learning is based on the assumption that two initiations are better than one. Actually, however, this assumption does not always hold true: unless an area of learning is appropriate to the children's developmental level and its content related to their needs, the second initiation will also fail to stimulate interest. Thus, it is quite unrealistic to supplement one initiation with another to achieve the desired results. Rather, it may be more practical, although admittedly difficult, to give up the area of learning altogether.

Characteristics
of an Effective Initiation

As noted earlier, there is always danger of going astray in initiating an area of learning. Confronted with a variety of types of initiations from which to choose, teachers become confused and uncertain about their selections. Intent on their desired outcomes, they force children to respond in ways that reflect these outcomes, listening only to those words they want to hear. Desirous of obtaining tangible results of the initiation, they rush through it in a mechanical fashion that defeats the purpose for which the initiation is designed.

Following is a typical example of the way a teacher can go astray in initiating an area of learning.

Mrs. Wood decided that her fourth-grade boys and girls needed to acquire more information about transportation. To prepare them for the area of learning she engaged her children in the following verbal interchange:

MRS. WOOD: How did you get to school this morning, boys and girls?

JIMMY: I rode my bicycle most of the way except I got off and walked up a big hill.

MRS. WOOD: What were you doing when you rode your bicycle, Jimmy?

JIMMY: I don't know. Exercising, I guess.

MRS. WOOD: Yes, but what do we say riding a bicycle is, Jimmy? What is it a part of?

JIMMY: Well, it's fun, especially when there's a whole bunch riding together and you're going someplace you want to go.

MRS. WOOD: You aren't answering my question, Jimmy. What other ways could you have come to school? Couldn't you have ridden on a bus or in an automobile? Who knows what we call all of these things?

SALLY: Ways to travel.

MRS. WOOD: Yes, but isn't there a special name that we call them?

SUSIE: Well, trains and airplanes are ways to travel, too. I flew in an airplane once. When I looked down at the ground it looked just like the picture in the front of our geography book—squares and patches of green and brown.

MRS. WOOD: You're getting off the subject, Susie. We're talking about ways of travel. Why did you fly in an airplane?

SUSIE: Because my grandmother said I should know what it's like to fly.

MRS. WOOD: Can someone else help us out? We've buses, airplanes, trains, automobiles, and bicycles—all ways to travel. When we are traveling, what are we doing? Aren't we transporting ourselves from place to place?

BILLY: I didn't know people were transported. I thought transportation meant things shipped in trucks.

MRS. WOOD: Anything moved from place to place comes under the heading *transportation*.

SUSIE: Maybe so, but it's still traveling to me.

Mrs. Wood's sole concentration was on the term *transportation*. She manipulated her questions to elicit this term. She believed that such a verbal interchange laid the groundwork for the area of learning to follow. Actually, of course, this verbal interchange neither motivated nor created a need for engaging in an area of learning focused on transportation. Rather, it was a fruitless conversation of little point to the children.

Such errors of judgment need not occur, however, if teachers are constantly mindful of the following criteria.

First, the initiation should capture the interest of all the children in a classroom, evoking wholehearted, enthusiastic response to the subject or problem under discussion. Interest is manifest in the children's facial expressions and in their willingness to pursue the discussion for an extended period of time. It is evident in their attentiveness and in the manner in which they concentrate on the discussion. Certain facets of the subject or problem will interest some children more than others, of course. Intensity of interest may also vary. But the interest of all the children, to some degree at least, is imperative to the success of the initiation.

Second, all the children should be able to identify themselves in the situation. Since the purpose of the initiation is to enable every child to see the personal values of the experience, this point is obviously of critical importance. Every child should be able to relate some of his past experiences to the subject or problem that is the focus of the initiation. Expressions such as these should be common to all children in the classroom: "I remember I tried that and it didn't work." "Our whole family went there last summer." "Oh, I saw that on TV." "That isn't the way to do it."

Third, the initiation should stimulate discussion among all the children. The discussion should be widespread, with no single child or group of children dominating it. Every child's ideas are accepted as worthy of consideration. Interaction flourishes in an atmosphere of give-and-take as children weigh and discuss the aspects of the subject or problem. There is evidence that children are thinking together, and reticent children participate as the teacher encourages them to do so.

Fourth, the initiation should help children recognize significant problems to be solved. Here again the importance of the criterion is obvious, for the identification of significant problems is the capstone of the initiation. Do the problems bear on the understandings identified as desired goals? Will they lead children into the problem-solving process and thus to generalizing and testing generalizations? Merely listing a series of questions may fall short of meeting these criteria.

For all practical purposes, there are two kinds of questions—those that seek information and those that stimulate inquiry. The first yields facts that are essential to the progress of the area of learning but do not in themselves lead to understandings. The second are thought-provoking questions that lead to a search for reasons and knowledge of cause-and-effect relationships. Note the following informational questions: What kind of food did pioneers eat? Did all pioneers live in log cabins? What kind of games did pioneer children play? Contrast them with these thought-provoking questions: Why were the pioneers so dependent upon their environment? Why did pioneers work cooperatively in carrying on their daily activities? Clearly, only questions of the latter type will engage children in the problem-solving process and lead them to the desired understandings.

Fifth, the initiation should encourage cooperative planning of ways to solve problems. Children's natural response to problems is to express ideas for solving them. Vague, tentative, often circuitous though their ideas may be, they are nonetheless a storehouse of possibilities for developing the area of learning. The initiation, therefore, should encourage free interchange of these ideas and group reaction to them. Moreover, it should help children look at their ideas in relation to the total group effort, thinking of them as "things we can do," rather than "what I can do." It must be clearly understood, also, that it is not the function of the initiation to plan ways to solve the problems that emerge from it. Planning ways to solve problems is the next step in the development of the area of learning. It is a unique and distinct process that requires its own techniques and procedures.

Every rule has its exceptions, of course. Not all initiations can meet these criteria wholly at all times. Yet, they are the essence of successful initiations. They are the goals that a teacher must try to achieve if he expects to build a firmly grounded structure for the area of learning he wants to develop.

The Role of the Teacher
in the Initiation

What is the teacher's role in the initiation? This question has been answered many times, and in many ways, throughout this chapter. But, as often happens when information is presented in bits and pieces, the role of the teacher in the initiation may still be unclear. Thus, to put it in sharper relief, here is a descriptive summary of this role.

The role of the teacher in the initiation is clear. In the main, he plans for children rather than with children. He leads them toward desired goals, sure and knowing in the process. But, at all times, he is flexible and adaptable, ready and willing to alter his plans and change his procedures.

In planning for the initiation, he clarifies the purposes the initiation will serve, determining the answers to such questions as these: What do I want the initiation to accomplish? Are many or only a few problems the desired outcomes of the initiation? Do I want to uncover children's virgin understandings about the area of learning and expose their ideas and misconceptions about it? Or is its purpose to strengthen interests that have become weakened for lack of nurture? Is arousing intense curiosity the goal of the initiation? Is it to give children a panoramic view of the subject—an overview of the content to be developed?

With the purposes clarified, he selects an initiation he hopes will fulfill them. He notes the special requirements of the initiation and takes steps to meet them. If, for example, he decides to introduce an area of learning with a dramatic-play initiation, he selects the situation or story to be enacted. He assembles or plans for the properties to be used in the enactment. In the same way, he collects and prepares materials for an arranged environment initiation. Before beginning a community experience initiation, he surveys the situation, activity, business, or project to be visited, arranges for his children to explore it, and makes plans for their transportation. As part of his planning, he familiarizes himself with the initiation process, making certain that he knows the procedures it involves. He lists samples of questions that will stimulate discussion in the initiation. He approximates the time to be spent on the initiation and plans his daily schedule accordingly.

When his plans are complete, all materials ready, and necessary arrangements made, he begins the initiation. Using the criteria for an effective initiation as his bench marks, he keeps the initiation on its course, directing it toward the desired outcomes. He is careful to cultivate critical thinking. Guiding, challenging, he helps the children evaluate the value judgments they reveal throughout the initiation. He guides his children as they formulate their problems but he does not dominate the process; nor is he guilty of verbally manipulating their problems to fit his preconceived ideas of what the problems to be identified should be. Rather, he helps children recognize which of the questions and problems are irrelevant, superficial, or trivial. He helps them differentiate between informational questions— "knowledge of" and "knowledge about"—and thought-provoking questions that lead to problem-solving activities. He strives, in short, to help children formulate problems that are significant to them and vital to the area of learning to be developed.

QUESTIONS FOR DISCUSSION

Refer again to the dialogue at the beginning of this chapter.

1. Why did the teacher choose dramatic play as a vehicle for the initiation?
2. How did the initiation help the children identify needs and problems?
3. What did the teacher contribute to the success of the initiation experience?
4. What did the teacher do in planning for the experience?
5. What other types of initiation might the teacher have used? Which do you consider most effective? What are the reasons for your choice?

SUGGESTIONS FOR CONSTRUCTING
A RESOURCE UNIT

Consider possible types of initiations and select one appropriate to your area of learning. Use the following questions to guide you in your selection:

1. Does your initiation grow out of a real-life situation?
2. Is your initiation the one most suitable for the area of learning to be developed?
3. Will it draw upon the past experiences of the children?
4. Will it capture their interest and involve them actively?

Indicate the steps by which teacher and pupils will carry out the initiation. Note the preliminary preparation the teacher will make for the initiation. Include specific information about the procedures and materials to be used in launching the initiation and in involving children in it. Specify procedures for engaging children in a discussion about the initiation and for stimulating critical thinking. Include sample questions that the teacher might ask to facilitate the discussion.

List a variety of thought-provoking problems (in children's language) that may grow out of the initiation and that will serve as the core of the area of learning.

3

Planning Cooperatively
to Solve Problems

MRS. JOHNSON: Yesterday, boys and girls, we found that we had many questions about the water-main break and the ways in which the news reached us. In fact, we used all our chalkboard space to record them. My, what a list!

JACK: Can we add more questions? I've already thought of something else we should investigate.

MRS. JOHNSON: Of course, I'm sure all of us will think of new problems to put on our list from time to time. But, just now, let's look at the list we wrote yesterday. Do you think we're ready to find answers to our questions?

SUSAN: We'll have to find a place to start.

ANNE: There are questions about so many different things. Can't we do something about that?

DONALD: And we jump around from one thing to another and then back again. The questions are really mixed up.

JACK: Maybe some of the questions can be put together. That'll leave more room for new questions later.

MRS. JOHNSON: Let's try to organize the list, then, to make it easier to work with. I'll write the new list on this piece of newsprint, and we can check off on the old list as we decide what to do with each question. Shall we try first to put together questions that belong together?

SUSAN: We have three questions that are almost alike: How does the telephone work? How do we send telegrams? How do we communicate by letter? Couldn't we just make them into one question: How do we communicate over distance?

ANNE: That's a good idea. Let's do that whenever we can.

MRS. JOHNSON: Do you all agree? Are there other questions that can be put together?

ANDY: Those about radio, television, and newspapers could be included in one question: How do we communicate with large groups of people?

DONALD: What about these two: What inconveniences are created when news is not received? What happens when communication breaks down? Wouldn't just one of these do? They mean the same. I like the second one better.

WAYNE: And to help find out about all the different workers we could ask, "Why does communication require the work of so many people?" One question can take the place of many that way.

47

DICK: There are some questions, though, that just belong by themselves, and we ought to keep them on the list.

MRS. JOHNSON: What do you have in mind, Dick?

DICK: Well, there's that one about what kinds of communication should be used for different purposes. That really ought to be on the list after the ones about communicating over distance and communicating with large groups of people. During the water-main break, lots of people had to decide quickly which was the best way to communicate with someone else.

MRS. JOHNSON: That's a good suggestion. We'll put that question up here just after the questions Susan and Andy helped us state. Are there other questions that cannot be combined with any others, questions that are important for us to investigate?

MARTHA: How does communication help people live better?

ROBERT: And don't forget the cooperation one: How does communication help people work together?

RUTH: And don't you think we should talk about how communication helps our country?

MRS. JOHNSON: Good, let's work at this job for a while longer. Then we'll have someone read the list we've decided upon.

. . . .

MRS. JOHNSON: Are we ready now? All right, Jane. Read the list for us, please.

JANE: 1. How do we communicate over distance?
2. How do we communicate with large groups of people?
3. What kinds of communication should be used for different purposes?
4. What happens when communication breaks down?
5. Why does communication require the work of so many people?
6. How does communication help people live better?
7. How does communication help people work together?
8. How does transportation depend upon communication?
9. How can we be sure that people understand us when we communicate with them?
10. Why is communication needed in a democratic country?
11. Why was communication long ago more difficult than it is today?
12. Why was communication so important in the early days of our country?

MRS. JOHNSON: Now we have a list that will be easier for us to work with. And room for new questions later on, Jack. Now, boys and girls, what's our next job?

PATRICIA: We'll have to think of ways to find the answers.

JACK: Where to go and what to see.

ANDY: What books to use.

FRANK: I've got an idea. My dad can get us into the television station.

MRS. JOHNSON: Just a minute, children. These are all good ideas, but should we consider each of them a bit more carefully and then make a record of those we may want to use? Patricia has suggested that we're ready to talk over ways to find answers to our questions. Andy, suppose you start us out with your idea about books.

ANDY: We'll need to read many different things to get some of the information we need. Maybe our social studies books have something in them to start on. Then there are probably books in the library. Miss Hampton can help us with reference books and things. Maybe Tim's dad can get some pamphlets from the telephone office.

MRS. JOHNSON: Suppose we start our plan this way: We can read books. Now, Ruth, you had an idea about places to go.

RUTH: Sometimes you can get better answers if you see something for yourself. We could visit the television and radio stations, the telephone office, the newspaper plant, and the post office.

SUSAN: I don't think we could all go to every one of those places. Maybe we could go together to one of them, and then committees could visit the others and report back.

ANNE: We wouldn't need to go to the newspaper plant. Most of us went last year when we were planning our room newspaper. It would be better to see something different.

MRS. JOHNSON: We'll surely have to consider your idea, Susan, and remember what you have just told us, Anne. We want to make as good use of our time as possible. I'll add to the list: We can visit places.

RONNIE: I think we could do some more dramatizing. We found out that we didn't know very much about communication when we played out the water-main break. Perhaps we could dramatize some of our ideas better when we have some real information—like how to use the telephone, how to give a radio program, and like that.

BILL: I've got an idea, Mrs. Johnson, as soon as you have Ronnie's idea on the list. How about making some telegraph keys—

WAYNE: Oh, boy, and an intercom set.

DICK: Yes, let's. It's a good idea. I can bring some tools.

MRS. JOHNSON: I can tell that some of the boys are enthusiastic about your suggestion, Bill. Which of our questions will your suggestion help us answer?

BILL: They'd show how the telephone and telegraph really work, at least partly. Mr. Baker, the high school science teacher, could lend us a hand. It would be great.

MRS. JOHNSON: Very well, then, we'll put your suggestion into our record.

. . . .

MRS. JOHNSON: That finishes the list, boys and girls, at least for the time being. Of course we may find some better resources later on, and maybe we'll decide not to try some of these. But it is a fine plan of action. Take another good look at it before we leave it for today.

Cooperative planning in social studies is the process that teacher and pupils use as they make plans to solve problems significant to them. It is based on a simple democratic principle that those concerned with a problem should share in solving it. It is supported also by evidence that democratic procedures produce more constructive and cooperative relationships among children than do autocratic methods.[1]

[1] R. Lippitt, "An Experimental Study of Democratic and Authoritarian Group Atmospheres," *University of Iowa Studies in Child Welfare* 16:43–194, 1940.

A critical view of world affairs today leaves little doubt that the skills of group planning are not yet well developed among the citizens of democracy, even though democracy itself depends upon such cooperative efforts. So important is the process of teacher-pupil planning that it has the support not only of prominent educators but also of persons in public life, who know from experience how essential are the skills of cooperative work.[2] Because the need for effective techniques in planning is so apparent in everyday living in the democratic community, the opportunity to participate in planning and to develop competence in it has value for every child. The area of learning in social studies provides a setting for cooperative planning that has meaning and purpose for the children.

Cooperative Planning in the Area of Learning

Cooperative planning is essential to the effective area of learning, functioning to give continuity and meaning to children's experiences. During the discussion that grows out of the initiation experiences, cooperative planning makes it possible for children to consider ways to achieve purposes and to make a tentative plan of action. As children move into a variety of experiences to solve their problems and to answer their questions, they cooperatively plan their activities and their methods of work. Throughout the area of learning, cooperative planning facilitates children's experiencing, helping them to work together skillfully and to move ahead from one undertaking to another.

FUNCTIONS OF COOPERATIVE PLANNING

Cooperative planning begins to function very early in the area of learning as the initiation creates a need for looking ahead and for proposing ways of proceeding. Cooperative planning in the planning session which follows the initiation, through the opportunities it provides for exchange of experiences and ideas, helps children to organize their questions and to identify their purposes. It contributes to increased and extended interest in the area of study. It encourages the development of a plan of action for future endeavors. Each of these services is fundamental to the unfolding of the area of learning.[3]

First of all, cooperative planning functions in helping children crystallize

[2] Louise Parrish and Yvonne Waskin, *Teacher-Pupil Planning* (New York: Harper & Row, Publishers), 1958.

[3] For a detailed description of the process of cooperative planning, see Lucile Lindberg, *The Democratic Classroom* (New York: Bureau of Publications, Teachers College, Columbia University), 1954.

their purposes. These purposes are often stated as questions, sometimes as problems, and sometimes simply as the things boys and girls plan to do. During the initiation, children's concerns are identified, needs revealed, and questions raised. The critical deliberations of the planning session that follows give substance and organization to these evidences of need and interest. To young children the teacher may say, "Have we listed all the important questions? Have we forgotten anything? Where shall we start?" He will encourage older children to think about such concerns as these: Will our plans lead us to a well-rounded picture of our subject? Are our questions thought-provoking and worthy of our attention? Do our problems need to be organized for more efficient study? What kind of problem should we choose for a starting place? Can some questions that are less important be investigated by individuals? The teacher also asks himself a vital question—the same question that was his concern in the initiation: Will the children's plans lead to the development of understandings, attitudes, skills, and behaviors that are desirable for them? Only through such analyses can children and teacher see their objectives clearly.

All this planning together quite naturally sharpens the interests identified during the initiation. The initial planning session makes its own contribution to the building of interest essential to individual and group effort and achievement. During the initiation experience, new interests are discovered or old ones vitalized, but it is in the planning session that follows that these interests are explored and extended. New phases of the problem may draw into participation pupils who were at first somewhat disinterested, while the point of view of all participants can be broadened as they think together about how they will find out what they really want to know. Cooperative planning that grows out of the initiation plays an important part in helping the group move ahead with enthusiasm and energy.

Children who participate fully in the initiation and in the subsequent planning usually move easily into the making of a plan of action. They suggest many activities that may be valuable in accomplishing their purpose. From all these possible experiences, they must make choices and come to some agreement about next steps. Children may ask themselves, "Which of these experiences will give us the best information? Which of them can be planned and accomplished in the time we have? Which of these experiences do we all need?" As discussion continues and decisions are made, the plan of action takes form. This plan may be a step-by-step outline of tomorrow's activity or it may be wider in scope, encompassing proposals for a whole series of experiences that children and teacher think worthwhile. Although this plan of action necessarily must be tentative, its development is one of the important results of cooperative planning. Consider how cooperative planning helped these first-grade children organize problems for study, extend interest in the area, and develop a plan of action.

Interest in the work of fathers began with the appearance of Sally's policeman father at the corner stop light at dismissal time. The next day there was some discussion about Sally's father, and several children began to ask her questions and to tell about the work of their own parents. Everyone was talking at once until the teacher calmly suggested, "Let's stop a moment and do some planning. Everyone is speaking without listening, and no one is really learning very much about the work our fathers do. You've been asking some questions, too, and I've been writing them down. Listen, while I read them from my list. Are all your questions here? What shall we do with these questions?"

"Now," challenged Mrs. Roberts a few minutes later, "how will we find the answers?" At this point the children were ready, the teacher thought, to think about some of the experiences that would help them acquire needed information. Dick suggested that each child could ask his father the answers to the questions; this idea was accepted and recorded as a sensible and practical idea. Rebecca thought it would be wise, if possible, to visit some of the places where fathers work—the police station, a grocery store, the airport, and a filling station. When the teacher asked what they should do about the fathers who worked at desks in offices, it was agreed that some of those fathers could come to school to tell about their work and perhaps bring with them some of the books and papers they used. It was not long before a plan of action began to take form.

Mrs. Roberts was aware, of course, that such experiences as those proposed by the children would extend over some length of time. She was certain, too, that new social studies interests would develop along the way, foreseeing at once that visits into the community, for example, would raise many new questions and perhaps develop into whole new areas of learning. The planning session following the initiation had started children's thinking in profitable directions in an area pertinent to their own lives, an area identified in terms of questions they had chosen to explore and planned ahead in such a way that pupils could know the direction their learning would take.

OPPORTUNITIES FOR COOPERATIVE PLANNING

Children's participation in planning is not completed, however, when the initial planning session is over. On the contrary, their planning experiences are only beginning. In drawing up their plan of action the children have made some tentative plans to use a variety of resources and to participate in various experiences to find the answers to their questions. Planning for work periods, for community experiences, for the use of materials and equipment, for ways of bringing the study to a close, and for evaluation—all provide further opportunities for cooperative planning.

Planning for work periods is one such opportunity. When children decide to work in small groups in order to survey several different aspects of a problem, to use a variety of references, to carry on simultaneously a number of different activities, or to accomplish any similar purposes, careful plans for the work period must be made. Teacher and children together decide what special tasks are to be undertaken, how the work groups will be chosen, how each group will plan and carry out its work, and how each will report the results of its efforts. In the cooperative planning session children discuss needed materials and their care, work space, and timing. They will need to agree upon some behavior standards to make it possible for several groups to work together without friction or undue confusion. All these aspects of planning for work periods are considered in cooperative planning sessions.

Planning community experiences is another opportunity for cooperative effort. If the children choose to survey the neighborhood community to secure some background information about their area of learning, they must plan the journey. The teacher asks these questions: What do we need to do before we can take the trip that has been decided upon? When shall we go? Where shall we go? What shall we look for? How shall we make a record of our information? And when the pupils return, they decide how to summarize the experience, how to share information with each other, and what experiences should follow. If an adult they met during their excursion can come to school with more detailed information, his visit must be planned. Who will talk with him to tell him our problems? Who will greet and introduce him? Who will lead the discussion period? These and other questions provide excellent opportunities for teacher-pupil planning.

Planning for the use of materials needed in the area of learning is a worthwhile cooperative activity. When pupils read from a variety of books and pamphlets, they need to plan together ways of recording information and sharing it with each other. When films are available, a small group of children preview them with the teacher before deciding which ones are to be shown to the class, and all pupils participate in setting up the questions that will guide their observation and listening during the showing. Children cooperatively plan a variety of exhibits, too—rocks, foreign dolls, simple machines, petroleum products, and the like—choosing suitable locations, arrangements, and labels. Cooperative planning of bulletin boards draws pupils' attention to the quality of their display and to its message. Materials, generally, become more meaningful to children when they participate in planning for their use.

Planning to bring an area of learning to a close offers children more opportunities to plan cooperatively. As they begin to draw together the important understandings gained from their study, research, and activities, they often suggest, "This is too good to be kept all to ourselves. Let's show it to someone." If teacher and children agree, the planning session is under way, with the teacher helping children to express their ideas and to explore them critically. Pupils come to some agreement about the type of presentation, they think through the task as a whole, they plan the steps to accomplish it, and they assign and assume responsibilities. As work progresses, plans may be changed and new problems arise; these new concerns call for more planning. If there are to be guests, a whole new set of responsibilities must be undertaken. Cooperative planning again becomes appropriate and necessary.

Planning for evaluation is yet another opportunity for cooperative effort. During their activities, teacher and children often stop to survey their progress. When projects are completed or experiences brought to a close, they plan ways of evaluating their success. If the study trip is to be thought through in retrospect, the standards of behavior drawn up by the group and the questions proposed for investigation serve as guides for thoughtful evaluation. Check lists cooperatively developed help children to assess their acquisition of new knowledges and skills and to evaluate work habits. Many of the materials they use must be evaluated in terms of the purpose for which they are using them. Does this book give accurate information? Is this kind of loom the best to use to demonstrate pioneer weaving? Can hand-made lantern slides tell about our trip to the airport better than the pictures we drew? During other evaluation sessions, reports to parents about the area of learning are developed in the classroom with children listing the important understandings they have acquired, the new skills they can now use, and the most worthwhile experiences undertaken and completed. There are almost endless opportunities for children to plan cooperatively for evaluation.

It is clear that there are many opportunities for cooperative planning in the area of learning. Children and teachers plan together their large- and small-group activities, they plan for community experiences, they plan for the use of many kinds of materials, they plan ways of bringing their study to a close, and they plan for continual evaluation.

CONTRIBUTIONS TO DEVELOPMENT OF THE AREA OF LEARNING

As the preceding discussion has already implied, cooperative planning plays an essential role in the development of the area of learning. Because the area of learning is more than teacher-made assignments and teacher-directed lessons and because it involves children actively in formulating purposes and finding ways to achieve them, it requires extensive cooperative planning. In the area of learning this kind of planning leads children naturally from one experience into the next, and, as it leads them, it unifies the group in a common purpose.

As children move ahead eagerly and purposefully, cooperative planning becomes the bridge from one experience to another. The planning of one activity almost inevitably starts the thinking on another; planning today's experiences usually suggests what must be done tomorrow; planning the work of one group frequently necessitates the planning for another group; planning how to improve working together points the way to using these suggestions in the next work session. Such teacher-pupil planning moves the group ahead and greatly facilitates the development of the area of learning. Note how the transition from one experience to another is provided by cooperative planning in this class.

Mr. Gordon's intermediate-grade pupils were exploring some concerns growing out of the polio vaccine shots the children were receiving. "What is vaccine? Is it medicine? Are there vaccines for other diseases? How long have we had them? What did people do about these diseases before vaccines were discovered? Why does everybody have to take shots? We read in the paper last week about a whole group of people who came down with typhoid fever; how did that happen?"

Because the children wanted more knowledge about these questions than they could uncover by casual inquiry, they began planning ways to secure authoritative information. Following decisions to visit the school nurse and local doctors, interview committees were set up, and plans for interviews were concluded. To check data gained from interviews, letters for further information were written to the state department of public health. When original problems were reconsidered and it became clear that historical information would not be forthcoming from sources already decided upon, plans were made to search for suitable materials in the library and to talk to adults who remembered when vaccines were relatively new.

As children became impressed with the facts they were finding, a campaign to encourage all children to get their polio shots seemed the logical next step. More plans for posters, chalk talks to class groups, and a leaflet to parents followed. And these in turn led to plans for appeals to adults through a radio announcement, plans for notes of appreciation for services received, and later plans for evaluation of their efforts. Cooperative planning here began with an identified problem and led children from one problem-solving experience to another.

Through such experiences as these, children begin to sense the involvement of their group in the pursuit of common goals. They begin to see the whole of what they are proposing to do. Plans become their own; goals are clarified. Each child sees the job ahead; each can see his particular part of it. This kind of unity is almost never obtained in the teacher-directed classroom. Each assignment, although it may be part of the whole the teacher envisions, is only a segment each child must complete. What lies ahead may be only guessed. The children who complete the present task are helpless to move ahead; the design of their progress has not been made known to them. In the area of learning where cooperative planning is an essential element, children not only move forward with security but also can use their time wisely. The superior pupil, because he knows the general plan, can choose related activities he feels will contribute to the study. Less competent pupils, because they helped to plan, know the value of the jobs they undertake. Children and groups work independently without calling upon the teacher for frequent direction. When children assume a portion of responsibility for the development of the area of learning, they are bound together by their cooperatively made plans. Planning cooperatively contributes to the development of an area of learning because it serves as a connecting link between experiences and as a unifying force directing the pupils toward agreed-upon goals.

CONTRIBUTIONS TO PROBLEM SOLVING

Throughout the area of learning, emphasis is placed on the solving of problems, problems related to the content of the area and problems related to the planning and carrying out of experiences. Skill in solving these problems develops as children have frequent and extended opportunities to pursue cooperatively the problem-solving process from beginning to end. These opportunities are best provided by cooperative planning. In every planning session, the development of problem-solving skills becomes a major objective: identifying problems, exploring sources of information, gathering data, determining possible solutions, deciding upon the best solution, and testing the decision in practical situations. Here pupils see the application of the scientific method to problems of everyday living and can acquire the skills of a systematic approach to problem solving that will be constantly useful to them. However, all these problem-solving skills require special competence and practice. Cooperative planning opens the way and sets the stage for each of them.

Cooperative planning promotes the problem-solving process by encouraging the identification and clarification of problems significant to the learners. Out of the initiation experience, of course, come the spurs to thinking and planning: How can we tell whether or not these stones are limestone? Why must we purify our drinking water? How can we reduce the running in our hallways? How do people learn to eat foods they don't like? How do forest fires affect us? These are some of the questions that lead children into problem-solving experiences related to the content of an area of learning. Operational questions offer equally good opportunities for problem solving: How can we organize committees so that there will be better working conditions for everybody? How can we find the tools we need for constructing the boat models? How can we darken our room enough to see Jim's color slides? The identification of such real problems through cooperative planning serves as an effective incentive for pursuing the problem-solving process.

Cooperative planning also makes possible the exploration of ways to solve problems. When there are real problems, children usually are eager to survey possible courses of action. They suggest various sources of information, list activities that will develop solutions, and plan special ways of working individually or in groups to gather needed data. As they move from one experience to another according to their plan, new problems arise, problems unforeseen and unplanned for; these problems then become the focus for new explorations and new experiences. As each problem calls into service research skills in locating information and critical evaluation of possible sources, the teacher assists by suggesting resources and techniques children may not know about and helps them to select those with the most promise. This cooperative exploration of ways to solve problems is good practice in an important aspect of problem solving.

When pertinent information has been gathered from a variety of sources, cooperative planning for next steps includes the sharing and evaluation of all collected data. During any data-gathering activity, children come together from time to time to note their progress and to exchange suggestions about what they are finding. When they feel especially successful with a problem, they participate in full-scale discussion before making plans to solve new problems or to engage in new experiences. During the planning and sharing session, they may discover that solutions to some problems depend upon the completion of an activity of some duration, or upon the results of an experiment that cannot be completed overnight, or upon the arrival of information from some distant place. They may find that some problems cannot be solved at all; these they mark for the future when better resources may be available. Such experiences in sharing and evaluation of information are vital to cooperative problem solving.

Through cooperative planning children move from a critical survey of the information they have uncovered to consideration of the possible solutions their data may suggest. Because the best solution may not at once be apparent, the group must identify various ways of meeting the problem and then evaluate each in light of its strengths and weaknesses. For example, the children who were exploring ways to reduce running in the hallways at school contributed several suggestions—that the principal be asked to warn the whole school and to promise some loss of privilege for misbehavior, that hall monitors be seated outside each classroom to apprehend those who were running, that posters showing the results of running in the hall be exhibited, and that dramatization of the present unhappy situation be presented in an all-school assembly to encourage all classes to consider the problem. Which of the solutions or combination of solutions would be most effective? The pupils were encouraged to weigh each idea carefully to determine its effectiveness in achieving the desired results.

When final decisions must be made, cooperative planning provides opportunity for the group to choose its course of action thoughtfully. Making a wise choice from many possible solutions demands that children evaluate objectively each proposed plan in terms of what they know about the situation, about the possible reactions of persons involved, and about the results they may expect. The merits of each proposal must be identified and considered. The children solving the hallway problem in their school had already made several generalizations that aided them in their decisions. Since their investigation had revealed that earlier suggestions made by the principal had not solved the problem, they decided that another warning from him probably would not be effective. They knew from their interviews with teachers that using students as monitors was not popular with the faculty and from their talks with students that young people did not like to be watched over by their friends. They concluded that their efforts should be spent in trying to help each class in the school become more aware of the problem and to encourage each group to make its own plans to do something about it. When this point in the discussion was reached, the posters and the dramatization for an assembly seemed to be the logical choices. It was cooperative planning, moreover, that had made possible the well-considered decision which resulted later in widespread interest in a school safety problem. Such decision making is the focus of social studies.[4]

The opportunity to make plans for testing group decisions is the final contribution cooperative planning makes to the problem-solving process. The wisdom of a proposed solution to a problem can be determined only upon its practical application to everyday situations. Some decisions, like the one about the safety demonstration, are simple to try and to test because observation can easily show whether or not one group is able to interest other groups in reducing a safety hazard. Similarly, planning to observe food habits in the cafeteria is a sensible way to determine how successful are children's proposals for learning to eat unliked foods. Some solutions, however, cannot be tried out so easily. Children may find that they cannot make plans to put their ideas into actual practice at once; they may need to be satisfied only with discussing their proposal with older persons. Whenever possible, of course, pupils should plan to test their solutions to problems in real life, for every successful application encourages them to attack the next problem with vigor and enthusiasm.

Thoughtful consideration of these essential problem-solving skills points up their close affinity to the procedures of the scientific method. As pupils work out the solutions to problems they have raised concerning basic human activities, they come to appreciate the values of a direct approach that has order and system. True, pupils will discover that sometimes problems are solved by trial and error or by chance, but in the main they recognize the value that lies in ability to make a frontal attack on the problems they identify as important to them. Moreover, these skills of problem solving are among the essential transferable skills being currently identified and emphasized.[5]

---

[4] Shirley H. Engle, "Decision Making: The Heart of Social Studies Instruction," *Social Education* (November, 1960), pp. 301–304; also in Byron G. Massialas and Andreas M. Kazamais (Eds.), *Crucial Issues in the Teaching of Social Studies* (Englewood Cliffs, N.J.: Prentice-Hall, Inc., 1964).

[5] Theodore O. Yntema, "We Must Also Teach Reality," *Chicago Daily News Panorama* (May 2, 1964), p. 2.

Characteristics
of an Effective Planning Session

The development of worthwhile planning sessions requires both teacher skill and pupil effort. Children must learn to plan. If children are accustomed to a high degree of direction and very little participation in planning their own affairs, cooperative planning requires of them a new orientation to the teacher and to the class group (see Figure 4). Perhaps the first step is to suggest a plan to children and to encourage them to discuss it. Do you think we can follow this plan? What part of it can we do best? Is there a better way of doing this job? At this level the teacher is asking pupils to react only to a decision already made, but after initial experience of this kind children may be given the greater responsibility of choosing between alternatives in accomplishing a job or solving a problem: Should we take care of the situation in this way or in that way? Pupils are encouraged to help make the choice. Later on they enter into planning much more fully as they share with the teacher the job of suggesting, evaluating, and deciding. And while children plan, the alert teacher considers the experience in the light of several useful criteria, pinpointed by the questions raised in the following discussion.

Is the planning unique to the area of learning that engages the attention of the pupils? Once children learn the skills of cooperative planning, they may fall into a pattern of planning that is dull and stereotyped. As they gain experience in planning, meeting with success in using certain procedures, and becoming acquainted with the expectations of their teacher, they may routinely suggest problems, plans, or techniques that in the past have seemed adequate. They may even be unconsciously encouraged in these habits by the teacher who loses sight of the values of cooperative planning that is spirited and thoughtful. The description that follows is typical of the pitfalls that may beset both teacher and pupils.

TEACHER: I'm sure it will be easy for you to plan what you want to know about Egypt; you've studied many other countries and know the important topics.

FIRST PUPIL: Well, first we have to know the location.

SECOND PUPIL: Then we should locate the large cities. We can make a large map like the one we made last time.

THIRD PUPIL: We need to know how they get food, clothing, and shelter.

FOURTH PUPIL: Yes, and about their transportation and communication.

TEACHER: Good, now what else would you like to know?

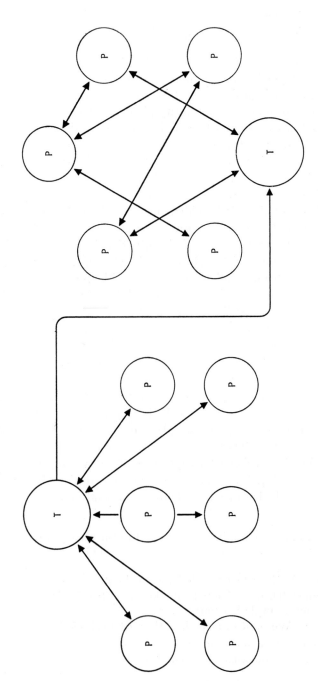

Figure 4

The roles of teacher and pupils are altered when cooperative decision making and mutual exchange replace teacher domination and pupil compliance.

SECOND PUPIL: Music, art, and religion would make good topics for special reports.

TEACHER: Yes, that plan worked well when we studied Mexico. Anything else?

THIRD PUPIL: How about comparing Egypt today with Egypt in ancient times. I saw a television program about it not long ago.

TEACHER: The study of the ancient world comes next year, so we wouldn't want to get into that, would we?

FIFTH PUPIL: Well, no, but we could find out what is happening in Egypt in the news and then try to explain it by what we can find out.

TEACHER: That's a good idea, but I really think your original plan to study various topics is best. It will cover important information quickly so that we can go on to other countries in North Africa.

A planning session that bears the earmarks of such repetitious planning contributes little to democratic process or to motivation of learning: in fact, it casts doubt upon the sincerity of the teacher and falls far short of involving pupils in any concerns vital to the subject under discussion. Rather, what is sought in cooperative planning is spontaneity, enthusiasm, and originality of thinking that indicate that the problems at hand have aroused the interest of pupils and challenged them to make plans that are relevant to the situation.

Are all children participating in the planning session? Participation that is as nearly complete as possible is essential to group unity and to the progress of the unit. An area of learning carried forward by only a few superior pupils or entirely by teacher suggestion is seldom accepted enthusiastically by the whole class. The teacher takes special care to involve all children in the planning by making sure that certain pupils do not monopolize the discussion, by being alert to possible contributions by children who are more reticent, and by calling into service information he has about the interests and abilities of various children in the group. On occasion children take time out to evaluate their participation in discussion by tabulating the number of contributions made by class members, by devising schemes for making sure that some do not do more than their share of the talking, and by calling to mind the importance of giving everyone who has an idea an opportunity to express it.

Pupil participation is extended when techniques of good discussion are emphasized. Children need to learn those techniques that give everyone in the group opportunities to share in planning. One class developed these suggestions for improving discussion and facilitating participation:

1. Listen to the one who is speaking.
2. Show that you are interested in the speaker.
3. Stay on the topic.
4. Do not repeat what has already been said.

5. Give everyone a chance to speak.
6. If you are talking too much, stop.

At times when the teacher was not needed at the chalkboard as a recorder, he kept a diagram of group participation by preparing a seating chart of the circle of children and showing by lines and arrows the direction of each pupil's contribution. Now and then he made this diagram at the chalkboard in front of the children. Follow-up discussion usually improved the amount and quality of participation during the next planning period.

Do children feel free to express ideas and suggest plans for solving problems? Freedom for children to express their ideas and to make suggestions is as important in the planning session as is wide participation. Each pupil must feel secure enough to share freely his thinking about all problems. He should not feel it necessary to apologize for any plan he suggests thoughtfully. The teacher in turn sets an example for the members of the group by accepting the ideas of each person, by leading the group to accept and consider all suggestions, and by avoiding any possibility that a child whose idea or plan is rejected will refrain from further participation. Children and teacher alike must learn those techniques that help everyone feel he can contribute a worthy and, therefore, acceptable point to the discussion. Without this freedom to express ideas and suggest plans children cannot plan cooperatively.

Are children drawing on past experiences for ideas to solve these problems? A good planning session encourages children to bring to bear upon problems of concern to them their own contacts with family life, with the community and its people, with travel, and with the natural environment. As they begin to relate themselves and their experiences to the new questions they have identified, they grow in self-confidence and enthusiasm. While the pupils reinforce this connection between the past and the present, they reveal to the teacher their special interests and capabilities, and they suggest resources of which the teacher may have been unaware. The problems children are exploring become more truly their own when they see the relationship between their old experiences and the new ones they are planning. Observe how one group of young children drew on past experiences to solve problems of the present.

The first-grade children at Fairview School, who were being constantly disturbed by some building construction next door to them, became interested in the kinds of machines making the noise. Because their teacher believed that the children could gain some important understandings about how work is done in the community and how machines help in this work, she encouraged their interest. Before their first discussion was ended and plans were completed for visiting the construction, Miss Fisher and her pupils had discovered some interesting facts about their own group. Seven fathers in the group worked daily with big machines. Four children had watched their own houses being built. One child had discovered that a steam shovel and a spoon had something in common. Every child in the room had used a kitchen tool or simple machine. Three had ridden on a tractor. These were the experiences the children could utilize in their study. Here were the answers to some of their questions. The area of learning, although new and challenging in a sense, was growing out of past experiences and knowledge; answers to new questions were to be found partly in old experiences recalled and related to the present. The productive planning period thrives on such a pooling of group experience.

Do the children accept the teacher as a participant in the planning session? In every planning group, of course, the teacher is an important working member. He encourages participation and helps children to put forth fruitful suggestions and to make decisions. When pupils sense that the teacher is not trying to direct their thinking into previously selected channels, when they are not involved in a guessing game to find out what the teacher wants, real acceptance and mutual understanding can result. When the teacher behaves not as the sole source of knowledge but as a person truly seeking with children the solutions to problems, cooperative planning becomes possible. The children look upon the teacher as someone who can help them test their ideas and then put these ideas into action. Consider the way in which the teacher in this sixth grade participates as a working member of a group.

Mr. Olson's boys and girls accept him as a regular group member. They are gathered informally near him planning a marionette show to complete their study of people around the world. At this point the children are choosing the countries to be represented in the dramatization, but thus far lively exchange of opinion has failed to produce the list. Now almost unconsciously the children are turning to Mr. Olson for guidance in making their decision. When he suggests that the pupils compile a list of all lands studied by the group and then work out a scheme to give everyone a chance to vote for his choices, the pupils agree and turn their attention to the problem of what to show and tell about each country. Mr. Olson reminds them that notebooks in which they have listed important understandings about each country may be helpful. This suggestion directs discussion into profitable channels, and before long committees are selected to make final plans for each scene. Deciding the type of marionette to use is the next item on the planning session agenda. When children begin to see that they do not really know much about constructing the various kinds of marionettes, they appeal to the teacher again. Mr. Olson asks, "Where can you find out?" This query encourages some library exploration; and after summarizing plans to date, the group adjourns to give committees time to work. Children's acceptance of Mr. Olson as a resource person, their lively exchange of opinion with him, and their pride in meeting problems cooperatively are all evidences of the quality of working relationships between teacher and pupils. Upon such rapport the successful planning session depends.

Are children weighing suggestions for individual and group activity? Although all individual and group ideas are accepted freely in such co-operative planning, children must evaluate carefully proposals for action.

Children learn to decide which plan will be most effective as well as which is practical and feasible. Unless children are trained in this aspect of effective planning, they are likely to accept and to act upon almost any suggestions seriously proposed by someone in the group. The teacher may suggest that children need to plan carefully before they begin the project, that they need to explore more than one way of accomplishing their objective, or that they need to consider the effect of their planning upon other people in the school. When pupils grasp eagerly at an idea and begin to put it into action without considering the time, money, or effort it may require or its effectiveness for the whole class group, the wise teacher encourages them to weigh each suggestion thoughtfully before accepting it as part of their plans.

That children do make these evaluative judgments in planning is evidenced in such comments as these, gathered at random from various groups: "The trip to Spring Mill would be better than one to Vincennes if we want to see how people in a pioneer village really lived." "We need more information about the United Nations before we can know what we want to find out." "We studied about our natural resources last year, so why don't we concentrate on conservation now?" "If we go to the telephone office, let's send our list of questions ahead of time; then our guides can be ready with the answers." "Jack's father works in the quarry; he would be a good person to help us plan our study of limestone." When children are carefully weighing suggestions for answering questions and solving problems, cooperative planning becomes increasingly effective.

Are children keeping records of decisions and plans? When arguments are settled and proposals accepted in a planning session, these developments should be recorded. Both teacher and children at times serve as recorders. They keep a permanent record of the problems that are accepted for study; they list the suggestions developed as a preliminary or suggested plan of action; they keep for future reference the committee and individual assignments and responsibilities. They record all developments that will be needed to facilitate the future progress of the group. Young children help to develop these records as the teacher uses chalkboard and chalk or newsprint and pencil to note their ideas. Older children can transfer their initial plans to more permanent wall charts, or teachers can provide copies for pupil notebooks or files. These records become useful reminders of group effort and progress and are the necessary tools to keep the group constantly aware of its direction. They encourage good use of time, help pupils avoid indecision and argument about past decisions, and provide a kind of running account of experiences. Keeping records accurately is an important aspect of cooperative planning.

In other words, an effective planning session meets several important criteria. When the planning is creative and unique to the problems under study, when children participate in it, when all feel free to contribute to plans, when children accept the teacher as a member of the planning group, when they are drawing upon past experiences for ideas to solve new problems, when they are evaluating their plans and keeping records of their decisions, planning cooperatively becomes a valuable learning experience for children.

Role of the Teacher
in Cooperative Planning

Although the role children play in cooperative planning is crucial, that of the teacher is even more important. Before the teacher can function well in this role, he must assume certain responsibilities for the control and direction of learning. Recognizing that cooperative planning must necessarily be subordinate to all-school curriculum planning in social studies, he guides children's planning toward desired goals within the framework of the social studies curriculum and makes sure that significant content will be utilized to achieve these goals. Understanding the role of cooperative planning in democratic group process, the teacher assumes responsibility for making it function significantly in children's experience. He is mindful, too, of his obligations to other teachers, to administrative personnel, and to parents to whom he must be ready to explain his methods of working with children.

In the planning session with children, the teacher has more particular responsibilities. He analyzes children's questions and problems, anticipates the direction of their planning, helps them see the need for planning and for thinking critically about their plans, and assists them in keeping records of plans and decisions.

In preparation for the planning session that follows the initiation, the skillful teacher carefully studies the problems children raised during the initiation experience. He evaluates them in the light of selected objectives, considers whether or not they should be reorganized for efficient study, selects the ones that will make good starting places for study, and identifies those that are appropriate for the whole group as well as those best suited to individual or small-group effort.

The teacher must first decide whether or not children's questions will develop important understandings, attitudes, and skills. Will the questions lead children to formulate some significant generalizations about basic human activities? Will they lead to attitudes that are appropriate for community life in democracy? Will they develop skills that improve the quality of children's living? If the teacher thinks that some of the questions are unimportant, he may encourage the children to leave them for the present in favor of concentrating on more significant problems. If an essential aspect of a problem has not been explored by the pupils, the teacher plans ways to focus attention upon it. If he feels that some phases of the problem touched by children's questions may be difficult for them to understand or impossible for them to solve, he considers ways to change the direction of their planning to more profitable channels.

The teacher then studies the children's questions to determine whether or not they need to be restated or reorganized. Some of the questions may be clearly related and can be regrouped for more efficient study. Children are likely to ask their questions in a problem area quite at random, moving swiftly from one aspect of the study to another and back again. The teacher plans ahead ways to help children regroup their questions; for older children this experience can contribute to an understanding of a simple outline. Younger children merely think together those questions that belong together while the teacher lists them in improved order. Children who have had much experience in planning sometimes organize their study problems as they go, putting together those that are related and combining questions as it seems wise. The teacher's preliminary consideration of the questions and problems prepares him to guide children more skillfully in the organization of their study.

As the teacher analyzes children's questions, he identifies those that are best suited to individual or small-group effort and selects those that should be given major emphasis by the large class group. Because he is careful to encourage all children to contribute worthwhile questions in the planning session, every list of questions will contain some items of special interest to only a few. Plans must be made for meeting these individual needs. On the other hand, the teacher's analysis of children's questions reveals those that are especially important for all children because of the understandings, attitudes, and skills that are to be developed. Those questions that provide background information in the area, that deal with important basic human activities, that pose questions that should concern everyone in the group, and that are essential to an appreciation of the special interests that may be developed are tentatively marked by the teacher for the consideration of all the children in the group.

Finally, the teacher explores children's questions to identify those that may be possible starting places for their study. What kinds of questions can serve this purpose? Because children usually need and seek background information early in their exploration of an area of learning, those questions that will encourage wide reading and investigation are marked for first consideration by the pupils. Because a good starting place can be a real challenge, the teacher carefully examines children's questions as he prepares to assist them in their selection of a worthwhile problem with which to initiate their study.

The teacher's analysis of children's questions suggested here is not designed to impede but to facilitate children's planning. Successful cooperative planning depends upon careful preplanning by the teacher, who has thought through the possibilities for organizing questions and problems and is ready to participate with children in making plans and decisions.

Not only in the early planning sessions but whenever new problems are raised during the progress of the area of learning, thoughtful consideration of children's line of inquiry makes it possible for the teacher to anticipate more easily the direction of their planning. As the identified problem is studied with possible pupil proposals in mind, the teacher has an early opportunity to plan ways to capitalize on resources children may discover, to secure support for what is good in their ideas, and to help them avoid disappointment if they plan impractical activities. When the teacher thinks ahead about the materials children may need and the activities they may suggest, he can be ready by subtle suggestion to guide children's thinking into profitable channels.

The teacher tries to anticipate the kinds of information children will need at each stage of their development of the area of learning as well as the difficulties they may have in securing materials. When a worthwhile question or problem calls for searching, the teacher makes a preliminary survey of the available resources, checking libraries and museums, visiting community facilities, interviewing, and exploring reading and audio-visual materials. When areas of learning fit into the framework of the social studies curriculum of the school and from year to year teachers have an opportunity to build up resources in broad areas of subject matter, the task of securing appropriate information is somewhat reduced. In any case, thinking ahead about materials saves time for both teacher and pupils.

The teacher also tries to anticipate the kinds of activities children may suggest to solve the various problems that are identified both at the beginning of the study and during its development. Thinking through the implementation of children's suggestions makes possible some preliminary exploration of their feasibility. If children want to embark on plans that are too elaborate to be practical, the teacher can be ready with a simpler proposal that will accomplish their purposes just as well. When children's plans would be needlessly expensive, the teacher can suggest ways of carrying out the activity more economically. When some of the effective methods of solving problems are not known to children, the teacher may propose that they investigate other ways to put their plans into action. The teacher knows that children will be interested in a great variety of experiences, only some of which can be undertaken. He can begin to make some tentative selections in terms of the richness of the experience and the contribution it will make to understandings, attitudes, and skills. Thinking through and evaluating possible experiences for children is an important part of the teacher's role in cooperative planning.

Because children may not always see the need for planning, the teacher serves the important function of pointing up this need. When children are eager to move quickly into problem-solving activities, the teacher suggests that they make certain that their problems and questions are organized in the most effective way possible and that each activity is carefully planned to ensure its success. Children can learn to plan skillfully, but teachers often must make clear the need for planning.

When children seem inclined to move into a particular activity without careful planning, the teacher inquires, "Do we have all the information we need before we start our project? Will we work as a large group or in small groups? What equipment and materials will we need? How can we avoid disturbing the class next door? Do you think we are ready to start our project this morning?" Such questions as these bring children to the realization that time and care are required in the planning of their activities. The teacher's questions help them realize the necessity for planning; and a successful activity can further reinforce their understanding of the importance of a good plan.

Children usually see the wisdom of planning and engage in it readily. A particular group, however, may not recognize this need and engage in an activity without careful planning. Evaluation of the product of this effort results in a realization that planning is a necessary part of any enterprise. At this point the teacher can tactfully assist pupils in rethinking the experience and encouraging the necessary planning.

If the teacher is successful in helping children see the need for planning, he can more easily encourage them to be critical of their own suggestions and to seek constantly to improve them. Where critical thinking is prized by the teacher, children think through their proposals more carefully and support them with more adequate reasoning. There are many evidences of critical thinking in the dialogue at the beginning of this chapter and many more in classrooms where children plan cooperatively ways of accomplishing their purposes in the area of learning.

An important part of the teacher's role in such cooperative planning is to recognize and commend good thinking, to note and approve thoughtful suggestions for procedure, and to suggest a pause for reconsideration of proposals hastily accepted. Children develop skill in critical evaluation of their plans only when the teacher guides this development.

All planning session decisions and plans are, of course, recorded for future reference, with the teacher often recording the first draft. Because the teacher has the skill necessary to record ideas quickly, he can facilitate the progress of the discussion as children concentrate on making plans. Keeping records of children's plans gives the teacher an opportunity to guide the questioning and planning so that ideas are expressed completely and clearly. The records that result are excellent resources for the teacher to study as he anticipates children's future planning.

During the initiation the teacher records the questions that are proposed by children. In this function as a recorder he has many opportunities to help children improve the quality of their questioning. If necessary he can rephrase a question to make its meaning clear. He can help children avoid questions that bring only a "yes" or "no" answer and encourage "why" and "how" problems instead. He can point out that some questions have already been asked and recorded. Here the teacher has an opportunity to improve children's questioning as he records their ideas.

During the planning session that follows the initiation the teacher also helps children record their plan of action and, later, their committees and study groups and their standards for working together. The recording of these plans and decisions while children are planning puts children's thinking into organized form for them to see and consider. Here, too, during the recording process the teacher can subtly suggest ways of making plans more understandable and usable. In some of these situations older children may take over the recording at the chalkboard as their classmates express their ideas, especially if the material to be recorded is not unduly complicated.

As these records materialize and accumulate, the teacher reviews and studies them in preparation for future planning sessions. As has already been suggested in this chapter, the teacher reconsiders children's questions to help them organize their study; he thinks through records of plans to anticipate needs and problems; he studies records of work groups to plan ways of promoting good interpersonal relations and suitable working conditions. Keeping records of children's plans is essential to the progress of the area of learning.

This brief analysis of the teacher's role in cooperative planning leaves little doubt about his importance in this ongoing process. He is the key to its success. He analyzes children's questions in order to assist them in organizing their study and activities. He anticipates the direction of children's planning—the kinds of materials they will need and the implementation of their plans for activity. He helps children see the need for planning and encourages them to think critically about their plans. He keeps records that will make future planning more profitable. In short, the teacher makes many important contributions to the fruitful planning experience.

Is the role of the teacher in cooperative planning too difficult a one for many elementary school teachers? Observation and research seem to indicate that all too few classroom teachers employ procedures that develop self-direction and democratic group process.[6] It is because of this obvious neglect that the extraordinary amount of attention given to cooperative planning in this chapter is relevant and justifiable.

Through cooperative planning, carried on under the guidance of a resourceful teacher, children may improve the quality of their work and study both in individual enterprises and in cooperative undertakings. The area

---

[6] Duane Manning, "An Analysis of the Relative Directiveness of Instruction," *Studies in Education*, Bulletin No. 2 (Bloomington: Indiana University, 1950).

of learning develops through cooperative planning and depends upon it for its successful implementation. Through cooperative planning children learn skills basic to working in a democratic group and take first steps in the process of problem solving.

QUESTIONS FOR DISCUSSION

Reread the dialogue that introduces this chapter and consider it in terms of these questions.

1. How did the planning session stimulate critical thinking among the children?
2. What function did the children's planning serve in helping them solve new problems?
3. What purpose will be served by the plan of action the children developed in this situation?
4. What did the teacher contribute to the planning experience?

SUGGESTIONS FOR CONSTRUCTING A RESOURCE UNIT

Using the materials listed in your annotated bibliography, select and record in outline form the information that will answer questions and solve problems raised by the children in the initiation.

An effective way to prepare a content outline for an area of learning is to structure it around the problems that children may identify in the initiation. These problems serve as major topics of the outline and provide a framework for organizing information essential to the area of learning. The topics of the outline may be the problems themselves, or the topics may appear as related statements.

Refer to the content outline in the resource unit in the appendix, noting the relationship between the major topics of the outline and the children's problems that precede the outline.

4

Experiencing
to Achieve Goals

FRANK: We are all set to go to the television studio, Mrs. Johnson. Last night when I told my dad that we want to visit, he said, "Just name the day."

MRS. JOHNSON: It's nice to know we'll be welcome, Frank. Possibly other boys and girls have ideas for carrying out our plans, too. Did anyone else talk about them at home last night?

SUSAN: I didn't tell anyone what we're going to do, but I know what I want to do. I want to have a TV show. Visiting the television station is all right if we could be in a show. They wouldn't let us do that, so I'd like to have a TV program right here.

FRANK: You have to know about television before you can put on a show— how people act, how to put a show on the air, and what commercials to have, and all that.

JANET SUE: Couldn't we do both? Visit the television station to find out about what Frank says, and then make up a program afterward?

RONNIE: If we're going to make up something, why don't some of us make up sign languages so we can communicate without people finding out what we are saying?

BARBARA ANN: Let's ask people about communication. I just love to interview people.

MRS. JOHNSON: All of those ideas have possibilities, but won't we need some general information about communication to do these things? Let's reread our problems and our plan of action. Perhaps that will help us decide on a starting place. Allen, will you read them for us?

ALLEN: Yes, I will. They're all in good order now.

MRS. JOHNSON: Yes, that's why we organized them.

ALLEN: 1. How do we communicate over distance?
2. How do we communicate with large groups of people?
3. What kinds of communication should be used for different purposes?
4. What happens when communication breaks down?
5. Why does communication require the work of so many people?
6. How does communication help people live better?
7. How does communication help people work together?
8. How does transportation depend upon communication?

9. How can we be sure that people understand us when we communicate with them?
10. Why is communication needed in a democratic country?
11. Why was communication long ago more difficult than it is today?
12. Why was communication so important in the early days of our country?

MRS. JOHNSON: Thank you, Allen. Did you notice that most of the questions ask for special kinds of information about communication? Are there any questions about communication in general?

BARBARA ANN: Well, one asks about different kinds of communication.

MRS. JOHNSON: Which question is that, Barbara Ann?

BARBARA ANN: What kinds of communication should be used for different purposes?

MRS. JOHNSON: Wouldn't information about different kinds of communication help us in finding answers to some of the other questions?

PEGGY: I guess we can't find out how communication helps transportation until we know about different kinds of communication.

ANNE: Now that I think about it, how can we find out about communication in early days without knowing the kinds of communication there are?

MRS. JOHNSON: That's true of many questions; isn't it? We need some general information about communication before we can begin to solve our problems. Let's start with Barbara Ann's question. Please read it again, Barbara Ann.

BARBARA ANN: What kinds of communication should be used for different purposes?

ALICE: Couldn't we visit lots of places in town to see what kinds of communication they have?

CHARLES: We could if we had the time, but it would take at least a week.

ALICE: But "visit places" is in our plan of action. It's third on the list.

MRS. JOHNSON: There are other suggestions, too, Alice. Read all of them.

ALICE: We can read books.
We can ask people.
We can visit places.
We can see films.
We can visit the museum.
We can play out some of our ideas about communication.
We can learn to communicate without words.
We can bring things from home.
We can have some real activities.

PATRICIA: Asking people would be faster than visiting places.

DONALD: Maybe so, but just finding people to ask takes time. Books are the quickest answer. That's something we can do right away.

MRS. JOHNSON: Even finding books to read takes time, Donald. But, if we all help look for materials, we should be ready to read tomorrow. There are several books about communication on our library table. I'm sure there are many others in the library as well as some in our own classroom.

ANDY: I'll look in the library, Mrs. Johnson. I'm returning a book anyway.

MRS. JOHNSON: Four or five of you might spend your free reading period in the library later this afternoon locating books. Jack and Charles, Ronnie, Philip —wouldn't you like to do that, too?

JACK: What kind of books should we get, Mrs. Johnson?

MRS. JOHNSON: Any with information about communication. There may be some that you won't care to read yourself, but other boys and girls may like them. Bring all you can find. Be sure to check through the encyclopedias and picture files. Both should have the kind of information we are looking for.

ANDY: I know how to use encyclopedias, because we have the Junior Encyclopedia at home.

MRS. JOHNSON: Would someone else look in the index of our social studies book for information about communication? Mary, will you do that? Our reading books probably have some material also. Some of you might look through them. Does anyone know of any other materials?

RONNIE: I saw a story about communication in my brother's sixth-grade reader. I think it was called "Communicating by Air" or something like that. Maybe they would let us use a few of their books.

MRS. JOHNSON: I'm sure Miss Adams would be glad to lend us several copies, Ronnie. Ask her tonight after school or tomorrow morning. Then there are books in our reading center. Surely several have something to offer. Susan, while others are exploring books, will you glance through the film catalogue for films we'd like to see. Let's stack everything we find on the library table, and I'll check with you before we leave tonight to see what you have found.

Experiences that are truly educative are the concern of the school. In social studies these experiences are the learning adventures that help children answer questions and solve problems and that lead them to understandings, attitudes, behaviors, and skills that are the goals of the area of learning, and ultimately to generalizations that are fundamental to social studies. Experiences are, of course, the essence of living, for the very nature of the changing environment is such that it continually impinges on individuals, causing them to react in some way to it. Experiences are a fact of life, too, because of the nature of the individual—a curious, exploratory, creative being who responds to his surroundings, learns certain things, forms certain attitudes, and relates himself to new circumstances in the light of past experiences. But social studies is concerned, not so much with experiences in general, as with those educative experiences specifically selected to meet teacher and pupil purposes in the area of learning.

Experiences and experiencing are highly regarded in the modern school, but sometimes little attention is given to their real meaning or justification. Experiences are those encounters with the human and physical environment that bring about change or growth in the individual. Experiencing is the personal involvement implied by such a definition of experiences. Experiences are more than activities, although the two terms are often used interchangeably for want of better synonyms. In reality, however, experiences and experiencing imply that something happens to the individual within as well as without; on the other hand, activities can be quite superficial—for example, reading a book without understanding the content or observing a theatrical production without being touched by its meaning.

Role of Experiences
in the Area of Learning

Experiences that will lead to the achievement of teacher and pupil purposes, and ultimately to more comprehensive goals, become the focus of attention as children explore ways to solve problems identified in the initiation (see Figure 5). In fact, the area of learning is a series of experiences moving forward in a smooth progression of undertakings toward well-defined ends and providing continuity of learning as each new experience emerges from experiences of the past and in turn carries over something of itself to a succeeding experience.

Experiences in social studies cover a wide range of interactions between the learner and the social studies environment—the world of the classroom, the library, the community, and the whole gamut of relationships between people and things. Labeled, these experiences are identified as planning; reading, listening, and seeing; contemplating; discussing; solving problems; constructing and processing; experimenting; and evaluating. Each of these is in itself a complex of processes, so that the educative experiences of social studies are so diversified as to defeat attempts at complete analysis. Nevertheless, since experiences play such a valuable part in learning, it is desirable to examine them in the social studies setting to emphasize their importance further.

RELATIONSHIP OF CONTENT TO EXPERIENCES

Experiences are important as the enterprises through which children learn about the content of an area of study. As noted earlier, social studies is a body of subject matter drawn from a number of disciplines—anthropology, economics, geography, government, history, social psychology, and sociology. In the modern social studies program, content from these fields becomes an integrated body of knowledge centered on significant problems and considered to be essential to living in a changing world. The search for solutions to problems concerned with basic human activities leads unmistakably to data drawn from a variety of aspects of man's relationships with others. Through their own data-gathering experiences pupils become involved directly with the content of social studies.

The relationship of content to experiences is an important element in much of the current discussion about social studies. There is a tendency to equate emphasis upon wide and varied experiences for the learner with

The Crucial Role of Experiences

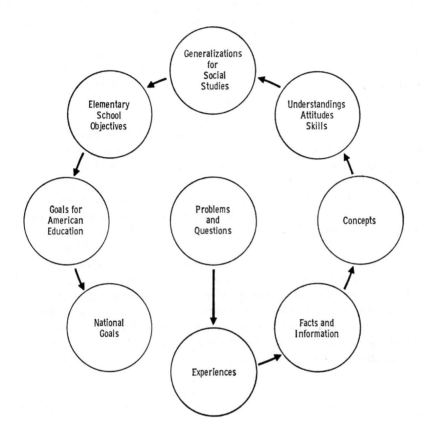

Figure 5

Experiences undertaken to solve problems and answer questions result in a hierarchy of learnings.

an absence of concern for significant content or to assume that concern for the teaching of content necessarily indicates a textbook-centered curriculum.[1] Complicating the dilemma is the fact that it is becoming increasingly clear that no one person can possibly know well all areas of subject matter that constitute social studies. Furthermore, frequently expressed dissatisfactions with social studies instruction center on the futility of confronting pupils with the superficial study of many areas of content for the

[1] John Jarolimek, "Curriculum Content and the Child in the Elementary School," *Social Education* (February, 1962), p. 59.

sole purpose of covering ground, a course of action that tends to reduce pupil experiencing both in breadth and in depth.

Scholars in the social science disciplines and authorities in elementary school social studies alike are suggesting a resolution of the dilemma by emphasis upon content that is selected carefully to illustrate and rein-force generalizations and is pursued as thoroughly as possible through methods of inquiry appropriate to the maturity of children and to the range of experiences open to them.[2]

The crucial nature of the content, components of which are facts, as a basis for the area of learning cannot be minimized, for facts provide the foundation of concept building and the evidence upon which to base gen-eralizations. Although the specific facts are likely to be less lasting than the generalizations they illustrate, without relevant content the working ingredients of critical thinking, problem solving, decision making, and gen-eralizing are missing. Obviously this content will vary in nature with the learning situation, its selection depending upon children's interests and needs, the social setting, and the teacher's background.[3] Moreover, this content will vary in quality—in clarity, authenticity, orderliness, and perti-nence—in response to the richness of the experiences that produce it.

Because some educators hold the view that engaging in varied experiences sacrifices the learning of content, it is necessary to reiterate that a problem-solving approach to social studies implemented through experiences co-operatively planned and developed is entirely compatible with the concept of organized content.[4] Furthermore, experiences in social studies should lead directly to organizing principles that demonstrate how things in the social world are related. No less an authority than John Dewey spoke clearly on the point, saying that "no experience is educative that does not tend both to knowledge of more facts and entertaining of more ideas and to a better, a more orderly, arrangement of them."[5]

From the children's point of view, of course, content is the knowledge they seek through their experiences and upon which they can base ten-tative conclusions. They read, explore the community, experiment, study maps and pictures, build and process, with an important objective in view —to locate, assimilate, and organize information and ideas for which they are searching.

[2] Byron G. Massialas, "Revising the Social Studies: An Inquiry-Centered Approach," *Social Education* (April, 1963), pp. 185–189.

[3] George W. Denemark, "Balancing Stability and Flexibility in Today's Curriculum," *The Indiana Social Studies Quarterly* (Muncie, Ind.: Ball State University, Autumn 1963), pp. 45–51.

[4] B. Othanel Smith, William O. Stanley, J. Harlan Shores, *Fundamentals of Curriculum Development* (New York: Harcourt, Brace & World, Inc., 1957).

[5] John Dewey, *Experience and Education* (New York: The Macmillan Company, 1938), p. 102. Used by permission of Kappa Delta Pi, an honor society in education, copyright owners.

DEVELOPING CONCEPTS THROUGH EXPERIENCES

Although experiences are the vehicles of concept building in social studies, helping children comprehend these concepts is no simple undertaking. Teachers frequently assume that words, because they are simple to read, are readily understood at various levels of abstraction. Common but complex terms, such as *climate, plain, industry,* and *transportation,* require more than skill in pronunciation. Even simple words when used in a social studies context may be strange. Consider the child's problem in deriving the meaning of *chairman,* a term commonly used in group process, from his notion of the word *chair.* To read or say aloud the needed word is no guarantee of understanding. Through the child's experiences meanings of words are broadened and deepened.

For example, children first meet the word *school* in the content drawn from their own school experiences, highlighted perhaps in the social studies area of learning. To the child whose contacts with school are limited, the word *school* has limited meaning; to him it means one school, his school, a building with desks and a playground, or a room and a teacher. After a time, through visits to other schools and through reading and discussion, the word encompasses more than one school. Later on, with more study and further contacts with the process of education, *school* may become a generalized idea or concept including very broad notions of the functions and values of school. Many concepts, such as *mountain, country, product, communication, map,* and *trade,* begin as new words in the pupils' vocabulary and gradually take on fuller and richer meaning as children have further experiences with them in social studies.

Many other concepts are less obvious and develop more slowly. *Cooperation,* for example, is a concept that is especially significant in social studies. What does the word mean to the first-grade child? He can pronounce it; perhaps he understands, in a simple way, when the teacher admonishes him to "cooperate by finishing your work quickly." He even uses the word himself, sometimes in anger when he threatens, "You'd better cooperate or I'll tell the teacher." But *cooperation* is a concept that grows slowly, gradually acquiring meaning through a study of community relationships, through knowledge of how the student council functions in the school, through reading about how nations of the world have worked together for certain objectives—in short, through a variety of purposely chosen experiences. Later, much later, the meaning of *cooperation* may become fairly clear to the elementary school child, but only maturity can bring full understanding. The content of social studies is made up of many such abstractions, of which *democracy, citizenship, freedom, loyalty, competition, international, communism, century,* and *government* are examples. Developing them becomes an important function of experiences.

The selection of experiences for concept development depends somewhat upon the ideas about something that the child has already acquired through previous experiences. Children's concepts are not always what teachers may expect. Their conceptions and misconceptions, built up previous to the initiation of a new area of learning, are often revealed in the initiation and in the cooperative planning period. Having some knowledge of pupils' present level of concept development certainly facilitates the selection of new experiences. Because children do not all develop a given concept at a given time, at the same rate, or in the same way, the teacher plans not one but many experiences with a new concept as the area of study unfolds.[6]

There are many concepts that must be developed in social studies, but some are so difficult and crucial that they need special attention. Time and space concepts are among those that are especially troublesome for children. Young children acquire some of them through their daily experiences —ideas of minute, hour, and day, as well as the association of various routines with certain hours of the day. "Today" is a familiar time concept used by very young children; "tomorrow" as something to come and "yesterday" as reference to the past follow a little later. But "last year" and "next year," "three weeks ago," or "on my next birthday" are hazy and formless for young children. During the elementary school years, however, children learn to tell time and to associate activities with times on the clock and with certain durations of time. All these concepts, imperfectly developed as they may be at this level, are derived from pupils' firsthand experiences in and out of school.

Older children also have problems in the development of time concepts. Their social studies experiences bring them into contact with the words *century, epoch, era, generation,* and *decade.* For a time such vague concepts as "in early times" or "long ago" may suffice for a particular purpose. But as pupils become more exact in their data gathering and as it becomes necessary to see relationships among events of the past, more precise concepts are needed. Span of time concepts develop through experiences specifically chosen to clarify them, and children need to meet such concepts in a variety of situations. Comparisons of the duration of events with the child's own life—"the journey westward took as long as your whole summer vacation" or "this happened when you were in second grade"—may help some pupils in concept development, but obviously these comparisons are of limited applicability. The development of concepts of chronology may also utilize the child's experiences. When the teacher says, "Tell in order every-

---

[6] For a detailed treatment of concept development see Arthur T. Jersild, *Child Psychology* (Englewood Cliffs, N.J.: Prentice-Hall, Inc., 1960), pp. 352–372. Also, Ralph H. Ojemann, "Social Studies in Light of Knowledge about Children," in Nelson B. Henry (Ed.), *Social Studies in the Elementary School* (Fifty-sixth Yearbook of the National Society for the Study of Education, Part II; Chicago: University of Chicago Press, 1957).

thing you did yesterday," he is helping pupils see sequence in previous events. The time line has been a favored device for expanding pupils' concepts of chronology to times past. Fortunately, as boys and girls mature, they begin to sense relationships among events and so develop better historical time concepts.

Space concepts are no less difficult. Very young children use freely such expressions as "a tiny little way" or "miles and miles" without very clear ideas about such concepts. Elementary school children need some reference points for concepts of area and distance, and experiences appropriate to their development can provide these reference points. An inch is about the length of the thumb from its tip to the first joint. A foot is about the length of a man's foot. The schoolroom door is about seven feet high. An acre is the area of a certain plot of ground well known to the children. A mile is the distance from school to a place everyone knows. A square mile is the space bounded by certain streets in the town. Ten miles is the distance to a town to which children have traveled. And so on. These are only representative of the reference points that may help pupils clarify ideas of area and distance.

Because social studies requires concepts of far greater areas and distances than those in the list just given, experiences with maps are the logical and necessary vehicles for their development. Although experiences with maps and globes are discussed more fully elsewhere in this book, it is pertinent to point out that maps and globes are the only practical way to represent ideas of space that the individual has not experienced personally. If maps can be related to personal experience, so much the better, but at least maps offer a useful tool in the development of space concepts. As pupils begin by making maps in which familiar areas and distances are reduced in size—a block city on the kindergarten floor or a map of classroom, shopping center, or farm on the primary-grade bulletin board—they clarify their concepts of inches, feet, and miles. Older children use the scale of miles on maps to interpret distance and area, and advance to the locational skills involving latitude and longitude. It is possible, however, to take too much for granted. Space concepts develop slowly and teachers may be misled about pupils' level of understanding. Planning for new experiences based on children's present level of development, accompanied by continual evaluation of the effect of such experiences, is probably the safest course for the teacher to chart.

Mrs. Johnson, in the dialogue at the beginning of this chapter, no doubt had some of the problems of concept development in mind as the children explored the experiences they might utilize in answering their questions about communication and as they tried to select a suitable starting place for their work. She had anticipated a great variety of terms the study of communication would unearth—*television, telegraph, emergency, message, newspaper, reporter, post office, broadcast,* and many others—some of them already familiar to children in varying degrees of abstraction. More difficult concepts fundamental to the area of learning were clearly implied in children's proposals for topics for study—*communication, transportation, democracy, cooperation, interdependence, change.* Concepts of time and distance surely would be needed in interpreting events and conditions of the past, speed of communication, and location of communication lines. Although Mrs. Johnson realized, of course, that many of these concepts were advanced and impossible to clarify fully, she looked upon the area of learning as an opportunity to introduce some of them and to extend those with which children had had some previous experience. Experiences finally undertaken by pupils become the medium for this concept development.

DEVELOPING UNDERSTANDINGS THROUGH EXPERIENCES

As experiences help children develop a variety of concepts, these experiences also confront pupils with situations in which relationships among concepts become increasingly evident. Generalizing then becomes feasible. For example, as pupils become acquainted with ways in which people live over the world, the words *food, clothing,* and *shelter* become general concepts covering a variety of specific cultural practices. At the same time pupils note the differences in land and climate with which these various people contend; in other words, *environment* becomes a general term signifying the conditions under which human beings live. Noting relationships between concepts of food, clothing, and shelter and the concept of environment, pupils can be guided toward a generalization similar to this one: *Environment affects man's way of living, and man, in turn, modifies his environment.*[7]

Pupils move toward the statement of such generalizations as they accumulate facts about a given question or problem; that is, while gathering sufficient facts for concept development, they begin to sense that certain relationships occur again and again. For example, older children learn facts about the goods that various countries send to other parts of the world, and the concept of *exports* develops; in the same way, the various products people buy abroad come to be known in general as *imports.* Encouraging pupils to see relationships, the teacher may say, "What do these facts tell us about the importance of exports and imports to the countries concerned with them?" The pupils may propose several ways of stating the understanding they are acquiring: *Every country depends on others for some of the things it needs. Few, if any, modern countries can supply all their own needs. Nations of the world are becoming increasingly interdependent.* Subsequently pupils will have opportunities to test the validity of their

---

[7] *Report of the State Central Committee on Social Studies to the California State Curriculum Commission* (Sacramento: California State Department of Education, 1961), p. 42.

statements by exploring further the ways in which nations are related to each other. Ultimately they arrive at a generalization of continuing and broader applicability in their world: *All nations of the modern world are part of a global interdependent system of economic, social, cultural, and political life.*[8]

It must be remembered, however, that children may not achieve these generalizations fully at any one time. There is ample evidence that young children do generalize from the facts they gather, sometimes illogically but usually sensibly from their point of view.[9] In fact, children may actually use an idea of structure in approaching new learning, although they do so somewhat unconsciously. Later on, children begin to be aware of certain relationships among concepts and ideas and may even recognize or identify these relationships. Ultimately they may state the relationships and show skill in illustrating them. Like concepts, generalizations grow in meaning with varied experiences and with the maturity of the learner.

To illustrate, consider the way in which children may move toward understanding of such a generalization as this one: *Cooperation is essential to happy and successful living in a group.* Children's first acquaintance with this idea comes from their observation and study of life in the family. They gather facts and develop concepts about roles played by various family members. They generalize that each person in the family must cooperate with others to make home a good place to be. Later pupils explore their school to find out how it operates and thus clarify concepts about people who work together in a common enterprise. They arrive at the understanding that many different people cooperate to carry on the work of the school.

In their study of community life, undertaken at another grade level perhaps, many facts emerge to strengthen the concept of cooperation. The people who provide food depend on others for transportation. Newspapers are assisted by various communication workers. Firemen need trucks in good condition. The city council helps community workers by enacting useful laws and regulations. Pupils now generalize further that cooperation in a community makes life better for its citizens.

In areas of learning that follow, pupils explore their expanding world, gathering more and more support for the idea of cooperation. They sense how nations cooperate and what happens when they do not. Throughout the elementary school years the generalization that *cooperation is essential to happy living in a group* becomes increasingly significant, an idea basic to the structure of social studies, discovered and tested by the pupils.

From this discussion it is obvious that generalizations are not all of the

---

[8] *Ibid.*, p. 41.
[9] Bernard Spodek, "Developing Social Concepts in the Kindergarten," *Social Education* (May, 1963), pp. 254–256; Kenneth D. Wann, "Children Want to Know," *Childhood Education* (September, 1960), pp. 8–12.

same degree of complexity. Note the increasing difficulty of the statements in the following list.

1. Farmers raise food.
2. People who live in large cities are dependent upon farmers for most of their food.
3. The kinds of food that can be grown in a region are limited by the natural environment.
4. Adequate food is essential to the health of the community.
5. A nation's economy is dependent in part upon the welfare of its farmers.

All these statements are based upon facts and information, but certainly they vary greatly in difficulty of understanding. The first is little more than a statement of a single fact, general rather than specific to a time or place, without emphasis upon a particular relationship between concepts. The second is a statement of relationship specific to a particular area of learning about how city people get their food. The third is much more inclusive, being a statement of relationship based upon much broader information than the first two. The last two involve concepts that are increasingly abstract—relationships that would be sensed only by more mature pupils.

For the purposes of this discussion it is convenient to think of all such generalizations as a hierarchy of knowledge that ranges from simple to complex. High-level or high-order generalizations may be thought of as statements of relationship like those quoted earlier from the California State Curriculum Commission. When used in this book the term *generalization* will refer to high-level, overarching statements of relationship that make up the structure of social studies. Lower-level generalizations that children make as a result of their involvement in certain areas of learning will be identified as *understandings*; these understandings will represent the specific knowledge goals of the area of learning. Ultimately children will draw upon a storehouse of these understandings in arriving at broad generalizations. In spite of the necessity for distinguishing generalizations from understandings, the process of arriving at either is essentially the same; and a multiplication of meaningful experiences is a prerequisite to the validity of the statements, regardless of their level of complexity and difficulty.

Helping children to develop understandings from facts and concepts through generalizing is a responsibility of fundamental importance the teacher must assume. For example, children gather certain facts about the work the policeman does in the community and from these facts concepts begin to emerge—general notions about policemen, law, traffic, protection, and arrest. The child can do one of two things with these facts and concepts. He can carry them about, at least for awhile, as a collection of facts and impressions in his mind, remembering them until study about another community helper crowds them out. Or he can, when the teacher asks what the study of the policeman tells about people who serve the community, formulate certain tentative statements of understandings.

1. People of the community depend upon each other for goods and services.
2. People who serve the community in special ways need the cooperation of all citizens.
3. The work of those who serve the community is determined by the kind of community in which they work.
4. As a community grows and changes, there are changes in the kinds of work done.
5. Each worker has a unique contribution to make to the welfare of the community.

The development of such understandings comes about best through problem-solving activities and results rather directly from the kinds of questions children seek to answer about the subject at hand. For example, in the usual stereotyped approach to a unit of work, children may ask such questions as these: What kind of work does the policeman do? How does he learn to do his work? How is the policeman paid? These questions will bring only factual answers. The policeman protects people and property. He is sometimes trained in a police school. His salary is paid from taxes. In other words, the results of this questioning are quite routine and terminal.

On the other hand, when the pupils are encouraged to ask thought-provoking questions, something more than casual information may result. Why does a community have to have policemen? How can the community help a policeman do his work? How does the policeman depend upon other people in the community? These more thought-provoking questions stimulate research and discussion that lead easily to the statement of important understandings about people who do the work of the community. For example, the pupils discover that the policeman depends heavily upon communication workers, especially in emergencies, that he frequently needs a doctor as he helps people who are injured, that he relies upon the garage mechanic to keep his cruiser car in good order, and that he counts on good citizens to alert him when there is trouble. When the teacher asks about the importance of other community people in the work of the policeman, the children have the basic knowledge from which to generalize that many persons in the community help the policeman do his work. They may also generalize or hypothesize that probably every community worker depends on others for help. As a result of further study the pupils can confirm or reject this broader understanding and others that have been identified. Such understandings are far more useful than mere collections of fact.

No doubt Mrs. Johnson, the teacher in the dialogue at the beginning of this chapter, had in mind certain important understandings about communication as she helped pupils explore content and experiences to find answers to their questions. As children suggested various sources of content and a variety of experiences from which to secure information, the teacher naturally saw each proposal in light of those understandings which she hoped to develop through the area of learning. While children were proposing various experiences, Mrs. Johnson evaluated their plan of action, considering its value in developing the understandings she had identified:

1. Because spoken language is our most common means of communication, every citizen must be able to speak so that others can understand him.
2. Skill and knowledge in the use of tools and materials is essential to communication.
3. Many workers contribute their efforts to make communication possible.
4. Mass media have extended communication to large numbers of people.
5. Some means of communication are more effective for certain purposes than others.
6. Democracy depends upon free communication among individuals and groups.

No doubt, too, Mrs. Johnson asked herself, "Will the content and experiences children plan contribute substantially to the development of these ideas? Will one experience be more valuable than another in developing certain understandings?" When there is reasonable assurance that major outcomes can be achieved, planning with children proceeds.

DEVELOPING ATTITUDES THROUGH EXPERIENCES

Experiences designed to develop concepts and understandings in the area of learning also make their contribution to the development of attitudes and values. Although there is much yet to be learned about the formation of attitudes, evidence indicates that they are acquired rather than inborn, influenced by knowledge and skill but not learned by memorization or from dictation. Attitudes seem to be products of children's interaction with their social group and of their participation with its members.[10]

Although it is difficult to define attitudes, it is possible to say that they represent a kind of readiness to respond—to see, to hear, to think, to act. In social studies, attitudes are often associated with such terms as *awareness of, respect for, desire to, appreciation of, willingness to, concern for,* and so on. Although there are little data to confirm a strong relationship between knowledge and attitudes,[11] the school is committed to the principle that if one knows and understands well he will hold appropriate and compatible attitudes. In other words, there is a strongly held view that the building of broad, well-supported understandings through varied and significant experiences can and should influence children's attitudes and values.

Experiences in the area of learning facilitate the development of attitudes in several ways. As pupils pursue their concerns in problem solving, exploring the community and meeting its people, identification with adults is a natural result. Since children form attitudes through association with adults, experiences that promote this interaction further attitude development. Through this identification children tend to take on whatever social

[10] William O. Stanley, *et al., Social Foundations of Education* (New York: Holt, Rinehart and Winston, Inc., 1956), p. 552.
[11] David Russell, *Children's Thinking* (Boston: Ginn & Company, 1956), pp. 193–194.

attitudes are exemplified in those they come to know well and to admire. Such identification can, of course, be extended to include persons from diverse groups beyond the community as children's problem-solving experiences invite such relationships.[12]

Experiences also open the way to the development of attitudes favorable to democratic group process as pupils cooperatively plan and undertake a variety of activities. Democracy can be understood and appreciated only through experiences with it; children must live democratically if they are to acquire attitudes characteristic of democratic individuals.[13]

Experiences also contribute to the changing of attitudes that children may have about people and things. Where the need to alter attitudes exists, the teacher becomes the agent for arranging situations in which pupils have opportunities to see a problem in a new light, to practice new approaches to old dislikes, to meet in new settings persons or things formerly viewed negatively, to feel new enthusiasms about something previously ignored or resented.[14]

Instruction in the area of learning is concerned, of course, with attitudes that lead to behaviors and skills—in other words, with attitudes that lead to action. Attitudes of respect and confidence in oneself should be evidenced in the way in which a child assumes leadership of his group at appropriate times, pursues his own learning to its proper end, and meets problems that arise in the development of the area of learning. Attitudes of respect and trust of others should lead to acceptance of and consideration for the thoughts and feelings of others in the daily meeting and communication that characterizes the elementary school classroom. Attitudes of concern for the welfare of others go beyond acceptance and understanding to dictate the need for concrete efforts to improve the life of the community and to contribute to those in need elsewhere. Attitudes of acceptance and appreciation of cultural differences should result in the seeking of many contacts with persons from varied groups, the development of genuine friendships in those groups, and diligence in learning more about them. It is clear that hearing or reading about or observing other groups cannot produce such attitudes. Pupils need many opportunities to experiment socially—in short, to experience social contacts—if these attitudes are to be realized.[15] These words by Kilpatrick spoken in relation to children's acqui-

---

[12] Edna Ambrose and Alice Miel, *Children's Social Learning* (Washington, D.C.: Association for Supervision and Curriculum Development, 1958), pp. 90–91.

[13] Lavone A. Hanna, Gladys L. Potter, and Neva Hagaman, *Unit Teaching in the Elementary School* (rev. ed.; New York: Holt, Rinehart and Winston, Inc., 1963), p. 76.

[14] Margaret M. Heaton, *Feelings Are Facts* (New York: National Conference of Christians and Jews, 1952), pp. 32–43.

[15] Lavone A. Hanna and Neva Hagaman, "Action Principles from Studies of Child Development," in John U. Michaelis (Ed.), *Social Studies in Elementary Schools* (Thirty-second Yearbook of the National Council for the Social Studies; Washington, D.C.: National Education Association, 1962), p. 47.

sition of the constituents of the good life are equally appropriate here: "Merely to learn about such matters will not suffice; nor will it satisfy merely to learn that they are counted morally desirable. These attitudes must be accepted to act on and live by."[16]

It must be pointed out, however, that experiences may create unfavorable, as well as favorable, attitudes if the experiences are carelessly chosen and without purpose in the eyes of the children. Such experiences may create dislikes or hostilities toward certain kinds of activity, for particular ideas or subject matter, or for people in the classroom group or on the outside. In fact, attitudes may in turn adversely affect emerging experiences, coloring children's eagerness to participate, their interpretation of findings, and their reactions to things, people, and ideas. The social studies area of learning, on the other hand, is a series of experiences designed to build positive attitudes through involvement in problem solving, attitudes that form a necessary bridge from understandings to behaviors and skills, from knowing to doing.

ENCOURAGING DESIRABLE BEHAVIORS AND SKILLS

The development of desirable behaviors and skills—the ultimate objectives of the area of learning—is the expected outcome of firmly established attitudes. Through experiences, children learn how to act in accordance with the attitudes they are acquiring. The pupil is more likely to demonstrate commendable behavior and skills if the understandings he has developed are impressive enough to produce attitudes that impel him to action now or in the future.

Opportunities to use knowledge—to try out new conservation practices, to develop a safety plan for the school, to initiate correspondence with a school overseas, to select better-balanced meals in the school cafeteria, to improve the use of reference materials in the school library, to solve a classroom problem through role playing—these and many more are provided in the experiences of the area of learning.

Experiences also serve as vehicles for the practice of a wide variety of skills in group process—exhibiting good human relationships, behaving democratically, performing as a responsible citizen, and assuming responsibility for the achievement of group goals. Through practice, these kinds of behaviors and skills become part of children's preparation for working and living not only in the school but in the world outside.

Mrs. Johnson undoubtedly had given some thought to behaviors and skills in relation to both content and group process as she tried to foresee how children's experiences would lead them to behave in certain ways. In addition to the development of skills in working together—a continuing

[16] William H. Kilpatrick, *Modern Education and Better Human Relationships* (New York: Anti-Defamation League of B'nai B'rith, 1949), p. 21.

emphasis in her classroom—she hoped her pupils would, as a result of their experiences in the study of communication, speak clearly in order to be understood, write their native language correctly, use communication devices properly, cooperate with communication workers in helpful ways, read printed materials critically, view television and motion pictures with discrimination, and speak forcefully to defend the rights of others. In the planning stage of the area of learning, Mrs. Johnson could not be certain about the outcomes of all the experiences pupils were proposing, but she was sure that without such experiences children would have few opportunities to put into use the skills they would be learning.

Role of Experiences in Problem Solving

Experiences play an important role in the problem-solving process. As pupils become concerned with a problem and plan a course of action they hope will lead to its solution, they depend upon experiences to provide opportunities for analyzing, sharing, and discussing and to provide facts and information needed in coming to conclusions and in generalizing upon what they have learned. These experiences not only assist in the solution of problems already identified, but frequently also create new problems that challenge pupils to move ahead to new fields, to seek out new resources, and to suggest new courses of action.

There is almost no limit to the variety of experiences in which children may participate as they embark upon the solving of problems and search for the data they need. The dialogue at the beginning of this chapter reveals some of the many types available for almost every group of pupils. When teachers and pupils realize the extent of these resources, solving problems and answering questions become delightful and challenging enterprises. Direct or firsthand experiences of most value to children seeking to solve problems in social studies can be conveniently grouped for overview here. Each of these types receives more thorough attention later.

Because of their importance in the process of problem solving, *group planning* and *discussion*, already treated in a previous chapter, are again emphasized. Experiences in group planning and discussion are the catalytic agent through which all other experiences develop and progress. They replace with democratic practices the authoritarian procedures of teacher assignment and pupil recitation. Through the experiences of cooperative planning and discussion, children become directly and personally involved in the identification and analysis of problems to be solved and actively participate in the pooling and evaluation of information upon which answers and solutions ultimately depend.

As the area of learning unfolds and pupils begin their problem-solving investigations in earnest, *reading* performs important services. It opens vast horizons of information unattainable through firsthand experiences and makes available an almost unlimited variety of sources. It provides background information in the area of study, leads to data useful in answering questions and solving problems, and supplies directions for developing projects of all kinds. Reading remains a time-honored experience in problem solving.

Because much of the content of social studies springs from the concerns and problems of the community, *community experiences* are logically an effective source of information in the searching process. Furthermore, living in democracy demands that children learn to assume the role of the citizen who knows how to meet and solve problems. Meaningful contacts with the community provide learning experiences through which children come to understand community problems and to participate in their solutions as real-life citizens. In other words, community experiences help pupils relate to the human concerns of neighborhood and town, serving both as an important source of information and as a laboratory for problem solving.

In the problem-solving process there are many opportunities for *construction* and *processing*. When significant questions and problems suggest the values of producing equipment and models and processing foods, materials, and other products, and when careful evaluation indicates that such activities will produce accurate information, pupils are encouraged to carry out their plans. Why did Indians use birch bark for canoes? What is the best kind of home to construct for our classroom pet? Why is raw silk expensive to produce in this country? What is a water wheel? How is cheese made? What would happen if the ingredients of this product were changed? Obviously the processing of materials and the making of equipment can contribute substantially to the investigation of questions and problems like these. Such experiences provide essential firsthand information, illustrate concepts difficult to understand through reading alone, and permit pupils to test hypotheses related to a problem.

Problem solving in social studies draws heavily upon *audio-visual experiences* whenever firsthand experiences are out of reach or impractical to achieve. As pupils follow many avenues of research in pursuit of facts and information, they turn to audio-visual materials when they need a panoramic view of the present, a living picture of the past, an intensive study of a topic or an idea, a pictorial record of an event, a dramatization characteristic of a period or a place, or on many other occasions when it is not possible to go to original sources for data.

Whenever the area of learning involves a search for science information, *experimenting* also becomes an important problem-solving activity. There are a number of problem areas in social studies that require the scientific approach. A study of conservation, for example, suggests the analysis of soil, experimentation with soil covers, studies of conditions for plant growth, to mention only a few. Study undertaken to improve diet and health often leads to feeding experiments and germ culture. Experiences with communication may naturally include experiments with sound and with various simple communication devices. These experiences are valuable for children in social studies because they stress the importance of the scientific method in problem solving.

Criteria
for Selection of Experiences

Even the very brief survey of experiences just concluded suggests that the profusion of experiences available to any group poses some serious problems of selection if the teacher is to guide children's problem-solving experiences so that they will be productive as well as challenging. There are, however, certain criteria that, if thoughtfully applied, can improve the selection of experiences in social studies. In achieving any given purpose the experiences chosen should pass the tests proposed by several searching questions.

Does the experience develop the content under consideration? This criterion is of great importance if use of school time for any given experience is justifiable. If the film *Shep, the Farm Dog* is selected to answer in part the question about how dogs help man, will it have accurate information easily understood by the pupils? If children visit the botany department of the university to see the greenhouse, will the excursion develop content concerned with the conditions for plant growth? If pupils re-create in their classroom the First Continental Congress, will the representation increase their understanding of the important content involved? If there is any doubt that the experience develops content under consideration, it probably should be discarded in favor of another that has more substance and purpose.

Does the experience develop understandings and concepts related to the area of learning? As has been already pointed out, understandings and concepts in social studies are the result of many and varied planned contacts with the content under study. Direct experiences that develop content are likely, if the teacher so intends, to deepen children's understandings and extend their concepts. It becomes necessary, however, for the teacher to think consciously about the understandings and concepts to which an experience will relate; otherwise, children may come through an experience with a collection of facts and information unrelated to any larger ideas. For example, a trip to the state legislature by an upper-grade group may yield information about how a particular state legislature operates on a given day. At the same time will it help children to generalize about how legislatures work or deepen their concept of the lawmaking process? And again, when a visitor comes to school to demonstrate spinning, will her visit develop the understanding that spinning by hand is difficult and develop as well such concepts as *carding, sliver,* and *fibers?* Every experience should develop easily recognizable understandings and concepts. If it does not, it may not be worth the time it requires.

Does the experience encourage problem solving and critical thinking? It is not enough that an experience in social studies develops content and the understandings and concepts drawn from it; it should also pose problems the children will need to solve and that will require critical thinking. These problem situations may relate closely to the content of the area of learning —determining the authenticity of cattle brands children wish to use in a study of ranch life, finding out how pioneer folk made hominy, testing corn in a seed tester, timing eggs in an incubator, checking the accuracy of a dinosaur drawing—or they may relate to ways of working together and to methods of carrying out activities. The occasions for problem solving and critical thinking in a well-chosen social studies experience are many. An experience that provides no such opportunities may be less than adequate.

Is the experience a true representation of the ideas it seeks to develop? The critical thinking children do about their experiences will do much to ensure that the experience itself is authentic or as nearly so as possible. The days of the sand table with its cut-paper objects are fortunately gone; teachers have come to realize that children can be misled by such productions. But misconceptions are still being encouraged—by the bulletin board about Korea where children mistakenly include temple scenes in Bangkok, the book that is obviously biased, the table display on silkworms with its paper larvae and moths, and the map that distorts its information. The experience that most effectively represents an idea reproduces the true fact as closely as possible; and when materials, process, or results are not authentic, pupils are made fully aware of the differences. An idea improperly represented may be worse than no representation of the idea at all.

Is the experience appropriate to the child's level of understanding? Appropriateness to maturity level is another measuring stick that is easily forgotten by the enthusiastic teacher who, in opening up an exciting new area of study, may forget that the children's ability to understand may not equal his own. The teacher will need to draw upon his own knowledge and past experience with children as well as upon his experiences with his present group of boys and girls in order to decide whether or not the experience under consideration will be in accord with pupils' ability to grasp its meaning. Will a trip to the atomic reactor be fruitful for third-grade children? Who should see a film on the Industrial Revolution identified as suitable for children eight to twelve? Can a current-events period that makes use of the daily newspaper be profitable for young children? These are the kinds of questions that must be answered by the teacher interested in selecting experiences appropriate to the child's level of understanding.

Does the experience spring from a previous one and will it lead to still another? Experiences in social studies are most effective when they come as the natural consequence of some identified need and when they serve as transitions to other experiences. A worthwhile experience seldom comes from nowhere; similarly, a worthwhile experience is almost never a dead end. Each experience must be considered in the light of its relationship to experiences that preceded and those that will follow. Each should contribute to the ongoingness of the area of learning. An experience unrelated to the main idea the study is developing probably would be better left to free-activity periods planned around other needs and interests of children.

Does the experience draw upon a variety of materials? Many experiences —reading to answer questions, arranging instructional bulletin boards, preparing special reports, reproducing or creating maps, planning a mural, writing a dramatization, and many more—require a variety of materials for successful completion. Others—taking a study trip, viewing a film, entertaining a resource visitor, conducting a community survey, and the like—require materials both for preparation and for follow-up experiences. And even more important, the development of understandings and the sharpening of concepts require that children explore and study materials of various types, treatment, and points of view. A single reference or source of information is seldom an adequate basis for a major generalization.

Is the experience practicable for these children? The last criterion, although not the least significant, suggests that each experience be considered in the light of the extent to which it can be carried on successfully in the local situation. It would be unwise to encourage children to embark upon plans for an experience that has little chance to be successful because of circumstances beyond their control. The teacher must consider school regulations about field trips, parents' attitudes toward various kinds of activities, the adequacy of available materials, and the response the administration will make to the action pupils take. He should also be sure that the conclusions he draws about such matters are correct and not merely assumed, for it is common to find teachers in the same school with different ideas about the kinds of experiences that can be freely encouraged. When the teacher finds out exactly what restrictions exist, if any, he plans with children accordingly. Reality always exerts some influence on the classroom situation.

The busy teacher may think the task of selecting experiences in accordance with these criteria is far too demanding; but if all experiences in social studies were carefully selected, the quality of children's experiencing would disarm the critics who think children should spend more time with books and less time being active. Not even the severest of them could dispute the value of an experience chosen to develop accurate content, understandings, and concepts; to encourage problem solving and critical thinking; to meet children's level of understanding; to stimulate new learning experiences; and to fit the demands of the local school situation.

Factors Determining
the Direction of Children's Experiences

Once experiences are selected in accordance with agreed-upon criteria, children and teacher set out to implement their plans of action. How do they begin? The point of departure pupils take greatly influences the course of events in the area of learning; and once a successful beginning is made, progress is closely related to the nature of the problem they are pursuing.

Several factors help teachers and pupils select a place to begin their study in an area of learning. The teacher recognizes that one of the most important of these factors is the pupils' need for background information. The problem chosen for initial consideration is usually one that will help pupils acquire this general background knowledge about the subject at hand, for the teacher recognizes that the group needs some common information upon which it can later build more specialized knowledge. Seldom does the good teacher encourage children to begin with a problem that is only a segment of the whole area of learning or to divide into committees that will immediately undertake the study of discrete phases of the particular area. Children need to extend the general background information partially uncovered in the initiation and to identify some of the understandings that can be drawn from this general information.

The initial study experience as well as the initial problem chosen should open up for children some view of the available resources for their study. In some groups, such as those in Mrs. Johnson's, reading on a general problem from a variety of materials may be an effective way to build the background necessary for further study. Sometimes a film or a field trip may provide a survey of the content and a common learning experience for the group. Whatever the starting point may be, teacher and children consider how they can best acquire general information that will help them to move ahead to more specific problems.

Selecting a place to begin study of an area of learning is influenced also by children's interests. If children undertake the initial exploration of content with enthusiasm, this experience will lead to another more readily. If the experience provides a broad enough base of operation, children can identify many areas in which they may want to make some personal investigations later. Cooperative selection of the starting place, even when it is rather firmly guided by the teacher, holds the most promise for enthusiastic acceptance. The illustration at the beginning of this chapter shows quite well how a teacher helped pupils see the wisdom of beginning with content and experiences calculated to build a good foundation for their later study.

Selection of initial experiences must necessarily be influenced, of course, by certain conditions the teacher recognizes and can call to the attention of the pupils if necessary. The availability of materials and equipment, restrictions of school policy, or limitations of room environment cannot be ignored in any realistic teacher-pupil planning. The task of selecting a good starting place for problem-solving experiences requires cooperative evaluation of each suggestion in terms of such practical considerations.

The direction their experiences will take, once children set out on their adventure in learning, depends largely on the nature of the problems they are trying to solve. Vital and significant problems will encourage creative planning and experiencing. Under the guidance of the resourceful teacher, pupils can evaluate for themselves the appropriateness of each experience they suggest, seeing clearly its relationship to what has gone on before and determining for themselves the contribution the activity is likely to make to solving a particular problem. If the teacher exerts too much influence, pupils may concentrate upon trying to identify what they think the teacher wants. On the other hand, if the teacher thinks with the children rather than for them, he can take advantage of their enthusiasms while he helps them to be increasingly purposeful and selective.

Obviously the direction of children's experiences in social studies cannot be predetermined by the teacher, but he does play an important part in helping children to select initial experiences that will open up many possibilities for future search.

QUESTIONS FOR DISCUSSION

Reread the dialogue recorded at the beginning of the chapter.

1. Why did the teacher encourage the children to explore many ways of solving problems?
2. How did the teacher help the children recognize a desirable starting place for their study?
3. What considerations led to the selection of reading as the initial experience?

SUGGESTIONS FOR CONSTRUCTING
A RESOURCE UNIT

Identify understandings, attitudes, skills, and behaviors appropriate to your area of learning. Refer to the content outline that you prepared earlier to make certain that it contains essential information for achieving desired outcomes.

Note the following guidelines for identifying and recording the understandings, attitudes, skills, and behaviors to be developed through your area of learning.

1. Understandings are the knowledge and insights that children acquire as they engage in the area of learning; understandings are stated in sentence form.

5

Reading to Build
Background
and Solve Problems

MRS. JOHNSON: Judging from the appearance of our reading table, boys and girls, we're ready to find the answer to our first problem about communication. Peggy, will you read the question we chose yesterday as our starting place?

PEGGY: What kinds of communication should be used for different purposes?

MRS. JOHNSON: The plan for our reading groups is on the chalkboard, but before we start we need to think of a good plan for recording the information we find in our books. Any suggestions?

RONNIE: Could each of us make a list of all the kinds of communication we read about?

CHARLES: We could, but that would answer only part of our question. We need to find out what the thing is used for.

MARY LOU: We could each write a story about the kind of communication we like best. That would be fun.

ALICE: We wouldn't have time to read much if we did that. We want to cover a lot of ground. Don't we, Mrs. Johnson?

MRS. JOHNSON: Alice is right, I'm afraid. Our scheme must be simple enough to allow plenty of time for reading and yet show clearly the answer to our question. What do you think, Susan?

SUSAN: Could we make a chart with a list of all the kinds of communication down one side and after each one a few words to tell what it is used for? Each of us could make a little chart as we read; then we could put all the different kinds together when we share.

MRS. JOHNSON: Let's try Susan's idea. It would be quick and would certainly show our information at a glance. Now let's check the board to find out what materials we start with and where our groups will work. See how smoothly we can get organized. Let me know when your group is ready.

ANNE: We're ready now, Mrs. Johnson. Is this little paper book with the green cover and the typing all we're supposed to have?

MRS. JOHNSON: That's all you'll need right now, Anne. We'll all use the books in the reading center later on. Your group has a special story.

DONALD: Where did it come from?

MRS. JOHNSON: I wrote it, Donald, just for your group. You'll be surprised to see how much information it has. Some of the information isn't in any of the other books. Can you find out what your story is about while I help the other groups get started? When I come back, we'll read the new story together.

DONALD: Sure. Looks pretty good.

MRS. JOHNSON (*moves to Frank's group*):   Can I help your group, Frank?

FRANK: Are we starting with our textbook? What pages?

PETER: Use the table of contents, Frank. I've found the right chapter already.

MRS. JOHNSON: "Talking Business" is the right chapter, Peter. But what would you have done if the table of contents hadn't told you so easily? Who knows?

MARY LOU: Index. Use the index. I'm sure I can find "communication" and "telephone" and "telegraph" and lots of other words like that in the index. Yes, right here under "communication" are all the pages and then it says, "See also cables, mail services, radio, telegraph, and telephone." This is just what we need.

MRS. JOHNSON: If you have all found the place, I think you are ready to read and to make your chart. I'll check with Wayne's group, and then I'll be back in a little while if you need me.

PETER: Don't worry; we know what to do.

MRS. JOHNSON (*moves to Wayne's group*): My, looks as though you're already at work with *Pioneering in Communication*. What have you found out about your book so far?

WAYNE: There's a separate story in it about almost every kind of communication. I don't think we'll have time to read every one of them. Will we?

MRS. JOHNSON: What kind of reading can we do when we want to find information quickly?

PATRICIA: We can skim to find the kind of communication and then skim to find out just what it is used for. We can read again more carefully when we look for answers to our other questions later.

MRS. JOHNSON: Skimming is very useful when you are looking for the answer to a special question. I think skimming would be a good way to read this reference, Patricia. Did you notice anything else about your book?

JANET SUE: It tells the history as well as up-to-date things. We can use this same reference again when we answer the questions about communication long ago—at least, it looks that way.

BILL: Look, here's the Morse code. That's for me. Can I make a telegraph key?

MRS. JOHNSON: But finish your reading first. If there are any difficult words, can you keep a list of them for us to talk about later? I think Barbara Ann's group may need me just now. (*Moves to the advanced readers, who are reading a variety of materials.*)

BARBARA ANN: These pamphlets are good, Mrs. Johnson, but there's a lot of information here. I won't have many different items on my chart. Is that all right?

MRS. JOHNSON: Yes, of course, Barbara Ann. You'll be our authority on telephones and telegraph. Allen, you can be the expert on the postal service;

Carrying the Mail is just the book for you. Did you have any trouble finding the right volume of the encyclopedia, Robert? Knowing the alphabet certainly speeds things up, doesn't it?

ROBERT: We're getting along by ourselves all right, Mrs. Johnson. All we need is time.

MRS. JOHNSON (*returns to group of slowest readers*): What do you think about your story now, Anne?

ANNE: It's all right, I guess.

MRS. JOHNSON: I'll sit with you so we can read it together. Can you read the first paragraph and find out the easiest way to communicate with someone?

DONALD: The easiest way is to talk to him, but you can't always do that.

MRS. JOHNSON: You're right, Donald. Let's read the second paragraph to find out another way to send a message. Do you see the word *message* in this paragraph?

. . . .

MRS. JOHNSON: I know most of you aren't ready to stop reading, but it will soon be time for recess. Should we see how much information we have for our chart? I'll keep a temporary record on the chalkboard, and we'll make the chart when we are all agreed on what it should include. Anne, do you want to suggest what we should have first?

ANNE: We ought to start with the easiest kind of communication. *Speaking.* But I can't think how you'd say what purpose it's for.

DONALD: It's used when you want to communicate with someone who is in the same room with you.

RONNIE: Then we could have hand and arm signals. We use them when we can see our friends but can't make them hear what we say.

MRS. JOHNSON: Good. Anne's group has us off to a good start. Who has the next item for the chart?

. . . .

MRS. JOHNSON: Do we have all the different kinds of communication on our chart and the correct purpose for each? Who can read it all while we make sure that we haven't omitted anything important?

CHARLES: This *was* a good question to start reading on, Mrs. Johnson. Look how many different kinds of communication we already know something about. Gives me an idea of something special I'd like to do—start a real newspaper right here in this room.

BILL: Wait'll you see my telegraph key. Anyone who wants to learn the code can help me operate it.

MRS. JOHNSON: Has this reading helped us in any other way, boys and girls?

PEGGY: We know something about where to get information to answer some of the other questions on our list. That's important, too.

MRS. JOHNSON: Can we have a committee of two to make our large chart for us? Then tomorrow we can take another look at it before we decide what to do next.

Skill in reading is highly prized in the American society, which from the beginning of formal education onward fosters in the child a desire to read. Its culture demands the ability to read—newspapers describing in detail the world of current events; thousands upon thousands of publications both rec-reational and educational; pamphlets, booklets, and flyers explaining every feature of the environment, natural or man-made; packages that line the shelves of every store; advertising for endless products and services; direc-tions to everywhere—in short, a multitude of reading materials in which it is possible to find out something about almost everything. The child soon learns that in these resources he can discover answers to many of his ques-tions, and as he grows older he perceives that his skill in reading is closely related to success in school and in life outside.

The democratic way of life also demands the ability to read, for reading is indispensable to an informed citizenry as a tool in gathering the facts and information needed in solving problems and in making defensible judg-ments and discriminating choices. The elementary school years are not too soon to learn habits of research that will help the thoughtful citizen keep abreast of his times and ready to participate in meeting its problems. Read-ing may be considered a way of life in America, a country whose educa-tional system and wide distribution of reading materials have given almost everyone the tools of reading.

In the social studies area of learning wide reading introduces children to a great panorama of information about the world in which they live, its past and present. From this reading children build background, gather evidence, weigh ideas, and draw sound conclusions applicable to the prob-lems that concern them. These experiences in reading for real purposes are good practice in the kind of reading well-informed citizens do when they search for facts that will help to solve the problems of neighborhood, com-munity, or nation. Because reading in social studies contributes to the development of skills needed for democratic citizenship as well as to the achievement of the purposes of the area of learning, its role is an impor-tant one.

Role of Reading
in the Area of Learning

The role of reading in the area of learning is really dual in nature. From the teacher's point of view reading is an important avenue to the achievement of the purposes of the area of learning, an avenue through which children widen the horizons of their world and become aware of those who share it with them. From the children's point of view, reading provides a source of information useful in their problem solving. It is not surprising that teacher and pupils usually plan to survey available reading materials rather early in the area of learning. Both recognize reading as a practical approach to building background and solving problems.

READING AS IT RELATES
TO THE TEACHER'S PURPOSES

Reading experiences make special contributions to the area of learning. They build upon other kinds of experiences children may have, vitalizing them and making them more meaningful, and they give children opportunities to experience vicariously many facets of living that cannot be a real part of their lives. Reading deepens children's understanding of the social world, helping pupils to identify themselves with its problems and processes. Reading experiences make other more practical contributions as well, enlarging children's acquaintance with a variety of materials and emphasizing the usefulness of reading in the search for the information and ideas needed in problem solving.

One of the most important of these contributions is the service reading performs in extending and enriching children's experiences. Through reading, the child can move from his personal experiences to a host of related adventures, as each of his own provides background for some other that he may know only through the printed word. In a similar way one reading experience leads to another, with every succeeding exploration enlarging the child's view and adding new detail, intriguing him to read on and to visualize many experiences in which he cannot actively participate. Children's visits to the railroad station, for example, may be only the beginning. How easy it is now to read more and more about trains, steam engines and diesels, passenger and freight trains, railroads that crisscross the country with goods and passengers, very little different from those that go daily through the community. Boys and girls who have toured the local newspaper office can extend this experience through reading to appreciate the operations on a great city daily with six times as many machines and a hundred times the circulation. Children can identify themselves with the life of the forest ranger as they read, building on their own experiences in the woods near the school or in the state park a few miles away. Such reading widens the horizons of the child's world and pushes back the boundaries of his own personal experience.

Reading further extends children's experiences by putting their classroom projects and activities into their proper setting. Reading can round out these experiences, telling what comes before and what comes after in real life, describing how the process is variously carried on in different environments, and showing what the activity means to real people. For example, weaving in primitive ways in the classroom raises other questions that can be answered by reading: How did early Indians color their yarns? What plants made the best dyes? How was the woven material used after it was finished? Setting up a sea-water aquarium affords fine opportunities for observing marine life in the classroom, but what really lies on the ocean floor? The diorama of Shasta Dam develops some concepts of its size and its location, but reading can make the building of a dam a great human undertaking of massive proportions. Constructing an adobe house on the playground helps children understand how people meet a basic need, but reading fills the house with people who plan and work together to solve the problems of daily living. In such ways books and reading extend the significance of children's projects and activities.

Whenever necessary, this reading in social studies can itself become a substitute for real-life experience. It brings to the child vicariously those experiences out of his life in time or place. It creates with words the steaming jungle of the Amazon, the frozen glaciers of the North, and the orange groves of the Far West. It describes, as well, the many processes in which men engage—the silversmithing of the Navajos, clockmaking in the Black Forest of Germany, or steel manufacturing in Birmingham and Pittsburgh. It tells how people outside the children's own community solve the problems of daily living as they meet the challenges of desert, mountain, or snow-covered steppe. Places, processes, and people come alive for pupils who cannot experience firsthand all the varied activities of today's world.

In a similar way reading makes the past live again. Many of the real-life experiences of another day can come into the classroom only through the printed word. Colorful descriptions of historical events, narrative or fictionalized, fill the past with real human beings who think and act in keeping with their times. Reading or listening to these accounts, well selected for their accuracy and appropriateness, supplies rich detail to clothe out-of-reach experiences in the fabric of reality and authenticity. Original sources, too, diaries or journals recording the experiences of real people, are useful in reviving the atmosphere and activity of days gone by. What can children find out about the real hardships of the Mayflower journey? Will the records kept by those on board re-create the uncertainties and discomfort? What was this community like when it was first settled? What will old newspapers tell us about our town one hundred years ago? Reading does bring the past to life. Carried there by skillful writers who through the printed word help children range far away and long ago, pupils ride the Viking ships, march with De Soto, sign the Declaration of Independence, and hunt for fur-bearing animals in the lands beyond the Mississippi.

When children have had a direct experience that is especially meaningful to them or that represents a highlight in their study of a problem, reading can help them to relive the experience and to gain new insights into its purpose. How many adults have eagerly read descriptions of places they have visited, noting how the authors' ideas agree with their own, hoping to discover what they missed seeing, or simply enjoying the experience in retrospect? When children have these same opportunities to read about things they have experienced, they seem to enjoy them as much. They like the more leisurely pace they can assume in reading; they have time to explore details they missed at firsthand; they feel again the sensations of sight and sound; they really understand what they are reading. Such reading enriches old experiences with new appreciation, understanding, and delight.

As children experience through reading, their social understandings are extended and deepened. Reading makes more meaningful to them the real focus of social studies—how people everywhere carry on their daily-life activities. They discover as they read, for example, that people in some parts of the world still live a very primitive existence, and that those in other regions have greatly changed their manner of living. Reading extends their appreciation of the effects of environment upon the ways in which people meet their problems and the influence of tradition and culture upon their solution to these problems. Between the covers of books they find real people planning ways to secure food, to find comfortable homes, to move from place to place, and to protect those they love. Concepts of family life are enlarged, because in books children can experience all kinds of families, seeing themselves in relation to their own as they read about others. Community life, past and present, becomes through reading a lively, cooperative effort in which workers of many kinds contribute to the general good. The concept of democracy is enlivened by stories of boys, girls, and adults who make its principles work in their daily lives. Becoming well acquainted, through reading, with people of another race or nationality sharpens children's interest in and understanding of people in their own communities who may differ in some striking way, just as it enlarges their awareness of world-wide problems growing out of discrimination and prejudice. Such wise use of reading in social studies helps children see themselves in relation to the social world and alerts them to socially acceptable ways of thinking and behaving.

Reading to build background and to solve significant problems also encourages children's acquaintance with a variety of materials. No longer is the social studies textbook the sole source of information for those who are exploring to find solutions to problems. In the reading activities of the area of learning pupils discover the wide range of materials that can be read for various purposes. First-grade children may skillfully read pictures to find out how to process bread at school or read from a chart how to make ice cream. Another group may use the teacher's professional text to find directions for constructing a relief map of salt and flour. A conservation bulletin from a state department may assist in a study of erosion. Sixth-grade boys and girls developing a "little United Nations" may search through a variety of publications to secure the information they need. Multiple textbooks, special references, trade books, pamphlets and bulletins, graphic materials, and current publications—all become tools for the pupils who are carrying on simple research in social studies. Moreover, this knowledge of reading resources, if properly developed, will be continually useful throughout school life and in adult society as well.

This functional use of many kinds of materials in social studies naturally emphasizes the use of reading as a learning tool. Printed materials often reveal information that possibly could be secured from no other source. When children discover that such helps are available, they go eagerly to them, persisting in their search until needs are met. How can an airplane model be constructed? Boys study diligently the directions on the carton. What is the inside story about new advances in medical research? An authoritative interview in a current magazine is suggested as a reliable place to find the answer. What kind of dress did pioneer women wear? Reading the encyclopedia produces the needed information in words and pictures. When encouragement and praise follow each successful use of reading in the search to answer a question, children strive to use many resources independently. The teacher ensures success by making certain that pupils have the skills necessary to efficient use of each new resource, emphasizing with children that one who can read and who knows how to use a variety of materials can learn many things quickly. Developing an awareness that reading is an effective tool for independent learning is one of the valuable contributions of reading to the area of learning. Such awareness is excellent motivation for improving reading skill. When a child wants to know something and knows that he can find out by reading, then learning to read assumes new importance.

READING AS IT RELATES
TO CHILDREN'S PURPOSES

Children, of course, use reading in the area of learning for very practical purposes. They read for the background information that gives them a survey of content in the field and helps them feel comfortable in the new area of learning. They read further to answer questions and solve problems which are the center of attention in their study. They read also to discover how to carry out many of the activities included in their plan of action.

The first reading children usually do in the area of learning is reading that will provide background information. Background reading gives children a general view of the area being considered, reveals certain segments of the topic in which they may have some special interests, identifies some of the vocabulary that will be needed in pursuing their study, and leads them to acquaintance with the content of a variety of materials. Reading together for background information provides a common experience for the group, holding its members together during the initial exploration and providing a vantage point from which smaller groups may take their cues. Background reading may also raise additional questions and problems for those children who during the initiation did not know enough about the area to feel special needs or interests.

This background reading may be accomplished in several ways. Sometimes children select from their proposed questions and problems a very general topic about which all may center their first reading experiences

For the most part, books selected for this experience are those that survey the content of the area rather broadly. At other times children do background reading as they locate reference materials to be used by the class, skimming quickly any likely references and marking the proper places. Although this kind of reading for background is often less thorough, it may be quite extensive. In some instances, however, the background reading may be actually background listening. The teacher's reading aloud to develop a common experience for the group is a very useful and widely used technique. Sometimes this background reading—from a colorful novel of a certain locale or an early diary or journal kept by a transcontinental traveler, for example—may actually be part of the initiatory experiences. In any event, the purpose of the background reading is the same—to stimulate interest and enthusiasm, to provide some working data, and to reveal the possibilities in the materials at hand.

The most important purpose for which children read is the gathering of data needed in the problem-solving process. This reading, of course, is extremely functional. If questions and problems raised in the initiation are pertinent to the lives of children and of concern to them, this reading will be self-motivated and purposeful. Pupils search for facts, weigh the opinions of several authors, check their own ideas against those of authorities, try to determine the authenticity of what they read, and share and compare their findings with those of others. Young children who do not have great skill in reading use their picture books, listen to adults read, or share charted information prepared by the teacher. Older children use materials suited to their reading ability and, if their maturity permits, take notes from a variety of sources, relating this information directly to the questions and problems under consideration.

Although all the children's questions and problems cannot be answered through reading, reading provides much of the information children want to know. At any one time a group may be using many different kinds of materials to answer questions about a certain interest. An intermediate group, for example, was learning about petroleum resources from a variety of printed materials. One small group pored over the publications of an oil company to gather information about prospecting for oil. Another used the encyclopedia to gather facts for a graph on world oil production. Another studied the science textbook to find out how oil is formed beneath the earth's surface. Another interpreted the printed report made by the local oil company as the result of a survey to determine present and future uses of fuel oil in the community. Although some of these references answered several questions, some were highly specialized and treated only one question. And, of course, the questions and problems that could not be resolved through reading became the subjects of other kinds of research.

Children read also for directions for carrying out a variety of projects needed in the solving of problems. This kind of reading may be the most purposeful of all. Children are challenged by projects and processes. Most of these activities, if they are to be authentic and truly valuable in developing the understandings of the area of learning, must be precisely carried out. Hence finding and reading reliable directions assume great importance as essential tools in helping children carry out their plans.

Directions for activities and projects come from a variety of sources. In one classroom a one-hundred-year-old cookbook supplies directions for making hominy, a pioneer journal helps children find out how to mold candles, an industrial arts textbook gives a method for making paper, and directions on the carton of the product are followed to make pudding. Often a resource person must be called in to develop with children the plans for making something or for carrying out a process; agreed-upon directions are usually recorded for later reading and reference. There is no doubt that this kind of reading is highly functional, reading that the child encounters not only in problem solving but almost daily inside and outside the school.

But reading does not stop at any of these points. In the problem-solving situation children return again and again to reading to substantiate conclusions drawn from many experiences, and they continue to read ever more purposefully to explore new interests and problems (see Figure 6). These reading experiences broaden horizons, lead to acquaintance with many materials, and identify reading as a useful tool in problem solving. Children recognize the values of reading in social studies because it serves their purposes well.

Reading Materials
in Social Studies

Problem solving in the area of learning is greatly facilitated by the availability of extensive reading materials of high quality. In fact, the development of critical reading depends upon children's having access to a variety of sources, of differing treatment and points of view, from which to gather and evaluate information. Furthermore, bringing to the classroom a wide range of materials that differ in levels of difficulty simplifies the meeting of individual differences that exist in every classroom group.[1]

TYPES OF READING MATERIALS

For many teachers the social studies textbook is the most readily available reference reading in social studies. Because many schools employ

---

[1] Alvina Treut Burrows, "Reading, Research, and Reporting in the Social Studies," in Nelson B. Henry (Ed.), *Social Studies in the Elementary School* (Fifty-sixth Yearbook of the National Society for the Study of Education; Chicago: University of Chicago Press, 1957), p. 196.

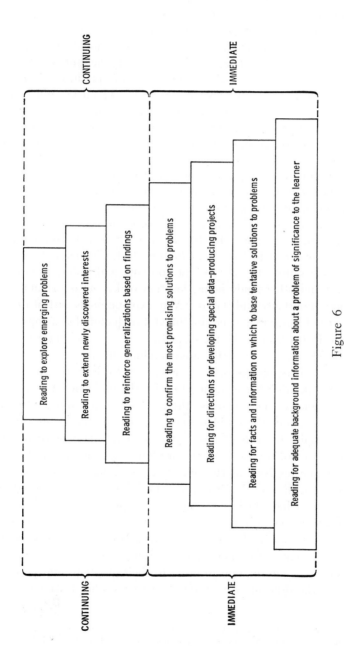

Figure 6

Purposeful reading in social studies carries the learner to reading experiences of increasing significance.

a series of textbooks in social studies as the basis for their social studies curriculum, teachers have come to rely on the textbook as the body of information considered essential by the school system that selected it.

Fortunately, textbooks in social studies have become increasingly attractive and well written, with liberal use of functional illustrations, charts, graphs, maps, and timelines. Authorities in the field of social studies have teamed up with successful classroom teachers to produce materials that are far more effective than the texts of years past. Teachers' guides that accompany the textbook generally reflect newer trends in social studies—emphasis upon basic generalizations, development of concepts, variety of experiences to supplement the reading, and evaluation techniques that go beyond testing of facts and information.

Because of the widespread adoption of the basic social studies text, it is realistic to consider the use of this resource in problem solving. Certainly the textbook affords for children in the group a common background of experience, serving also as an overview of content or an introduction that may give rise to questions for further investigation. Furthermore, it is frequently convenient to have available for all pupils materials that illustrate basic study skills—use of table of contents and index, interpretation of headings and other study helps, location of key ideas in paragraphs, construction of outlines, and the like. Map exploration as part of the initiation of an area of learning may be simplified if each child has a copy of the map in hand. Instruction in the use of pictures, charts, and graphs is also easier when all children can use the same graphic aid.[2]

Some teachers, on the other hand, prefer to delay the use of the basic textbook until all other searching to solve the problems of an area of learning is completed; they then use the textbook as a summary that pulls together ideas about the problems investigated. At this point children have an opportunity to evaluate the textbook in the light of their other wide reading, to compare and contrast information, and to check authorities.

Use of the textbook as the sole source of information in social studies has, however, distinct disadvantages.[3] Because it presents a single point of view, children have little opportunity to explore other approaches to the area of learning or to bring together a variety of data on which to base the solutions to problems. Furthermore, having all read the same book, pupils have little incentive for discussion or sharing of ideas; indeed, they have no other source of information to bring to their questions and problems.

One of the difficulties in using the social studies textbook as the only

---

[2] Howardine Hoffman and Armen Sarafian, "Instructional Resources," in John U. Michaelis (Ed.), *Social Studies in Elementary Schools* (Thirty-second Yearbook of the National Council for the Social Studies; Washington, D.C.: National Education Association, 1962), pp. 227–228.

[3] *Ibid.*, p. 227.

reference source resides in the readability of the content.[4] There is evidence that textbooks for a particular grade are comfortably read by only a part of the children at that level; and that in a given series of textbooks, readability is not always continuous from level to level, and, in fact, may vary considerably within any one book.[5] The problem is further complicated by the needs of superior readers who may not find in the textbook the detail or depth they are seeking in their search for information. If the teacher is doubtful about the reading level of the text, he may consult the results of the publisher's check on readability, or he himself may apply one of several well-known techniques to secure this information.[6] In any case, it is safe to assume that the textbook will not meet completely the reading needs of all the pupils in the class. Hence difficulties can be expected if there is but one text selected for the entire group.

Another and perhaps more serious concern created by the use of the basic textbook in social studies is that, no matter how well conceived the textbook may be, it tends to determine the areas of learning in social studies and limits attempts to meet the needs of particular children in a particular community. Putting the textbook into the hands of each child is frequently interpreted to mean that every child is responsible for learning and remembering all the facts it contains. Under such pressure teachers feel constrained to limit other kinds of investigative experiences in favor of giving more time to direct study of the text.

It is not inevitable, of course, that the use of the basal social studies textbook should limit the experiences of pupils. It is possible to make the textbook function as a valuable tool in children's problem solving.[7] A creative teacher can find ways of encouraging pupils to pursue concerns cooperatively identified, even though the textbook necessarily occupies a central place in the social studies program.

Many schools, on the other hand, supplement the single text or replace it with a variety of textbooks that include information about the areas of learning commonly developed at a particular grade level. When this approach is possible, small sets of textbooks that vary somewhat in level of

[4] Roma Gans, *Common Sense in Teaching Reading* (Indianapolis: The Bobbs-Merrill Company, Inc., 1963), pp. 138–139.

[5] V. E. Arnsdorf, "Readability of Basal Social Studies Materials," *The Reading Teacher* (January, 1963), pp. 243–246.

[6] Edgar Dale and Jeanne S. Chall, "A Formula for Predicting Readability," *Educational Research Bulletin*, V. 27, 11–20, 1948; Lester R. Wheeler and Edwin H. Smith, "A Practical Readability Formula for the Classroom Teacher in the Primary Grades," *Elementary English* (November, 1954), pp. 397–399; and Victor R. Randolph and Clarence D. Samford, *Teaching Elementary School Social Studies* (Dubuque, Iowa: William C. Brown Company, 1957), pp. 220–223, for a description of the Yoakam technique.

[7] For a treatment of the use of the textbook by authors who have also written an elementary textbook series, see Ernest W. Tiegs and Fay Adams, *Teaching the Social Studies* (Boston: Ginn & Company, 1959), pp. 89–94, 360–63, 310, 328.

difficulty, augmented by single copies of other reputable texts appropriate to the scope and sequence of the social studies program, can provide more adequately for individual differences and make possible greater breadth and depth in the fact-gathering activities of groups and individuals. This extended variety of text material encourages pupil search and provides opportunities for generalizing from a broader base of information, for evaluating sources of information, and for exchanging ideas and points of view expressed by various authors.

When information in depth about a subject is desirable, the unit text is a useful tool. The unit text is a booklet or pamphlet that treats a single topic—Brazilian coffee, pioneer homes, agriculture in early days, life in Switzerland, petroleum, Alexander Hamilton, and so on. Because several copies of any one of the booklets may be purchased at less cost than a single copy of a textbook, such resources greatly extend the variety of information and points of view available for various work and study groups. Such booklets fill a real need for varied and flexible materials; moreover, the possibilities for new titles and new themes are endless.[8] They are eagerly read by bright students who want pertinent facts quickly and by slower readers who may be easily discouraged by longer books.

Of special usefulness are the increasing numbers of trade books on almost every subject of possible interest to children. Printed largely for single-copy purchase, these books are found in school and public libraries and in the possession of many of the pupils. Books of fairy tales and poetry from other lands help pupils gain new insights into the hearts of the people they are studying. Do-it-yourself books make available techniques for projects and construction activities. Biographies of famous people are being used in interesting ways in social studies programs.[9] Books about community problems, ways of living around the world, occupations, historical events, and adventure of all kinds facilitate problem solving because they include detail not found in the usual textbook, detail that stimulates the imagination, supplies the stuff from which concepts are developed, provides additional data to support generalizations, and adds zest to the process of search.[10] A variety of these resources encourages exchange of ideas and tends to encourage wide reading as children share their findings.[11]

In almost every area of learning, however, children must turn to specialized references for certain kinds of information. Although many of these

[8] Vincent R. Rogers and Raymond H. Muessig, "Needed: A Revolution in the Textbook Industry!" *Social Education* (October, 1963), pp. 167–170.

[9] Ralph Adams Brown, "Biography in the Social Studies," in Michaelis, pp. 343–355.

[10] Burrows, pp. 201–202.

[11] For aid in selecting trade books related to the growth of the United States and to life in countries around the world, see Ruth Tooze and Beatrice Perham Krone, *Literature and Music as Resources for Social Studies* (Englewood Cliffs, N.J.: Prentice-Hall, Inc., 1955).

references are of advanced reading level, young children can learn that there are special sources for certain kinds of facts. For factual information about famous persons, special holidays, living around the world, important industrial processes, or a topic like education, religion, or government, the encyclopedia is a useful tool. Encyclopedias especially adapted for young people are now in wide use. Third- and fourth-grade children are not too young to learn the skills necessary to locate information and to read, with the teacher's help if necessary, the facts pertinent to a problem. In a similar way children learn to recognize an information almanac as a printed record of a great variety of facts, published annually to keep it up to date. Whether the pupils need to know the dates when the states entered the Union or the wheat production of a certain region in any given period or the kinds of currency used in various countries, they should think of the information almanac as a readily accessible source of facts. For older children various government reports supply data pertinent to the area of study, and an atlas becomes a similar authority in matters of geography and weather—possible air routes over the North Pole, the location of an obscure island mentioned in a travelogue, the scene of a striking event, or wind and ocean currents. When difficult words impede reference reading, dictionaries are useful, the picture dictionary for the very young and the junior dictionary for children in the intermediate grades.

If resource materials in the classroom are limited, teachers and pupils find a variety of pamphlets useful. Many of these pamphlets, distributed by governmental, service, or commercial agencies, frequently contain up-to-date data not available in textbooks or standard references which require much longer periods of time for preparation and publication. Such sponsored materials, of course, should be used only when they have direct bearing on the problems being investigated and when they represent conscientious effort to provide accurate information useful to pupils.[12]

Reading resources in social studies would not be complete without first-hand sources—diaries, logs, personal narratives, and documents. Although many of these materials may be uncovered by resourceful pupils and teachers in their search for information about the real world of the past, librarians are usually delighted to help in such search. Once located, out-of-copyright materials may be freely copied and used. Although many of these sources may at first appear to be of difficult reading level, wise teachers can select and occasionally adapt if absolutely necessary the paragraphs that will enrich children's understanding of an area of learning. Father Marquette's own description in his diary of the country along a great river, an Indian's account of his tribe's first reaction to a train crossing the prairie,

---

[12] Joint Committee on Cooperation with Business and Industry of the National Council for the Social Studies, *Sponsored Resources for the Social Studies* (Washington, D.C.: National Education Association, n.d.), pp. 2–3.

the true tale of a covered-wagon journey described by a despairing traveler, and the exciting story of a steamboat explosion told by an eyewitness are but a few of the firsthand accounts hidden on library shelves. Old maps of the community, an early schoolteacher's class record book, or a facsimile of the newspaper that announced an exciting event impart reality to historical information that cannot be secured effectively in any other way. These source materials supply the answer when children ask, "What was it really like?"[13]

In contrast to these materials from the past is a wealth of current publications—newspapers and magazines. Alert teachers, continually watching for pertinent articles in the press, are seldom disappointed. Only recently a single popular magazine included a striking account of an American battleground, a word portrait of a famous American, a description of a vital community project, new developments in gardening, information about several foreign lands—all of which might at one time or another be useful in providing information about or insight into a problem. Newspapers, too, afford up-to-the-minute accounts of pertinent happenings—the city cleanup campaign, safety needs in the community, and events of national or international concern. If pupils are deeply involved in problem-solving experiences that have their inception in the real-life situations of the present, current information from newspapers, when read critically, adds a new dimension to reference reading. News accounts of current affairs shed light also on excursions children may be taking into the past, making possible speculation about cause and effect, helping to illustrate how events of the present are often a consequence of what has gone before.

Comparatively new to the array of possible resources are the programed materials beginning to appear in social studies. Although such programs are intended usually for individual instruction when mastery of information or skills is the goal, programs that relate to content useful in problem solving can be an interesting change from other forms of printed materials and a challenge to pupils engaged in independent study of certain facets of a problem. Although programs were developed originally for use with teaching machines, the programed text requiring no mechanical device is gaining favor. In these texts, information is presented in small increments in frames to which the pupils must respond in some way, with the content so arranged that learners may test their knowledge immediately step by step. Several programed texts are available for the elementary grades, and undoubtedly there will be more.[14]

To all these reading materials may be added the children's contributions—pupil-constructed materials. These include charts of group and committee

[13] Maxine Dunfee, "The Stamp of Reality," National Education Association Journal (April, 1952), pp. 227–228.

[14] For titles, see Center for Programed Instruction, Programs, '63 (Washington, D.C.: Office of Education, U.S. Department of Health, Education, and Welfare, 1963).

plans, directions, standards, new vocabulary, and important dates, developed by individuals or groups of children during the area of learning and used as needed during its progress. In addition to such charts there are maps, graphs, and diagrams constructed by pupils to clarify important points in their study. Permanent records of experiences appear in the form of logs, diaries, scrapbooks, all of which may contain reading materials useful for future reference. Similar records bequeathed by last year's pupils can be effective guides to improvement during the present. One group left a day-by-day log of an experience in planting and caring for a garden. Because these pupils recorded their difficulties as well as their progress, the group who followed them in a similar project had some direct information about what to do and what not to do. Pupil-constructed materials have a special appeal that cannot be discounted.

Children need to develop some standards for their written records. If they keep in mind that others will use these records, they can be encouraged to work for clarity, legibility, and good form. Simple, direct sentences are most appropriate. Correct usage and structure are essential. Good arrangement on the page or chart will help to give their material the prestige usually enjoyed by the printed page; spacing, adequate margins, and good quality of material for permanent records contribute to a pleasing appearance. Children often take great pride in their contributions to the reading materials available in any area of learning.

The many types of reading materials available in social studies—books, references, current publications, teacher-prepared as well as pupil-written accounts—are impressive in number and variety. When these materials for an area of learning have been explored, the teacher faces the problem of identifying those that are best suited to the particular problem-solving situation. How well the teacher chooses materials for individuals and groups determines in part the effectiveness of reading in the area of learning.

CRITERIA FOR SELECTING READING MATERIALS

The selection of reading materials for problem solving is the responsibility of both teacher and pupils. They must be concerned with the answers to at least three questions: Is the reading material authentic? Is it suited to the developmental level of the children? Is it the best available material for the purpose? The implications of these questions are explored in the paragraphs that follow.

Only reference materials that are authentic make a lasting contribution to problem solving, because only such materials help pupils build correct concepts and make accurate generalizations. And although the task is difficult, pupils, with the help of the teacher, can assume responsibility for evaluating materials, making at least a beginning in this important area.[15]

[15] Burrows, pp. 195–196.

What questions can pupils and teacher try to answer in determining whether or not a printed resource is properly accurate?

Who are the authors of the article, book, or pamphlet? Are they qualified to write on their subject? Are they free from special interests that would influence the content? Do they have firsthand knowledge of their subject? How did they gather their information? Children need to come face to face with inconsistencies, contradictions, and differences of opinion and to make selections based upon good judgment. The kind of analysis sometimes required in this evaluation is a challenge to children and emphasizes the fact that a statement is not necessarily true just because it is printed.

When was the material written? Was it written at the time the event happened? If the material deals with data that are pertinent to a current problem, how recent is the information given? Is more recent information available? For example, sixth-grade pupils studying water-power resources could not agree on the amount of cultivated land under irrigation in the United States until someone suggested that checking not only the source of the data but the recency of the report might settle the debate. Even the newest textbook is likely to be a year or two behind the figures of an annual government report. A current article about displaced Indians written by an associate of the Bureau of Indian Affairs, for example, was found by another group to have later information than the last official report of the bureau itself.

How does a description or narrative or compilation of factual information compare with similar sources? How does it compare with other materials written about this same region, or about this same process, or about this same historical event? How does it compare with information given or written by an expert in the field, by an eyewitness to the happening, or by a native of the country being described? If there is great inconsistency in the information given by any one source when others seem to be in general agreement, children should investigate the source carefully before accepting it.

These points to consider in determining the reliability of reading materials are especially appropriate to use in evaluating the many free and inexpensive materials available today. Because these items are prepared by specialized agencies, public and private, particular attention must be given to the reputation of the groups preparing the material, to their purposes in writing, to the point of view of their material, and to their use of advertising. A useful guide list for evaluation of sponsored materials is now available.[16] Resources that successfully pass all the necessary tests included in such an evaluation can be of considerable help to a group of children faced with limited sources of information for their study.

[16] See guide list in Joint Committee on Cooperation with Business and Industry, pp. 6–8.

Reading materials that pass the test of authenticity must then be reconsidered in terms of the developmental level of the children for whom they are intended. Materials that are simply written, that emphasize a few big ideas rather than many, and that are well illustrated by words and pictures are most effective for the young reader or for the older child who does not read well. All children read most efficiently materials that use uninvolved sentence structure, that explain carefully the meanings of key words as they occur in the text, and that identify the most important ideas of each section or paragraph. Although the teacher can learn much by observing children in their individual selection and use of reading materials, children and teacher together can come to some sound judgments about materials that seem most appropriate in achieving the purposes of the area of learning. These cooperative decisions are especially pertinent when materials for various study and exploration groups are chosen.

Whether materials related to the area of learning are scarce or plentiful, teacher and children must choose from those available the ones that are most appropriate to the purpose of their investigation. Efficient research to answer questions and solve problems requires accurate, clearly presented data, such as can be found in atlases, almanacs, encyclopedias, special pamphlets, and bulletins. Surveying of background information draws upon materials that treat in a general way various important aspects of the problems being considered. For specific activities and projects, children need directions found in special references like handbooks, cookbooks, and craft books; for a study of community problems, newspapers and magazines are important sources of current information; and for a better understanding of real people in varying environments, well-written trade books are often superior.

Children should become familiar enough with the various materials at their reading level to recognize quickly where to begin the search to meet a particular need. Until pupils acquire adequate skill in selection, cooperative evaluation through discussion of materials promotes its development. As children select, compare, discard, or retain printed materials for study, they learn to evaluate them in terms of their usefulness. The teacher may begin by saying, "Where can we find incidents in Daniel Boone's life that we would like to dramatize? How can we check the truth of the stories we select? Will the encyclopedia help us?" Or when factual information is needed, the teacher may ask, "Where will we locate facts about uranium production in the world today? Is a current magazine our best source of data? Why would you use the information almanac?"

Through many evaluation experiences children become proficient in selecting materials suited to their needs. Which of the materials will give facts in well-organized and easy-to-use form? Which are likely to give many specific details about one phase of the problem? Which will tell a little about all aspects of the study? Will illustrations clarify important ideas?

What kinds of references have the most useful pictures? Where can we find good stories that use facts as a background for the action? These are only a few of the questions that children and teachers try to answer as they become skillful in selecting materials that are needed at any particular point in the area of learning.

As a result of continual evaluation the selection of reading materials can be vastly improved. Authentic reading materials appropriate to children's maturity in reading and to their purposes in the area of learning are essential to critical thinking and problem solving. Criteria for selecting reading materials should be conscientiously applied to printed information in all its various forms by both children and teachers.

Role of the Teacher
in Planning Reading Experiences

In any profitable reading experience in social studies the teacher plays a prominent part. Because reading in the area of learning is purposeful and directed toward specific goals, both pupils and teachers seek progress toward these objectives. A well-planned reading session in which children are searching for information of concern to them and using materials suited to their reading ability depends largely upon the thought and effort expended by the teacher, both before and during the reading experience.

IDENTIFYING INDIVIDUAL DIFFERENCES
IN READING

Prerequisite to the success of reading experiences, no matter for what purpose, is the selection of materials suited to the reading level and interests of each pupil. Identifying these individual differences is the teacher's first responsibility. What techniques will assist the teacher to assess each child's reading ability and to determine the nature of his interests?

Both formal and informal evaluation techniques help the teacher make a judgment about how well each child reads. The standardized test in reading, for example, usually evaluates the child's level of comprehension, his speed, and his understanding of vocabulary. In interpreting the results of such tests it is well to remember that they give at best only an estimate of the child's probable success in reading. Under pressure of the test situation some children read more efficiently and some read more poorly than they normally would. Furthermore, the teacher should examine the test to see whether or not the reading selections include the kind of material the pupil will be reading in social studies.[17] Such an examination will no doubt throw

---

[17] Cooperative Sequential Tests of Educational Progress, Educational Testing Service, Princeton, N.J., include a reading test based on a variety of reading selections of the kind pupils meet in their daily experiences.

additional light on the usefulness of the reading test score as a predictor of success in reading social studies materials.

The informal reading test also makes its contribution to the teacher's knowledge of the child's ability to read in social studies. One such informal test uses social studies texts spanning several grade levels, from each of which is chosen a paragraph or page of similar kinds of materials that do not put undue emphasis on proper nouns. As each child is tested individually, the teacher asks him to read first the selection from the level that then seems to be his social studies reading level. While the child reads, the teacher notes smoothness and pronunciation and asks questions to check comprehension. If the child reads with success, the teacher tries him in a text selection at the next higher level, and so on. If, on the other hand, the child experiences difficulty in reading the first selection chosen, the teacher moves step by step to lower-level text selections until he locates one the child can read successfully. Through such a technique the child's social studies textbook reading level can be estimated quite successfully.

A similar procedure using vocabulary taken in an orderly way from the social studies text can reveal something of the child's reading level. In this type of individual informal test, the child pronounces, and uses in sentences, words chosen systematically—every tenth noun on every tenth page, for example—from the text at his expected level. The teacher moves up or down to similar vocabulary lists from various text levels until he finds the one at which the child performs most efficiently. Such techniques as these that utilize the social studies text will probably reveal the previously mentioned fact that many textbooks are somewhat above the reading level of the children for whom they are intended. At the same time the child's comfortable reading level becomes quite clear.[18]

Such test information about children's reading level is, of course, supplemented by careful teacher observation. The wise teacher arranges his school day to allow adequate time to observe children as they work and study and makes definite plans to record for future reference any evidence about reading abilities that may be helpful in planning. As a simple method of finding out the level of the child's ability, he frequently makes available a variety of social studies books and encourages each child to find those he can read independently. As the pupil shares what he has chosen and relates it to the area of learning, it is not difficult for the teacher to judge whether or not the child is understanding the content and using successfully the new vocabulary of the area.

Observation during research reading provides further evidence of pupils' ability to read in the area of learning. When groups of children are reading

---

[18] For further suggestions that can be adapted for social studies, see Arthur W. Heilman, *Principles and Practices of Teaching Reading* (Columbus, Ohio: Charles E. Merrill Books, Inc., 1961), pp. 161–164.

together in social studies, the teacher may say to a pupil, "Read the sentence that tells why the coastal lands are well suited to truck farming," and on another occasion, "Read and tell why early trains were called iron horses." Sometimes the teacher is interested in determining children's skills in summarizing as he suggests, "Tell in your own words the important idea in the paragraph," or "Read the paragraph and tell what question it answers." When the teacher is not actively working with any one of the groups, he moves about to others, noting difficulties and answering questions, observing study habits, and evaluating the success children are having with the materials they are using.

Teachers, of course, formulate some judgments of children's reading ability in social studies from their observation of the performance of each in the developmental reading program in his group. Knowledge gained here helps the teacher to identify individual differences in reading, prepare to meet any difficulties wisely in social studies, and anticipate special ones that may arise later because of inadequate reading skills. The teacher knows that the pupil's performance in the functional reading of social studies is usually no better than his performance in the daily reading classes, except in those instances when certain children, highly motivated by purposeful reading in the content areas, seem for the moment to excel themselves.

Observation reveals not only children's skill in reading but their interests as well. As the teacher moves about in the school library or among children who are selecting books in the classroom reading center, he has excellent opportunities to note where children's interests lie. A record of books children read at home or in their free time at school will show clearly what children read when they are free to choose. Sharing periods in which children discuss their experiences will suggest to the alert teacher books and materials that will be of interest to pupils in social studies. Taking note, too, of reading materials boys and girls bring from home may provide some guidelines for the teacher as he selects challenging materials for the planned reading experiences.

Informal inventories of children's reading in social studies, made at the close of a previous area of learning, furnish some additional data about interests. Such inventories or interviews may have revealed what materials children think most useful for finding various kinds of information, which are most pleasing to read, and which contain the most interesting content. Real interest in the reading is a powerful motivating force for investigation in social studies. The teacher wisely capitalizes upon children's interests whenever he can do so profitably.

Knowing the kinds of materials children are able to read and the kinds of materials they find most interesting and useful is an invaluable aid to the teacher as he adapts reading materials in social studies to meet individual differences. It is evident, of course, that the teacher himself must be acquainted with all the materials that children will use; in no other way

can he be aware of their difficulty or content. Children will read successfully only if they are reading comfortably and are finding out what they
want to know about problems that concern them.

ADAPTING MATERIALS TO MEET DIFFERENCES

What does the teacher do with this knowledge of children and materials in planning reading experiences? Often he plans to group children
so that those who are of about the same maturity in reading can read similar materials and thus share information among themselves. He then must
determine which of the materials about a particular problem is best suited
to each of these groups of children.

The teacher plans carefully for the group of children making normal
progress in reading at their grade level. He may suggest that these children
first read the regular textbook and share its information with others in the
group. Or these boys and girls may use several small sets of textbooks that
treat the problem under consideration. If these children can read independently, they may use a study guide prepared by the teacher to check their
own comprehension or focus their attention and note taking on questions
and problems raised in the initiation. There may be one or more groups at
this level, depending on the available materials and the number of children.
Using several small sets of texts is usually more satisfactory than using only
one, for children can read from different points of view and gather somewhat varying kinds of information to share later. As these children increase
their understanding of the content of the area, they begin to explore more
widely among a great variety of materials, selected cooperatively and related to children's special interests in the area of learning.

The superior readers can be challenged by materials of more advanced
level. Although it may be desirable for them to read together first from
some one source, they can move swiftly to other materials. Individuals in
the group can read special pamphlets or booklets; some can search for the
answer to a single question in a variety of sources; others can explore special
facets of a problem. Many can locate information in encyclopedias, visit
the school library for additional help, and even prepare reading materials
for others. Each pupil in this group needs some definite responsibility in
relation to the problems and questions raised by the entire group. He can
be encouraged to explore rather widely to fulfill this responsibility.

Selecting reading materials for the less successful readers, however, often
poses problems for the teachers. If books of easier reading level are not
available in the area of learning, the teacher may need to adapt more
difficult materials by rewriting or he may prepare original materials. Usually
such special accounts, particularly if the teacher writes into them some
information not found easily by other readers, are read with great interest
by those who may otherwise feel unsuccessful. The materials can be illustrated by pictures cut from magazines and made attractive with unusual

cover sheets. Carefully guided work with easy-to-read information is excellent preparation for moving on to the more difficult book materials. As the teacher writes for these children and studies with them, he lays a foundation in basic understandings and vocabulary that children will need when they read other printed resources.

Slow readers in a fourth grade who were studying conservation of natural resources were unable to read with ease any of the many materials that were available for the study. The teacher saw this situation as a good opportunity to write for them information that would give them some facts about the questions and problems identified by the class and that would introduce them to the basic vocabulary they would meet in later reference reading. The account given here is part of the one used by the teacher in this situation.

SAVING AMERICA'S TREASURES

Most boys and girls know how to save things.
They save their money.
They save candy they want to share with others.
They try not to waste their school supplies.

Countries must learn to save, too.
America has many wonderful treasures.
America has acres and acres of forests.
America has rich soil.
America has coal and oil and iron.
America has many wild animals and flowers.

But our people have not taken very good care of these fine things.
The forests have been cut down to make room for farms.
Some of them have been burned up by great fires.
Not enough new trees have been planted.

Some of our best soil has been washed away.
Some of it has been worn out.
Many farmers do not use the soil wisely.
We have used some of our minerals very fast.
Some of them may not last very long.

For the slower readers described in the dialogue at the beginning of this chapter the teacher chose to write a sketch that would include a bit of information that most of the other children in the class had no opportunity to know at this particular time. Because these children needed to feel important to the group, the teacher sacrificed giving them a survey account of various kinds of communication in favor of one that would bring them some special attention. The article included here contrasts quite strikingly with the one previously cited.

THE NEWSPAPER

People read the newspaper to find out what is happening around them.
It takes many people to make a newspaper.
Some people get the news for the newspaper.
Some people write the news.
Some people print the news on newsprint.
Others put the paper together.
Still others put the newspapers on trucks.
Trucks take the newspapers to newsstands on many streets.
Some trucks take the newspapers to nearby towns.
Some newspapers are sent by mail.
Newsboys take the newspapers to homes in the morning.
Many people read newspapers in the morning.
Many people buy newspapers at newsstands.
The newspaper is interesting to read.
Many kinds of people read newspapers.

Reading groups such as those just described are extremely flexible. Although it is true that many of them are planned by the teacher in terms of children's reading level, there are times when reading groups formed about projects and processes pull together pupils of varying ability in reading. A group of boys, for example, searching out directions for building some kinds of model boats may actually read quite difficult materials in order to reach their objective. On other occasions, the reading venture may be an individual search for the answers to unanswered questions, with the teacher moving about helping pupils read successfully. And sometimes small groups cluster spontaneously about the child who is fortunate enough to find just the right reference to take care of a difficult question. The emphasis throughout reading in social studies is purposefulness. Grouping and other such techniques are only means to an end. If children read enthusiastically and effectively, the teacher can expect no more.

Effective reading in the area of learning does not come about by chance. With the teacher rests the responsibility of identifying individual differences in reading ability and interests, selecting and adapting materials to meet these differences, and grouping children for successful research among the many printed materials available in the area of learning.

ENCOURAGING AND GUIDING READING IN SOCIAL STUDIES

When the reading groups are planned, the teacher begins by encouraging children's enthusiasm and interest in the reading. His introduction of the reading task, his own acquaintance with materials so that he can honestly recommend them, and his planning so that the groups can function effectively give children the feeling that the reading is important and worthy of being well done. The teacher sets the stage, reviews with the children the purposes of the reading, helps them fix firmly in mind the questions and problems under study, helps them find a pleasant environment in which to work, and then lets them know that he is there to assist when he is needed. Under such circumstances the reading and research period can proceed smoothly.

The teacher then must make sure that children have command of all reading skills they will need in their independent or group reading. If the skills have been previously taught in the regular reading class, he helps the group see their usefulness here. If the needed skill has not been taught, he must provide the instruction. When the entire class needs such instruction, social studies reading halts long enough to establish control of the skill— locating material in an index, taking simple notes, reading maps, or whatever it may be. These many skills and suggestions for their development are included later in this book in a discussion of related skills.

Before the groups actually separate to undertake their various responsibilities, they may need to think together with the teacher about ways in which groups can work well by themselves. They may recall the successes and failures of the last reading period, identify some particular problem of working in groups that they need to solve, or simply review previously developed standards for successful group work. Here the teacher helps children move ahead to more successful small group effort.

When the reading groups, large and small, are ready to work, the teacher moves rather quickly from one to the other to make sure that each group knows how to start and what to do. He plans to spend somewhat more time helping the slower readers begin, to put the better readers as much on their own as possible, and to check as needed with those who can read independently with only occasional help from the teacher. If the teacher plans this moving about skillfully, he can avoid wasting his own time and that of pupils, he can give help where and when it is needed, and he can encourage truly independent work. Moreover, if he does not feel that he must be actively working with some group every minute of the time, he has an opportunity to observe pupils as they read and groups as they function. Information gathered through this kind of observation is essential to planning future reading experiences.

After reading groups have spent some time at their planned tasks, some individuals or groups may bring up special problems that need to be solved. A new question about the content may call for the assistance of the school librarian. A reference appropriate for the work of one group may be discovered by another and a transfer of books made. The child who has forgotten how to help his group work efficiently may require the teacher's special reminder. Children who complete their responsibilities must be encouraged to explore other materials or to move to activities and projects suggested by their reading or previously planned by the class.

Now and then during the reading sessions teachers and children may come together to share resources or to answer primary questions that motivated the general reading. Out of these discussions come decisions to move to more specific topics and questions. When children are embarked upon serious study of their questions, this coming together at intervals helps the group assess its progress, identifies the questions that are being answered, and emphasizes the answers or solutions that have thus far eluded the pupils. A lively class discussion serves to evaluate the progress of the group and to move it along in its search for information.

It is evident that the teacher plays a key role in the development of the reading period in social studies. Although teachers plan with pupils ways to secure materials, the questions and problems to be explored, the responsibilities of good working groups, and the environment in which they will read, the teacher's greater knowledge of children's abilities and needs and his skill in organization make him an indispensable part of the planned reading experience.

QUESTIONS FOR DISCUSSION

Read again the dialogue at the beginning of this chapter and consider these questions and problems:

1. How did the teacher provide for individual differences in the reading experience?
2. What were the specific purposes for which the children were reading?
3. How did the variety of materials used contribute to the children's interest in and desire to explore the problems?

SUGGESTIONS FOR CONSTRUCTING
A RESOURCE UNIT

Select the reading experiences that will develop understandings in the area of learning. Refer to your annotated bibliography for specific resources to be used. Include experiences that will build background information, help pupils answer questions and solve problems raised in the initiation, and provide information for carrying out activities and projects.

Describe the reading experiences that will fulfill the above functions, clarifying the exact purpose of each experience, the kinds of grouping that may be needed, the specific resources and materials to be used in the experience, and the activities of the children engaging in it.

Consider, at this point, the format you will use for recording not only reading experiences but the direct and related experiences to be incorporated in your plan later. Note the usefulness of devising a scheme that clarifies relationships among experiences, particularly problem-solving and related experiences. The charts of experiences in the resource unit in the appendix illustrate one such scheme.

6

Drawing
on the Community
to Solve Problems

MRS. JOHNSON: Here is the chart Susan and Charles made for us. Do you like it? Does it show what kinds of communication are used for different purposes? Making this chart certainly gave us a good opportunity to find out about communication in general, didn't it?

SUSAN: When Charles and I were making the chart, we noticed that some kinds of communication work best between two people and some kinds are used to communicate with lots of people at one time.

CHARLES: That's right, and the chart shows why people didn't learn about the water-main break by letter or newspaper. When you want to tell something to many people fast, you have to pick out the best way.

MRS. JOHNSON: What kinds of communication on our list are used to communicate with large groups of people?

ROBERT: Television and radio if you are in a hurry.

FRANK: Why don't we start finding out about television? It certainly told us what we needed to know the morning the water main broke. My dad's all set to let us visit the station.

MRS. JOHNSON: Which of our questions would such a visit help us answer, boys and girls?

RUTH: It would tell us how we communicate with large groups of people. And we did put visiting places in our plan of action.

ANNE: We need some firsthand information now. Most of us have watched television, and all of us read something about it earlier this week.

MRS. JOHNSON: What will we need to do if we are going to visit the television station?

RONNIE: We'll have to decide when to go.

ANDY: Are we going to ride or walk?

JACK: And we have to get permission.

MRS. JOHNSON: Is that all? Why are we going?

SUSAN: We will have to decide what we want to find out. They're too busy out there just to have us wandering around.

MRS. JOHNSON: Susan's right. There's no reason for going unless we have a real purpose.

DONALD: I know what I'm going to find out. How did the TV put on the map showing the water-main break?

MRS. JOHNSON: Shall we make a list? Let's start with Donald's question. How does television send out pictures, maps, and signs? What else?

PATRICIA: I'd like to know if television gets the news over the teletype just the way they do at my father's newspaper office.

RONNIE: The plays are the most interesting. I'd like to know how the actors put on a play, how they set up the scenery, and things like that.

BILL: I'd like to know just how we get a picture on our TV set. I expect it's complicated, but I'd like to know.

. . . .

MRS. JOHNSON: Now that we have our list of questions, do we have volunteers to go with Frank to see his father and make arrangements for the time? I think we could go any morning next week, perhaps early in the week if it's convenient. Will you, Peter, and you, Bill? Now, whom else must we ask?

ANNE: We have to write notes home to get permission to go. Can't we do that this afternoon in language arts class? We have so much planning to do this morning.

MRS. JOHNSON: That's a good idea. We'd better add that to the list of things we planned to do today so we won't forget. Now, anything else that needs to be done? How shall we go? What are the possibilities? Frank, what would you suggest?

FRANK: I usually take the bus when I go down to meet my dad. We could take the South Walnut bus right here at the corner, and then we'd have to hike a little way at the end. Not bad, though. Costs fifteen cents.

MRS. JOHNSON: How many think we could go that way? We'll mention the money in our letters home. Well, then, that's settled. Any other plans?

WAYNE: We'll have to make sure that someone is responsible for each of our questions. When we get out there, we'll be so busy looking we'll probably forget what we went for.

MRS. JOHNSON: Have you a plan in mind?

WAYNE: Each one of us could take a question, and if no one tells us the answer as we go around, we could be sure to ask it before we leave. We'd better write that question down, though.

DONALD: I'll take the question I put in the list.

PATRICIA: And I'll take mine.

MRS. JOHNSON: Perhaps this idea will work. If you are willing to be responsible for a special question on our list, will you sign your name beside it when you leave the room for recess? If you don't have a special question, then you can listen carefully to help us double-check on all the answers. Have we forgotten anything?

PEGGY: Our standards. We can't forget our standards. There are some in this room that always have to be reminded about how we're supposed to act.

MRS. JOHNSON: It's probably a good idea for all of us to review the things we always try to remember on a trip. We do want to be welcome visitors. Will you get the list we made for our trip to the greenhouse, Peggy? Let's think about what we should do to make this trip pleasant for everyone.

MARTHA: Mrs. Johnson, I thought of something else. Could we take our sketch boards with us? We'll want to draw pictures when we get back, and we could start getting some ideas.

MRS. JOHNSON: Of course, Martha. Will you see that everyone who wants a sketch board and paper is taken care of? Now let's think through our list of the things that make a successful trip. Are you ready, Peggy? And then we'll review all our plans to see if we've forgotten anything important.

. . . .

MRS. JOHNSON: Come on in. Let's all sit down and talk a little about what we have just been doing. It was a good trip, wasn't it?

ROBERT: I think most of our questions were answered. Could we check to see? If any one was left out, Frank could ask his father tonight.

MRS. JOHNSON: That's a good plan, Robert. Shall we do that now or wait until this afternoon when we're more rested?

DONALD: Just listening to all the words those television men used wore me out. But I found out what some of them are. Kinescope, boom, transmitter, monitor—pretty big words.

JANE: We should add them to our dictionary of communication words.

MARTHA: I started a sketch of the inside of the studio. If someone would help, we could draw in the things Donald is talking about and name them right on the picture.

JACK: I'll help. I'll draw the picture of the outside of the station.

ANDY: I'd like to know if the radio station is like the television station. Could a committee go visit the radio station to find out? I kept thinking all the time that the radio station is probably just like this except for the cameras.

MRS. JOHNSON: We seem to have several good ideas of things that we ought to do next. How many of you found the answer to your special question?

ROBERT: I found the answer to my question, but then I kept thinking of new questions to ask.

MRS. JOHNSON: Do you think then that the trip was worthwhile? Did it help us answer our question about how we communicate with large groups? Who could tell us one important big idea you learned from the trip?

SUSAN: Well, I learned that television is a very good way to communicate with people in an emergency.

ROBERT: —and when you want to show people as well as tell them something.

ANDY: I found out that most of our television is paid for by people who want to sell things.

BARBARA ANN: I found out that it takes many people to put on just the littlest kind of television show.

MARTHA: I found out that a good artist is needed at the television studio—making scenery, painting signs, and planning costumes.

JACK: Television is very expensive. Even one camera costs more than a thousand dollars.

FRANK: I learned that when a television show goes on it has to be just right. There isn't any way to correct the mistakes that are made.

BILL: I was surprised to find out how many television shows are really just films that have been made in other cities. We were lucky to be there for a live show.

MRS. JOHNSON: All these ideas you brought back with you should help you to appreciate television more than ever. Were there any problems about taking the trip that we need to discuss?

Community experiences are a natural way for children to gather data for problem solving, for such experiences are part of every child's growing up. At a very early age children begin to explore the community as they accompany parents and friends about their village, town, or city to shop, to attend school and church, and to find recreation. Adults outside the family are also a part of each child's environment—the oil station operator who fills bicycle tires, the sponsor of the softball team, the church school teacher, the Brownie leader, the traffic policeman on the schoolhouse corner—these and many other members of the community enter the child's world. From these contacts the child learns something of the life around him and begins to develop some concepts about the community.

It is not only the local community that impinges upon the child's life. Today's children with their families are highly mobile. On vacation or in seeking new homes, they move from place to place, seeing changing landscapes and cities of all sizes. Efficient modern transportation is able to carry them swiftly from one end of the city to the other, here and there throughout their state, and even far away. From these forays beyond the confines of home, the child continually enlarges his concepts of community people and their ways of living.

Relationships between school and community are equally strong. The good school reflects its community, responding to its unique characteristics and alert to its problems. As the community and the school interact, children move freely between the two, with no feeling that life outside is vastly different from life within the school. The community becomes a part of school life when the school assumes its proper role as an aspect of community living.

Values
of Community Experiences

To achieve the purposes of social studies, the child must become a real part of the community in which he lives, interact with it, and contribute to it. To become an effective citizen the child must become a responsible member of the community with civic attitudes and ideals compatible with the spirit of democracy.[1] There is no more effective way of

---

[1] John B. Niemeyer, "Education for Citizenship," in Nelson B. Henry (Ed.), *Social Studies in the Elementary School* (Fifty-sixth Yearbook of the National Society for the Study of Education; Chicago: University of Chicago Press, 1957), pp. 221–222.

becoming this kind of person than through practicing what such a person will do. The social studies area of learning, through a variety of community experiences, offers the child the laboratory in which he may experiment with life in the community and begin to find his place in it.

Furthermore, as an important source of information in problem solving, community resources are unusually appropriate. Children's contact with the community produces data that are authentic because they are drawn from real sources. If children are carefully guided in their listening and observation and in the subsequent formulation of generalizations, the first-hand information they have collected can be an invaluable aid to satisfying their search for answers to questions and solutions to problems. Furthermore, community experiences are mutually enriching as they bring children and adults together in the consideration of various aspects of life in the community (see Figure 7). Such intimate relationships between community and child set the stage for and contribute substantially to problem solving in the area of learning.[2]

Although everyone recognizes that a child is not an adult and cannot function as an adult member of the community, it is equally evident that a person who has had no contact with community life is not likely to develop a deep interest in its development or problems. Thus it is that social studies in the elementary school assumes the major responsibility for this orientation to community life and depends broadly upon experience in the community and with its problems to bring children into closer relationships with the human environment. How do community experiences achieve this relationship?

Venturing into the community gives children an opportunity to observe and sometimes to participate in the basic human activities that characterize living in the social group. Children can go almost everywhere under the careful guidance of the school and of cooperating community groups— asking questions, gathering data, and pooling information. They can investigate many phases of human activity in the community. Visits to telephone, newspaper, and telegraph offices clarify ideas about communication. Study trips to airports and other transportation centers, as well as rides in a variety of vehicles, show how people and goods are moved about. Production and consumption can be understood better when pupils see the stores, markets, and factories of the community. Education, government, religious activities, protection, and conservation are all there for children as they venture forth, sometimes hearing, sometimes seeing, or sometimes taking part in the life of the community. Many opportunities to observe and to experience basic human activities are within the reach of boys and girls

---

[2] Edward G. Olsen, "How We Learn and So Should Teach," in Edward G. Olsen (Ed.), *The School and Community Reader: Education in Perspective* (New York: The Macmillan Company, 1953), p. 130.

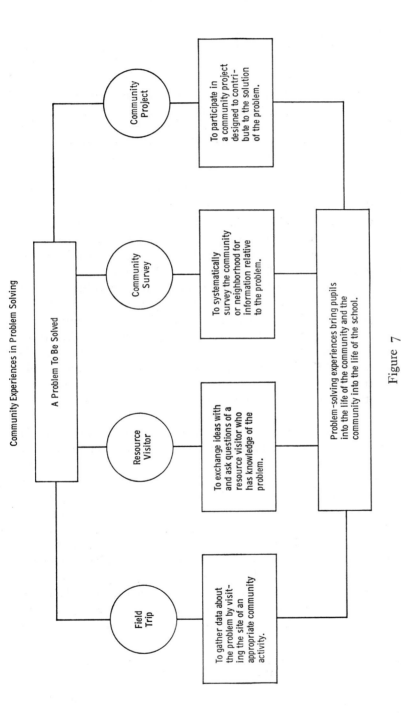

Community Experiences in Problem Solving

A Problem To Be Solved

Field Trip — To gather data about the problem by visiting the site of an appropriate community activity.

Resource Visitor — To exchange ideas with and ask questions of a resource visitor who has knowledge of the problem.

Community Survey — To systematically survey the community or neighborhood for information relative to the problem.

Community Project — To participate in a community project designed to contribute to the solution of the problem.

Problem-solving experiences bring pupils into the life of the community and the community into the life of the school.

Figure 7

Community experiences induct children into community living and prepare them for participation in solving community problems.

if the school does not neglect this vital avenue toward more knowing citizenship.

Community experiences also help children realize that there are certain group processes necessary to living in democracy.[3] As they move about outside the school or draw the community into the classroom, they can and should become aware of behaviors and attitudes necessary to the life of the democratic community. They should not fail to note the air of cooperation that generally pervades offices and industry, community services, and projects. They see with new appreciation the importance of the responsibilities each community adult assumes in the life of the group. They note the concern for others illustrated by drives and campaigns, by the protective work of government, and by daily acts of kindness and compassion undertaken in the city. They find people of the community busy with problem-solving activity—identifying, gathering facts, and discussing.

Relationships between young people and community are strengthened when there is a sense of need, a problem to be solved. The community has many problems about which boys and girls can be aware. Some of these problems are ones to which they may contribute solutions, others are problems they can begin to think about now and do something about later, and others are beyond their level of understanding. But if community experiences are planned to produce learning, they can encourage children to consider the particular problems associated with the various activities they are encountering. Traffic problems, safety problems, protection of public property, community beautification, conservation, and law observance are but a few to which children can actually make a contribution appropriate to their level of development.[4] A problem shared builds interest, concern, and a feeling of kinship; the principle works well when pupils and community are thrown together in the consideration of vital problems.

Many of the community experiences described in this chapter provide a common meeting ground for children and adults. They create situations in which pupils must assume the role of adults—as interviewers, as hosts, or as dignified visitors. Children and adults talk together intelligently about the activity in which the adult is involved. Children can see adults as sympathetic, dedicated individuals and recognize their importance in the community; adults can see children as maturing young people, searching for facts and ideas, growing into the citizens of a few years hence. Each sees the other in roles somewhat different from the usual family relationship; they communicate not as adult and child but as two groups interested in mutual concerns, the children stretching to be adult for a time, the adults

---

[3] W. W. Staudenmaier, "Organizing for Learning," in Olsen, p. 117.

[4] For example, see Effie G. Bathurst, *How Children Use the Community for Learning* (Washington, D.C.: U.S. Department of Health, Education, and Welfare, 1954), and a classic, Paul R. Hanna, *Youth Serves the Community* (New York: Appleton-Century-Crofts, Inc., 1936).

trying to make their work and life understandable to younger persons. The occasion can be delightful and satisfying all around.

Because community experiences are quite likely to be specific, a visit to a particular newspaper or an interview with a certain government official, children frequently need to turn to books to find out whether or not the local information they have assembled is generally applicable to other communities. For example, when junior high school students interviewed their city mayor, they learned that because he had a city manager his duties were different from those of mayors in many neighboring communities. He recommended to them some available reports of his yearly duties and suggested that they secure and read reports of similar kinds from communities differently organized. The visit of a group of younger children to the local weekly newspaper revealed that, unlike newspapers in larger cities, it made relatively little use of wire news services so important to the large city dailies. Reading several city newspapers and comparing them with their own community paper clarified the differences more fully. After the visit of a foreign student to a classroom of older children, pupils were stimulated to check facts in their social studies book against those given by their guest, a search which finally resulted in the return of their friend to help check the accuracy of other reading resources. Another pointed example of how a well-planned experience leads to more and better reading!

Community experiences often stimulate reading through children's interest in some detail or aspect of what they have heard or seen that may not be perfectly clear to them. When the child says upon his return to the classroom, "What I don't understand is why—or how—," then reading may be the key to more complete information. Although the facts and ideas gleaned from a community experience are usually authentic, it is quite likely that some children will not find in the time allowed the depth of information they demand. Then reading supplementary material assists them in their continued search and emphasizes once more the importance of reading as an aid to learning.

The values of community experiences are, in fact, so many that it is difficult to see why they were so long neglected in favor of reliance upon textbooks.[5] No doubt there was a time in the villages and towns of a century and a half ago when boys and girls were a more integral part of community life and of the human activities that comprise it, when their food, clothing, and shelter were locally produced, and when they themselves had a hand in many homemaking and community crafts. At any rate, the situation today is vastly different. Wise use of community resources can help present-day boys and girls relate themselves to a mechanized society and a somewhat more decentralized home life.

[5] An excellent example of the use of the textbook with disregard for a community problem appears in Herbert B. Bruner, "The World outside Our Doors," in Olsen, p. 71.

Types
of Community Experiences

The possibilities for contacts between children and their environment are numerous and varied. Every casual encounter can qualify as a community experience if it results in new understanding and knowledge about the world in which the child lives. But for the purposes of this discussion, attention will be centered on several unusual kinds of community experiences that teacher and pupils plan and carry out cooperatively and through which they expect to answer questions or solve problems.

STUDY TRIPS

The study trip usually comes to mind first as the teacher thinks about worthwhile experiences for his pupils, for it is likely to provide the most direct and accurate information available to pupils in their problem solving.[6] Armed with questions for which they are seeking answers, children venture forth, following well-made plans for securing data and looking ahead to the opportunity to use the community in their study.

Mr. Curtis's class of fifth-grade boys and girls are involved in a study of conservation needs in their neighborhood. They have noted that every rainstorm washes the street full of the red clay soil from a housing area adjacent to the school and that mud from the school ground is running in rivulets all over the paved drives and walkways. Today they have decided to explore the neighborhood more carefully to see if the soil erosion problem goes beyond the close-at-hand school environment. There are several questions to answer, questions identified and agreed upon by the group. Where is soil erosion most apparent? Under what conditions is it occurring? Are there any evidences that erosion is being controlled in any way?

Because the pupils already have built some background from their reading about the causes of soil erosion and methods of control, Mr. Curtis is rather certain that the pupils can work independently in gathering this information. As a result he encourages the pupils to divide themselves into four groups, each group to cover an area within a radius of four blocks of the schoolhouse. A rough sketch map of the area on the chalkboard helps in marking off the route each group will take. Each invites a parent to join the walk, although the children do not plan to involve their guest directly in their problem-solving activity. They recognize that for safety and in observance of school rules they need adult company; they have learned from experience how to treat their escort courteously, explaining their work and its purpose and following suggestions he may give for keeping the group together.

This study trip immediately requires that pupils look closely at their neighborhood with a specific objective in mind, that they record carefully their find-

[6] Lavone A. Hanna, Gladys L. Potter, and Neva Hagaman, *Unit Teaching in the Elementary School* (rev. ed.; New York: Holt, Rinehart and Winston, Inc., 1963), pp. 256–263.

ings so that they can be reported later, and that they learn to generalize from their collected data. Furthermore, the contact they have with the accompanying parent gives practice in clarifying their work to an adult.

Such trips as these have a variety of objectives—kinds of work going on in the community, industries and stores, local organizations in operation, governmental offices, man's use of the natural environment, exhibitions, and museums, to name but a few. Some are complex undertakings requiring elaborate transportation, full-day planning, and additional adult helpers. These longer journeys—trips to historical sites and special events beyond the local community—not only have exciting destinations to be explored for problem-solving data but also offer valuable opportunities for observation of the environment along the way.[7] Some field trips are shorter and more easily-planned visits to factories, radio stations, newspaper plants, wholesale and retail establishments, libraries, and the like. Still others are simple to undertake and may be embarked on almost at the moment of conceiving the idea—the walk around the block to see nature and man getting ready for winter, the trip downstairs to see how the school building is heated, the journey to the neighbor's garden to see some spring plant coming through the earth, the walk through the park to gather some needed specimens, or a period of sitting on the steps outside the school to record the kinds of transportation used by people passing by. The variations are almost endless.

Planning the study trip involves the pupils in many decisions. On the basis of what they need to find out to solve a problem they have previously proposed, they may suggest available community resources and with the teacher's help evaluate suggestions in terms of what will serve their purpose best, what their own background of experience dictates, and what arrangements will need to be made. When the objective is identified, they set up the kinds of information they expect to find and make plans for recording it and using it when they return. If permissions from school, home, or industry are needed, they plan to get these—sometimes through letters written in the language arts period or through telephone calls or interviews. Before departure pupils draw up specific plans for their conduct and review again their plans for fact gathering. Unless all these are well planned, the trip will have little chance of real success.[8]

RESOURCE VISITORS

Resource visitors to the classroom give pupils an opportunity to discuss problems with an adult expert in an intimacy that is not usually pos-

---

[7] For an interesting observation guidesheet for a school journey, see Zoe A. Thralls, *The Teaching of Geography* (New York: Appleton-Century-Crofts, Inc., 1958), pp. 155–158.
[8] Stephen M. Corey, "Tested Criteria for Using the Community," in Olsen, p. 160

sible on the study trip. Children can share their own knowledge, check its accuracy, and extend their undertsanding of the subject through the experience of meeting and talking with a person they have invited to their classroom.

Li Wong came to the third grade of a university laboratory school to see the silk worms the children were raising in their study of the materials man uses for clothing. The moths had already begun their work of cocoon-spinning; in fact, a number of pale yellow and pale green cocoons clung to the stick hutch the children had erected, and several adventurous moths had chosen to fasten themselves underneath the ledge of the table. The children posed a question for the visitor. "Can you help us get the silk off the cocoon? We have made a little reel according to directions. We know we are to soak the cocoons in soapy water. But the job is more than that. Can you help us?"

Came Li Wong's reply: "It has been a long time since I helped my mother do this in our home far from here. But I remember what she did, and I'll tell you. Then we'll all try. You are right to put the cocoons in hot water. My mother used to have great baskets of cocoons to pour into the water all at once. Then you need a little brush. Use the brush to turn the cocoons over in the water as you gently brush. If you are lucky, the brush will pick up some silky threads. Do this until you find the end of the thread put there by the moth. Once you have the end, the rest is easy. It will be best if we can find the ends of several cocoon threads, so that we can wind several at once. They will be stronger that way. Now, let's have a try at the job." It is not difficult to understand why the children's eyes followed so closely the long slender fingers in their search for that elusive end of silk thread!

The resource visitor is brought to the classroom rather than visited on a field trip when it is the person and his knowledge or experience that is needed rather than acquaintance with his environment. Community helpers of all kinds come to the classroom—the policeman, the postman, the nurse and doctor, an artist, a musician, or a writer—bringing with them the tools of their trade, wearing their special gear, and armed with experiences to relate. In most communities today there are also persons from faraway places—foreign students, new residents from other continents, or special visitors to churches and community organizations. These individuals can extend children's acquaintance with the rest of the world and deepen their understanding of the brotherhood of man as they and the pupils build bonds of friendship through the sharing of experience.

The resource visitor creates an especially happy situation if he likes to help children find answers to their questions and if he has been well briefed about the study in progress and his contribution to it. Although children may have a number of suggestions for inviting resource visitors, the teacher seldom encourages an invitation until he is sure that the person who will come has a lively interest in the education of children, skill in talking with young people, and valuable information for which pupils are searching.[9] Following the decision and the issuing of the invitation, pupils plan for the visit much as they do for their field trips, with special attention here to extending the courtesies of their classroom to a special guest. Questions to be discussed, plans for recording information, and ideas for follow-up experiences are all part of the preliminary consideration.

Pupils may undertake interviews as a method of collecting data when it is not convenient for the resource person to come to the classroom or when seeing the resource person in his proper setting—the mayor in his office, the librarian among her books, the chemist in his lab, the custodian in his workroom—may add considerably to the value of the information he can contribute. Under such circumstances the children go to the person with their questions and problems, observing him at his work, and bringing back impressions of the locale as well as the information sought. Obviously, it is often not feasible for an entire class to interview a single person. A small group may go with the teacher after school or during school with a parent as guide. Several groups may go out on various interviews at the same time, each with special responsibilities to the rest of the class. Although the planning is similar to that for the resource visitor or the field trip, the interview requires some special techniques that must be developed ahead of time. Here the skills of meeting and interviewing people become important for the class to master.

Largely because of the skills involved, older children are likely to show more initiative and ingenuity in interviews than young children, although the latter can begin them in the company of adults, their teachers or parents. One class of sixth-grade pupils exploring community government interviewed through small groups the mayor, the chief of police, the water commissioner, the park commissioner, the street superintendent, and the fire department chief. One group returned with a map of the community's water system; another had taped the interview with the mayor; another had made arrangements for the entire class to see a fire-fighting demonstration; another had accepted for the class an invitation to visit the city council—all these opportunities were in addition to the facts they secured from those they interviewed.

COMMUNITY SURVEYS AND PROJECTS

A broader view of the community than that afforded by a field trip or contact with a resource person is provided by the survey in which pupils look at their local environment to study some aspects of a problem that seems pertinent to them. Although the survey itself may be quite specific in character, during its development pupils may be in touch with persons

---

[9] Victor R. Randolph and Clarence D. Samford, *Teaching Elementary School Social Studies* (Dubuque, Iowa: William C. Brown Company, 1957), p. 284.

in many kinds of work, homes in several neighborhoods, or officials with varying responsibilities. They take the serious role of trying to find out something important about their community; they approach adults with an important objective in mind. A variety of survey experiences may suggest themselves to the classroom teacher. Some of the more common were part of the experiences of children in this particular school.

During Fire Prevention Week, all the children of Adams School undertook a fire-hazard survey of their homes, an activity resulting from an intensive study of the causes of home fires and a desire to find out how many homes were in potential danger. Older children developed the questionnaire and instructed children at all grade levels in the meaning and use of the simple instrument. In their study of recreation facilities in their community fifth-graders became interested in the possibilities of a new swimming pool in their section of town. Encouraged by a sympathetic town council, they canvassed the neighborhood to determine the number of potential users of such a facility. At election time intermediate-grade children volunteered to knock on doors and remind people to vote. During a safety campaign led by another class, a survey of the number of bicycle riders in school and the safety of their routes to school was made and reported to the whole student body.

Community projects, sometimes suggested by surveys, make a special contribution to helping children feel that they are participating in community life. In the area of learning when pupils encounter some community problem that begs for solution, they frequently suggest that something be done about it. Although it is not always possible for children to accomplish worthwhile results, there are some community problems they can undertake. When they ask what can be done, then is the time to explore the possibilities. Often the results are surprising. Children in one group found to their delight that their carefully worked out plan for a traffic overpass was acted upon favorably by an alert city planning board. Fourth-graders who canvassed from house to house to collect clothing for Korean children were deluged by contributions. Third-grade children who took their laboriously knitted bed cover to the veterans' hospital were received by ceremonies quite beyond their expectations. Another group that had prepared a clever puppet to earn Red Cross pennies was invited to appear before adult organizations all over town. These experiences reap rich rewards in building closer relationships between children and community and deeper understanding of how people live and work together.

In addition to these major community experiences, there are, of course, many other occasions when pupils and community may come together. Whenever these are planned as part of the social studies area of learning, they have potential for helping the child take his place in the life about him and for making problem solving an experience in living as well as in studying.

Identification
of Community Resources

Although the wealth of community resources is obvious, opportunities to use these resources are sometimes neglected simply because busy teachers have little definite knowledge about them. How to make this important information accessible to teachers is worth some exploration and suggestion.

The community survey is a fruitful way of finding out what the community has to contribute to problem-solving experiences in social studies. Such a survey may be undertaken by the teachers of a school or by the teachers of an entire system, and boys and girls may also have rewarding experiences in taking part in the search.[10] The first task is to identify the types of resources that are likely to be available—field trips, resource visitors, persons to interview, community agencies, community special days, community projects, needed community studies, radio, television, and library resources. Teachers then share the responsibility for ferreting out examples of each type in the community. Then, prior to setting out on their exploration, teachers—and pupil volunteers if they are to take part— agree to find certain types of information about the various kinds of community resources. Data for each of the possibilities are recorded for the office file. Information cards for certain of the resources may look like the cards shown here.

Resource Visitor
Name:
Address and phone:
Subject:
Time available:
Has child in school: Yes _____ No _____
Grade level:
Comment:

Community Project
Type:
Date needed:
Person to call:
Equipment needed:
Expense: Length of Time:
Age of children:
Educational value:
Comment:

---

[10] Howardine Hoffman and Armen Sarafian, "Instructional Resources," in John U. Michaelis, *Social Studies in Elementary Schools* (Thirty-second Yearbook of the National Council for the Social Studies; Washington, D.C.: National Education Association, 1962), p. 232.

Visual Resources
Title of aid:
Content:
Firm or person:
Address or phone:
Availability:
Grade level:
Educational value:
Comment:

School Resources
Name of person or material:
Subject:
Location:
Availability:
Arrangements needed:
Grade level:
Educational value:
Comment:

Similar cards can be made for every type of community resource; and when these are conveniently filed in the school office for ready reference, the problem of how to locate a suitable community resource is solved. If teachers who use a suggestion from the file are encouraged to add their comments to the card, in due time the practical values of the resources can be easily determined at a glance.

An industry questionnaire may be an efficient way to gather information needed for that portion of the information file dealing with the business community. Although the content of the questionnaire may vary from school to school, the following is typical of the kind that may result in useful returns.

INDUSTRY SURVEY

Our school is aware that it is important for children to become well acquainted with their community. Knowing the important kinds of work that are done in the city is a valuable aspect of their education. Please fill out the following questionnaire in order that we may make the best use of any services you have to offer.

What is the name of your company?
Where is your company located?
What does your company do?
Do you permit excursions through your plant?
Have children gone through your plant in the past?
If trips are permitted, how many children may come at one time?
Whom should we call concerning plans for coming to visit?
Is there a phone where he can be reached?
Is an interview with this person possible?
How long does the excursion take?

Is there any charge for your services?
Can someone come to speak to us before we take the trip?
Is there any special apparel children should wear or bring?
What season of the year, day of the week, and time of day would be most suitable?
Are any of the following facilities available for children?
_____ a cafeteria where children may buy lunch
_____ a place where children may eat lunches they bring
_____ rest rooms
_____ a place to put their wraps
Do you have any of the following?
_____ free literature for teachers' use
_____ free literature for children's use
_____ free film for class use
_____ free pictures, models, exhibits

Thank you!

Every school has a great store of talent in its patrons, a wealth of experiences and abilities to share with children who need authentic information to assist in problem solving.[11] Indeed, each classroom in reality has many teachers if they can but be found and intrigued into participation. The parent interest survey by means of a questionnaire is often the answer to locating possible contributors and stimulating interest in helping. Miss Smith used the following check list to explore the resources among her parents.

PARENT INTEREST SURVEY

Dear Mr. and Mrs._____,
    We are aware that our parents can make the school program more helpful and valuable by sharing their interests and abilities with children. Although we may not be able to utilize all your suggestions in any one year, won't you help us by marking and returning the check list?

Miss Smith

YOUR NAME
ADDRESS   PHONE

Would you be willing to help with any of the following?
_____ transportation for a field trip
_____ cooking at school
_____ sewing at school
_____ sewing at home
_____ gardening at school
construction and crafts at school
        _____ art activities
        _____ ceramics

---

[11] Committee on Human Resources of the Metropolitan (New York) School Study Council, *Fifty Teachers to a Classroom* (New York: The Macmillan Company, 1950).

_____ weaving
_____ woodworking
_____ other
_____ dramatics at school
_____ folk dancing or games at school
_____ sports
_____ music
_____ room improvement (painting, construction, decorating)
_____ laundering at home
_____ lunch program at school
_____ parties at school
_____ typing at home
_____ library at school

Would you be willing to come to school to share in your travel experiences?

_____ in the eastern states   _____ in Mexico
_____ in the South   _____ abroad
_____ in the Southwest   _____ places of interest in Indiana
_____ in the Northwest   _____ others
_____ in Canada

Do you have photographs of your trip that you can share?
_____ slides
_____ movies

Do you have collections from your trip?
_____ souvenirs
_____ other things

Do you have any special interest, talent, or hobby that you would be willing to share with the class?
_____ playing a musical instrument
_____ drawing, painting
_____ singing
_____ pets
collections
_____ insects
_____ antiques
_____ rocks
_____ other kinds
_____ photography

Would you be willing to share some of the interesting aspects of your work with the class? _____ If so, what is your occupation? _____

With what age level children would you most enjoy working?
_____ first and second grades (6–7 year olds)
_____ third and fourth grades (8–9 year olds)
_____ fifth and sixth grades (10–11 year olds)

When are you free to come to school? _____

Thank you!

Criteria for Selecting
Community Experiences

As has been previously suggested, community experiences should not just happen. Because they are time consuming, they can be justified only if they are well selected and yield understandings, attitudes, and skills consistent with the goals of the area of learning. To guard against the selection of community experiences on the basis of interest or variety or opportunity alone, a wise teacher checks each selection carefully against defensible criteria.

Does the community experience provide answers to children's problems? It is obvious that a community experience must bring pupils closer to their informational goals than they would otherwise be if the experience is to be selected as a worthwhile activity. To ensure this result demands that the teacher know the situation well in advance of the children's contact with it and that he lay the proper foundation with the persons involved. Children necessarily must go with definite purposes in mind and with a plan for making sure that they know when their questions have been answered. Care in planning for the gathering of information forestalls any feeling on the part of the participants that the trip is only a lark or a holiday from school and dispels fears of parents that children may be wasting their time when they are away from books.

Will the experience contribute to children's understanding of basic social processes of group living?[12] Although the contribution of the community experience to answering children's questions is important, the teacher is likely to be more concerned with its relationship to his goal of developing understanding of how people live and work together in democratic society. The examples cited here can pass this test, because children, rubbing elbows with members of the community, see for themselves how the community works—how the people make a living, how they provide the things they need, how they take care of what is theirs, how they help others, and so on. To make certain that children know what they have seen is the responsibility of the teacher and one of the purposes of the discussion which follows every planned community contact. What were people doing? Why were they doing it? When children can answer these questions with understanding, they are giving evidence that the community experience has met an important test.

Is the experience the most appropriate for the purpose? In other words, does it provide for better learning than can be achieved by other methods

---

[12] Earl S. Johnson, *Theory and Practice of the Social Studies* (New York: The Macmillan Company, 1956), p. 431.

within the classroom? The teacher is always faced with the problem of guiding children to select the best way to reach their goals. If there are any possibilities at all, pupils almost always suggest field trips; preference studies with sixth-grade pupils show that field trips are the most popular of all social studies activities.[13] Only through cooperative planning can teacher and pupils explore the values of a proposed trip. Information that can be efficiently garnered from books should be sought in that way—a field trip would be a waste of time. On the other hand, reading about conservation practices in the community is no substitute for observation and consultation at the conservation site.[14] When there is a conflict of opinion about the choice of experiences, clear thinking and exposition of ideas by those who hold various points of view can be a valuable experience in decision making.

Will the experience provide opportunities for cooperative planning?[15] Whether or not the community experience meets this criterion depends largely upon the teacher. It is possible, of course, to direct children through a community experience without encouraging any participation on their part. If this approach is used, one of the values of community experience is lost: the teacher is demonstrating that the best way to get things done is to plan each detail and ask children to follow his plan. The ingenuity, enthusiasm, and interest so conducive to developing contacts between pupils and adults in the community are thus overlooked, and the whole takes on the nature of an assignment rather than of an adventure. Does every community experience offer opportunities for cooperative planning? Probably so, but if the teacher feels that these opportunities do not exist the experience probably should be forgotten.

Can the experience be easily planned and executed? It must be noted that although this criterion is included it is secondary to all other considerations. Perhaps it would be better to ask whether or not the experience is worth the time and trouble it takes. It is equally unwise to involve children in an activity that is physically dangerous, that may produce unpleasant reactions in the neighborhood, that may disillusion young children about adults, that may be considered trivial by parents, or that in any way cannot be justified in terms of what it requires of teacher and pupils. With the great wealth of community experiences readily available, there is no point in holding out to children the possibilities of some experience that has difficult or unsavory aspects.

[13] Harriet M. Foley, "Preferences of Sixth Grade Children for Certain Social Studies Activities." Unpublished master's thesis, Boston University, 1951, as reported in W. Linwood Chase and Gilbert M. Wilson, "Preference Studies in Elementary School Social Studies," *Journal of Education* (April, 1958), p. 17.

[14] Corey, in Olsen.

[15] See Ernest W. Tiegs and Fay Adams, *Teaching the Social Studies* (Boston: Ginn & Company, 1959), pp. 468–470.

The importance of careful selection of community experiences cannot be overemphasized. If there were fewer possibilities, the task would be easier. Awareness that the most spectacular or impressive may not be the most effective may well save the teacher and his pupils wasted time and energy. On the other hand, a rich community experience may be worth its weight in textbooks!

Planning
for Community Experiences

Every successful community experience comes as the result of careful planning by both teacher and pupils. The teacher plans ahead so that he can better guide the children in their planning. When both agents do their work well, the values of community experiences are considerably enhanced.

ROLE OF THE TEACHER
IN PLANNING COMMUNITY EXPERIENCES

The teacher knows that modern emphasis upon cooperative planning does not relieve him of his responsibility for prior and supportive planning as children move in the direction of the community experiences involved in the pursuit of a problem. Previous discussion of cooperative planning sought to make clear that the teacher who does not look ahead to anticipate children's planning cannot make the most of their ideas. A clear distinction between the responsibilities of the two parties is helpful in defining the sphere of each.

Because the understandings, attitudes, and behaviors to be developed in the area of learning have been clearly defined by the teacher, it is his responsibility to survey community experiences appropriate to these purposes. In fact, he is more competent to do so than anyone else. Although the children will have identified some near-at-hand, specific purposes, the teacher alone is the one best able to take the long view of why certain activities are to be undertaken. He may not decide definitely upon a particular activity but will be ready with pertinent facts about its possibilities. If pupils suggest the activity or if he feels that its value should be called to their attention, he will be ready to give necessary guidance.

When teacher and pupils have cooperatively selected the community experience that will best suit the purpose as seen from their respective points of view, the teacher begins to think in terms of building appropriate background for the experience. In doing so, he will probably ask himself some of the following questions. What contacts have children already had with the proposed experience? Are there books and other materials that will prepare them for what is to come? films? pictures? objects? How can these be used in the preparation period? What do children need to know before they embark on the new activity? The answers to these questions may suggest that several class periods should be used to familiarize children with the coming experience so that their understanding of it will result in better participation and better utilization of what they see and hear.

And then before the preliminary discussion of the experience, the teacher plans the nature of this period. With teacher guidance, children will identify the purposes of their trip or the interview or the guest hour. They will make specific plans for carrying out the affair. And most important of all, they will clarify exactly what it is that they are trying to find out. Essentially, the well-prepared teacher thinks through all these aspects of the discussion before the meeting with the children, being ready in this way to help them move ahead successfully toward the important task of completing their plans.

Before the event takes place, the teacher thinks ahead to the follow-up experience, trying to foresee what leads pupils may wish to pursue and what next experiences will be logical and valuable. Often these new experiences emerge from cooperative evaluation of the success of the children's understandings. Did we learn what we wanted to know? Where do we go next? What new facts do we need? Can we summarize what we learned in an interesting way? Is there someone in our school who will want to know about our experience? To this discussion the teacher brings the ideas he surveyed in preliminary planning and stands ready to assist pupils in identifying next steps.

And, of course, the teacher anticipates problems that may arise at various stages of the activity and prepares to cope with exigencies that may develop. Although it is not possible to prevent minor upsets, careful planning on the part of the teacher will ensure that the adults involved are prepared, that necessary arrangements can be made with parents and the administration, that places to visit are able to care for child guests adequately, that physical needs of children can be easily met, and that the general atmosphere of the experience is conducive to cooperation and learning.

All these phases of preliminary planning by the teacher are easily identified in the preparations Mrs. Field made for a study trip with her fourth grade to a historical spot in Indiana. In their discussion of ways to see history close at hand the pupils suggested an excursion to some place where the people they had been reading and talking about actually lived and worked. Mrs. Field accepted the suggestion and asked the children to be ready next day with definite ideas about where to go and what to do. Before the opening of the planning session, Mrs. Field mentally explored the possibilities in the surrounding territory. Because she was familiar with the environment, this part of her preparation was easy; but she did more than catalogue in her mind the historic sites available. She considered which might have the most impact upon children's learning and which would be best managed in the time available and at that season of the year.

Mrs. Field came to the teacher-pupil planning session with several good destinations to suggest but mindful that the children might propose something even better, especially since they had been encouraged to discuss the project with their parents. Under her guidance and as a result of cooperative choice making, the class decided to make their goal a field journey to Vincennes —the home of William Henry Harrison, the site of the George Rogers Clark monument, a famous bridge over the Wabash, the old cathedral dating from the French era, and the legendary home of "Alice of Old Vincennes." The great variety of attractions in this city sent both teacher and children on a search for detailed information about each aspect of the area they hoped to visit. Mrs. Field put on the reading table some original narratives she had written about the site, copies of Alice of Old Vincennes, leaflets from the Memorial, a description of Vincennes written by schoolchildren, and pamphlets from the Vincennes Chamber of Commerce, as well as supplementary texts and reference books. A film depicting Clark's journey to Fort Vincennes through the flooded wilderness helped children relive that trying experience; several scenes were dramatized in the classroom as pupils tried to catch the spirit of those historic days.

Then Mrs. Field began to think about specific teacher-pupil planning for the trip. She determined ahead of time the transportation facilities, checked with the park commission about best times to visit, secured permission from school officials, and went into the discussion ready to help pupils identify questions to be answered at the site and set up standards for their conduct. She anticipated that there would be new words, especially proper names, to be reviewed. And, of course, letters for parent permission would need attention in the language arts period. Although the trip was yet to be undertaken, Mrs. Field thought about what might happen upon their return, how pupils could evaluate their learning, what records of the journey would be particularly appropriate, and what might be the values and possibilities of sharing the adventure with others. Mrs. Field knew from years of successful teaching that a community experience, whether simple or complex, requires careful and continual planning.

ROLE OF PUPILS
IN PLANNING COMMUNITY EXPERIENCES

As the chapter on cooperative planning made clear, pupils have an important role to play in planning their experiences, and, if they are to secure the important values inherent in a well-executed community experience, their planning continues throughout. In a sense their planning parallels somewhat the planning and preparation of the teacher. They are able to plan because the teacher has planned. They have a resource person to guide them, to help them evaluate their ideas and plans, and to assist in implementing those plans.

Although the teacher determines the basic purposes of the community experience in terms of over-all objectives of the area of learning, children play a part in identifying their own purposes and in selecting the experience that will best meet these goals. Children's purposes will, of course, be quite specific—an idea they wish to illustrate, something they plan to do, and facts they wish to locate, all in pursuit of a problem or question. For example, pupils are interested in learning how fish are raised in a hatchery. How can this purpose be achieved? There are several possibilities—to read from the encyclopedia, to discuss the question with someone who knows about fish hatcheries, or to visit a nearby goldfish hatchery. Which will give the most accurate information, which will make most clear the nature of the operation, and which will provide the answers to children's specific questions? Often the question is not which will be used, but in what order these sources of information should be explored. Cooperative planning and evaluation of the possibilities of each will ultimately lead to a tentative selection. Pupil participation in the selection of the experience contributes to pupil acceptance of the plans as their own and personal involvement in implementing the choice.

Acquiring a background of information for the experience then becomes the responsibility of each pupil as the group prepares to follow through on its plans. With the teacher's help children identify what it is they need to know in order to be intelligent visitors or interviewers or survey makers. They suggest books to read, persons from whom to get advice, and consultation in the family circle. They listen to and discuss information the teacher or another pupil may contribute.

And during these preliminary activities questions begin to emerge to serve as the basis of exploration during the community experience itself. These the pupils identify, mark as important or cast aside, organize, and record. They suggest ways in which information may be gathered during the community activity and anticipate the form in which it may appear. Knowing that it is possible to forget one's responsibilities when the experience is unusually interesting, they plan how each pupil will make sure that all essential information is secured and returned to the next class session. Various techniques may be tried from time to time. Often the responsibility for each question is taken by a small group or by an individual, armed with paper and pencil for taking notes. Sometimes every child takes the entire list of questions, making notes as the answers come to his attention. For very young children the teacher may keep the record as children discover the information they need. Whatever the specific method used to implement the idea, pupil participation in planning what is to be found out impresses children anew with the purposefulness of the enterprise.

Children further implement their plans by participating in many of the decisions that are involved in making arrangements for the experience and in planning how they will take care of themselves. Although the teacher generally makes sure beforehand whether or not an activity is possible in terms of various permissions needed, children learn here that one clears all his plans with those who are likely to be concerned with making them successful. In the language arts period they write letters home, interview the principal, and often formally get in touch with other adults by letter or telephone. Whether the trip is a riding or a walking one, safe routes and sensible safety behavior must be studied and agreed upon by the group. Their own conduct as recipients of community attention—whether they are hosts or visitors, interviewers or listeners—has a full-dress rehearsal.

Through the planning of the venture teacher and pupils are in partner-ship, thus assuring better understanding of its purposes and full coopera-tion in making it a success. It is possible that the values of the planning, alone, would make such community experiences beneficial, even if there were no other positive results. Certainly, in the development of democratic group process, skill in discussing and evaluating plans is highly desirable.

Appraisal
of Community Experiences

In view of the frequently repeated criticism that learning through experiences is wasteful of pupils' time and unproductive of learning, it is well to consider evaluating community experiences rather carefully in terms of two criteria. Do community experiences reinforce children's learning? Do they encourage interest in further learning and lead to new learning activities?

When the community experience comes to an end, pupils and teacher gather together to check on their findings and to plan for next steps. Often the first order of business is to find out whether or not questions were an-swered to the satisfaction of everyone. In the question-answering period teacher and pupils have an opportunity to organize the facts they gathered, to share with each other the wide range of information they have discov-ered, and to relate their learning to the problems being studied. Often this information is much more effectively discussed than that gathered, for example, from reading, because pupils have exchanged ideas with adults and have attended more closely to the results. Through restatement of ideas and facts in the class discussion, the important learnings are clarified in the minds of pupils and become more truly their own. The extent to which pupils profit from community experiences in terms of new facts, information, and ideas is an effective measure of success.

The acquisition of new vocabulary as a result of field activity is very likely to become evident during the evaluation period. In fact, it may be useful to compile a list of the new words and to encourage children to prac-tice their use during the follow-up discussions. Pupils seem to take pride in calling things by their right names, and the teacher should not be sur-prised if, on the return from a field trip, they are using quite expertly many terms not previously a part of their vocabulary. As in Mrs. Johnson's group, whose television-studio field trip is described at the opening of the chapter, children often find acquisition of vocabulary through firsthand contact with things much easier than acquisition through reading and dictionary use. The value of the community experience can certainly be measured some-what in the development of new vocabulary.

Although the development of concepts is closely related to the acquisition of new vocabulary, concept development as used in this discussion goes beyond recognizing the special meaning of a word. The knowledge that a certain musical instrument is called by a certain name or that a particular worker in a factory is designated in a special way is not evidence of concept formation. If the community experience helps children handle words at more than a concrete level, then it is contributing to the building of concepts. For some children a visit to a factory develops the idea that *factory* is this particular factory visited; if the community experience and the follow-up discussion are effective, pupils may understand *factory* to represent those cooperative activities in which men and machines create useful products. Similarly, *city government* should, as a result of a firsthand experience, come to mean something more than an office building in which city employees work. It is apparent that the teacher needs to play a significant role in directing the follow-up discussion so that concept development is facilitated.

The formulation of understandings growing out of a community venture can be effective evidence for the evaluation of the experience. What did we learn from the experience? What big ideas impressed us as we looked, listened, and explored? What did you notice about the way in which the whole dairy operation proceeded? What can you say about the way in which factory workers performed their jobs? What do the objects brought to us by our resource visitor tell us about the skill of his people? What conclusions can you draw about life in the early days of our city by our study of these old newspapers? If, during the sharing and discussion, pupils can extract generalizations that can be applied to other similar situations, the community experience will have made a significant contribution to learning.

Ideally, before any such experiences are undertaken, the teacher will anticipate what may happen when children return to the class to mull over their activity and plan what needs to be done next. The extent to which the experience does bear fruit of a useful kind will be a measure of its real value to the ongoing activities of the study. What kinds of experiences should the successful community experience motivate?

The best of these is never a dead end, for any community experience worth the time required to develop it should uncover almost as many new questions as it answers. Every group should return to the discussion period with new questions of how and why. When these unanswered questions and unsolved problems are uncovered, a search for solutions seems logical. Naturally the teacher must judge whether or not these leads are significant and worth extensive exploring and whether or not individuals or small groups can take care of the inquiry through research activity. But whatever the course, the most effective community experience is likely to pose one or more new problems to be solved.

Certain types of community experiences may be so impressive and valuable that children will feel the need for making permanent records of them. Although not all community experiences that are worthwhile may result in the need for some kind of record, certainly evidence of their worth can be drawn from children's interest in capturing their experiences permanently. Pupils' expressed feeling that here is an enterprise valuable enough to keep in some concrete form tells something of the satisfaction they had in planning and executing the activity and promises well for the permanence of the learning that occurred. Scrapbooks, logs, exhibitions, assemblies, and illustrated reports are but some of the forms these records may take.

Often the cooperative development of the record of a community experience results in the desire to share it with others. The experience that was simply too good to be kept within the class group is likely to have been worthwhile. When this sharing emphasizes answers to significant questions, new vocabulary, concepts, and important generalizations, there is further reinforcement of learning as it is communicated to others who are less informed. Happily, too, such sharing helps children hold up for inspection an experience they have planned and helps them to see it from a different point of view.

The desire to share an experience with others or the need to improve subsequent enterprises may generate a very useful critical analysis of the community experience. When children check their accomplishment against their original plans, when they analyze their conduct of the undertaking in terms of the standards they have set up, and when they take note of things to remember next time, they are participating in an activity that is a significant consequence of the stimulating venture into the community. Were there no considerations of this kind, the teacher could well assume that children either did not feel very much a part of the planning or else that they did not think the experience warranted any concern about how it was implemented. The depth of children's analysis of their experience is a key to what it meant to them.

The good elementary school is part of the community in which it exists, and to it every day come the young citizens of the community. Through the area of learning the schoolchild comes to understand his community —how its people live and work, what its problems are, and what his role is now and in the future. Community experiences provide the bridge between school and community and the resources through which the child develops increasingly mature understanding of what it means to be part of a community group. In like manner, the community comes to know the work of the school, what its pupils are studying and doing, and it learns to contribute to that learning in a variety of ways. The social studies classroom is as big as the community if teacher and pupils take advantage of all that the world outside the school has to offer.

QUESTIONS FOR DISCUSSION

Reconsider the dialogue at the beginning of the chapter, using it as the focal point for discussion.

1. What part did children take in selecting the community experience?
2. What preparations for the trip did the teacher and the pupils make?
3. How did the trip lead to other experiences in the curriculum?
4. Why was the trip to the television station a particularly appropriate experience?
5. If there had been no television station, what experiences might have accomplished the teacher's and children's purposes?

SUGGESTIONS FOR CONSTRUCTING
A RESOURCE UNIT

Describe the community experiences that will be needed in developing your chosen area of learning. Since these experiences often require larger blocks of time than some other types of experiences as well special arrangements that involve time and effort on the part of persons outside the school, the importance of careful selection and planning cannot be overlooked.

As you consider the community experiences that will best achieve the purposes of your area of learning, consider the amount and kind of planning that will be required and include in your description the steps to be taken in planning the experience. Answering such questions as these will help to make the description clear:

1. What is the purpose of each community experience?
2. What preplanning will be necessary?
3. What steps in planning will children take?
4 What will children do in carrying out the experience?

7

Constructing
and Processing
to Solve Problems

BILL: Mrs. Johnson, I'm ready to get started on my telegraph keys. The book you gave me gives directions for making a good little set. It is hard to read, but I think several of us boys can figure it out.

MRS. JOHNSON: I think many of us are ready to try making some equipment to communicate with, Bill. Wayne, how about your idea for an intercom set? Ronnie, are you still interested in signals?

RONNIE: Alice and Anne and I want to make a set of signal flags like the ones the Navy uses. We saw a picture where they were signaling planes to come in for landings on an aircraft carrier. I think the encyclopedias show the way to use the flags.

CHARLES: Susan and Pat and I want to try making a linoleum block print for the masthead of our newspaper. I have a good hobby book that shows how to do it.

RUTH: We read about how electricity helps in communication, but most of us girls don't know much about it. Could some of the boys help us find out about batteries? We could find out how doorbells work—that's communicating.

MRS. JOHNSON: We have a number of ideas here for finding out more about how communication works. Should we plan some work periods when we can try these things?

PEGGY: It'll take more than one.

MRS. JOHNSON: Yes. We can plan how to get started and then plan to use several days for the work. Groups can report now and then so we'll know how everyone is getting along. What groups shall we have? We've already suggested these. I'll write them on the board.

1. intercom set
2. telegraph key
3. signal flags
4. block print for newspaper masthead
5. batteries and bells

What do we need to plan first?

MARY LOU: What each group has to do to get ready to work.

MRS. JOHNSON: How do we start?

JANET SUE: We'd have to read to get directions first.

WAYNE: Then plan what materials and tools we need.

PEGGY: And who's supposed to bring them.

PATRICIA: And where we'll work.

JACK: We'd better have a chairman for each group, too.

MRS. JOHNSON: How shall we decide who will be in each group?

CHARLES: Some of us have already made some plans, but we'd be glad to have other people join us.

MRS. JOHNSON: Suppose we record on the chalkboard the plans that have already been made, and each person can decide which group he wants to join. If we have five groups, how large will each one be? Yes, not more than six or seven in each. Can we have a second choice in mind so one group will not be larger than the others? Perhaps you can sign up for the group as soon as you come in from recess. Then we can have our group planning meetings immediately after that.

. . . .

MRS. JOHNSON: Now that each group has had its planning session, are we ready to report our plans? Shall we start with the group making the telegraph keys?

BILL: I'm chairman of the telegraph group because it was my idea in the first place. But the others elected me.

MRS. JOHNSON: What are your plans? Are you ready to go to work?

BILL: We found directions in two or three places, but we decided to use the ones that are in the book you showed me yesterday. It's by Craig. We read the directions, and we think we know just what to do in the right order. We made a list of the things we need—two sort of thick boards, three large nails, two pieces of tin that have to be cut in a special pattern, some sort of knob, and wire. Each of us will bring one of these things.

MRS. JOHNSON: Do you need any tools?

BILL: We plan to ask Mr. Swanson in the shop for a hammer and for tin shears. We need a table to work on. Then we're ready to start.

MRS. JOHNSON: Good, Bill. Let's see now. You chose a chairman; you found your directions; you listed the materials and who would bring them. Yes, your plans seem to be complete. Now, how about your group, Mary Lou?

MARY LOU: I joined the group with the batteries. I'm like Ruth. I need to know more about electricity. Ruth's going to be chairman, but Donald said he'd teach us. Jack's going to help, too.

RUTH: We found some charts in our science book that show how to wire batteries to bells. We need some batteries, some wire, and bells. Do you think Mr. Baker in the high school science room would lend us the right things? We probably can work in the reading corner if no one else wants it.

MRS. JOHNSON: Do you think the ringing of the bells will disturb others?

MARY LOU: We'll just have to be careful. We can't work in the hall. That would be worse.

MRS. JOHNSON: If you are careful and everyone else knows your problem, it probably will work out all right. We can try it to see. Is the block print group ready? Charles, do you think your group can locate some linoleum scraps for your masthead before tomorrow?

CHARLES: Yes, Mrs. Johnson. We thought of a better idea after we reported.

MRS. JOHNSON: Good. Now that all groups have reported their plans, what's the next step for each group?

MARTHA: We have to get all the materials in. Each chairman could check off his list as soon as we come in with them in the morning and then report to you when everything is ready.

MRS. JOHNSON: A good idea. Let's hope everyone remembers his special responsibility.

. . . .

DONALD: We're all ready for our work period, Mrs. Johnson. If Ronnie's group forgot to bring big scissors, I have an extra pair.

MRS. JOHNSON: Does each group know what it's going to do? And where to work? Ronnie, is your group going to move a table into the hall where you can spread out the cloth for your signal flags? Ruth's group in the reading center? Remember the sound, won't you? The block-print group can use my desk—it's all cleared for you. The telegraph group—yes, back in the corner will be fine for you. How about the intercom, Wayne?

WAYNE: Mr. Swanson said he'd help us get started in the shop if it's all right with you, Mrs. Johnson.

MRS. JOHNSON: That's fine, Wayne. You'll have plenty of room there. Come back in an hour, or sooner, if Mr. Swanson has other things to do. We'll have brief progress reports before lunch.

WAYNE: All right, we're on our way.

MRS. JOHNSON: Suppose we all find our places and go to work. I'll come around to help if you need me. Will you need to plan a bit before you start?

SUSAN: Mrs. Johnson, the signal flag group has a problem already. We each want to make a set of flags. That's two apiece. We have enough cloth, but our rulers aren't right to measure for them.

MRS. JOHNSON: There's a yardstick in the coat closet and a tape measure in my desk drawer. Will either of them help you out?

. . . .

MARTHA: Mrs. Johnson, Bill thinks that just because he's chairman we all have to do just what he says. He says girls don't know anything about telegraph keys.

MRS. JOHNSON: Perhaps we'd better talk a bit about what a good chairman does. I'm sure Bill wants other people to enjoy making the keys as much as he will. How does a chairman help his group?

. . . .

DONALD: Mrs. Johnson, we have the batteries and bell hooked up, but the bell doesn't ring. I think these batteries aren't any good.

MRS. JOHNSON: What should we try to do before we decide that the batteries are dead?

MARY LOU: Let's read the directions over again while you're here, Mrs. Johnson. Maybe we made a mistake. It says, "Take two pieces of electric wire. Scrape off the insulation for about three quarters of an inch at the ends of the wire." Did you do it on both ends of both wires, Jack? Maybe that's the trouble.

MRS. JOHNSON: What difference would that make, Mary Lou?

MARY LOU: Donald showed us the covered wire. If the covering is left on the end of the wire that is wound around the battery posts, I don't think the current could go through.

. . . .

MRS. JOHNSON: Now that each group has finished its project, shall we share what we have done? Do you have any ideas about how we could do this?

FRANK: The members of each committee could demonstrate their equipment.

BILL: And tell what they learned about how we communicate with it.

MARY LOU: Ours would be a little different because electricity used in lots of communication doesn't come from batteries like the ones we used. But I think we can explain about currents and like that.

SUSAN: We can show how a block print is used. A real newspaper makes a metal plate, but the idea is the same.

MRS. JOHNSON: Does each group need a few minutes to plan its report? Perhaps we should also discuss any problems you had in trying to work together. We want to make our next work periods better if we can.

Constructing and processing and taking apart and putting together are natural activities of children. Their play environment and the toys provided for them encourage creative use of materials and equipment. At home children not only engage in those activities on their own, but also mimic adults around them—sawing, pounding, sewing, mowing, mixing, and stirring.

Children are immensely curious about how things work: they want to see inside, to shake, to pull ,and to separate. Equally strong is the drive to contrive, to make something in their image of the real thing—two crossed sticks for an airplane, a tunnel of blocks, or a castle of wet sand. The reality of the constructed object is in the builder's mind and not necessarily in the appearance of the object. It is the doing and the imagining that are important to the child.

In their explorations of materials, children have important experiences in testing out their ideas about how things work, what happens when ingredients are mixed, and how pieces of things fit together. They put their hunches and guesses to work and by trial and error grow in their control of the environment.[1]

These experiences are especially appropriate today, when the child seldom sees at firsthand the construction or processing of many of the goods and products he uses daily. Basic knowledge of what goes into the many things he uses at home and school is not readily available unless the need is recognized and met by understanding adults. Here social studies provides the environment for this learning, and the problems children raise set the search in motion.

Many of the questions and problems raised by children in social studies can best be answered by direct participation in constructing objects or processing foods and other materials. To encourage children to solve prob-

---

[1] Laura Hooper, "The Child—The Curriculum—The World of Materials," *Childhood Education* (May, 1955), pp. 443–445.

lems through this kind of experiencing is appropriate to their need for exploration and discovery and essential to successful development of concepts and understandings in social studies.

Values of Construction and Processing

Experiences in construction and processing are an important part of a good school day for children. Because they provide children with still another method for answering questions and solving problems, construction of authentic tools, equipment, objects, models, and dioramas, as well as the processing of materials used in everyday living, past and present, is the direct experience that contributes vitally to the area of learning in social studies.

In spite of widespread acceptance of the values of construction and processing by those who work with children, these experiences are, however, very much the focus of discussion among those who believe that time spent on "activity" robs pupils of more valuable opportunities to concentrate on the content of social studies.[2] Presently, with increasing emphasis upon intellectual aspects of the curriculum, it becomes even more important that teachers select construction and processing activities critically in terms of the extent to which they help children discover the relationships implicit in the structure of social studies. Only through many kinds of experiences can pupils move from concreteness to the abstractions so essential to generalizing. What, then, are the special contributions of construction and processing experiences to learning in social studies?

PROBLEM SOLVING THROUGH CONSTRUCTION AND PROCESSING

Construction and processing experiences make significant contributions to problem solving. They yield authentic data about basic human activities; develop appreciation for products and processes by making them concrete; clarify vocabulary, concepts, and understandings, thus giving meaning to reading; and encourage exploration and discovery (see Figure 8). Although construction and processing share some of these values in common with other experiences in social studies, children's love for doing, their interest in manipulating, and their pride in producing make these experiences particularly appropriate and successful learning activities. Awareness of how these experiences facilitate problem solving is essential to their improved selection and utilization.

---

[2] Fannie R. Shaftel, "Industrial Arts in the Social Studies Program," in John U. Michaelis (Ed.), *Social Studies in Elementary Schools* (Thirty-second Yearbook of the National Council for the Social Studies; Washington, D.C.: National Education Association, 1962), pp. 212–218.

Values of Construction and Processing

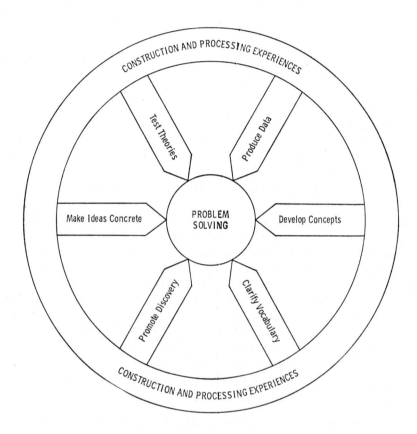

Figure 8

Pupil involvement in reproduction of authentic objects and processes contributes significantly to problem solving in the area of learning.

Construction and processing, first of all, offer information about the basic human activities around which many of the concerns of children revolve. How people carry on the processes of daily living is the subject of many of the questions and problems pupils identify in the area of learning. The opportunity to re-create or reproduce a process or product provides work experiences that show more clearly than any other kind of learning activity how man has solved the problems of living in his environment and how he continues to change and improve these techniques. Reading may bring a vivid description of a process, the community may provide opportunities to observe, but in both the child is at best only a spectator. In construction and processing the child can become a participant in the process and sense more personally the important relationship between the worker and the work done.[3]

Construction and processing also develop a new appreciation for processes and products. Children today enjoy a vast supply of objects and materials acquired with no effort on their part. They are rather far removed from the industries and crafts that provide most of the comforts of daily living. Only through actual participation in production can children begin to sense the social significance of a product and the principles basic to its development.[4] Even though children's techniques may differ somewhat from commercial or professional procedures, pupils can identify themselves with the process or construction enough to feel more keenly its requirements and more respect for its results.[5]

Experiences in making objects and materials further aid problem-solving ability by clarifying concepts and deepening understandings. It is important to remember that children's learning is multisensory and not confined to the study of verbal symbols emphasized so much in a strictly intellectual approach to content. Before generalizing becomes possible, children need many concrete experiences upon which to base their ideas about the way of life in any country or region.[6] It would be simple to tell children the answers to their questions, or to cite suitable references, or even to show them pictures or objects. But the secret of discovering a concept, or arriving at an understanding, is the opportunity children have to integrate knowledge drawn from direct experiences with that drawn from verbal sources. Construction and processing through repeated contacts with a concept or an understanding at increasingly higher levels of thought give children a vehicle for proving that a statement is true and serve as the authority on which children can base at least tentative conclusions. The sometimes vague understanding pupils may have gained from other sources crystallizes, as doing takes over where listening, reading, or watching leave off.[7] When the teacher inquires about what important ideas have been learned from an experience in construction or processing, the pupils begin to put into words the thoughts they were formulating as they worked. Note how experiences in weaving deepened understandings of the process for an elementary school child.

[3] Mary-Margaret Scobey, "Role of Industrial Arts in the Elementary School Program of Social Studies," *Elementary School Journal* (January, 1955), pp. 288–293.

[4] *Ibid.*

[5] For an extensive list of processes that illustrate ways of meeting basic needs, see Edith P. Merritt, *Working with Children in Social Studies* (San Francisco: Wadsworth Publishing Company, Inc., 1961), pp. 236–238.

[6] Shaftel, pp. 212–218.

[7] Ruth D. Tomlinson, "Let's Look to Proof for Authority," in *Children Can Make It!* (Washington, D.C.: Association for Childhood Education International, 1955), pp. 46–47.

Sarah's first experience with the concept of weaving came when she used a simple loom set with nails and strung with cord or yarn. She put the needle in and out from one side to another, alternating the "overs" and "unders." From this activity she was able to make certain observations. In weaving there are up and down threads. The weaver makes the cross threads go over and under. When the weaving is finished, there is a piece of cloth. At a later stage, Sarah used a small table loom, putting the shuttle through and pulling the beater against the woven portion. Did her concept of weaving enlarge and her understandings about it deepen? Of this there can be little doubt. When Sarah's class went to visit an adult weaver and the children were encouraged to try to operate the foot pedals of the big loom, Sarah's understanding of the process was enlarged still further. Her experiences helped her to generalize in these ways. On large looms it is possible to weave fine cloth in a variety of intricate patterns. Skill and patience are required to complete hand-woven articles. Materials woven by hand are often more prized than machine-woven ones. In these processing activities the child's concept of weaving and the understandings she was able to formulate about it were generally enriched and extended.

Furthermore, construction and processing stimulate children to experiment with materials as they put into form objects or processes in which they are interested. Although specific directions for making models and carrying out many processes are available,[8] at times pupils have only pictures or a very meager description on which to depend. Then they may need to test out their ideas about how a simple machine works or how lye changes grease into soap. In some situations, children can investigate substitutes for unavailable materials and experience occasionally the discovery of a new process. Construction and processing offer frequent challenges to pupil ingenuity.

As the area of learning unfolds, pupils with high interest in particular facets of the problem being explored may choose to pursue these special avenues of inquiry through the use of a variety of educational media. Their search in depth often suggests appropriate construction and processing. These individual projects provide a challenge for the learner as he strives for authenticity and accuracy, and their successful completion enriches the knowledge and understanding of all group members who share them. An unusual film, "Learning Is Searching," describes these "side studies" most effectively and emphasizes their special contributions to problem solving.[9]

Since problem solving in social studies is largely an effort planned and executed by the group, construction and processing activities that pupils plan offer unsurpassed experiences in working and learning together.[10]

[8] Older but useful references for model building are Louis V. Newkirk, *Integrated Handwork for Elementary Schools* (Morristown, N.J.: Silver Burdett Company, 1940); and C. J. Maginley, *Historic Models of America and How to Make Them* (New York: Harcourt, Brace & World, Inc., 1947).

[9] "Learning Is Searching" (New York: New York University).

[10] Ernest W. Tiegs and Fay Adams, *Teaching the Social Studies* (Boston: Ginn & Company, 1959), p. 125.

Although very young children are individualists, as they grow older they become more capable of sustained participation in a group and more aware of the values of group effort. Moreover, daily life in the community demands that children learn to be cooperative, able to work with others in pursuit of a goal. Construction and processing experiences provide the environment and motivation for the practice of group process skills.

Thus, for several reasons, construction and processing are an important part of every effective social studies program. Evidence of these experiences can be found in the classrooms of every good elementary school.[11] To omit them is to neglect a valuable avenue to learning and problem solving.

Kinds of Experiences
in Construction and Processing

Values previously ascribed to construction and processing are most fully realized when teachers are aware of the wide variety of useful experiences from which children may choose and when they guide children in the development of activities that meet certain criteria. Good results are likely to follow careful exploration and judicious selection of experiences.

Almost every area of learning gives pupils opportunities to make the things they need in their study or to carry out processes suggested by the content of their questions and problems. Constructing tools and equipment, making models and dioramas, making cloth and clothing, and processing these and other materials are among the most valuable and practical of these activities. Information about each of these types of experience will be useful to teachers as they prepare for cooperative planning of construction and processing activities in the area of learning.

MAKING TOOLS AND EQUIPMENT

The construction of tools and equipment needed in the area of learning provides purposeful activity leading directly to important understandings, attitudes, and skills. Man's dependence upon his tools and his inventiveness in solving mechanical problems are well illustrated through children's efforts to devise equipment for various processes.[12] Children gain not only appreciation of the way in which such equipment makes possible various projects and processes but also satisfaction from the opportunity to use something they have made for a real purpose. These tools and equipment are often those that are not readily available in the environment, representing, instead, unique requirements of the classroom situation, equip-

---

[11] Edgar Dale, *Audio-Visual Methods in Teaching* (rev. ed.; New York: Holt, Rinehart and Winston, Inc., 1954), p. 118.

[12] Scobey, pp. 288–293.

ment used in earlier times, or devices found in cultures that differ from the children's own. In pursuing problems raised during the initiation, primary-grade children may find it necessary to make many objects—cages or shelters for pets, furniture and curtains for the reading center, counter surfaces for a cookie sale, incubators for hatching baby chicks, containers for terraria, or flower boxes. Intermediate-grade children may need other tools and equipment that require more mature skill in construction. Candle molds and wicks for dipping candles, reels for removing silk from cocoons, butter churns, spinning wheels and looms, sundials and shadow clocks, paper-making frames, musical instruments, windmills, and water wheels are only a partial list of the tools and equipment that may be essential to carrying out plans in the area of learning.[13] To provide for children the simple equipment they can make for themselves is to deprive them of experiences that test skill and independence and that develop important understandings about tools and machines and their relationship to man's creative activities.

CREATING REPLICAS, MODELS, AND DIORAMAS

Constructing replicas, models, and dioramas can be equally valuable and stimulating as children pool information related to their problems and give it substance. Replicas are intended to be lifelike re-creations of important objects being studied; models are usually thought of as smaller representations of objects that cannot be conveniently brought into or reproduced in the classroom. Although the distinction between the two is sometimes difficult to define, both serve to clarify concepts and understandings. In a similar way, dioramas, which are three-dimensional scenes of objects, animals, and people in their natural environments, play a part in bringing meaning to the area of learning.

Primary-grade children can construct, although sometimes crudely, a variety of objects that are in a sense replicas or models. The playhouse, the bus made of blocks, the train fashioned of great wooden packing cases, the post office, the grocery store, and the greenhouse are usually life-size and from the children's point of view quite lifelike. When children need to show a great expanse of territory—the layout of a farm, a railroad freight yard, the stores and other buildings of a community, traffic hazards near school, airports, and harbors—they construct smaller items to represent their ideas. Although these objects are models of a sort, they are often only streamlined versions of the real things, with their simplicity the result of young children's disinterest in exact duplication. For replicas and models alike, the children's imagination happily supplies all missing details. As children use these creations in dramatic play or explain them to visitors,

---

[13] For directions, see *Children Can Make It!* (Washington, D.C.: Association for Childhood Education International, 1955).

they clarify their own understandings of important human activities that bring the models and replicas to life.

Intermediate-grade children, however, because they are growing in manipulative skill and are becoming more interested in producing objects and goods that are real, construct many kinds of replicas and models that are beyond the abilities of primary-grade children. Such environments as the pioneer living room, a tropical hut, the colonial kitchen, a Mexican market place, or a western ranch home complete with trappings and furnishings have been reproduced successfully with all the attendant values of bringing to life other times and places. Although these children do not need visual representations as much as they did in the primary grades, well-chosen activities of this sort bring new interest and deeper understanding to the area of learning. The constructing itself helps children relate their learning to reality.

Because older children can follow with reasonable skill the directions for making a variety of things, the construction of authentic models becomes possible in the intermediate grades; and the model itself becomes more valuable in developing accurate concepts and understandings. These models have at one time or another been constructed by intermediate-grade children: oil derricks with movable parts, pioneer log cabins with canted chimneys, covered wagons, Viking ships, flatboats with paddle wheels, totem poles, hornbooks, lumbering equipment, human figures, and animals. Cooperative planning will reveal many other possibilities for constructing objects useful in helping the groups answer questions and solve problems.

When detailed planning for the making of models gets under way, older pupils search for pictures, sketches, or descriptions of the article or arrange to observe the real thing in action. They can then draw the item, showing the necessary views, and proceed to selecting materials most appropriate to the construction. Clay, plaster of Paris, papier mâché, wood, and metals are among the possibilities for preparing the model.[14] Each of these materials has characteristics that make it especially appropriate for certain kinds of models. Art personnel in the school are good sources of help in selecting and preparing materials for these projects.

Dioramas are usually popular with older children. In them they can combine interest in detail and a sense of the dramatic with their greater skill in using materials. There are many variations of the diorama and an infinite variety of materials that can be used in their construction. One that children seem to like begins with a cardboard or pasteboard box, turned with its opening on one side. The background is planned and finished first, either directly on the inside surfaces of the box or on a curved sheet of heavy paper if a rounded interior is more suitable to the scene. Then the

[14] For helpful directions, see R. Murray Thomas and Sherwin G. Swartout, *Integrated Teaching Materials* (New York: David McKay Company, 1960), pp. 433–441.

environment is completed: rocks, twigs, soil, and bits of sponge are used in the outdoor scenes; sticks, stones, plaster of Paris, or sawdust and wheat paste provide building materials; and miniature furnishings are added to interior scenes. The animals and people who inhabit the diorama are fashioned from pipe cleaners, clothespins, balsam wood, or clay and arranged in the foreground. A well-executed diorama is especially effective in helping children see relationships between living things and their environment.

Appropriate subjects for dioramas are almost endless. One fifth-grade class made a series of them to illustrate the growth of California, depicting in sequence the early explorers, life in the mission, ranching in dry country, the orange groves of modern times, and the building of a great irrigation dam. Children in a fourth grade, who made their diorama to represent animal life in prehistoric times, developed clay figures of dinosaurs against a background of abundant plant life, inserting in the back of the box a beautiful transparency of a waterfall. Boys and girls in an older group re-created in a diorama the United Nations General Assembly complete with murals on the walls and booths for instantaneous translations. Nimble fingers, patience, and imagination can help children illustrate in the diorama important understandings from the area of learning. In turn the completed diorama becomes an effective device for teaching others.[15]

MAKING CLOTH AND CLOTHING

Among the many other worthwhile things that children can construct or process are cloth and clothing. Because the processing of cloth is a fundamental activity in almost every culture and the clothing of a culture is so representative of the culture itself, children often find that these two kinds of experiences are needed in order to understand fully those about whom they are studying. Although these activities vary greatly in difficulty, both primary- and intermediate-grade children can perform them if there are real purposes for the work and a real use to which the products can be put.

Young children, for example, find that their problems about what makes a house suggest the need for a rug for the playhouse. How can they make one? Their participation in Junior Red Cross activities calls for a wool lap robe for a disabled veteran. What are the possibilities for weaving one? The need of a local children's hospital for bedding poses a problem. What can children create as their contribution to meet these needs? In each of these situations children and teacher cooperatively explore ideas. They survey their own skills in relation to what they would like to do. They make plans to learn new skills the teacher thinks are appropriate to their maturity.

[15] For other ideas, see Thomas and Swartout, pp. 430–431, and James Brown, Richard B. Lewis, and Fred F. Harcleroad, A-V *Instruction* (New York: McGraw-Hill, Inc., 1959), p. 275.

Older children can become as much interested in the process of making cloth as in the product. Hanging a Navajo loom from a crossbar on the classroom wall and stringing it with yarn are but the first steps in helping children understand the patience and skill essential to the creation of a fine piece of handicraft. When they try their own hands at carding and spinning wool, heckling flax, or making dyes as colonial and pioneer women were compelled to do, they can appreciate more clearly than ever before why cloth and clothing were cherished possessions not to be gained easily or worn carelessly. Those classrooms that are fortunate enough to have environments suited to the raising of silkworms become laboratories of living evidence that tedious and painstaking effort alone can produce unbroken strands of silk from a fragile cocoon.[16] A piece of cloth becomes something more than an object of utility when children participate in processes related to its creation.

Fashioning cloth into clothing is almost certain to be suggested when children who are exploring ways of living in other places plan to translate into something tangible their findings about native costumes or dress. Although it may be wise in some instances to search for real examples of the clothing being studied, it is quite possible for intermediate-grade children to produce some authentic items related to the area of learning. A study of Japan suggests kimonos, obis, and wooden clogs; serapes, rebozos, and large hats are part of Mexican life; articles of straw are common to the Chinese; squaw skirts and boleros turn the girls into Navajos; breech cloths and shell necklaces make the Sioux dancers look the part; full skirts, ruffled bonnets, knee breeches, and powdered hair bring colonial life to the fifth grade. Appropriate dress not only demonstrates what one is learning but also helps the wearer to feel the role and the place and the time.

When children become deeply involved in making clothing representative of the groups about which they are studying, most teachers feel the need for expert help. Accurate pictures and descriptions are absolutely necessary. If there is no attempt to be authentic and if children are not fully aware of the necessary substitutes, the activity will contribute little to a real understanding of the relationships between a people's dress and their culture and environment. A skillful parent or two, as well as the high school home economics teacher who may be available for a work period now and then, can be of great assistance in helping children turn their ideas into reality. As children carry their plans to completion, the teacher has excellent opportunities not only to teach some useful skills but also to increase children's awareness of the purposes and understandings to be achieved by the work in progress.

[16] For directions, see *Children Can Make It!* pp. 51–53.

PROCESSING FOOD AND OTHER MATERIALS

Food and other materials can also be processed successfully and profitably in the elementary classroom. The processing involved in most of the products children know and use is not generally part of their experience. Although in earlier times children were more actively engaged in many of the processes that led to the satisfaction of needs, most children today have few responsibilities of these kinds and few opportunities even to observe them. The challenging area of learning usually raises a number of questions that can be best answered meaningfully through processing of various kinds.

Many problems about how man meets his need for food can be solved by processing foods in the classroom. Man's use of a single plentiful crop to furnish a variety of foods is illustrated by the pioneers' conversion of corn into hominy, corn bread, parched corn, and cornmeal mush. The ease of cooking with packaged foods is demonstrated when children make soups and simple desserts. Steps in a process are clearly defined when children follow directions for making cakes or cookies. The preparation of vegetables picked in the school garden builds an awareness of land-to-table relationships. Recipes from around the world bring to the classroom the unique foods enjoyed in other places—Mexican tortillas, English crumpets, shish kebabs from the Middle East, and countless others. New ways of doing things, new appreciations, and new taste experiences are the natural results of such food-processing experiences.

Food preparation, of course, requires some equipment and skills. If the school does not provide simple utensils and implements, a group of teachers can make a collection to be shared as needed; or as a last resort children can volunteer to borrow needed articles. If the school encourages food-processing activities, a storage cabinet on wheels with work space on the top provides a convenient way to move equipment from room to room wherever needed. If a portable oven and a hot plate are not part of this unit, the school kitchen or the stove of the nearest willing mother can be called into service.

Children can see how other needs, too, are satisfied by changing raw materials into useful goods. Many of these processes can be undertaken in the classroom. Making pottery in various ways builds concepts and understandings about dishes used in everyday kitchens, about the coil pottery of the Indians, and about the clay bowls of Mexico. Certainly no study of colonial or pioneer life is complete without quilting, molding candles, and making soap. The development of paper and the binding of books enrich the story of early civilizations as well as bring new understandings to the study of communication. Processing characteristic of foreign people can be reproduced in the classroom—basketwork, batik, jewelry designing, lacemaking, oriental writing, carving, abacus calculation, block printing, and making toys are but a few of those that have contributed to children's appreciation of peoples of other countries. Life on the farm becomes more meaningful when children plant grains and vegetables, gather in an orchard harvest, or raise chickens and other animals. These processes are all appropriate when they help children find satisfying answers to their questions.

Teachers who need help in guiding processing activities will find a number of suggestions with precise directions in various craft and industrial arts books.[17] Art consultants and home economics teachers are usually ready to give needed assistance. Parent helpers find working with children pleasant and enlightening. A survey of the special interests of school patrons will often reveal photographers, weavers, painters, model builders, culinary artists, and seamstresses. The materials required for processing can usually be secured through school funds, but if necessary pupils can bring needed resources from home. Equipment can be obtained from similar sources, and, as suggested before, in some situations children can profitably construct essential equipment.

CONSTRUCTING MAPS AND GLOBES

Problems that depend for solution upon seeing spatial relationships between man and his physical environment often can be clarified through map making and globe construction. Although commercially prepared materials serve this purpose well on most occasions, there is sometimes need for special representations unique to the problems children are solving. An excellent British film, "Near Home," for example, shows clearly how pupils' intensive study of their community led them to make, first, a simple sand-table model of their environment, followed later by a scale relief map when the need for seeing accurate relationships became clear.[18]

When pupils need a map especially related to the problems they are studying, they can produce their own. Young children begin their map making with very tangible layouts—blocks arranged on the classroom floor or perhaps toy objects set up in a sand table to show some aspects of the environment.[19] Later outline maps of an area may be spread out on the floor, outlines large enough for children to walk on, ensuring proper orientation to direction and a feeling for various locations to be added.[20] When children have grasped the idea of the purpose of their map, they can move

[17] Frederick Gordon Bonser and L. C. Mossman, Industrial Arts for Elementary Grades (New York: The Macmillan Company, 1923); Marthann Alexander, Weaving Handcraft (Bloomington, Ill.: McKnight and McKnight Publishing Company, 1954); and Irma Littler Paine, Art Aids for Elementary Teaching (Minneapolis: Burgess Publishing Co., 1959).

[18] "Near Home," British Information Service.

[19] Rose Sabaroff, "Mapping Experiences in the Early Grades," Journal of Geography (October, 1958), pp. 360–367.

[20] Zoe A. Thralls, The Teaching of Geography (New York: Appleton-Century-Crofts, Inc., 1958), p. 34.

toward semipictorial symbols to represent what was formerly shown concretely. Eventually an accurate base map of a region can form the background for symbols that become increasingly abstract.[21]

When pupils need outline maps not readily available in the sizes or materials they require, smaller maps from various references can be projected and traced in the desired dimensions. Such maps form the basis for relief maps of papier-mâché or salt and flour, on which children may plot various facts about features of the environment they are encountering in their study and from which they can form tentative conclusions about the region they are exploring.[22] These outlines can also be developed into product, vegetation, or land-use maps useful in illustrating and emphasizing various relationships that emerge in the process of problem solving.

Other types of map construction can provide useful resources for problem solving. One group of fifth-grade children constructed a globe six feet in diameter with a papier mâché surface; the globe became a continuing project as they used it to test their ideas of relationships suggested by their search for information about the world and its people. Small globes can be built around beach or large rubber balls, fishermen's glass floats, tree ornaments, or other spherical objects. These also are covered with papier mâché of sufficient thickness to keep the globe from collapsing and then are finished with paint or plastic to give a smooth surface.

Although the maps pupils construct cannot be entirely accurate because of obvious limitations, experiences children have in planning and executing them provide geographical and mathematical problems that are stimulating and valuable.

The preceding discussion has suggested only a few of the construction and processing experiences that help pupils gather data for problem solving. Tools and equipment made and used by children, models and replicas reproduced with concern for authenticity, cloth and clothing representing varying methods of processing or differing customs, products processed step by step by methods both old and modern, and maps and globes on which children may try out their ideas of relationship are the practical results of children's search for answers to their questions about how things are made and used—and why.

Criteria   .
for Selecting Experiences

Because there are many opportunities for construction and processing in the area of learning and because it may be impossible to carry out all the activities that may have promise, teacher and children must be selec-

---

[21] Sabaroff, *op. cit.*
[22] Thomas, and Swartout, pp. 409–413.

tive in their planning. There are some important questions to be answered when choices about activities are being made.

Is the activity the most appropriate one to use in achieving the teacher's and the children's purposes? The teacher's purposes, of course, reside in the understandings, attitudes, and skills that are to be developed in the area of learning. The children's purposes are centered in the question they wish to answer or the problem they need to solve. The construction or processing selected must be the one that will best satisfy basic objectives and most adequately achieve children's goals. The teacher bears initial responsibility for this selection, anticipating the suggestions pupils will make and guiding them to understand that all experiences are not equally valuable in answering questions and solving problems.

Is the activity suited to the children's maturity level? Because primary-grade children cannot use heavy tools, carry out projects that require detailed and accurate representation, nor sustain attention for a long period of time, their experiences must be different from those that can be undertaken by older children, who have greater facility and staying power. Young children's attempts to assemble small models from kits, sew puppet costumes that must be durable, create slides on small pieces of glass, or carry to completion a long tedious job are usually disappointing. Teachers of small children are more successful in encouraging construction and processing when they make available big boxes, big blocks, and big brushes, and when they encourage children to make something that can be assembled or taken apart with relative ease and speed.

Older children find the range of suitable construction and processing experiences much wider. Their more skillful handling of tools and equipment, their ability to work independently and persistently for longer periods, and their greater interest in accuracy and precision lead them into more difficult projects. Although the teacher avoids encouraging activities that are obviously beyond the abilities of the children, boys and girls in the intermediate grades are frequently more resourceful and successful than teachers expect them to be. Careful observation of children at work will provide the data most teachers need in judging the suitability of certain building and processing experiences for children of any given level of development.

Is the activity truly representative of the concepts it develops? Since the purpose of the experience is to develop certain understandings and concepts, it is doubtful that the purpose will be accomplished if the activity fails to re-create the process or reproduce the product in its original forms. In re-creating many home processes at school, especially those of the present, there is usually little problem of authenticity. Baking cookies, making pudding, arranging a dish garden, caring for a pet, and hemming a curtain are examples of processes that vary little from home to school. Such experiences are closely related to the concepts they develop. Objects children construct to clarify their ideas or to manipulate in finding the answers to questions usually offer no problems. If the object serves its purpose and children obviously know how it differs from the thing it represents, then incorrect concepts are not likely to develop.

When, however, changes are necessary in a processing method, when substitutions of materials must be made, or when the results of the processing are not truly realistic, children should be fully aware of the differences between their processes or products and those in real life. For example, the churning of butter at school in a hand churn immediately raises the question of how butter is made in a dairy: obviously few homemakers today churn their own butter. If young pioneers make soap with commercial lye, they must develop in some other way the concept of the ash leach early settlers used in making lye. The pottery baked in the school kiln fails to suggest the difficulties of baking pottery in the outdoors, just as the electric plate in the classroom is far removed from the fireplace of colonial times; these are differences that must not be passed over. One group of children who searched diligently for a substitute for white deerskin finally chose heavy unbleached muslin, carefully explaining to everyone the reason for the change. And another group found that when no mulberry leaves were available silkworms would for a time subsist on lettuce. When the experience can be authentic or when all necessary deviations are fully understood by the participants, it can be more easily justified as a means of developing concepts and understandings.

In the use of models, especially, the differences from real life should be made clear. It is the responsibility of the teacher and of the pupils who are demonstrating the use of the model they have made to emphasize that the model merely represents something that cannot be brought into the classroom: the danger of creating misconceptions must be avoided by pointing out the relationships between the model and the thing for which it stands.[23]

Is the activity feasible and practical? Some teachers avoid construction and processing because they feel that these experiences are not worth the time and effort they demand. There is no doubt that much valuable time can be wasted on experiences that have little to contribute to the area of learning. It is also true that the activity may be so elaborate that before completion the law of diminishing returns with regard to learning may set in. In some of these situations it may be that more real learning will result and less time will be consumed by the careful fabrication of a few components of a product than by the construction of the complete product; for example, the piecing of several quilt blocks in authentic pioneer patterns may be more practical and as fruitful in learning as the making of a complete quilt of a single pattern or the simulation of such an item with other than real processes.[24]

---

[23] Dale, p. 119.
[24] Tiegs and Adams, p. 125.

Because it is discouraging for children to make plans they cannot realize, the teacher must consider the matter of practicality before he and the children begin to plan. The teacher may ask certain questions about the proposed experience: Will it be possible in the time available? It is worth the effort it will require? Can the necessary materials be secured? Is the experience compatible with school policy? If extra help is needed, are there some adults available? These and similar questions avoid disappointments that come when children and teacher are impractical in their planning.

Implementing Construction and Processing Experiences

Knowing the values of construction and processing is fundamental to helping children engage profitably in these experiences, but this information alone does not guarantee successful group participation. The function of teacher-pupil planning, the role of the teacher in setting the stage, and the development of the plans in the classroom are all important to the success of these experiences.

TEACHER–PUPIL PLANNING OF CONSTRUCTION AND PROCESSING

Throughout the area of learning, teacher-pupil planning helps children move forward to new interests and experiences, unifying pupils toward common purposes and encouraging cooperative effort. Nowhere does teacher-pupil planning make a more effective contribution than in executing construction and processing activities. In this cooperative effort children and teacher together select the experiences best suited to the purposes they wish to accomplish, make plans for securing the necessary information and the needed materials, and decide upon appropriate procedures for carrying out their plans. Each of these planning sessions is crucial to the successful implementation of construction and processing experiences.[25]

In executing these experiences, teacher and pupils first select the particular activity best calculated to achieve their purposes. When children begin to explore ways to find answers to the questions raised in the initiation of an area of learning or to any of the subsequent problems that may arise, they soon discover that they must select from among many activities those that contribute most to meeting their needs. Their approach to the selection problem is usually quite direct. Because their goals are close at hand, they ask such questions as these: Will the activity answer our question? Can we carry out the plan in the time we have? Can we get materials? Can we make it real? Is there a better way to answer the question?

[25] Lavone A. Hanna, Gladys L. Potter, and Neva Hagaman, *Unit Teaching in the Elementary School* (rev. ed.; New York: Holt, Rinehart and Winston, Inc., 1963), pp. 347–349.

Teacher-pupil planning inevitably leads children from the selection of a purposeful activity to a search for necessary information. Although the teacher may have given thought beforehand to possible sources, teacher-pupil planning helps children think together about how they will secure the information they need. Each suggestion is evaluated carefully and accepted or rejected by the group. Thinking critically about various proposals encourages children to plan carefully before investigating rather than to begin an unplanned, haphazard, and time-consuming search for help. Such teacher-pupil planning also demonstrates to children that a group of persons thinking together frequently can produce more fruitful suggestions than individuals working alone.

A profitable search for information encourages children to begin making plans for securing materials and equipment and arranging for their use. During the planning periods they will ask and try to answer such questions as these: What materials do we need for the activity? Where will we get them?[26] Who will be responsible for bringing each of them? What tools will be needed? Do we have the necessary equipment? Can we borrow what we need? Will the equipment require any special care? Children must think through each of their activities, checking carefully on all essential materials and equipment. Meeting these problems in general discussion encourages children to assume responsibility and to recognize the importance of planning. The group can move forward when all are informed about progress and plans.

Teacher-pupil planning continues to function as children consider ways to put their decisions into action. At times all the children in the class may cooperatively engage in the same construction or processing, but on other occasions several different activities may be going on simultaneously. In either case the planning must be thorough. If several groups are to work, where will each be located? What will small groups do when they finish the day's plan? How will groups, large or small, secure help when they need it? How long will the work period be? Will there be progress reports? Consideration of the answers to these questions will help children see the importance of over-all planning for the work period and will provide happier working conditions for everyone.

SETTING THE STAGE FOR CONSTRUCTION
AND PROCESSING

Although cooperative planning bears a large part of the responsibility for facilitating construction and processing, the teacher's role is an important one. Because he understands the abilities and needs of his children, knows available resources, and has skill in helping groups organize and

[26] Frances M. Berry et al., Uses of Waste Materials (Washington, D.C.: Association for Childhood Education International, 1949), suggests many useful and readily available sources.

work together, he makes several important contributions to the success of the work period.

In setting the stage for construction and processing, the teacher checks carefully children's needs for certain materials and equipment. The children assume responsibility for securing the things they need to carry out their plans, but the teacher must be ready to assist in the task. Without taking from children the obligations they have agreed to assume or making their work too easy, the teacher helps them know what resources will be helpful and how difficulties in securing them can be overcome. When certain items can and should be purchased with school money, the teacher makes the necessary arrangement for children to do their own buying. The teacher comes to the work period prepared to supply essential items should the forgetfulness of any one child spoil the plans of the group. He gives thought to hazards that may be incurred in the use of equipment as well as to the care and storage of all materials and tools.

Essential to children's success in various industrial arts activities is the development of skill in the manipulation of tools and materials. Children are quite aware of this fact: ineptness is seldom acceptable to them. They want to know how, and they generally want to gain skill in the doing. If the teacher is unable to teach children how to use needed tools or materials, he can usually call upon a parent or another teacher to show children the correct technique. When this basic information is well understood, the teacher can provide opportunities for children to practice the skill. Tools and scrap materials readily available in the classroom workshop can be used at odd moments when the noise they make will not disturb others. Subsequent cooperative evaluation will encourage better manipulation of tools and increase pride in good workmanship.

Young children need special help in learning to manipulate materials and tools. Short attention span, limited physical strength, and lack of small-muscle coordination influence the selection of experiences for these children. As they move through the primary grades, improved facility makes possible more refined manipulations.

Primary-grade children use very simple tools—hammers, saws, C-clamps, and hand drills—and easily handled materials—lumber from wooden crates and boxes, small wooden and cardboard boxes, plywood, tin cans, dowel rods, nails, sandpaper, paint and brushes, and a variety of odds and ends found at home or at school. For processing they need such equipment as containers of various sizes, measuring cups and spoons, wooden spoons and rods for stirring, and an electric plate; the materials used in the processing usually can be secured from home or community at the time they are needed. Older children can use more adult tools, adding to their equipment the brace and bit, the plane, and the vise. Adequate storage for these tools and equipment can be planned cooperatively by teacher and children and constructed with the help of older boys and girls, custodians, and parents.

Increased security in the use of tools and materials should be accompanied by concern for their proper care. Children can cooperatively develop standards for cleaning and storing all kinds of equipment needed in construction and processing. One group developed this chart as a reminder for use during work periods.

ARE YOU A GOOD WORKMAN?

1. Remember that there is a right way and a wrong way to use every tool. Are you using the right way?
2. Remember that there is a right way to care for every tool. Do you know how to care for the tool you are using?
3. Remember that there is a place to store every tool you use. Have you returned your tools to their proper places?
4. Remember to return borrowed tools as soon as you have finished using them. Is someone else waiting to use the tool you borrowed?

Implementing children's plan for organizing their work period is also part of the teacher's role in setting the stage. Only with the support and cooperation of the teacher can children make any realistic scheme for carrying out their plans for construction and processing. To be ready to give this support the teacher anticipates what children may propose. He considers possible rearrangement of classroom facilities to reduce noise and confusion.[27] He explores the various areas where projects can be carried out—table and other work surfaces, unused space in hallways or on stair landings, possible areas in coatrooms and storage spots, and portions of the classroom that can be cleared. He thinks through carefully the kinds of groups that can perform successfully in each of these locations—which group will need to be near running water, wastebaskets, or heat; which group may need to work where its activity will not disturb others; which group can work on its own away from close teacher supervision; and which groups must work near each other in order to share equipment. The teacher plans his own activity during the work period—how he will move from group to group when his help is needed, how he will take note of significant pupil behavior, and how he can encourage independent effort and good workmanship. Children need effective teacher guidance as they learn to organize their work sessions and carry out their plans. A well-organized and orderly period is the natural result of the teacher's successful implementation of children's planning.

When plans have been completed and children are ready to begin their work, the teacher contributes further by anticipating the problems that may arise during the activity period and planning some tentative courses of action. Because of his knowledge of how children work, the teacher is

[27] Berry *et al.*, pp. 344–346.

often able to foresee difficulties that may interfere with children's progress. Will an aggressive pupil dominate a group of which he is not the chairman? Will a restless one wander from group to group disturbing them and accomplishing no work of his own? Will children have difficulty using a particular tool? Will directions for certain processing activities be confusing to pupils? What can be done if some important piece of equipment or some essential material is not ready in time for the work period? For each of these and similar problems the alert teacher formulates possible solutions. He may forestall some difficulties if he thinks through the pattern of the group at work and sets the stage for it successfully. If a real problem develops, he is ready to step in at a crucial moment with just the right kind and amount of help.

In these several ways—studying children's needs for equipment and materials, helping them carry out their plan of organization for work periods, and anticipating problems that may develop during work time—the teacher sets the stage for construction and processing in the elementary school classroom. Thus he complements his role in pupil-teacher planning with his role as a facilitator.

EVALUATING EXPERIENCES IN CONSTRUCTION AND PROCESSING

Teacher-pupil planning, supplemented and supported by the teacher in his role as a stage manager, usually brings children successfully to the work session, eager to begin and as eager to finish. The beginning of the work period requires a careful survey of plans and equipment; the work session itself moves ahead with one problem after another successfully solved; and finally the products and processes are completed and results can be shared and evaluated. To suggest what happens at each of these stages of development in construction or processing may be helpful to the teacher who is anticipating similar experiences in his own classroom.

When children come together to put their plans into operation, the teacher encourages them to take a few minutes to check their plans to see that all is in readiness. As a class group they make sure that everyone knows the over-all plan for the period, its purposes, the length of work time, and the follow-up activity for the day. If a difficulty arises and it appears that the work period cannot proceed until it is removed, the class cooperates to restore proper working conditions. If discussion shows that the general plan is understood by the pupils, this initial checkup is followed by a similar survey in each small group. The chairman helps the group review its work plan, to check its materials and equipment, and to verify directions. A careful check on plans before work begins is good insurance for a profitable work period. Observe how careful planning helped one group successfully develop a processing experience:

Ten-year-old children who were creating simple costumes in the spirit of the early settlers of their state had made plans to work as a total group in preparing the garments and dyeing them in appropriate colors. At the time set for the activity, the children met in a brief planning session. They checked to make sure that bolts of muslin for the costumes were ready and that each child knew how to cut out the simple items—skirts and rebozos for the girls and sashes and bandanas for the boys. A special committee that had come early to prepare the tubs of dye reported that all equipment was ready in the art room. Since all children would not dye costumes at the same time, children reviewed the order in which each would complete his part of the process and decided on work that could be done in the art room by those who were waiting their turns. The children tried to visualize their plan in action, realizing that good plans help ensure smooth-running work periods.

During the work period teacher and pupils together meet various problems that arise. Although the teacher may have anticipated and thus avoided certain problems, it would be impossible for him to foresee all difficulties or emergencies. He may discover that one group needs a skill its members do not have. Another may be handicapped by a stubborn group member. Another may experience failure because its members have not read directions carefully. A minor accident may interrupt the activity in some other group. The wise teacher helps children meet these problems as well as they can. He may plan with the children to practice the needed skill at their first free period. He may sit in with a group experiencing poor working relationships. He helps those who are having problems in carrying out their activity discover their mistakes and learn from their failures. He encourages children to change equipment or to try a different tool. In all these situations children learn to adjust to the circumstances or to overcome the difficulty and to move ahead in their activity. A work period without problems would be rare indeed; one in which frustrations of various sorts are successfully met provides useful experiences in critical thinking and problem solving. Note how problems that arose in this work group gave these children real opportunities to meet minor adversity and to plan ways to resolve their difficulties:

A primary-grade group preparing for a pet show had its share of knotty problems to solve. The work period had been cooperatively planned, and on this day everything seemed in order for the work period. Amid the sounds of busy activity, however, came hints of trouble. The teacher hurriedly answered an emergency call from a group that was just discovering that its homemade terrarium was leaking moisture. A check of the directions by committee members revealed they had forgotten to reinforce the corners of the glass container they had put together. The boys and girls building the cages for small pets could not make the cages rest firmly on the floor; the shop teacher who came in for a few moments helped them discover that they had not accurately cut the lengths of wood needed for the frame. Members of the parrakeet committee, who had stopped their work to enjoy the antics of their pet, were encouraged by the teacher to return to their task of cage-cleaning. Then those in the reading corner preparing talks about pets to be presented in the show asked for a little more quiet, a request relayed to other groups by the teacher. Meanwhile, the overly ambitious aquarium group had a floor to mop in the process of getting a watery home ready for the goldfish. Did these problems make the work period disorderly or unsuccessful? When children plan their work period, they expect problems. They plan in general how they will meet their difficulties, and they derive satisfaction from solving their own problems.

Sharing the results of the work period in construction and processing is often the most satisfying part of the experience. Here children see the products of their work and can report the success of their efforts. Of course, not all groups will finish their tasks at the same time. The teacher helps children plan how to proceed to other experiences when they have completed their particular contribution. He may suggest that a group report its results at the first opportunity after work has been completed, or the children may plan to wait until all groups have finished. Sharing results may take many forms. If the objects constructed are essential in developing certain concepts important to the study or to carrying on other activities, children will probably demonstrate the use of the things they have made. The products of processing will no doubt be put to use—the food eaten, the clothing modeled, the paper tested with writing tools, and so on. Sharing the results of construction and processing experiences is important to children, who need to have tangible evidence of a purpose realized. Consider the satisfactions that must have come to these children who found that the product of their work was proof of their success:

Children in a first grade tested their efforts to prepare a simple, well-balanced meal in a most delightful way. They decided to eat the meal on the spot! According to plan, small groups had prepared various parts of the meal. The carrot group had scraped most diligently. The soup mixers had successfully followed the directions on the can. The gelatine dessert committee had turned out a firm and colorful dish. The apples had been polished with care. And altogether it was a tasty combination, expertly checked against simple diet charts and passed with a high rating. The luncheon speeches were the reports made by each committee chairman—how the groups worked, what problems they met, and what suggestions they had for "next time." The results of the processing activity, as well as the results of working together, were received enthusiastically.

Intermediate-grade boys and girls, completing some processes characteristic of Indians who had inhabited their state in early days, decided to report with displays and bulletin boards. The potters displayed their bowls attractively on a table, adding necessary captions for explanation. The food-drying group displayed their wares, hanging dried corn overhead and arranging other dried products on the bulletin board below. Samples of dyes made from seeds, nuts, and plants were displayed in tiny glass vials and accompanied with samples of cloth colored with the dye. The relief map showing the location of early Indian tribes occupied another center of interest. When the children turned their attention to discussing the questions and problems that led to the processing experiences, the displays were concrete illustrations of the information being shared.

On another occasion primary-grade pupils reported the results of their activities in a somewhat different way. Their job of solving rainy-day recess problems had resulted in the construction of a number of quiet games to be played in the classroom. They chose to report by assembling in small groups and moving about from one game to another trying out each of them—ring toss, tenpins, ball in the cup, and puzzle fun. Making real use of the objects constructed or the materials processed brings pleasures to children and easily opens the way for pupil-teacher evaluation.

Cooperative evaluation is a vital part of all experiences in construction and processing. Because all these activities are undertaken for specific purposes, pupils must consider whether or not they have achieved what they set out to do. Children and teacher ask, "Did we accomplish what we intended? Is the product of our work useful? Did the processing help us to understand better our reading about the subject? What important understandings have we gained from our construction work?" These questions relate, of course, to the process and to the product, the two aspects of the experience most pertinent to children's concerns. The teacher, however, will also encourage attention to another phase of the experience, asking, "How well did we work together? What problems did we encounter? How can we improve our next work period?" Careful evaluation of the work period and its product not only emphasizes the fulfillment of purposes but also serves as a connecting link with the next activity and helps children to plan ahead more realistically.

Planning and executing experiences in construction and processing afford excellent opportunities for teacher-pupil planning and evaluation. The teacher's role in preliminary planning and in facilitating the progress of the work period itself is an important one. The successful work period is not a matter of chance. Children and teacher must learn to plan and to carry out their plans efficiently. When there are failures, the next work period offers an opportunity to try again. The values of democratic group process combine with the values of construction and processing to make these experiences essential to problem solving in social studies.

Questions for Discussion

Reread the dialogue used as an introduction to this chapter.

1. What determined the selection of the construction experiences described in this situation?
2. What steps in planning for the work period did these children take?
3. How did the teacher and children solve problems that arose in the work period?
4. How did the children use resource materials in carrying out their plans?
5. What skills were needed to further these experiences?

SUGGESTIONS FOR CONSTRUCTING
A RESOURCE UNIT

Review the preceding chapter noting types of construction and processing experiences that may be adapted to your area of learning. Note also that the construction and processing experiences identified in this chapter contribute directly to the development of desired learnings.

Identify a number of such experiences using these criteria in selecting each:

1. Is the experience the most appropriate to use in achieving the teacher's and children's purposes?
2. Is the experience suited to the children's maturity?
3. Is the experience truly representative of the concepts to be developed?

Identify the function of each experience and the directions, materials, and equipment needed to implement it.

8

Using Other
Educational Media
to Solve Problems

MRS. JOHNSON: We are making good progress in our problem solving, boys and girls. Our reading, our visit to the television studio, the reports and demonstrations from our groups, as well as all our other experiences, have clarified many ideas for us. Let's look at our list of problems to see which one we should explore next.

ALLEN: After the work on our newspaper and our trip to WTTV-TV all of us ought to know how to communicate with large groups of people. We can check that one off.

BARBARA ANN: But I've been thinking that we could do more with what we learned about television. A long time ago we talked about maybe having a television show. Could we do something about that?

MRS. JOHNSON: Put those ideas away for the time being, Barbara Ann. At the moment we are deciding on our next problem.

BILL: I know we are, Mrs. Johnson, but couldn't we talk just a little bit more about television? I saw a big show last night that started me thinking. I just couldn't figure out how they did so many different things on a television stage like the one we saw. My father said that the program was probably on film or video tape that had been made quite a while ago. I think we were lucky to see a live show when we went to the studio. A film wouldn't have been nearly so interesting.

MRS. JOHNSON: Why do you say that, Bill?

BILL: Oh, it's more fun to see real people acting.

JANET SUE: Not always. There are some films on television that are more exciting than live shows. They have more scenes and more action.

MRS. JOHNSON: They didn't tell us at the studio why some television shows are on film or tape, did they? Does anyone know the reason?

RONNIE: Probably they don't cost so much.

SUSAN: I know they can't always get the people for a live show when they want them. If the show is on film, it fits in any time.

MRS. JOHNSON: Filming or taping are ways of making a permanent record that can be used many times. And as Janet Sue said, if there are many changes of scene, it's easier to do ahead of time outside the television studio.

176

PEGGY: Some of my favorite programs are not live. I can tell from the way they start.

MRS. JOHNSON: All of you have learned new information from a film, haven't you? Is that a possibility to consider in finding the answers to some of our remaining questions?

SUSAN: Yes, Mrs. Johnson. Do you remember when we first began to study about communication? I looked at our film catalogue to see if I could find anything we'd like. Then I forgot all about it. I did find some I think we could use. Wait a minute; I'll get the catalogue.

MRS. JOHNSON: While Susan is looking through the catalogue, let's go back to our questions. Which ones haven't we answered? What are they, Andy?

ANDY: The one about how transportation depends on communication and two more about communication in early days.

ANNE: The very last one was my question. The more I find out about communication today the more I wonder what people did when there wasn't any television or radio.

SUSAN: We could see *The Newspaper Story*. It's about the way a newspaper is printed.

MRS. JOHNSON: Do you think seeing a film is the best way to find out about the newspaper?

JACK: Not better than going to the newspaper shop.

MRS. JOHNSON: Is that the only film you think we could use, Susan?

SUSAN: No, here's one that tells the story of the pony express. It tells how mail was carried in the early days of our country. Wouldn't that answer our last two questions?

MRS. JOHNSON: Perhaps it would help. Would you like me to preview the film to see if it will serve our purpose? Susan, would you like to see it with me?

. . . .

MRS. JOHNSON: Susan made a real discovery when she found the film about the pony express. We are going to see it the first thing this afternoon. What should we look for in this film?

RONNIE: First of all, I want to know what a pony express is.

PEGGY: How did it start?

FRANK: Where did it go? I've been trying to find the route on the map ever since we mentioned the film.

MRS. JOHNSON: Let's list the questions on the board. I'll write them as we think of them.

1. What is a pony express?
2. How did it start?
3. Where did the pony express go?
4. How much did it cost to send mail?
5. What kind of mail was sent?
6. How long did it take to send a letter?
7. When was there a pony express?
8. How did it work?
9. How long did the pony express last?
10. What kind of people worked on the pony express?

You may not know some of the words used in the film. Let's discuss them now. "Relay" is the first word.

. . . .

ANNE: Ten days to send a letter 2000 miles! It doesn't take that long now to send air mail letters to foreign countries.

MRS. JOHNSON: That's true, Anne. It not only took a long time to deliver mail, but also cost a great deal. Two of our questions are answered already. What of the others? Did the film answer them, too? Do you know what a pony express is now, Ronnie? Can you trace the route on our wall map now, Frank?

. . . .

MRS. JOHNSON: I think we are agreed that the film gave us some interesting information about the way people communicated in the early days of our country. Let's sum up that information in several general statements. Who has one ready?

BARBARA ANN: I do. It took a long time and was expensive to send letters in the early days of our country.

JACK: The men who carried the mail went through many hardships to deliver it.

ALLEN: People who handled the mail in the early days of our country were as careful about protecting it as we are today.

. . . .

MRS. JOHNSON: Have we answered to everyone's satisfaction the questions about the pony express? Should we confirm our ideas by using any other sources of information? Perhaps we should check our picture file and the collection of recordings in the library. Sometimes it helps to see things from more than one point of view. Who will do that for us?

PAUL: I can take care of that job.

MRS. JOHNSON: Very well, can you report back this afternoon? Now, do you think the information about the pony express will give us all the facts we need for the answer to our question about communication in early days? Do we need to search further?

Children live in a world of sight and sound that they accept casually as a phenomenon of everyday life. Since they have never known a time without motion pictures, radio, and television, constantly being bombarded by mass media of communication is a normal circumstance. In town and country, billboards exhibit visual symbols of things people must eat, wear, and do. The radio accompanies many automobile rides. Television is an almost constant companion. Children move confidently through this environment, hearing, seeing, and reacting.

Through these avenues of communication children have incidental visual and auditory contact with a variety of basic human activities, vicariously experiencing the life of the doctor, the cowboy, the patrolman, the sailor, and many others. Children look in upon scientific investigations, listen to analyses of the news, and visit faraway places that were once all but unknown to their parents. Although these contacts are often unguided and disorganized, through them children do acquire many new ideas. They build a store of information and form impressions they take with them to school and that help them successfully bridge the gap between books and real life.

It is in keeping, then, with children's out-of-school experiences that a variety of educational media should be drawn upon in problem solving, to dramatize ideas not easily grasped in the abstract and to substitute for firsthand experiences not available or feasible.[1] The values of some of these media—community resources, construction and processing—have already been considered, but the special contributions to problem solving made by films, filmstrips, and slides, recordings, pictures, maps, charts, diagrams, artifacts, and specimens are the focus of this chapter.

Influence
of Selected Educational Media
Upon Learning

In an age of mass communication by television, radio, motion picture, and illustration, few teachers question the potential usefulness of these media or doubt their influence upon learning. The current widespread interest in all kinds of illustrative materials and projection techniques is impressive and not to be written off as a passing fancy. Certainly pupils who cannot even imagine a world without these resources accept them enthusiastically, if uncritically, as a normal part of their school day. Even so, it is neither necessary nor wise to use audio-visual resources just because they are popular and available. As a foundation for careful selection and well-planned use it is important to be aware of the special services that experiences with educational media perform in the improvement of learning through problem solving.

It is common knowledge, well supported by research that extends over more than forty years, that children learn from pictorial representation and in fact learn more in terms of standardized test measures than they learn from verbal materials alone.[2] What does this research mean for problem solving? It means that these media open up new avenues of information and that, used in effective combination (the multiple-media approach), they

[1] Howardine Hoffman and Armen Sarafian, "Instructional Resources," in John U. Michaelis (Ed.), *Social Studies in Elementary Schools* (Thirty-second Yearbook of the National Council for the Social Studies; Washington, D.C.: National Education Association, 1962), p. 220.

[2] Charles F. Hoban, Jr., "Research on Motion Pictures and Other Media," in *Newer Educational Media* (University Park: The Pennsylvania State University, 1961), p. 2.

establish facts and ideas more firmly and more efficiently than can text materials used by themselves. In other words, a multisensory attack on information and ideas improves children's understanding of the printed and spoken word by taking advantage of impressions acquired through all the senses.

True, the printed word remains a prime source of information in problem solving, and children's learning in school is still characteristically verbal.[3] The newer educational media cannot and should not replace these printed sources of information. Words and pictures belong together; printed sources and pictorial representations complement each other.[4] This relationship leads the teacher to see educational media not as opposed to each other as in some kind of competition, but to consider how such media may be used in a constellation to provide for pupils sources of data for which they are searching and to create a kind of learning milieu within which pupils experience multiple stimuli.

These varied stimuli clarify concepts, rendering them both concrete and meaningful. They provide data from which pupils may draw conclusions and ultimately to generalize. Research indicates that reading and pictorial resources used together help children develop principles that are understood and can be applied to new situations and problems. One such experiment describes how a second-grade class built and extended to various industries the understanding that machines increase production; through the interplay of a variety of educational media children were involved in a dramatic and dynamic experience from which they were able to derive an impressive idea.[5]

Visual and auditory media that present a continuity of scenes or ideas are also a special aid to learning, helping children organize ideas about a problem or a process. Children who have acquired a jumble of facts in their searching can see these facts fall into place as they experience a well-organized visual or auditory presentation. Facts of history are integrated and take on life through recorded drama; the sounds of the city are interwoven into a recorded pattern from which other distractions are eliminated; the water cycle or the process of erosion can be captured by visuals and compressed to an understandable sequence. Nature can be made to stand still or to double its normal pace. A long span of history can cross the screen, bringing to the children a new feeling of control over time and facts and a sense of the logical organization of information around a topic or problem or idea.

---

[3] Fred P. Barnes, "Audio-Visual Materials in the Learning Process," *The National Elementary Principal* (January, 1961), p. 7.

[4] Hoban, pp. 4–5.

[5] Hoffman and Sarafian, pp. 221–224.

Extending Experience
through Audio-Visual Resources

As children embark on problem-solving activities, they naturally utilize their own experiences, drawing upon them for facts that will be applicable to the problem situation. Frequently, however, these experiences are inadequate or unreliable sources of information and must be supplemented or replaced by better ones. Since personal experience can seldom reach into the past or beyond the limits of firsthand contacts, other resources must be available. Sight and sound captured on film or tape, pictures, and a variety of graphic representations make the extension of experience a reality.

When firsthand experiences are not possible, substitutes are a necessity. For example, if children find a visit to the local newspaper plant inadequate to answer their questions about how the press secures its newsprint supply, a film can provide a detailed clarification of the process of papermaking. Pupils who live in eastern Connecticut can use the old seaport and museum at Mystic as a primary resource for the study of whaling ships and whaling, but for Iowa boys and girls one of the sea chests sent out by the seaport is a logical and useful substitute for the reality of a visit to the village. Watching a butterfly emerge from its cocoon is an exciting experience, but one not often captured in the classroom; a film can show the toilsome process in a fraction of the time it usually requires—a substitute that, through time-lapse photography, actually improves upon direct observation. Thus, in many situations the film or picture or recording is a competent stand-in for the real thing.

Such experiences also serve to widen children's horizons, taking them beyond their own experiences and putting them into other times and places they could not know on their own. Certain types of materials have the capacity to re-create for the child events and environments that are beyond his personal knowledge; and when they are peopled with human beings with which the child can identify himself, for a time he is actually there, absorbed by the sights and sounds of another community. Teachers have only to observe the effect upon children of a wide variety of television offerings to note how broad their experiences are and how much they learn about the world and its problems even from casual viewing. Obviously, many of the problems for which pupils seek solutions have roots that range far from the local scene and require data that daily life experiences cannot provide. The child's everyday experiences are the foundation upon which he builds his learning, but certainly they are too narrow to serve as the only source of information for all the ideas with which he may be emotionally or intellectually concerned. The vicarious experiences made possible through various instructional resources stretch considerably the walls of the child's world.

Needless to say, the burgeoning of new media multiplies significantly the sources of information available in any problem-solving situation (see Figure 9). As pupils move from study and recitation of a textbook to problem solving, the single text is no longer adequate for data gathering. The increasing expansion of all kinds of instructional materials makes it possible for pupils to check the accuracy of one source against that of another, compare a word description of a process with a visual, verify data shown on a graph by studying other graphic representations, explore the dimension of sound through a recording to supplement visual impressions, or collect a variety of different types of data to support an important generalization. Imagine the interest of pupils in historical events that can be explored through books, dramatic recordings, and filmstrips, all coordinated to enlarge children's view and deepen their understanding.[6] Or their enthusiasm in exploring other countries and other times through books, picture series, and filmstrips coordinated to present facets of a problem through a variety of stimuli.[7]

It thus becomes clear that experiences that complement the printed page offer distinct advantages in enhancing children's learning and in broadening their horizons. When carefully selected and well planned, their educational value is assured. It remains for the teacher to learn as much as possible about the great variety of materials available and to consider criteria for their selection; otherwise, the value of the resource may be lost through uncritical acceptance and careless utilization.

Experiences
with Selected Educational Media

Each of the instructional materials that children may use in problem solving has particular and unique contributions to make to the area of learning. The teacher asks many questions as he anticipates children's planning. For what purposes can each of the media be used? Where can the materials be found? Are the experiences easily implemented? What utilization suggestions are important to know? How can media profitably be used in various combinations?

---

[6] For example, see the many titles in the series that includes Landmark Books, Enrichment Records, and Enrichment Filmstrips (New York: Enrichment Teaching Materials).

[7] For example, see the many titles in the Classroom Pictures, Filmstrips, and Matching Textbooks series (Grand Rapids, Mich.: Informative Classroom Picture Publishers).

The Multimedia Approach

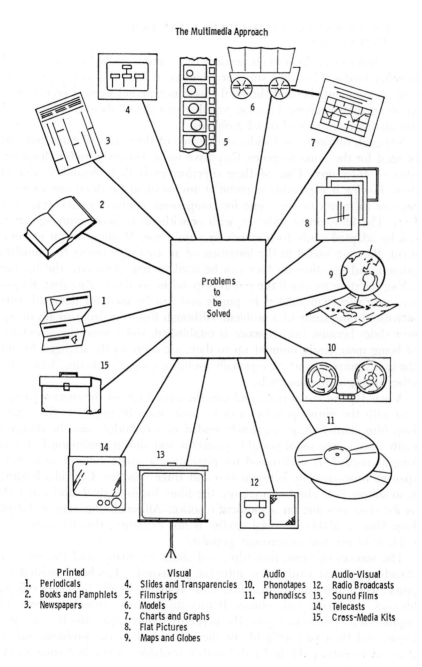

Printed	Visual	Audio	Audio-Visual
1. Periodicals	4. Slides and Transparencies	10. Phonotapes	12. Radio Broadcasts
2. Books and Pamphlets	5. Filmstrips	11. Phonodiscs	13. Sound Films
3. Newspapers	6. Models		14. Telecasts
	7. Charts and Graphs		15. Cross-Media Kits
	8. Flat Pictures		
	9. Maps and Globes		

Figure 9

By providing a range and variety of resources the multimedia approach extends children's opportunities to solve problems.

EXPERIENCES WITH FILMS, FILMSTRIPS, AND SLIDES

Films can perform many services that cannot easily be accomplished by other media. They do a superior job of re-creating the past, putting life into environments beyond the local community, condensing a process into an observable sequence, bringing together vast detail about a subject, and stimulating discussion of social problems.

Although filmstrips and slides share some of the values of films and can be used for the same purposes, they have some distinctly useful characteristics of their own. One of their superiorities is their flexibility: during their showing it is possible to pause at any moment for discussion or questions or to return to any scene for comparison, contrast, or rechecking of facts. The filmstrip or slide set, with or without an accompanying script, can be adapted easily to teacher's or pupils' use. Without script or comment, they are useful in the initiation of an area of learning to stimulate interest and questioning; they can be used in test situations, the teacher asking question to which the pupils respond in speaking or writing. Projectors are easily manipulated by pupils and can be used for data-gathering activities in the study of a problem. Although filmstrips have an advantage over slides because the sequence is established, slides have the advantage of being more easily brought up to date, are more easily arranged to suit the user's purpose, and are especially useful in projecting maps, charts, and other such graphic materials.

A new type of visual that combines the advantages of the motion-picture film with the filmstrip, which can be easily used by pupils, is the 8 mm loop film. This film, permanently loaded in a cartridge, may be dropped easily into a very small portable projector and shown continuously for as long as needed. It is designed for presenting a single concept in a short span of time—usually between two and three minutes. Cartridge-loading is so simple that children may use the films for individual study, as well as for class viewing, on a moment's notice. Although the current list of loop films available in social studies is not extensive, this promising aid is likely to become increasingly popular.[8]

The sources of films, filmstrips, and slides are many, and the number already produced easily runs into the thousands. Teachers, assisted by pupils when appropriate, may find films available locally in school offices, libraries, industries, and colleges. If lists are not to be found, teacher and pupils can cooperate in writing the necessary letters requesting lists or catalogues and then prepare a file of the aids suited to the problems under study. A recently published index makes available for the first time an in-

---

[8] *Source Directory, Educational Single-Concept Films Available in Magi-Cartridges* (Burbank, Calif.: Technicolor Corporation, June, 1964).

tegrated list of professionally produced instructional materials conveniently catalogued according to topics commonly part of the curriculum.[9] Educational films and filmstrips prepared by industries and other agencies and lent free of charge are also listed in guides brought up to date annually.[10] Family films and slides often record interesting and useful information that pupils can use at school. Children usually take special pride in these contributions to the area of learning.

Films, filmstrips, and slides are extremely popular and stand high on the list of experiences listed as favorites.[11] They are certain to be suggested by pupils in cooperative planning. Pupils should be involved in identifying the purpose for using the visual aids and in planning the follow-up experiences; they should be active, not passive, participants. With such cautions observed, experiences with films, filmstrips, and slides can render service commensurate with the time and effort their use requires.

EXPERIENCES WITH PICTURES

Experiences with pictures are so commonplace in the area of learning that their values may be overlooked; in fact, pupils may actually fail to make effective use of pictures for this very reason. In the initiation of the area of learning, pictures with challenging captions help to arouse interest in a problem and to stimulate thinking about it. Research groups find pictures useful in the interpretation of the printed word and in the building of meaningful vocabulary. Pictures passed from hand to hand, displayed before the class, or projected are often employed by committees in their reports. In the culminating experience, pictures serve as illustrations in scrapbooks and diaries, function in bulletin board summaries, and convey ideas to others in a variety of exhibits.

To be completely useful, however, pictures must be read. They must be read as thoughtfully as the printed page is read. When problem solving provides the motivation for reading pictures, children use them to discover clues about land forms and climate, economic development of an area, relationships of work to environment, cultural likenesses and differences, density of population, characteristics of historical periods, and so on.[12] When

---

[9] Educational Media Council, *Educational Media Index* (volumes for preschool and primary [grades K–3] and for intermediate [grades 4–6]; New York: McGraw-Hill, Inc., 1964). Lists strips, phonotapes, flat pictures, phonodiscs, videotapes, programed instruction, slides, models and mock-ups, kinescopes, cross-media kits, maps, and charts.

[10] See *Educators Guide to Free Films* and *Educators Guide to Free Filmstrips* (Randolph, Wis.: Educators Progress Service, published annually).

[11] Harriet M. Foley, "Preferences of Sixth-Grade Children for Certain Social Studies Activities." Unpublished master's thesis. Boston University, 1951, reported in W. Linwood Chase and Gilbert M. Wilson, "Preference Studies in Elementary School Social Studies," *Journal of Education* (April, 1958), p. 17.

[12] Zoe A. Thralls, *The Teaching of Geography* (New York: Appleton-Century-Crofts, Inc., 1958), pp. 83–84.

these clues are confirmed through comparison with other sources, children recognize the usefulness of reading pictures as an aid to problem solving.

Pictures are the most readily available of visual materials; both teachers and pupils can contribute to what may become an extensive collection clipped from magazines and gathered from agencies that offer such materials without charge. To obtain the materials currently available, children can make the contact with airlines, embassies of foreign countries, museums, industries, publishers of encyclopedias, and similar groups. The industry and community surveys suggested earlier will identify appropriate materials in the local community.

But flat pictures create difficulties in storage not encountered in the use of films, filmstrips, and slides. Unfortunately, pictures come in all shapes and sizes; and although the larger pictures are usually more prized, the difficulty of keeping them in good condition increases proportionately. Here, too, is a practical problem that pupils may assist in solving. Many classes keep a file of pictures in regulation filing folders, indexed in accordance with a plan cooperatively reached. Oversize pictures may be stored in a large shallow drawer or in a large folder of sturdy cardboard. Whether pictures are permanently mounted depends on the teacher; some store pictures trimmed but unmounted until time of display and others feel that a heavy, permanent mount protects the picture. A compromise may be reached in terms of the value of the picture: pictures that cannot be readily replaced and are of superior quality may be put on sturdy mounting so that handling by pupils and repeated display will not damage them.

EXPERIENCES WITH RECORDINGS

Listening to recordings can add the dimension of sound to many of the problems children explore in the area of learning. Recordings bring to the classroom resources that cannot be made available in any other way. Developing understanding of people of other times and places, for example, through sharing their arts, can be accomplished with the many recordings currently available—a rich storehouse of folk music, folk tale, and dance from every corner of the world and from the pages of America's history.[13] Dramatizations of great historical events combined with authentic music develop the feeling of times past and breathe life into history. There is currently available an extensive collection of historic events in dramatic form with new titles appearing regularly.[14] To hear the words that made history and to know as well the events that prompted them is to become a more active participant in the events themselves.

[13] See Folkways Records, Folkways Records and Service Corporation, 117 West 46th Street, New York, N.Y.
[14] See Enrichment Records, Enrichment Teaching Materials, 246 Fifth Avenue, New York, N.Y.

Recordings both on disc and on tape are becoming more numerous. In addition to those commercially prepared for school use, other reputable agencies are producing recordings of various kinds. Transcriptions of radio programs are often available. Some schools are building a library of tapes made from outstanding radio programs and are recording on the spot local incidents and happenings of national interest when the situations are unusual enough to warrant such preservation. Here, as in other types of materials, there are many free items.[15] A well-chosen library of recordings, with equipment readily available and in good working order, serves as a useful resource for large and small groups searching for information. If an area can be provided for individual listening, the use of tapes and recordings becomes much more flexible.

The successful utilization of recordings hinges primarily upon children's motivation to listen attentively and to make use of what they hear. The purpose for listening must, therefore, be crystal-clear. Developing listening habits, of course, is of critical importance, and pupils need to be aware of the progress they are making in this basic skill.

To achieve the most flexible use of recordings children should be taught to operate the recording machine independently. Tapes must be handled carefully, for a miscalculation may erase the content irretrievably, and discs must be protected against breakage.

Tape recorders have special appeal to pupils because they can make their own originals. In their search for information children find the taping of an interview a useful way to take data back to the class. They tape preliminary tryouts of their reports and panel discussions, playing them back for criticism and improvement. With the help of an adult they can tape an important evening or week-end radio broadcast or television program for later use at school. They tape explanations to accompany murals or exhibits or put on tape a dramatization they would like to leave for the class that follows. Teachers and children are daily finding new and fascinating uses for the tape recorder.[16]

EXPERIENCES WITH RADIO AND TELEVISION

The viewing of television and the use of radio must be considered important tools in problem solving. From the point of view of quantity, commercial television certainly has much to offer. Although research shows that teachers make few attempts to use television materials in the classroom, they agree that there are educational values for social studies and that improved concepts and deeper interest are probable results of tele-

[15] See *Educators Guide to Free Tapes, Scripts, and Transcriptions* (Randolph, Wis.: Educators Progress Service, published annually).
[16] *The Tape Recorder in the Elementary Classroom* (St. Paul: Educational Service Department, Minnesota Mining and Manufacturing Company, 1955), pp. 24–30.

vision viewing in this content area.[17] In spite of criticisms of television program quality, through these resources children have many extraordinary opportunities to meet the world and its people. There is adequate evidence that intermediate-grade children, for example, draw from "westerns" an amazing amount of information and a rather deep understanding of the day-to-day life of pioneers—their food, transportation, family life, difficulties, and hardships.[18] Radio and television accounts of current events are particularly useful because of their immediacy and on-the-spot reporting— national elections, visits of important persons to foreign lands, national problems and crises. Research indicates that even third-grade children can be guided to improve their understanding of current events through classroom utilization of out-of-school radio and television newscasts.[19] Unfortunately, commercial radio and television programs cannot be deferred to an appropriate time in the curriculum; but they can be consumed, discussed, held in memory, or, as previously suggested, taped and stored. Frequently, the scripts of unusual programs are available from broadcasters and sometimes the transcriptions as well.

In some communities lessons for the elementary classroom are being produced for radio and television. Research generally has been favorable to such instruction, and a large body of data supporting the values of television instruction is being accumulated. Teachers have been open-minded and eager to experiment, but certain difficulties in caring for individual differences, overcoming inflexibility of schedules, and promoting active learning and problem solving on the part of the consumers have not yet been solved fully.

There is, however, general optimism that educational television can be of great assistance in problem solving when it brings to the classroom persons, places, documents, and artifacts not available locally, especially through video tapes that can be used in more flexible ways than the original telecasts.[20] Static drills, lectures, and other highly verbal presentations seem to have little to commend them to the participants in a dynamic area of learning. On the other hand, the television camera that reaches beyond the walls of the classroom can bring to children authentic visuals and sounds of great value. To make these programs true assets, they must be used with the same suggestions and cautions appropriate for films, filmstrips, and recordings.

[17] Rowland Dean Klink, "A Survey of Uses Made of Commercial Television Programs by Teachers in the Elementary Schools of Indiana." Unpublished dissertation, Indiana University, 1958.

[18] J. D. McAulay, "Western TV Programs and Elementary School Social Studies," *Social Education* (April, 1960), pp. 169–171.

[19] J. D. McAulay, "Mass Media and Third-Grade Social Studies," *Childhood Education* (November, 1964), pp. 120–122.

[20] Hoffman and Sarafian, p. 238.

EXPERIENCES WITH REALIA

Working with realia or representations of realia helps to make concepts meaningful to children. The word for an unknown object, or even for one vaguely familiar, is easy to overlook in a paragraph of difficult reading; but the thing itself, attractively displayed and free to be touched, is seldom ignored. The strength of an impression depends upon the vividness of its presentation. When real things can be a part of the child's experience with a new idea, there are lasting benefits in understanding and remembering.

Things are interesting to most people. The crowds that throng every museum and fair attest to this fact. People like to see things for themselves and children are no exception. When the object is known, children recall their own experiences with it with enthusiasm; when it is unknown and presented in an intriguing way, they eagerly ask questions. A previous chapter pointed out how useful objects, specimens, and models are in stimulating interest in an area of learning; the initiation of a new study is very likely to involve real objects of some kind. Because children are explorers at heart, an unfamiliar thing is usually the subject of mental and sometimes of physical dissection.

Whenever pupils are aware of some object, device, artifact, or tool that has an important part to play in what they are learning, there are usually many questions: What is it made of? How does it feel? What size is it? How does it work? How is it made? Can we make one? Without the object, pupils must depend upon words and pictures, which are useful but at best incomplete. Try describing with words, for example, the taste of a mango, the texture of linsey-woolsey, or the operation of a steam engine. When there are comparisons to be made, opportunities to investigate real things make better judgments possible. How did lighting in the pioneer home differ from lighting in homes today? How are Mexican foods different from common foods in this country? Moreover, when problem solving requires the development of an idea or a process, objects and specimens are invaluable to show concretely each step in the sequence. When children are trying to determine how environment affects the lives of people, articles of clothing, pottery, tools, equipment, and food bring the study to life. Facts can be found in reading, but concrete representations of these facts are highly valued by pupils who want to see and touch and find out for themselves.

Not only do materials from real life stimulate interest in the initiation and help pupils form accurate concepts in problem solving; they also play their part in the summaries children make of the area of learning. These real things usually appear in the displays and exhibits children prepare in order to share what they have learned. One group of children arranged specimens of rocks and plants they had used for dyes and paints in their camping experiences. Another exhibited homemaking equipment in a pioneer corner in their classroom. Another set up a working model of an oil derrick, together with samples of petroleum products to tell the story of oil production. Both in committee reports and in class exhibitions, such resources continue to teach the reality of the things about which pupils are studying.

The sources of these useful articles are numerous and obvious. Many of the most useful can be found in the homes of parents and can be located through the parent survey previously mentioned. Those who have traveled, or who have hobbies or a high interest in certain kinds of work or community activity, may have on hand a number of fine resources— collections of stamps and coins, dolls from other countries, realia from a particular foreign land, objects used in days gone by, old books and other printed materials, souvenirs of past events, and specimens of various kinds. All these may lie unnoticed by pupils until their interest in the area of learning recalls them to mind or until the teacher discovers their availability. Audio-visual centers in public schools and museums often have useful artifacts to lend to classrooms. A number of cities have museum collections for children, some of which travel back and forth to schools upon request and others that are permanently located but are arranged with children in mind and are available for close inspection and handling. Children themselves locate valuable articles on their excursions into the community, coming back from the newspaper office with samples of news in various stages of collection and printing, from the farm with samples of products or types of soil, or from the dairy with empty cartons to represent all the kinds of products prepared there. These objects and materials take on added meaning when children find them in their original settings. Resource visitors, of course, frequently come with materials that children have an opportunity to examine closely under the guidance of an authority. There are some free exhibit materials, chiefly from manufacturing companies, that show samples of products or various stages in their development.[21] Available for purchase by schools are some kinds of specimens and models if their use warrants the expenditure and if they are not available from any other source.[22]

Children must realize, of course, that useful as specimens and objects are, they lose some of their reality when brought from their natural or cultural setting to the classroom. Consequently, pupils must re-create the setting through other audio-visual aids in order not to acquire, or pass on to others, a distorted or "half-view" of the thing under examination.[23]

[21] *Elementary Teachers Guide to Free Materials* (Randolph, Wis.: Educators Progress Service, published annually).
[22] See Educational Media Council, *op. cit.*
[23] Edgar Dale, *Audio-Visual Methods in Teaching* (rev. ed.; New York: Holt, Rinehart and Winston, Inc., 1954), p. 120.

Pupils need to do careful planning whenever they borrow materials and objects for use at school. They think first about how to display the material in an appropriate manner; they make rules for handling it with reference to its value and fragility; they make sure of their facts in preparing informative captions if they are to take over this responsibility. When the materials are to remain permanently in the school, pupils can help the teacher plan proper storage so that their usefulness will not be impaired by careless treatment. And, of course, paramount is the children's awareness of what is to be learned from the materials; identifying the important ideas that can be drawn from the experience of using the materials will emphasize for pupils that aimless handling of materials, no matter how interesting, makes little contribution to their search for information and ideas.

EXPERIENCES WITH CHARTS, DIAGRAMS, AND GRAPHS

When children use charts, diagrams, and graphs, they are working with visuals that are sometimes verbal as well as graphic. Charts especially tend to be highly verbal and yet have their content arranged to show relationships—classification, order, sequence, summary—more clearly than the printed page. The teacher may prepare such charts because he wishes to put before children some information that is not easily understood through paragraph reading, that is not readily available in material they can read, or that would take an undue amount of time for oral explanation. In the development of an area of learning concerned with natural resources, for example, a sixth-grade teacher prepared a number of charts to help his pupils in their problem solving. Among them were a list of leading oil-producing states and their annual productions, types of commercial woods accompanied by silhouettes of the trees and samples of the wood, an outline of steps in the refining of crude oil, a list of important minerals with identifying descriptions, a classification of various hard and soft woods, and a list of the by-products of coal production.

Pupils themselves suggest ideas for many charts used in the area of learning. Throughout their problem-solving activities their progress is recorded on charts that display the questions they plan to answer, their plan of action for solving their problems, reports of their experiences, vocabulary lists needed, standards for excursions and various work activities, and summaries of information. Usually the children plan the content, and then the teacher or selected pupils prepare the charts. Older pupils assume such responsibility more often than younger children because of the difficulties that arise in spacing, arrangement, use of special writing materials, and printing. These charts keep before children a record of their work and also inform visitors and other pupils and teachers of what is going on in the room.

Diagrams often combine with chart material when graphic techniques are used to present information that cannot be clearly seen through reading or discussion. In the diagram various relationships are shown by lines, sketches, and geometric figures. A second-grade teacher prepared a number of diagrams to use in a study of the community—the progress of milk through a dairy, the various duties of the community policemen, a side view of a large department store showing its many services, the system of water distribution in the city, and a scheme for crossing the street at a busy intersection. These diagrams were prepared from the teacher's own knowledge or were enlarged and simplified, when necessary, from diagrams given in various adult materials. Although older children can prepare such diagrams, especially for use in committee or individual reports, those prepared by the teacher are usually more truly representative of the ideas to be conveyed.

In their search for data children also find graphs helpful. Research shows that pupils in the early elementary grades can use simple graphs to make comparisons and draw conclusions from certain kinds of information.[24] The picture graph is the easiest for young children to interpret in their problem-solving activities. In the picture graph a small picture is used to represent a fixed quantity of something, and the number of symbols appearing in each row of the graph represents the total for that category. For example, in a picture graph showing the number of workers engaged in various community jobs, a tiny drawing of a man, each drawing representing 100 workers, is repeated the proper number of times to represent the workers in each occupation.

Pupils can move easily from the picture graph to interpretation of the bar graph. The bar graph, like the picture graph, is an effective way to show comparisons. On the bar graph quantities are indiciated by bars of varying lengths in either horizontal or vertical position. For example, third and fourth-grade children might use bar graphs to discover the length of time required to cross the country by various means of transportation or the production of corn in leading farm states.

The line graph is better suited to older children because its representation is not quite as clear-cut as that of the bar graph and because of the type of information it usually presents. The line graph is generally used to illustrate trends or progress: decrease in polio cases in the United States, growth of population in the community, and so on. Pupils frequently meet the line graph first in spelling or arithmetic, where they develop one to show their progress from week to week or from test to test. From such

<hr />

[24] Ruth G. Strickland, *A Study of the Possibilities of Graphs as a Means of Instruction in the First Four Grades of the Elementary School* (New York: Bureau of Publications, Teachers College, Columbia University, 1938).

line graphs, which they plot themselves, they can learn to interpret those that appear in their social studies reading.

For data that deal with the parts of a whole, the circle graph can be used by pupils who have the necessary background in fractions. Circle graphs used in the upper grades may show such information as how a farmer uses his land, how school tax money is spent, how state industries are distributed, and the like.

Through frequent experiences with charts, diagrams, and graphs, pupils come to appreciate the values of these techniques for condensing and graphically presenting a body of data, acquiring at the same time skills that will be continually useful in the learning process.

EXPERIENCES WITH MAPS AND GLOBES

When children need graphic representations to help them understand the earth and its surface, experiences with maps and globes are indispensable. In recent years pupils' needs for such activity have been considerably extended by their own broader contacts with the world through improved communication and transportation and by the general increase in public concern for the rest of the world, a concern that children feel both at home and at school. Certainly the area of learning capitalizes on this place-consciousness and affords many motivations for the use of maps and globes.

The purposes for which maps and globes are used in the elementary school are many, but perhaps they can be characterized by the kind of information sought by pupils. Maps and globes are used to find direction "to and from" in relation to the poles and the equator. They are the tools of location for places on the earth's surface in relation to other points and in terms of hemispheric divisions, latitude and longitude, and the like. They clarify distances between places by means of the scale of miles and through the tracing of great-circle routes. Maps are superior to most globes in showing the features of a region—area, elevation, land forms, rainfall, and temperature—and they are used almost exclusively to show relationships between physical features and the human use of land. On the other hand, only globes can develop important concepts of time growing out of the earth's rotation and revolution. Most of children's experiences with maps and globes will fall into one or another of these uses.

Maps and globes to be used in such ways may be purchased from a number of reputable map companies. Usually these can be ordered subject to approval, and teachers and pupils can take advantage of the opportunity to use the map before deciding to buy it; careful selection over a period of time can result in a useful collection. The most practical maps and globes have just the amount and kind of information needed by pupils at a given level in problem-solving experiences in social studies; their symbols and legends are clearly printed and easily understood.

Because it is impossible for most teachers to have an unlimited supply of maps and globes, a knowledge of some of the most useful ones may help them in their selection. Globes, of course, are especially important because they are intended to be accurate models of our planet. Primary-grade children need a simple globe that shows the land and water areas; with this globe they can have informal experiences locating their home and their country as well as places about which they hear in their daily contacts with adults and with radio and television. A more detailed globe with political and physical features presented in uncluttered fashion is needed for formal instruction in the use of globes above the primary grades. At least one of these globes should be mounted on its axis to show the proper inclination of the earth. The project globe, which has a slated surface and outlines of land and water areas, has limitless possibilities for encouraging pupils to develop various kinds of representations that can be removed and replaced at will. Currently, teachers are becoming interested in individual globes of the cradle type that can be used by groups of children who are developing skills in interpreting globe symbols.

Wall maps are equally important because, unlike globes, they show larger views of small areas of land and thus permit a study of the details of a portion of the earth's surface. Primary-grade pupils can have informal experiences relating locations they find on the globe to a very simple map of the world and then to an equally simple map of the United States; these experiences, often casual, are always an outgrowth of children's daily activities. These same maps can be used by older children for beginning work in reading maps, but these more mature boys and girls can use a world map that shows somewhat more detail; later they will be able to compare maps needed in their problem-solving activities in terms of the various types of projections. Pupils need wall maps of all land areas that may be a part of the area of learning—appropriate continents, regions, or states—with emphasis upon the physical or physical-political rather than on political features alone. Other wall maps can be added to the classroom or school collection as required.

When children need these maps and globes in problem solving, they are highly motivated to discover their uses. There are some special keys, however, to success in the development of map and globe understandings. Teachers are more successful if they recognize that maps, unlike other visual aids, are intended for repeated or extended use. Their information cannot be extracted in a single showing; on the contrary, a long period of exposure is required for the development of thorough understanding of even the most simple maps and globes. Under such circumstances the element of newness can be utilized only in children's first few meetings with a map; other motivations must be provided if interest and desire to learn are to be sustained. These motivations develop first as a result of pupils' need for map information of a certain kind, need that arises from their search for the solution to significant problems. Why is the air route to Japan shortest over the great-circle route? Why do Kansas farmers plant wheat in the winter rather than in the spring? How did pioneers use natural land features in their westward journeys? In what latitude does cotton grow best? How was our school postman's route determined? Why is it difficult to measure accurate east-west distances in Canada on a flat map of the world? Which route will be best for our bus trip to Vincennes? How can we use a map to show where soil conservation is most needed in our community? Every introduction of the use of maps and globes in the classroom will be more or less effective in terms of its relationship to some such significant question that pupils are investigating. The wise teacher makes the most of every opportunity for children to have personal contact and experience with maps and globes, to share information gleaned from them, and to formulate appropriate generalizations. When pupils seem inclined to venture into making their own maps, enthusiastic co-operation and adequate materials are the responsibility of the teacher. In such an environment, boys and girls begin to feel pride in their growing ability to use map materials and a sense of satisfaction in using these unique tools to find answers to important questions in the area of learning.

NEW EXPERIENCES WITH EDUCATIONAL MEDIA

Thus far, experiences with a variety of educational media have been considered discretely in order to discover the peculiar strengths and weaknesses of each in relation to children's need for them in problem solving. In actual practice the trend is toward the combining of media into a kind of frontal attack upon a given problem or idea. In the not too distant future when children begin the exploration of a problem area, they may very likely be able to draw upon a package or "system" of educational media, designed, planned, and ordered to lead to certain selected understandings. For example, Los Angeles schools are using an instructional package designed to develop concepts about the state of Hawaii; the plan includes filmstrips, recordings, realia, books, and a teacher's guide that outlines the precise way—both sequence and method—in which the items are to be used.[25] Although one may be concerned about the limitations on problem solving of so direct and planned an approach, particularly if it is extended someday to whole courses of study, the instructional system idea certainly reinforces the multiple-media approach, which is most appropriate for children in the search for facts from which understandings are derived.

The new emphasis upon organized and systematic use of a constellation of educational media serves, at the very least, to focus attention upon the values of related and integrated experiences as over against isolated, un-

[25] James D. Finn and Elinor Richardson, "The Principal Faces the New Technology," *National Elementary Principal* (January, 1961), p. 22.

related, and nonintegrated learning experiences. Potential for integration is in part a measure of the value of any instructional resource.[26]

From the foregoing discussion it is clear that there are almost unlimited experiences that can facilitate problem solving and make learning more exciting and lasting. It is also evident that in almost every category there are materials and equipment to meet, in some degree at least, the needs of even the least favored of schools. With such a variety of media from which to choose, the task of selection and effective utilization may seem almost monumental. Actually, however, selecting, planning for, and using these many resources is less a task of impossible proportions than it is one of judgment and skill.

Selection of Experiences
with Educational Media

When there are such varied instructional materials available to pupils, the problem of selection becomes increasingly significant. Guidelines for selection conscientiously used help to ensure choice of the right resource for the right occasion. The questions that follow are practical tests that may be applied to each proposed experience.[27]

Is the experience particularly suited to the purpose for which it is to be used? The experience may be interesting and colorful, it may add variety to a dull subject, or it may be enjoyable, but these are scarcely adequate reasons to enable it to pass the test of purposefulness. Selection with purpose in mind implies that the study in progress has a definite direction and that children are seeking an identified goal.

Will the experience develop understandings basic to the content of the area of learning? Throughout social studies, emphasis is placed upon the development of understandings that children can apply continuously to human life in this world, and each new experience, too, must make its contribution to the reinforcement of these central ideas toward which the area of learning is moving. Many materials being developed today tend to center facts and information on important generalizations, but to the teacher falls the task of leading children to extract and formulate these ideas from their seeing, hearing, and touching experiences. In fact, children's whole orientation to the experience is the teacher's responsibility: pupils will engage in the experience at whatever level the teacher encourages and makes possible—for fun, for facts, or for ideas. If the experience does not contribute to the acquisition of understandings toward which

[26] Carolyn Guss, "Selecting Instructional Materials" (Bloomington: Indiana University Audio-Visual Center, mimeo).
[27] Ibid.

problem solving is directed, then it may not be worth the time or effort required to develop it.

Will the experience present correct information? It may be unnecessary to mention explicitly the criterion of accuracy, for all teachers would agree that inaccurate information may be more undesirable than no information at all. If problem solving is to be encouraged, then the experience must provide correct and dependable information. However, it may be difficult for teacher or pupils to determine whether or not facts derived from the experiences are reliable, and under these conditions they may have to rely on some exterior evidences. For example, the integrity and reputation of the producer are important clues to the acceptability of commercial materials. If the author is identified, his reputation for careful production can be investigated. When the information does not agree with other reliable sources, discrepancies can be checked with authorities. This kind of activity can be especially valuable for older children, who need to learn to discriminate among various sources in terms of the faithfulness to fact that each shows. The importance of previewing materials before use has special reference to this matter of accuracy of information. It is easier to eliminate an aid than to explain away its inaccuracies to pupils, except on those occasions, of course, when the teacher feels that children are ready for such an evaluation experience.

Will the experience encourage further reading and investigation? Some educational media are dead ends—they seem to tell all, and they give the impression that there is no more to be learned. Probably there are uses for such materials, but the helpful ones make it known that there is much more to be learned, that the problem is not yet solved, that there are other facets worthy of exploration, that there is need for class discussion, that it is time to return to books for further clarification, or that there may be something in the community that will shed light on the subject. Although the material or aid itself may not suggest such follow-up activities, the nature of the content should be such that there is intellectual challenge for the future. The use of a recording may suggest the need for using pictures, for checking with a person who has experience with the content, for reading for verification of facts, or for checking on a topic of interest to some of the listeners. A picture may suggest an interview with a community person, an appropriate television program on the same subject, a visit to a similar spot in the environment, or more pictures showing detail missing in the first one. As an earlier chapter pointed out, part of the value of any experience is the bridge it builds to another one.

Can the experience be used successfully in the situation? The experience can be no more successful than the quality of the film projection, the clarity of the sound track on the recording, the ease with which children can see the picture, or the availability of the equipment. In earlier parts of this chapter there are suggestions for successful utilization of various materials.

It is no doubt true that some teachers think audio-visuals are not worth the time and trouble they take to secure them, arrange for their use, and return them to their storage places. If rooms cannot be darkened adequately, if the record player cannot be heard by the class, if pictures are too small to be seen by the group, or if for some other reason the audio-visual experience will result in loss of interest and attention, then it is probably well to think through the situation carefully with a view to avoiding such difficulties or making substitutions. After all, even though all other criteria are met, the audio-visual experience can be rendered useless through ineffective presentation.

Planning and Using
Experiences with Educational Media

It is in the planning for and use of audio-visual experiences that the teacher has an opportunity to apply the criteria just described. Like Mrs. Johnson, in the dialogue that began this chapter, the teacher bears the ultimate responsibility for the success or failure of every experience.

ROLE OF THE TEACHER IN PLANNING
AND UTILIZATION

Selecting the appropriate educational resource is basically the teacher's task, although he may be assisted in a variety of ways by the pupils as cooperative planning moves the area of learning ahead. In selection the teacher takes into consideration children's needs in problem solving and their level of intellectual development. At the point of selection and prior to the preview the teacher must rely upon his knowledge of his pupils and whatever information is available about the proposed materials. Some schools have developed a useful record-keeping system to which teachers add their opinions of each resource they use, reacting in writing to its content, level, and effectiveness for various purposes. Other teachers, and pupils as well, may then refer to the file for suggestions before selecting items for preview.

The best check on the wisdom of the selection is the preview. Until the material is actually seen or heard, there is no way to know for certain that it will fulfill the purposes for which it is intended. If the preview indicates usefulness, other activities on the part of the teacher will add to the completeness of his preparation. Preview is an excellent opportunity—in fact, it may be the only opportunity unless there is an adequate guide accompanying the material—to identify the important ideas and to relate them to problems being investigated and to extract those words and concepts that will need special attention in the classroom before and after the presentation. Mrs. Johnson found such a vocabulary in the film about the pony express, and so will every teacher who previews thoughtfully. The preview is the time to note questionable data, confusing situations, or content un-related to the children's study. If the material seems unsuitable in any way, even at preview time it may be discarded and selection begun anew.

Following the preview the teacher takes steps to provide for effective presentation. If bringing equipment into the classroom or moving the group to a special room may be distracting, the teacher anticipates prob-lems that may arise. Planning the environment ahead of time—a display space that all can see, blinds drawn for projections, suitable extension cords where needed, chairs arranged comfortably—will make possible a smooth transition from whatever activity the pupils are engaged in to the new experience. Even the best of materials if introduced or used haphazardly may produce only discouraging results.

The most important steps in planning are yet to come, however, for no amount of physical arrangement can make up for lack of thought about how children are to be introduced to the experience itself. The teacher plans to help pupils see the relationship of the new activity to the problems they are now studying, become acquainted with the vocabulary they may encounter, and recognize what they are to look for as they use the resource. Some thought may also be given to what may be done with the information and ideas later. In short, the teacher plans to introduce the experience in such a way that children will feel anticipation and pleasure as they engage in this natural continuation of their search for information needed in problem solving.

In his planning the teacher tries also to anticipate the follow-up activi-ties, although the children's ideas and reactions may alter these plans some-what. The teacher in general, however, plans to encourage children to identify the important ideas they have been exposed to, to test whether or not the experience helped with their problem-solving activities, and to sug-gest how they can use what they have learned. And, of course, there will be time to discuss misconceptions and answer questions about troublesome details. If the experience is likely to lead to further research, community activities, or construction experiences, the teacher thinks ahead to be pre-pared for implementing the ideas of the pupils.

All this is to say that casual presentation and exhibition of films, pictures, or other instructional materials is not enough; research in mass media gives complete support to the emphasis upon well-thought-out plans for the introduction and follow-up for every such experience.[28]

ROLE OF CHILDREN IN EXPERIENCES
WITH EDUCATIONAL MEDIA

In spite of the emphasis upon the teacher's role in the planning and development of each experience, the children's participation in it has the

[28] Hoban, p. 6.

greatest impact upon the learning situation. What children do and what they think in each stage of the development of the experience are extremely important. Being aware of the process going on will serve to point out to teachers that an active learning situation rather than a passive one is sought.

There are occasions when pupils themselves can participate in the selection of instructional materials appropriate to their purposes. Searching for suitable titles, they may survey lists; they may interview school personnel in charge of such aids for the school; they can study with the teacher several possible experiences, making a cooperative decision about the best one to use in a given situation. Sometimes boys and girls can be efficient previewers with the teacher. Their reactions, questions, and difficulties can be most useful in helping the teacher decide whether or not the entire class group should use the materials. Children are quite insightful about what other children will like and use, and they delight in being called upon to take part in such decision making.

An important consideration in pupils' use of audio-visual materials lies, of course, in the relationship of the experience to children's needs in problem solving. It has been pointed out that there are four basic principles of effective learning from pictorial and graphic representation.[29] Pupils must, first of all, be searching for something they need or want to know. This principle is the basis of motivation in problem solving. Second, when the pupils are exposed to the instructional materials, they must notice something; serious attention is essential, and the materials must attract and hold that attention. Third, pupils must respond in some way to the presentation. Intelligent questions and requests for a second showing are kinds of evidence that pupils are responding to the ideas presented. Fourth, pupils must find in the aid what they are looking for. There must be a reward in terms of the purpose they identified in making plans for the experience. These principles, in fact, reinforce problem-solving processes as teachers and children cooperatively appraise the learning obtained: What big ideas were emphasized? What special information was made available? What questions about content must be cleared away? What other aids can reinforce what we have learned here? Cooperative evaluation of this kind impresses pupils with the serious intent of each experience and develops a new appreciation of the values of various types of resources. Moreover, evaluation makes perfectly clear the function of the experience in the area of children's exploration and gives them a sense of accomplishment and progress.

In the follow-up period, pupils may identify unanswered questions and new problems as well as review what the material has contributed to their

[29] Neal E. Miller, *Graphic Communication and the Crisis in Education* (Washington, D.C.: Department of Audio-Visual Instruction, National Education Association, 1957), pp. 64–103.

original purpose. In fact, as already pointed out, profitable experiences always lead to something else—new ideas to explore, new paths to be investigated. The most valuable part of the experience may be a pupil's concern for pursuing an idea further or involvement in finding the answer to a new question raised by what he has just seen or heard. In this case, learning becomes dynamic rather than static, and what is ahead is even more challenging than what is past.

Clearly, experiences with newer media of instruction have a place in the problem-solving activities of social studies. Learning by these experiences is frequently more efficient than learning by verbal methods alone, and, used together with reading and telling, audio-visual materials of instruction do much to enhance the understanding and interest of pupils. The skillful use of these materials in problem solving will do much to demonstrate their indispensability and to encourage the expansion of school resources.

QUESTIONS FOR DISCUSSION

Study the dialogue that introduces the chapter and use the following guides to discussion.

1. Why did the teacher and children choose a film as a source of information?
2. How did the film help children to make generalizations?
3. In terms of the criteria for selecting audio-visual experiences was the film a good choice?
4. In a cross-media approach what other experiences would be useful in deepening these children's understanding of the historical development of communication?

SUGGESTIONS FOR CONSTRUCTING
A RESOURCE UNIT

Because resources in many areas of learning are often quite extensive, your task in selecting experiences with various educational media is both easy and difficult. Easy, because of the many possibilities; difficult, because of the need for careful selection in terms of purpose.

It may be useful to explore the many and varied experiences for your area of learning and then to select and describe those that seem most appropriate at this state of your thinking and planning, holding other ideas in reserve until you and the pupils plan the area of learning.

When you have tested each tentative selection against the criteria given in the chapter above—with special attention to purpose and accuracy—describe the experience. For each, indicate the contribution it will make to the area of learning, the exact materials to be used, and the procedures to be followed. If you have not already done so, include in your annotated bibliography complete data about all commercially prepared educational media which you think may be useful in the area of learning.

9

Enriching an Area of Learning through Creative Activities

DONALD: We've almost finished coloring our mural, Mrs. Johnson. Come and look at it. We think it looks good. What do you think?

MRS. JOHNSON: I agree with you. It looks fine. I am amazed at how much information about communication you've been able to crowd into it.

ALICE: There was a lot to put into it, too. Doesn't it look nice spreading across the back of our room? It looks big, but we still couldn't put in all the inventions and happenings in the development of communication from the past to the present.

MRS. JOHNSON: Yes, I heard your committee discussing that problem. You seem to have worked it out very well. How did you do it?

MARILYN: Two ways. We tried to choose the inventions and happenings that were very important. Then we had to see if anyone could draw them for the mural. That wasn't so hard to decide. Mark likes to draw people. The printing in the mural is mine. I guess you know that. Jack is good at drawing all kinds of things. The radio and television sets are his.

MRS. JOHNSON: Can you guess what I especially like about your mural?

ROBERT: No, what? Tell us.

MRS. JOHNSON: Its originality and imaginativeness. Who thought of a scroll with Chinese writing to show that the Chinese were the first people to use paper and ink? And the television tower reaching nearly to the top of your sheet and all those houses at the bottom with antennae on their roofs. Whose idea was that?

WAYNE: Mostly we've forgotten whose ideas are in the mural. You gave us some help. Don't you remember? Mrs. Sinclair was lots of help, too. She knows many things about art, but she didn't try to tell us what to do. The committee worked together. Everyone made suggestions. We'd talk about them, and the ones we liked we put in the mural.

CHARLES: It took longer to make our mural than we thought it would. Just try coloring that much and you'll know why. It was a job. But I'm glad we used crayon instead of chalk. It'll stay nice for a long time.

WAYNE: We still have a few more things to do to it. If there is time to work today, we should just about finish it up.

* * * * * * *

JACK: Musical instruments and the tape recorder? What for, Mrs. Johnson? Are we going to make a tape recording of some of the music we know?

MRS. JOHNSON: Not exactly, Jack. We're trying out something new today, something I hope you'll enjoy. Push your desks to one side and all sit on the floor in a circle. Let's move the table with the instruments on it into the center. I'll sit in the circle, too. We'll take a minute to get settled.

MARK: Are we going to play all the instruments?

MRS. JOHNSON: I'm not sure. Maybe we'll play all of them, maybe we won't. It depends on how many ideas you have for using the instruments. You had lots of good ideas for your mural, "The Communication Story." You feel that it is very complete, don't you? And it is. All except for one very important part of communication.

PEGGY: I suppose we should have put more people in it. Communication isn't communication without people.

ALICE: More people! How could we? We put in all there was room for. Did we miss some kind of communication, Mrs. Johnson?

MRS. JOHNSON: No, it's nothing you've overlooked. You couldn't put them in your mural, but without them the communication story isn't complete. Your mural needs sounds, all the sounds we associate with communication.

MARILYN: Sounds! What kind of sounds? You mean like a radio playing?

MRS. JOHNSON: Yes, people talking in loud voices and soft voices, telephone ringing—no two sounds alike. Each sound identifies some special kind of communication.

RONNIE: Like the clicking sound of the teletype machine in the newspaper office?

MRS. JOHNSON: That's it, Ronnie. What is that sound? Can you make it with one of these instruments? The sticks, perhaps.

ANDY: Telegraph keys make a sound something like that. Give me the sticks, Ron. I'll try the Morse code. You know some of the code, Pete. Get some more sticks and send me a message. I'll see if I can answer it.

ALLEN: Doesn't a fast-rolling drum beat sound like a pony express rider racing his horse? Listen.

MRS. JOHNSON: That's fine. Ideas are beginning to come. Susan, do you have one?

SUSAN: I was just going to ask if you've ever stood by a telephone pole and listened to the wires humming. Sometimes I imagine I can hear people talking. Other times it's just a zinging sound like the zing of an auto harp. Like this.

MARY LOU: Isn't the policeman's whistle a communication sound?

MARK: The siren on the fire engine certainly is. At least it communicates to my dad. When he hears one, he pulls over to the side of the road in a hurry.

MRS. JOHNSON: Could you put all these impressions together into a single musical composition?

ANNE: I know. Something like our "Dance of the Raindrops"?

BARBARA ANN: Let's call it "The Communication Story in Sound" and our mural, "The Communication Story in Pictures." Oh, I like that.

JANET SUE: That's what the tape recorder is for, isn't it, Mrs. Johnson?

MRS. JOHNSON: Yes, I thought we might record each of our impressions of sound on tape today and decide tomorrow how we can use them.

* * * * * * *

MRS. JOHNSON: During the past month we've accumulated much information about the telephone and many important things we want to remember. But, unless we find some way to help us remember this information, I'm afraid we'll soon forget it.

ALICE: The story I wrote about using the telephone helped me remember how to use it.

PATRICIA: Writing my story helped me, too.

MRS. JOHNSON: One of the reasons we wrote the stories was to summarize and record what we learned about telephone usage.

PEGGY: It would be fun to take one of our stories and make a play out of it. Wouldn't that be a good way to remember the important things we've learned?

ALICE: We could just act it out the way we did the water-main break or we could write down a play on paper.

SUSAN: Let's not act it out without writing it. You remember things better when you write them. Everybody thought Mary Lou's story about the telephone was best. It would make a good play.

MRS. JOHNSON: How do you want to write your play? All together or turn it over to a play-writing committee?

SUSAN: Wouldn't it take too long to write it all together? It goes faster when there aren't so many people.

JACK: Who would be on the committee?

MRS. JOHNSON: Anyone who's interested in working on it, I suppose. Are you, Jack? Susan is, I know, and Mary Lou, of course. Who else? Pat and Ronnie? Barbara Ann? Any other boys? You, Mark? How many is that? Seven? That's a good working committee. Can you get together during your free time this afternoon and sketch out some ideas for the play?

· · · · · · ·

SUSAN: We're ready with the main ideas for the play, Mrs. Johnson. We couldn't get started right away because we tried to find some way to have as many of the class in it as we could.

MRS. JOHNSON: I'm glad you thought about class participation in your planning. We're eager to hear what you have in mind.

SUSAN: We chose Mary Lou to tell you what we've decided because it's her story.

MARY LOU: Well, you remember my story is about Mary, a little girl who liked to talk on the telephone. She always talked a long time and never wanted to stop. She talked loudly, she didn't give the other people a chance to say anything, and she slammed the receiver in people's ears. Mary's manners were so bad that her mother finally had to scold her. Then Mary pouted, "I'll never use the telephone again!" Immediately a strange voice said, "Yes, you will, Mary." "Who said that?" Mary asked, looking around. There Mary saw a little man with a body that looked like a telephone. He was sitting on the window sill. He was very angry at Mary. His ears hurt and his body ached from the way she had treated him. "I'm going to teach you a lesson," he said. In the rest of the story he does all the things to Mary that she did to other people. It ends with Mary changing her bad telephone manners to good manners.

PATRICIA: It's a good story. The characters will be Mary, Mary's mother, and the telephone man. The class can tell what is happening in the play with choral reading. You remember—the way we did it last week.

Throughout time man has sought to enrich his life by engaging in a variety of creative activities. Only recently, however, has he begun to look at the concept of creativity with a scientific eye. Today his concern with this concept covers many fronts that range from purely academic consideration of the creative act to speculation about certain kinds of research on creativity. For example, "The most fertile area of this work will most likely come about in terms of ways of using creativity for substantial learnings in basic subject areas and for ways of using creativity as a means of fostering needed mental health factors."[1]

Yet, lack of research notwithstanding, the majority of those concerned with social studies instruction share the belief that "enrichment [creative] experiences contribute to the development of feelings and shades of meaning which are an inseparable part of basic concepts, attitudes, appreciations, and the thinking processes";[2] that "enrichment activities should be an integral part of units of instruction";[3] and that "they should be used to contribute directly to the development of basic generalizations, attitudes and appreciations."[4] Moreover, those who believe that creative activities should be an integral part of a social studies area of learning can draw support for this belief from the current consensus on creativity and its cultivation. Note these major points of agreement:

In children, creativity is a universal; few, if any, human beings are born without some creative potential.

Although the aptitude for creativity is inherited, the development of this potential is primarily a matter of learning.

Creativity is manifested at many levels and takes a variety of forms of expression.

Creativity has no subject boundary lines; it is operative in scientific and social settings as well as in those that are esthetic.

Developing the creativity of all children is a major responsibility of the educational enterprise.

[1] Gladys Andrews, "Releasing Creativity—Extending Curriculum Opportunities," in Robert S. Fleming (Ed.), *Curriculum for Today's Boys and Girls* (Columbus, Ohio: Charles E. Merrill Books, Inc., 1963), p. 460.

[2] John U. Michaelis, *Social Studies for Children in a Democracy: Recent Trends and Developments*, Third Edition. © 1963, by permission of Prentice-Hall, Inc., Englewood Cliffs, N.J., p. 526.

[3] *Ibid.*

[4] *Ibid.*

In short, it is generally agreed today that all children are potentially creative, that creativity can be nurtured, that it is diverse in its modes of expression, that all curriculum areas are embryos of creativity, and that the nurture of creativity is the school's inescapable task. It is therefore both pertinent and desirable to consider the concept of creativity in relation to the social studies curriculum. To that end then, this chapter explores ways and means of enriching areas of learning through creative activities.

Creativity— its Nature and Cultivation

First consideration is the answer to the question: What is creativity? The extent to which this concept can be defined is limited, of course. In general terms, however, creativity is the ability to see (or to be aware) and to respond;[5] it is an awareness of previously unnoticed relationships; it is the ordering of ideas that are disorganized and seemingly unrelated. It is believed to be a constellation of knowledges, attitudes, abilities, and skills, all of which are interrelated. Fundamental to creativity is a rich reservoir of knowledge—words, facts, generalizations, and principles—to draw on in implementing the intellectual abilities that are important to creativity. Attitudes such as curiosity about the environment, open-mindedness, willingness to try out new ideas and to spend long periods in executing them are also basic to creativity. So, too, are certain intellectual abilities—comprehension, application, analysis, and evaluation—abilities that involve both critical (reflective) thinking and creative (imaginative—intuitive) thinking. And skill in using tools and materials effectively is likewise essential to the process of converting ideas into observable form—skill in using the voice and the body, as well as skill in using art materials and construction and writing tools.[6]

Conceivably creativity exists in some degree, to some extent, in all children and is unique in each individual, being in essence personal. In some children the creative urge is strong enough to find expression. In others it is under the surface waiting for an opportunity to disclose itself. As creativity is nourished, it thrives and flourishes; as it is oppressed, it declines and withers. Nourished, the childhood roots of creation grow in force, and the creative man emerges. Oppressed, they lose their power, and the creative man who might have been never comes into being.[7]

---

[5] Erich Fromm, "The Creative Attitude," in Harold H. Anderson (Ed.), *Creativity and Its Cultivation* (New York: Harper & Row, Publishers, 1959), p. 44.

[6] Mary Lee Marksberry, *Foundation of Creativity* (New York: Harper & Row, Publishers, 1963), pp. 7–9.

[7] Hughes Mearns, *Creative Power: The Education of Youth in the Creative Arts* (New York: Dover Publications, Inc., 1958), pp. 267–268.

Certainly no teacher can be indifferent to these facts. To nurture creativity in children is an inescapable responsibility. And rarely has it been so inescapable as now, when the needs of modern society and the survival of democracy call for large numbers of creative adults, and when that call grows increasingly urgent and demanding.[8]

However, it is one thing to accept responsibility for nurturing children's creativity, but quite another to bring it to fulfillment. To do so is a real achievement not to be taken for granted but to be worked for constantly and diligently. Most teachers willingly encourage and even plan for nurturing children's creativity. But the constant nurture of creativity, carried on continually, calls for a special effort and a climate that germinates ideas and that provides free unrestricted opportunity for their expression.

Ways that Creative Activities Enrich Social Studies Learnings

Of all areas of the curriculum—with the exception of the creative arts, of course—none is a more natural habitat for nurturing creativity than social studies. Both the content and the method used to develop learnings in social studies are in themselves germinal of creativity. Consider first the content of the area of learning. Implicit in all social studies content is man's creativeness in transforming his environment and making visible the love for the world in which he lives. Any area of learning that furthers a child's understanding of man's struggle to survive and progress, therefore, also illumines the importance of creativity in this struggle.[9] And in so doing it gives the child insight into what it means to be creative and why creativity is a gift men prize.

So, too, the method of developing learnings in social studies fosters creativity among children. Such learnings are acquired by search and discovery. Innovation, exploration, and experimentation are encouraged. Geared to individual differences, pursuit of individual interest, and freedom of expression, its emphasis is on the uniqueness of children. Certainly among the goals to be achieved in social studies nurturing creativity is high in priority.

Furthermore, to the degree that an area of learning in social studies is a habitat for creativity, learning in the area is enriched. Learnings take on new dimensions, deepen, and multiply as creative activities flourish. Thought processes are organized, motivation for learning increases, mean-

[8] Andrews, p. 404; also, E. G. Reed, *Developing Creative Talent* (New York: Vantage Press, Inc., 1962), p. 18.
[9] Harold H. Anderson (Ed.), *Creativity and Its Cultivation* (New York: Harper & Row, Publishers, 1959), p. xi; also Reed, p. 29.

ings become more lucid. There is, in short, a reciprocal relationship between areas of learning in social studies and the creative activities carried on in them.

DEEPENING KNOWLEDGE

Creative activities enrich social studies learnings in many ways. To begin with they deepen children's knowledge of the content under study. The desire to express creatively the ideas they are accumulating about a subject often motivates children to dig deeply and search widely for information. In the process they not only acquire new facts about the subject, but also add new words to their vocabulary and thus deepen their knowledge of the key concepts they wish to express creatively. For example, fifth-grade children engaging in research on the life of the English people during the Crusades are acquiring a variety of knowledges about the subject. Seeking to express their ideas, they produce numerous creations that are outlets for their ideas. A boy, having found a book illustrating various English coats-of-arms, decides to design a family crest for the door of his family's station wagon. To do so he needs more information about English seals-of-state, crests, and coats-of-arms. What kinds of information were symbolized in them? What purpose did they serve? How were the colors used in them chosen? Did colors have special significance? Discovering that he does not have all the information he needs to create his design, he undertakes the task of obtaining more knowledge—more facts, more concepts, and more vocabulary. In the same way a girl uses her knowledge of pioneer life to create a soap figurine of a pioneer woman. And a group of children draw on their concepts of mountain ranges to paint the backdrop of an original play about life in a Colorado mining town at the turn of the century. Like the boy, these children turn back to find answers to questions they cannot answer and thus deepen the knowledge they already possess.

CLARIFYING MEANINGS

A second way that creative activities enrich areas of learning is by making many abstractions that are unclear to children more meaningful to them. Abstract ideas, words, and concepts take on meaning when they are expressed creatively. The abstract becomes concrete, the unclear is clarified, and that which is without meaning is understood. The child who is told or reads that a masthead is a necessary part of the front page of a newspaper and later learns that it is also a necessary part of a ship may quite understandably be confused. Much of this confusion disappears, however, as he carries on creative activities that clarify these terms. Working with a group, he writes to the editors of the nation's leading newspapers to request copies of their mastheads and information about their history. Later the group dramatizes several of these historical accounts in a short enactment that portrays the decisions involved in selecting a newspaper masthead. A creative experience also clarifies the meaning of masthead as a part of a ship. Writing an imaginative story about a sailor who watches over his ship from his crow's-nest close to the masthead, the child sees the importance of the masthead to the ship's operation and begins to understand that "masthead" is a word of several meanings. Moreover, when children consider abstractions from a creative point of view, they often discover their meanings. What is more important, they understand them. Cultural terms—names of articles of clothing worn by peoples of other countries, for example—mean little to the child when he first encounters them. But when he concentrates on the creativity that an article reflects, he perceives it in a new light, seeing its artistry, its ingenuity, and its craftsmanship. And often with this perception comes insight into the reasons for wearing it. Typical illustrations of this point are the sari worn by Indian women, the Malayan sarong, the Eskimo parka, and the Latin American poncho.

EXPRESSING FEELINGS

Another way in which creative activities enrich areas of learning is through the opportunity they provide for the child to express his sensory reactions to knowledges he is acquiring and thus to transform learning from an experience that is largely intellectual to one that is emotional as well. Expressing whatever he feels about these learnings in some kind of creative activity is a satisfying experience that adds richness and fullness to the learning. Every child is unique in the feelings he has about the learnings developed in the area. Learnings may elicit positive emotions from one child; negative ones from another. What to one child may be an interesting geographic locale may seem quite drab to another. One child, for example, may feel that the Mississippi River is a destroyer of life and land, whereas another, thinking only about the river boats and the showboats that once floated on it, feels the romance and adventure of the river. Note the range of sensory reactions a group of fourth-grade children expressed following a period of learning about the jungles of the world. One child felt their beauty and tried to express this beauty in a finger painting that was a splash of brilliant color—many hues of green, brilliant reds, and oranges. Another wrote of its dangers:

> The jungle's dark and gloomy,
> Animals creeping round;
> So you must be on the watch
> For a snarl or any sound.
>
> Stumbling through the jungle
> Is not a pleasant thing;
> Snakes crawling on your legs,
> You fear their deathly sting . . . .

But to another child the jungle was an enchanting place.

> Jungle, jungle, deep dark jungle,
> Where distant drums play mournfully
> And rapids of the Congo sing;
> Villagers pass along the paths
> Chanting happily a native song;
> Streams, paths, flashes of color, birds,
> Light peeping through tangled growth,
> Making jagged, weird shadows on moss-
>   covered ground.

INTERNALIZING LEARNINGS

In addition, creative activities add depth to learnings children are acquiring, for they serve to augment internalization of these learnings and thereby increase their permanency. By using these learnings in creative ways children repeat them, reorganize them, recapitulate them, and in this way fix them. One of the most important factors involved in the process, of course, is that fixing learnings, when done in a creative setting, is a pleasant, satisfying experience for the child. Probably in most instances he is scarcely aware that his creation is a summary of his knowledge or that in making the creation he has reviewed knowledge acquired earlier. As an example, the script of a play that children write is in effect the re-use of ideas and information they have obtained from their study. The fifth-grade boy who wrote the following poem certainly internalized his knowledge of Greece as he wrote.

> Greece was a country of wisdom and grace
> With armies cruel and soldiers bold,
> Who fought for land and power.
> Beautiful buildings splendid and high
> Of marble and stone significant;
> Practically surrounded by water was Greece,
> Sailing ships bringing goods from afar.
> Garments called togas worn over the shoulder,
> Sign of a citizen at the age of fifteen.
> Slaves that were captured in the wars were sold
> To people of wealth their work to do.
> Rich landowners kept hundreds of slaves;
> They made them plant and dig in the soil.
> Slaves of value those who were trained
> To write letters and Greek children to teach.
> Olympic games held in honor of Gods
> Those who entered must have done no wrong.
> The festival opened with offerings beautiful
> Made of gold and ivory with carvings inside;
> At the foot of the altar they laid their gifts.

When to school the Greek children went
With lanterns in hand to guide their way,
They wrote on a tablet covered with wax,
Writing the words with a stylus sharp.
Truly a country of wonders was Greece.

To sum up, creative activities give life to an area of learning. They give it color. They give it interest. They convert passive, vicarious learning into dynamic, meaningful experiences. They clarify and illumine meaningless abstractions. They recapitulate and reinforce learnings. All together these are compelling reasons for making creative activities an integral part of an area of learning. In fact, it is doubtful that the desired outcomes of an area of learning can be fully achieved without them.

Ways that Creative Activities Contribute to the Social Goals of an Area of Learning

Not only do creative activities enrich social studies learnings—the knowledges and understandings being acquired in the area; they also contribute to the social goals indigenous to any area of learning that contributes to the objectives of social studies. To the point is the goal of citizenship. Implicit in the term *citizenship* is a concept of a creative person, one who is a genuinely free person, capable of making wise decisions, an individual of initiative, originality, and, above all, capable of creativity in human relations. Such a person is one who is continually in the process of becoming his best self—an adequate person, a creative person. Creative activities contribute to the development of this "adequate person" the child is seeking to become. When carried on as an integral part of an area of learning, they open up opportunities for children to identify and nurture their creative potential. They expand children's interests in creative ways. They encourage experimentation with materials. And they foster creativity in human relations.

IDENTIFYING, DEVELOPING, AND PERFECTING ARTISTIC TALENTS

Particularly for children whose potential artistic talents are under the surface, creative activities related to an area of learning are the opportunity for release of this potential. Such activities, in fact, often make the difference between artistic talent developed and perfected or artistic talent bottled up and undiscovered. As stated earlier, a child whose creative potential is undeveloped never fulfills the promise of becoming the creative man. This is society's loss; even more important, it is the child's loss. But in classrooms where creative activities are an integral part of an area of learning there is opportunity for children to try out their artistic talents, to discover the character of these talents—to tune in, so to speak, on the esthetic urges that beat most strongly for release. If the child derives satisfactions from his tentative effort to express himself artistically—if he receives recognition for it, if he accepts it as an achievement of worth, and if it has deepened self-understanding, then he is encouraged to nourish this talent. In this way, then, what in the beginning was only a potential becomes a reality. Creative activities that go on during an area of learning act as detectors of children's artistic talents; such activities provide the opportunity for expressing these talents and the incentive for perfecting them.

DEVELOPING AND EXPANDING INTERESTS

It is a different, more personal, and far more specific level of attention that children give to subject matter that interests them. On this level children become self-motivated and move out under their own power to satisfy their curiosities. Moving out in this fashion, they begin to extend their life space, developing new interests and expanding continuing ones.

Every child seeks this kind of experience. Most of his energies are directed toward finding out what life is like, in answering the whys of the phenomena that puzzle him. As he encounters new, interesting, and sometimes intriguing knowledge in an area of learning, he is motivated to pursue this interest creatively. A child's interest in learning another language often springs from the experience of singing songs in this language. His interest in ceramics may have originated in a story he read in social studies about the great kilns in England. Children who pursue interests in creative ways and who invent and innovate in the process satisfy their need for status with their peers as authorities on their area of interest. And most important, when children pursue new interests or expand continuing ones through some form of creative expression, they are setting the foundations for the worthy use of leisure time in adulthood.

EXPERIMENTING WITH MATERIALS

There is no better opportunity for a child to satisfy his need to explore and to experiment with things than in an area of learning that offers the incentive and freedom to carry on creative activities. It is not unusual to observe a child so absorbed in trying out materials as he seeks to express his ideas in a creative way that he is oblivious to everything that is going on around him. "Would the picture look better if I'd put paint on in thick gobs?" he may be asking himself as he daubs chunks of paint on his creation. "Would this yellow and blue make the shade of green I want for my trees?" "How can I make the painting in my book look faded and old?" another one may ask as he experiments with a variety of papers and dyes.

Or another who desires to produce a special sound may experiment with numerous kinds of musical instruments in his search for it. And another who wishes to create a three-dimensional effect on a mural builds up some of the surface with papier-mâché before painting the scenes he is creating.

These are merely a sampling of the ways in which children experiment with materials as they seek to transform social studies information and ideas into some kind of creation. Such activities put children's senses to work, sharpening them, refining them. As they experiment with materials, they smell, they taste, they listen, and they feel. Punching, pinching, poking, sniffing, tasting, looking, cutting, folding, molding, shaping, measuring, stirring, dipping, pounding, through trial and error, through exploring, and through experimenting, they reap the satisfactions that come from achievement, that come from bringing ideas to the surface and shaping them into a creative product. And, in addition, they are enriching their knowledge of material resources for creation.

FOSTERING CREATIVITY IN HUMAN RELATIONS

No man, no woman, no child can live without the help of his fellow men. For this reason it is important that every individual learn creative ways of getting along with others. Discussed at length in an earlier chapter, the development of effective human relations, nonetheless, warrants further treatment here. It is axiomatic, of course, that children learn by doing. Learning to work creatively with others, learning social skills and processes, is largely a matter of practice. Particularly it is a matter of practice in situations that are as functional as possible. Working together and playing together while engaging in creative activities related to areas of learning, children learn to meet and solve problems. They are able to test themselves in group situations, to take stock of their social behavior, and to measure it in terms of desired results. Moreover, they see at firsthand the results of creative, cooperative effort.[10] The following report of a group's efforts to write a play is a most revealing account of human relations operating creatively. Exactly as a member of the group wrote it, here is the account:

OUR PLAY

In January, we chose four groups of people, each group with a topic. What these groups wanted to do was to make a play. We were studying about Greece. One group took schools, one trade, one a market place, and one war. All of these things were of Greek civilization. The topic my group had was war. And in this group were Carol, Katherine, Frances, John, and Tom.

There is social studies in the morning, and during that time different groups would go down to the play room to practice; but before we could go down there we first had to write the play. The first day our group didn't get much

---

[10] Arden N. Frandsen, *Educational Psychology* (New York: McGraw-Hill, Inc., 1961), p. 466.

done, but most of the groups got more done than we did. In the morning when it was time for social studies, our group went over to the table; Carol brought up the idea of how to start, and we took her idea.

After we had quite a bit written in two days, we thought it wasn't good enough. Katherine said, "Why not have a school?" Frances, who had not been there the first two days, said she didn't like the idea either. Carol said she thought we should have a thought topic as we couldn't show the war because we didn't have enough people. You see all of the other groups had six people and we had only five people. It was pretty hard to show it. We still kept on our same play. The next morning our group was on the davenport thinking about our play, and David brought up an idea which we liked very well. He said, "Since we can't show it, let's tell about the war in the story. Have someone tell about it."

We went over to the table and put a new ending on the story. We liked the ending better. We fixed it so that when we were making merry, the king would call for the storyteller, who would make up a story which he could learn and tell.

It was the next day in social studies and our group was going down to the playroom to practice. A violin teacher was down there, and he was going to use the room so we went upstairs to the first floor. We were going to use the music room, but there was a class in there so we came upstairs. Our teacher was out by the door. She said we could get the screen and use the hall. We got the screen and put it out in the hall. The hall was quite narrow, but it was good enough to practice in. We got the chair ready and went through the play. This was going to be our last practice. After we went through it once, we went through it again. Our teacher came out in the hall to tell us we should give our play that afternoon after music, but Carol said that she couldn't because she was going to Marysville with Miss Jackson to play the piano on the radio. So we couldn't give it that afternoon but were supposed to give it the next morning. I had forgotten all about it the next morning until our teacher said that the group on war was to give their play. We went out in the hall. Tom said, "Where is my cup to drop?" Carol said she forgot to bring one, and she went out to the art room and got a cover for a jar.

Tom said, "Where will I put it?"

Katherine came out and gave a little introduction; then I came in and sat down. After the play we went out in the hall, and I found out that I forgot the cup. Then we went to be criticized. Our teacher said we might use it in the big play.

Creative Activities
Related to an Area of Learning

Creation excites creation. The more creative acts a child experiences —his own or others—the more creative he becomes. The greater the succession and variety of perceptions of the world and its people that an area of learning develops the more raw material from which to create. Exposed to an abundance of material from which to create, given time and freedom for it to incubate and the media with which to transform subjective ideas into form and symbols, a child's creative output increases in quantity, improves in quality.[11] Together these facts point the way for teachers to plan and implement experiences that enrich learnings in social studies at the same time that they nourish children's creative potential.

Where, then, does a teacher begin his search for the media of creativity? In other words, what are the means by which children can find creative outlets for their thoughts, their ideas, their feelings, their pictures, and their songs?

The media of creativity are the countless materials in the environment that wait for the fingers of the innovator and the mind that will reorganize and synthesize them into new form and substance. They are music—songs, ballads, musical compositions, and musical instruments. They are arts and crafts—paints, paper, pencils, cloth, wood, wire, and metal. They are creative dramatics—plays and stories dramatized, dramatic play enactments, and choral speaking. They are rhythms—rhythms with things and rhythms with bodies. They are stories to write, poems to write, and plays to write. They are literature—stories to read and to enjoy. These are the media of creativity.[12] Each is a sensory experience, unique in symbol and expression. Each is infinitely varied in the forms it can take.

EXPERIENCES WITH MUSIC

Certainly no child needs to be denied any of these media since all are increasingly available in his environment. Consider the first of the media listed above—music. Music is a universal medium of communication. Among peoples of the most primitive cultures and among peoples of the most civilized cultures it is a mode of expression. The folk music of a culture is often a direct reflection of the effect of geography upon the people and upon their customs and occupations as well. Singing the folk songs of a culture, especially singing them in the language in which they are written, children are transported in spirit to this culture and in the process feel a kinship with its people. Listening to music recorded in a particular culture serves the same purpose. What child listening to a recording of Honunoo music from the Philippines—chants, rituals, lullabies, trail calls, courting songs, and animal calls, played with flutes, gongs, musical sticks, Jew's harp, bamboo buzzers, and bamboo zithers—would not feel the creativity of its people and perhaps be enchanted enough to make a bamboo musical instrument for himself. Recordings that feature the bagpipes of Scotland, the fiddlers of the Ozarks, the music of South Pacific Islands, ceremonial music of the Navaho Indians, and many similar recordings beget children's creativity and enhance their enjoyment of an area of study.

[11] Mearns, pp. 269–270.
[12] Miriam E. Wilt, *Creativity in the Elementary School* (New York: Appleton-Century-Crofts, Inc., 1959), p. 7.

Older children who have acquired some skill in composing music use their knowledge of a particular locale in creating musical compositions that reflect the character of that locale. For example, the clang of cable cars in San Francisco, the foghorns in the bay, Chinese merchants talking together, the calls of the fishermen docking their boats, clicking heels on sidewalks, honking horns—all of these are the sounds that make San Francisco the city that it is. Children create music easily and naturally. Is there a child who has not embellished his piano practice with musical interpretations of his own or who has not added words to a familiar song or created music to give color to play? By drawing on this natural behavior, teachers not only add life and meaning to social studies but also nurture children's creative potential. In addition, every community has within it people with special musical abilities who welcome opportunities to share their music with children in a classroom.

At any level of maturity music adds enrichment to social studies. All children, the young and the older, given the opportunity and the guidance, can create music—songs, rhythms, dances. Moreover, for some children whose academic abilities are limited, music related to an area of learning is a rewarding means of building concepts of social studies. Too, these children often have special gifts in music—beautifully coordinated bodies, clear bell-like voices, and a keen sense of rhythm—that give them the prestige they otherwise could not achieve.

The following anecdote illustrates the way in which one child's spontaneous musical creation inspired children to create an interpretive dance related to their study of primitive man.

"Mrs. Brown, some of us fourth-grade girls have an idea we think the class would like. Want to hear it?" Sue asked expectantly.

"An idea about what?"

"It's about a piano piece Shirley made up. It sounds just the way we think primitive music sounded."

"We think maybe she could play it before our caveman play," suggested Mary Lou. "You know, like the overture an orchestra plays before the curtain goes up."

"Do you remember your piece well enough to play it this morning when everyone gets back from band practice?" Mrs. Brown asked Shirley.

"Of course, I do," Shirley answered.

The children were later than usual in assembling that morning. Finally when they were settled and ready for the day's work, Mrs. Brown announced, "We've been waiting for all of you. Shirley has an original musical composition that the girls think will make a good introduction to the caveman play. She is ready to play it now."

Shirley settled herself at the piano like a famous concert pianist whose audience waits breathlessly for his performance. She played her composition and then, scarcely finished, jumped up from the bench excited and glowing.

"I have a new idea. Why doesn't Donald get his drum and beat out the rhythm like a tom-tom while I play the piano. That would really make primitive-sounding music."

"Try it, Donnie, try it," the boys urged.

So Donald brought his drum from the hallway where he had left it, and as Shirley played, he picked up the accent of the music with his sticks. The children enthusiastically approved the new composition; later Shirley scored her music, and it was added to the script of the play the children were writing about primitive man.

One afternoon weeks later following a rehearsal of the play, Pat exclaimed, "Couldn't we do a pantomime dance to Shirley's music? If she'll play it and some of the boys and girls will act out the motions I tell them to, we can make up a dance."

Several children readily volunteered. Shirley played her music, and Pat, with suggestions from others, interpreted it in motion.

Several tryouts later, during which some movements were added and others eliminated, Pat made a narrative record of the dance. Pat's synopsis of the dance follows, and the music that inspired it is reproduced on page 218.

THE GREAT HUNT

An Interpretive Dance of the Life of a Primitive People

Men and women dressed in primitive costumes are seated on the ground making the motions of scraping skins and shaping tools.

Suddenly a tom-tom is heard beating in the distance. Soft at first, it grows louder and seems to be moving nearer to the gathering.

Workers look up, startled, alert. They turn their heads toward the sound.

Messenger, carrying spear, runs to the group, out of breath, as though he has been running hard. Stops, points into distance.

Music begins. Tom-tom plays soft accompaniment. Workers rise, pick up spears, and follow messenger.

Two women remain, move in crouching position to rhythm of music. Messenger motions them on.

Music crashes loudly. Messenger throws his spear as though striking a "bear."

All jump for joy as they gather around the fallen bear. Several go through motions of cutting up the bear. They put pieces of meat on their shoulders and, carrying their load, move rhythmically as they follow the messenger back to camp.

They drop their burden around the fire. Women join them. The music grows faster and faster. Then gradually it slows up. The dancers drop cross-legged to the ground. They eat greedily, throwing the bones away. Movement.

They yawn and rise sleepily. Slowly they all file away to bed.

Tom-tom softly dies away!

EXPERIENCES WITH ARTS AND CRAFTS

Like music, art activities enhance children's learnings in social studies, foster creativity, and contribute to social and emotional development. In fact, much of what has been said about the values of integrating music and social studies applies also to experiences with arts and crafts. Production of art objects and consumption of art in a variety of forms continue to increase among the peoples of America. Increasingly, for example, industrial products are evaluated in terms of their beauty as well as their effi-

ciency. The examples of art in everyday life are limitless. Communicating
ideas through art media is an effective practice among many kinds of
services and industries. Indeed, the environment in which today's children
live is one that abounds in opportunities for art experiences. Pictures and
illustrations in books often convey more successfully than words the ideas
and concepts to be learned. The art of a culture—its paintings, sculpture,
and architecture—offers clues to the concerns, the customs, and the values
of that culture and thus contributes to a child's understanding of it. The
crafts of a country offer a wide range of learnings about the country. Take
Mexican silver and jewelry, for example: What forces brought about its

production? Who are its producers? What problems are there in making and selling it?

But it is in the child's own artistic efforts that the fullest values of integrating art and social studies are realized. As noted and illustrated many times in this chapter, art experiences add new dimensions to children's learnings about areas of learning. When first-grade children draw simple pictures of activities at the fire station, they are creating an objective symbol of their knowledge of this community function. When sixth-grade children with more skill and knowledge about art techniques paint pictures of such epic events as the Chicago fire or the San Francisco earthquake and the fire that followed it, they are converting a whole complex of ideas about fires in a locale into a concrete form that illumines these ideas.

Because in arts and crafts experiences the emphasis is on symbolic representation of ideas rather than on the authentic reproduction emphasized in construction experiences, children's imaginations have free expression. Consequently, art experiences do much to induce children to be original in their creations, in the form of these creations, and in the materials they use for them. When children feel free to try out and experiment with their creations, the quality of these creations improves and output increases.

In arts and crafts, as in music, there are many ways for children to express themselves artistically. For individuals, there are art media that lend themselves to individual effort—drawing, coloring, painting pictures, modeling, carving, weaving, designing, illustrating, and similar media of art expression. For groups, there are murals like the "Communication Story in Picture," which was described in the dialogue at the beginning of this chapter. By depicting social studies ideas, scenes, and events, murals and friezes further social studies learnings. By drawing on the talents of many children, they are, in effect, cooperative enterprises in miniature. And they provide opportunities for children to use their special abilities. Dioramas, the three-dimensional displays that are so frequently seen in modern museums, are yet another form of art expression that enhances learnings in social studies. Peep shows, properties, costumes, and scenery for plays and puppet shows—these also foster creativity and in so doing make social studies more meaningful, more exciting, and more rewarding to the learner.

EXPERIENCES WITH LITERATURE

Literature is a magic carpet that takes children all over the world. Through literature—stories, narratives, and poems—a child travels in his imagination to places far and near. Through it he learns to know people and to give them shape and form and color. Like a stereoscope, literature adds a new dimension to information and in so doing deepens the meaning of this information. Literature, more than any other single resource of learning, is the firebrand that lights the way to knowledge about peoples, events, and places.

The repertoire of literature in the area of social studies is as varied as it is voluminous. Lavishly illustrated books and recordings of renowned actors masterfully recounting events of past history beckon children to read and to listen and to react to what they read and hear. Is there a boy or girl reading Carl Carmer's A *Flag for the Fort* who would not glean new insights into the meaning of words in "The Star-Spangled Banner"? Is there a child studying the history of the Civil War who would not respond to Charles Laughton's moving reading of "The Gettysburg Address"?

The teacher who uses literature to enrich social studies learnings goes a long way toward resolving the problems of children's differing abilities to cope with and internalize these learnings. Gifted children, dissatisfied with the meagerness of information in textbooks about subjects that interest them, find the stimulation they seek in literature, not only literature printed in their own language but in foreign languages as well. These children's growing facility with such languages as French and Spanish makes it possible for them to read simple stories written in these languages. Reading the story of Joan of Arc is an interesting experience for any sixth-grade girl. But to read this same story in simple French as a young French girl reads it is an experience in fellowship.

Slower children, too, find satisfactions in literature. Children who encounter difficulties reading social studies textbooks often find it possible to obtain essential ideas from the context of stories that are structured on the information presented in the textbook. Carried forward in their reading by the flow of action words in a story and by words that evoke visual images, they are able to extract meaning from the printed page. Or freed from the tedious drudgery of identifying symbols, they find pleasure and meanings in literary recordings of social studies content that is beyond the limits of their reading ability.

In addition, using literature to enrich social studies content provides teachers with a much-needed opportunity to help children become discriminating assimilators of information. Here is the opportunity to teach children to distinguish fact from fiction, to differentiate between information that is truth and that which is fanciful, and to evaluate information in terms of the author's purposes.

Truly literature in social studies is a resource of great potential in enriching social studies learnings. Indeed, not only does it give life to these learnings; through developing an appreciation of the creativity of others, it also encourages children in their own efforts to be creative.

EXPERIENCES WITH DRAMATICS

Creative dramatics opens a child's eyes to see and his heart to listen and understand. Play-acting, he pushes out the boundaries of his life space, expressing in imaginative make-believe his ideas, his concepts, and his feelings about human living. Transported by the evocative magic of play-acting, he puts himself in the place of other people. He feels the cold of a Chinese boy who stands huddled and freezing, pleading for a morsel of food. He cries as a little boy cries for the schoolbooks his father cannot afford to buy. And in so doing, he develops at least a glimmer of insight into what it is like to be someone else.

Creative dramatics may be spontaneous and unrehearsed or formally structured with lines of a script read or memorized. Dramatic play unfolds spontaneously without plot. It utilizes the dramatic elements of characterization and dialogue. Empathy is strong in a dramatic play enactment, with the actor taking on the character of the person he is fashioning. Engaging in dramatic play, children explore in their own way the activities and relationships of human living for the purposes of acquiring needed information and skills.

Dramatic play lends itself to many learning situations in the area of learning. One of these, the dramatic play initiation, has been described in detail in an earlier chapter. Dramatic play is also an effective tool for evaluating the results of instruction in social studies. Used as a tool of evaluation, dramatic play makes a galaxy of learnings observable and thus reveals the degree to which children are internalizing the knowledge they are acquiring. When learnings are few, enactments are simple. As children accumulate more learnings, enactments become more accurate and more complex. In some instances this spiral culminates in a structured dramatization that summarizes significant learnings to be derived from the area of learning. In this case, of course, the activity is no longer dramatic play but formal dramatization with a plot, planned scenes, and a recorded script.

Most important, perhaps, are the insights into the meaning of social consciousness that result from dramatic play enactments. Not only do these enactments illumine the responsibilities of democratic citizenship; they also provide children with an understanding of the problems of community living and a realization of the importance of participating in community activities.

Dramatizations of prepared scripts do not reveal children's virgin concepts about people and situations as clearly as dramatic play enactments do, but they are nonetheless effective in nurturing social studies learnings. As previously noted, scripts that children write and then enact summarize and make permanent learnings to be derived from an area of learning. Like dramatic play enactments, dramatizations shed light on human motivations and behavior. For example, children who dramatize a play on the discovery of America must feel the tension and the joy of the event and thus develop new understandings about it. And children who create a play based on Nicholson's moving article, "The Return of the Unknown Soldier," and then play out their script certainly should acquire new concepts about the worth of the individual in the American democracy.

All of which is to say, let children be actors and acting they will learn.

Let them engage in creative make-believe acting, and they will learn what no teacher can teach them. Let them play-act the understandings to be assimilated in social studies, and that which is unclear is understood, and the remote becomes near and alive.

Possibly the talent for teaching engendered in creative make-believe is bred in the bone; possibly it is acquired. But whatever it is, teachers who use it as a master key open doors of learning through which children can enter into the lives of others, through which, in short, they gain insights into the human relationships so necessary to their survival.[13]

Criteria for Selecting Creative Activities

At this point it is well to recall the fact that creative activities in a social studies area of learning serve two basic purposes: they enrich learnings evolving in the area of learning, and they further the social goals that inhere in it. It is the first of these purposes that is of most importance here: creative activities enrich social studies areas of learning in several ways. First, they offer opportunities for expressing ideas and feelings about the content of the area; second, they give life, interest, and color to the area of learning; third, they reinforce the concepts and understandings to be obtained from the experience. Achieving these values or these purposes is by no means a haphazard, incidental process. On the contrary, there are quite specific criteria for selecting creative activities that will enrich social studies learnings.

First, does the creative activity grow out of or relate to the area of learning? This criterion may seem at first glance to be so obvious as to be superfluous. The fact is, however, that failure to consider this criterion in selecting creative activities that will enrich areas of learning is one of the most common mistakes that teachers make when they seek to further social studies learnings through creative activities. To enhance social studies learnings, to give them depth and meaning, to add life, color, and interest to them, and to reinforce concepts and understandings in the area of learning, creative activities must be clearly, unequivocally related to the learnings. Only when the relationship between the learning and the activity is clear is there social studies value in the activity. To be sure, there may be values other than those related to social studies, but they are of little concern here. Perhaps an illustration will serve to bring this point more sharply into focus.

---

[13] Adapted from H. L. Sagl, "Dramatic Play: A Tool of Learning in Social Studies," in John U. Michaelis (Ed.), *Social Studies in Elementary Schools* (Thirty-second Yearbook of the National Council for the Social Studies; Washington, D.C.: National Education Association, 1962), pp. 208–209.

The fifth-grade children who spent several weeks in a search to find out why large cities are located on waterways discovered that during the settlement of the West the Ohio River functioned as major highways do today. They learned that the needs of the settlers stimulated new industries and services in ports along the Ohio River and that, without this river, movement to the West would have been even more hazardous, even more tedious, than it was. Among the creative activities that were rooted in this knowledge was an epic poem in which these children, writing cooperatively, tried to eulogize the importance of the Ohio River. Using Carl Sandburg's "Chicago" as an inspiration, they wrote of the beauty of the river, of its hazards, and of its history. Later they used their poem as a choral reading. A group of these children also created a pictorial map of the geographic area through which the Ohio River flows, illustrating it with pictures that depicted life on the river a century ago. Others assumed the role of persons who lived during that period and in this role wrote letters that described the events and experiences encountered during a boat trip from Pittsburgh to Cincinnati. Each of these creative activities was clearly related to the knowledge that the Ohio River was U.S. Highway No. 1, a river of vital importance to the settlers who used it. Each creative activity served to express this concept of the importance of the river in the lives of people. The end result, of course, was to gain deeper insights into the reasons for this importance. In other words, and quite logically so, to enrich knowledge in areas of learning creative activities must be derived from this knowledge and must utilize the basic ideas inherent in it.

Second, does the creative activity have a clearly defined purpose? This criterion may be controversial from one point of view: there are many who believe that creative activities need no purpose to justify them, that in themselves they have such value that justification for them is not necessary. But again, it is important to recall that the focus in this chapter is not on creative activities *per se* but on creative activities as a vehicle for enriching social studies learnings. In this light, therefore, the purpose of the activity is of utmost importance. If a creative activity is to enhance specific learnings, its purpose must be identified at the outset of the activity. How else can children know whether or not their creative expression truly enriches the learnings they have acquired in a particular area of learning? Failure to identify the purpose of the creative activity may result in aimless, disorganized activity that not only leaves the child devoid of satisfaction in his efforts but offers little opportunity for him to evaluate his creativity.

Third, will the creative activity make a worthwhile contribution to the area of learning? This criterion also bears examination. Why should the creative activity make a worthwhile contribution to the area of learning? Again the answer is that the primary reason for engaging in the creative activity is to enrich the learnings in social studies. It stands to reason that some creative activities are more enriching than others. Some, in fact, may even bring very little enrichment to the desired learnings. Thus, when selecting creative activities, a teacher must necessarily consider the contribution the creative activity makes to the learnings implicit in it. When selecting creative activities related to areas of learning, he must weigh the contributions of one type of activity against those of another, asking himself such questions as, "What kind of creative activity will deepen children's insight to the greatest degree?" The teacher whose group was studying the Westward Movement, for example, encouraged pupils to write an epic poem about the Ohio because he saw it as an especially effective way of helping children feel the importance of the river. Thus, in selecting creative activities to be carried on in connection with an area of learning, the unique contribution of the activity is always of necessity a matter of concern.

The fourth and last criterion needs no defense and very little explanation. Does the creative activity have significance for children? Without question children's efforts and the quality of their products are closely related to the significance they attach to the activity. If they rate it high on their hierarchy of values, they will expend great energy on it, working painstakingly for long periods of time to achieve their ends. It is therefore most important that children recognize the significance of the creative activities they engage in and that they accept them as activities that will enhance the knowledge they are acquiring in the on-going area of learning.

Role of the Teacher in Planning and Carrying on Creative Activities

Because creativity is the product of experience rather than a magical inborn quality of inheritance, because ideas are the source of creation, and because certain social and cultural milieus favor or hamper creativity, the teacher is a decisive factor in determining how much or how little creativity there is in his classroom. If a teacher has an over-orthodox, narrow notion of what constitutes creativity, he tends to look on its possessors as a favored few to be set apart from the rest of the children. As a result he not only denies his responsibility for developing the potential creativity of the other children in the classroom but may even insist that there is nothing he can do about it. Fortunately, teachers with this point of view are diminishing in number. Fortunately, many of today's teachers believe that they should and can nurture children's creativity. Yet the fact remains that too few children are participating fully and freely in the experience of creation.

Perhaps this state of affairs is to be expected because there are so few absolutes to tie to in nurturing creativity. There is little evidence, for example, that security is as essential to creativity as many people believe it to be; or, for that matter, that a high IQ is a prime requisite.[14] But

---

[14] Frank Barron, "Creative Vision and Expression," in Alexander Frazier (Ed.), New Insights and the Curriculum (Washington, D.C.: Association for Supervision and Curriculum Development, 1958), pp. 296–297.

teachers can operate within the framework of the facts about creativity as they know them, using these facts as guides in planning ways to encourage children's creativity.

A point of departure for any teacher seeking ways to nurture children's creativity is to examine his own attitudes and beliefs regarding creativity. Does he believe that it is the heritage of all children, and of not just a favored few? that the capacity to be creative is inherent in all children, though the utilization of that capacity may be hard work? that all children have a longing to do or make things that give their feelings form and substance? that the creative potential of every child is as unique in form as children are unique in their personalities and character? Only if his answer to these questions is strongly affirmative, and only then, will he be able to nurture creativity in his classroom. Only then can he create the kind of atmosphere that encourages children to express themselves freely, an atmosphere in which even the creativity of those whose talents are few and ambitions simple is expressed.

CREATING AN ATMOSPHERE FOR CARRYING ON CREATIVE ACTIVITIES

There is every indication that an atmosphere that nurtures creativity is one in which a child is free to innovate, to be different, and to be marginal. It is an atmosphere where creations are accepted at their face value and where children do not feel compelled to defend their creations or to justify their deviations from prescribed standards. It is an atmosphere where children and teacher alike are alert to the ideas and thoughts that are evolving in learning situations in the classroom. And it is an atmosphere pervaded with flexibility and spontaneity. It is, in short, an atmosphere in which children know that their creative efforts, no matter how eccentric, will elicit the interest and encouragement of teacher and peers.[15]

What can a teacher do to create an atmosphere that engenders children's creativity? For one thing, he can make it possible for his children to share the ideas and experiences they are acquiring as they engage in an area of learning. It is through interaction, through exchange of ideas, that the urge to create comes to the surface. Sharing their experiences, children whet the creative urges of one another and garner new ideas for expressing them. Some children, left to themselves, would never create, but when they share their ideas and experiences, they are encouraged to do so. Some children need evidence of acceptance or recognition of their ideas to express themselves creatively. Hence teachers who make it possible for children to share ideas and experiences contribute to creative expression among children. Recall how creative ideas emerged and took shape in the group that wrote the script described earlier on the subject of wars in ancient Greece.

[15] Marksberry, p. 21.

Certainly one of the most important elements of an atmosphere that nurtures creativity is time—time to take notice of thoughts, time to reflect on these thoughts, time to respond to them with some kind of feeling, time to do something with these thoughts and feelings, time to experiment when a first try does not turn out right, time unrestricted and unlimited, time for creativity to blossom, to grow, and to ripen. Any growth—physical, mental, emotional, or social—takes time. Creativity cannot be rushed. It cannot be streamlined. It cannot be forced. Thus, of all the elements that a teacher can contribute to an atmosphere of creativity, time is of the essence.

GETTING STARTED ON CREATIVE ACTIVITIES

When a teacher has built up a rich background of ideas about the content of an area of learning, he has set the stage for creative expression. But for many children an atmosphere conducive to creativity is not enough to release their creative urges. It takes more overt action on the teacher's part to set their creativity in motion. And the more inhibited a child is, the more overt this action must be, particularly in dramatics and rhythmic activities, where there is fear of appearing ridiculous in the eyes of peers. For these children specific suggestions for getting started may be needed. The teacher, of course, takes his cues from the nature of the content and the children's reactions to it. For certainly some content lends itself to one kind of creative expression better than to another. The poetry cited earlier, for example, seemed for some to be a most satisfying way to express feelings about the jungle.

If the creative activity is to be a group activity, that is, one in which all children are using the same mode of expression—either poetry, drama, narration, or music—the teacher discusses the activity with the children, inviting their suggestions and exploring its possibilities, making certain as he does so that the suggestions remain fluid. Acting as a leavener, such a discussion often brings children's ideas about a subject to the surface where they find a creative outlet.

There are, however, other times when a teacher remains in the background, suggesting ideas only as they are sought. His function in instances where a creative activity originates with the children themselves is to facilitate its expression. For example, in a classroom where creativity is encouraged and children think creatively, such comments as the following are typical: Couldn't we write a play about pioneers to show how they lived? Some of us thought we could write music for our poem, "Faraway Places," so we could sing it as well as speak it. Wouldn't Mary's story about the ways people use the telephone be a good story for us to act out? I wish we could paint a big picture of interesting things that were going on in Indiana during the Civil War. Why don't we write stories about a runaway slave? We could tell about the underground railway and how it was used to help slaves escape. Usually a teacher counters such queries with remarks like these: What did you have in mind? Why don't you find several others who might be interested in your idea and go to work on it. I'll help you when you need my help, and others will too, I'm sure.

In other words, the teacher plays an active, not a passive, role in inaugurating creative activities in the classroom. By no means, however, is the teacher's role a dominating one. On the contrary, from all that has been said it should be clear that here, as throughout most of the development of a social studies area of learning, the teacher's role is a leadership role. Too often, however, teachers interpret this to mean "hands off." But few creative activities just happen. They must be planned for and guided in their execution.

CARRYING ON CREATIVE ACTIVITIES

As children carry on creative activities individually or in groups, the teacher continues to act as a leader. He is ready to give assistance as assistance is needed. He is a resource of knowledge and skill to whom children turn for help with their special problems. But he does not force the child who is engaged in a creation to accept his ideas. He may suggest; in fact, a teacher nourishes children's creative efforts through his suggestions. Obviously, the line between suggestions and domination is a delicate one that teachers with more rigid, preconceived notions of ways to express ideas may find difficult to maintain. Yet at all times they must realize, and act accordingly, that there is no right way, no wrong way, no best way to express ideas creatively.

QUESTIONS FOR DISCUSSION

Use the dialogue at the beginning of the chapter as a basis for discussion of the following:

1. How did the creative activities described in the dialogue grow out of the area of learning?
2. In each instance why was the creative activity particularly appropriate to the children's purposes?
3. What new interests and talents did these creative activities identify?
4. How did the teacher's role in these experiences differ from her role in construction and processing?

SUGGESTIONS FOR CONSTRUCTING
A RESOURCE UNIT

Analyze each of the problem-solving experiences you have planned and note opportunities for expressing creativity. Identify and describe appropriate related experiences that capitalize on these opportunities. Use the following questions as guides in describing each experience:

1. What creative arts—writing, art, music, and dramatics—serve as vehicles for children's expression of feelings, ideas, and interests growing out of the problem-solving experience?

10

Developing Skills
Related to an Area
of Learning

MRS. JOHNSON: The design for your newspaper masthead is very interesting, Charles. What comes next in your committee plan?

CHARLES: Many of the people in our class have been asking about the newspaper and want to help on the committee. If everyone wants to, maybe the whole class could work on it. It would be better than if Pat and Susy and I do it by ourselves. We've found out there's more to making a class newspaper than we thought.

MRS. JOHNSON: Several groups have finished the projects they've been working on. Let's see how many want to help with the newspaper. I see the hands of many volunteers. Perhaps we could all make plans and then find out how we can take care of the special responsibilities. Planning together will help us all to feel that the paper belongs to us. What will we need to think about?

SUSAN: I want to be a reporter like my father.

MRS. JOHNSON: Do you mean that we'll have to decide what newspaper workers we'll need? We certainly will have to have reporters.

JACK: We'll have to decide on the parts of our paper—society page, sports news, television programs, and like that.

CHARLES: We'll have to find out how it can be printed. My committee can't make linoleum blocks for the whole thing. The masthead was enough.

MARY LOU: And where we'll get the paper and how much we need.

PEGGY: And whether we'll sell the papers or give them away.

MRS. JOHNSON: You're going pretty fast, Peggy. We can decide that matter when the paper is ready.

MARTHA: I'll be glad to do the art work if there is any.

MRS. JOHNSON: Thank you, Martha. Now let's see, what comes first? Jack mentioned the parts we need in our paper. And then Susan suggested the workers. Yes, Ruth, the editorial staff checks the material and puts the paper together. What's your idea, Pat? A publishing committee to look after the printing and distributing? Yes, you'd be a good chairman for that because if we need help we could ask your father. I know several other parents who would probably come to school if we need them, too. Peggy's mother is publicity chairman for the PTA; she'll know how to write news articles correctly. Do you think she'd come, Peggy?

PEGGY: I'll ask her. Can I do the PTA publicity for our newspaper? I can get all the information from my mother.

* * * * * * *

MRS. JOHNSON: Our editorial committee reports having some difficulty with the news articles you are writing. They asked me to help them find out why they can't understand some of your ideas very well. We discovered that almost everybody needs to review how to write a good sentence. Since all of us will take a turn at writing news, perhaps we should spend our language arts time today reviewing. Can someone suggest how we could start?

ROBERT: Could the committee show us some sentences that aren't right? We wouldn't have to know who wrote them. Then we could really see what's wrong.

MRS. JOHNSON: That's a good idea. We can select some troublesome ones and put them on the chalkboard during recess. Any other ideas?

ALICE: There's probably something about writing sentences in our language arts book. I'll look it up and have it all ready for class.

ANNE: There will probably be some sentences in the book to practice on after we've studied the ones on the board.

RUTH: Then all of us who wrote news articles had better get our news and go over it. Maybe someone who isn't writing this week could be our partner and help with it.

MRS. JOHNSON: We'll try out these suggestions. It may not take us long to get our good sentence writing habits back again. There's the recess bell.

* * * * * * *

MRS. JOHNSON: Boys and girls, let's use part of our mathematics period this morning to help our newspaper publishers with a problem. Patricia and her committee asked me for help, but I think this is a problem our class can solve together. What's the situation, Patricia?

PATRICIA: We have to decide what kind of paper to use for our newspaper. Mr. Stevens says the school will buy the paper for us, but we should spend as little money as possible. We can make our copies on the ditto machine or on the mimeograph machine. Ditto paper costs 95¢ a ream; mimeograph paper is 78¢ a ream. We need a sheet of ditto carbon for each page or a mimeograph stencil. Carbons are 3¢ and stencils are 12¢.

MRS. JOHNSON: Is there anything else to be considered besides the cost?

CHARLES: Things that are mimeographed last longer. Ditto things fade out. But the news would get old anyway, so I guess that wouldn't make much difference.

MRS. JOHNSON: What do we need to do, then? Figure out the costs of both methods? Have you estimated the length of your paper? Four sheets? How many copies do we need? For the whole school? Then we'll need 240, won't we? What do we do first?

WAYNE: See how many newspapers we can get from a ream. I'll look up how many sheets in a ream in the dictionary. Is that r-e-a-m? I have it. Five hundred.

ANDY: That's easy. If there were 400 sheets in a ream, we could get 100 papers from a ream. The other 100 sheets make 25 papers. One hundred twenty-five from one ream.

WAYNE: Two reams would be 250 copies. It'll take almost 2 reams of paper.

MRS. JOHNSON: Now, how about the cost of 2 reams of paper at 95¢ and two reams of paper at 78¢?

FRANK: Just add them up, 95 and 95. Other one, the same way.

MRS. JOHNSON: Good, shall we do it that way?

JANET SUE: If it's finding 2 ninety-fives, I think you could multiply like finding 2 sevens, but the numbers are bigger than we've had.

MRS. JOHNSON: That's good thinking, Janet Sue, but right now adding is a good way. We'll know which method of publishing the paper is cheapest in just a minute. Of course, we have to add in the carbons or the stencils.

JANET SUE: When can we learn how to multiply with two numbers on top, Mrs. Johnson?

*   *   *   *   *   *   *

MRS. JOHNSON: Boys and girls, I think we need to devise some plan to help our newspaper writers spell the special words they need in their articles. All of us who aren't writing are glad to help, but I'm sure we spell some of the same words over and over for different people. If our newspaper is to go on for several issues, we may as well work out a system now. Do you have any ideas?

DONALD: The dictionary would help, but I can't read it.

ANNE: Neither can I!

FRANK: Could we make a dictionary that everyone could read?

MARTHA: Do you mean a big one for the whole class? I'll decorate the cover.

MRS. JOHNSON: Fine, Martha, but let's do a little planning first. How could it be done?

ALICE: We could make big pages out of heavy paper.

MRS. JOHNSON: Yes, but can you suggest any special plan for the pages?

PEGGY: They have to go A, B, C, D. We could have a page for A words, a page for B words, and so on.

MRS. JOHNSON: That seems sensible.

RONNIE: Yes, but I don't think we'll need pages for X or Z.

MRS. JOHNSON: Then what?

ROBERT: When someone needs a special newspaper word, you could print it on the right page. Then when someone else needed it, he could look and not have to ask.

ANNE: During newspaper writing time, we could hang all the pages around the room; then everyone could see them.

MRS. JOHNSON: A fine idea. Do we have some volunteers for getting the book ready? Martha has already offered to do the cover. Bill, do you have another idea?

BILL: Some of the words that people use over and over we ought to learn to spell. Like *newspaper*, *sports*, *weather*, and *program*. I almost know them already.

MRS. JOHNSON: I think you're right, Bill. We'll watch to see what words are most often needed and include them in our weekly spelling lists. Do you want to be on the committee with Martha, Anne, and Robert?

Experiences that develop skills related to the area of learning in social studies, unlike experiences with community resources, educational media, construction and processing, and reading, do not directly answer questions or solve problems identified by the children. These related skills are essential to the area of learning, however, because they facilitate pupils' search for solutions to group concerns, making possible the location and interpretation of data, the recording and reporting of information, thoughtful discussion of facts and ideas, and improvement in the quality of the problem solving that goes on in the area of learning.

Role of Related Skills
in the Area of Learning

The successful development of an area of learning is possible only when children have command of the skills essential to carrying out the plans they make. When the area of learning is concerned with real problems, it calls for the use of many skills.[1] Related skills in communication, in quantitative thinking, in critical thinking, and in group process play an important role in the area of learning. As children crystallize their concerns in the form of questions and problems, set about to gather the necessary information to meet these needs, and work together to carry out their plans, they use skills with real purpose. The reality of the problem that requires the use of related skills helps pupils to recognize their importance and to see a need for learning them.

These related skills are the tools and techniques children need to carry on the problem-solving activities of the area of learning. They are the means by which children accomplish their purposes and move ahead to new experiences. When children plan cooperatively with the teacher, they need group process skills; when they embark upon research to find answers to questions, they must know how to locate and evaluate information; when they make excursions into the community, the skills of speaking and listening are vital to communication with those whom they visit. These skills make it possible for children to participate effectively in direct experiences selected to solve problems and to develop understandings, attitudes, skills, and behaviors in social studies.

Some of the skills drawn into areas of learning are quite well developed in periods of the school day especially devoted to them. Although good teachers make an effort to relate these skills to real life, it is not always possible at the moment to find the appropriate situation in which to use

[1] For a thorough analysis of skills involved in problem solving in elementary-grade classroom situations, see John E. McGill, "Organizing the Social Studies Program," in *Social Studies for Children* (Washington, D.C.: Association for Childhood Education International, 1956), pp. 26–31.

the newly learned skill. The area of learning can enhance the values of these skills in children's eyes as the problems they are trying to solve require their use. The area of learning can provide the meaningful practice essential to developing facility in the use of skills. The following description of a first grade at work illustrates how skills facilitate problem-solving.

When there were signs on the school playground that tree surgeons were doing something very strange to an old willow that had been children's favorite climbing tree, the first grade was distressed. Heated discussion about the cutting of the tree followed the discovery and threatened to continue for the rest of the school day. The teacher, feeling that some action was called for, encouraged the children to find out more about how trees are cared for and protected; in the meantime, she learned that the favorite tree that had started the discussion would remain standing, at least for the present. A variety of experiences began to take shape; in each, related skills were used. A letter dictated to the teacher and copied from the chalkboard asked the municipal botanical garden for information about the protection of local trees. Careful printing of labels for the leaf and twig display further reinforced children's newly acquired writing skills. Skills in questioning and listening were practiced by a special committee delegated to interview the tree experts who were examining all the trees in the school neighborhood. Numbers became functional when stamps for letters were purchased and money was collected for a new tree to be planted near the schoolhouse. Many such skills already learned were called into service as pupils pursued their concern about the trees on their playground.

The area of learning also creates a need for learning new skills. Experienced teachers recognize that skills are most easily learned when there is a need for them and when they can be put to use immediately. When children have taken an important part in planning their social studies experiences and are vitally interested in translating their plans into actions, they recognize the importance of learning new skills. Children seldom ask, "Why do we have to?" The teacher almost never finds it necessary to say, "Someday you will need these skills." The children need them now in the area of learning. They are ready to learn skills that will help them achieve their purposes.

The first-grade boys and girls who were studying about the care of trees found that they needed new skills not yet part of their resources. A trip to the library for more books about trees introduced them to the card catalogue; a few of the more mature children were encouraged to help the librarian use it to locate new books. Learning to use the picture dictionary helped children do simple but independent reading, and learning to use the telephone properly became important when pupils decided to invite guests to the tree-planting ceremonies. New vocabulary began to appear—names of trees, parts of trees, and tools used by tree experts. In addition, the whole series of experiences emphasized new needs for knowing how to work together and how to solve problems. Although none of these related skills answered directly questions and problems identified by pupils, each one played an essential part in facilitating the planning and implementation of experiences directed toward learning more about trees and their protection.

Types of Related Skills
in the Area of Learning

The area of learning offers excellent opportunities for the development and reinforcement of basic skills, whether they are taught in social studies or in other periods in the school day. A variety of communication and number skills, as well as skills in critical thinking and group process, is essential to the development of problem-solving experiences planned by pupils and teacher (see Figure 10). In fact, skill development in social studies has been considered so important that the National Council for the Social Studies has in recent years devoted two complete yearbooks to their treatment.[2] Specific focus on these skills here may enlarge and extend the teacher's awareness of opportunities for their effective use.

COMMUNICATION SKILLS IN THE AREA OF LEARNING

In solving problems and answering questions *communication skills* are almost constantly in use. Communication begins in the initiation, where children identify their needs and problems and make plans to meet them, and continues throughout the series of experiences. Planning, investigating, sharing, recording, and evaluating can be fruitful experiences only when participants communicate adequately. Speaking and listening, reading, and research make major contributions to social studies; without them the area of learning could not be developed.

Skill in writing is needed in many phases of the area of learning. Effective writing comes only when the pupil has something to say and the skill with which to say it. Social studies provides the occasion and the content for many writing experiences, and the teacher makes available the necessary instruction and opportunities for practicing this skill.

The writing experiences of very young children are, of course, limited by skill in handwriting and spelling. Some children plan their writing with the teacher, dictate to him, and copy the product from chalkboard or chart. Other young children, with teacher assistance or the aid of the picture dictionary, begin to write on their own. Boys and girls who were finding

---

[2] Helen McCracken Carpenter (Ed.), *Skills in the Social Studies,* Twenty-fourth Yearbook of the National Council for the Social Studies (1953) and Helen McCracken Carpenter (Ed.), *Skill Development in Social Studies* (Thirty-third Yearbook of the National Council for the Social Studies; Washington, D.C.: National Education Association, 1963).

out what makes a house used their new writing skills in a variety of ways. They helped the teacher list behavior standards planned for their trip. They arranged and labeled with appropriate signs the samples of materials used in the building of a house not far from school. They wrote invitations to their families asking them to view the playhouse they had constructed; and they wrote thank-you notes to the architect, carpenter, plumber, and electrician who had explained the work on the new house nearby. They wrote a cooperative summary of their visit to see the new house. Through frequent use they learned to spell some new words—*house, wood, door, roof, paper, glass, saw,* and *stone.* All these experiences not only demonstrated to children the usefulness of writing, but reinforced incidentally the connection between reading and writing in communication.

Older children meet similar situations, but since they write more skillfully, they can match their own need for writing much more effectively than young children, who must depend upon adults for assistance. These more able pupils can stay with a writing task for a longer period of time, independently use their language arts textbooks as references when needed, and express ideas with greater freedom from the physical task of putting words on paper. Their greater maturity is evident in the experience of a fifth-grade group exploring the water-power resources of an important river in their local environment. These boys and girls wrote letters asking permission to visit the power station and dam and the local factories that used the electricity. They outlined important points from their background reading about the industries of the region. They took notes like seasoned reporters on their interviews with the government power commissioner, the foremen of factories, and parents who were factory workers. They printed their own charts of questions, standards for group work, and important vocabulary. They incorporated into their spelling lessons commonly used words from their study—*kilowatt, turbine, generator, horsepower, electricity, hydroelectric, conservation,* and others. Business letters, thank-you notes, and invitations they handled smoothly when needed instruction and guidance were provided. At times several language arts periods in succession were devoted to carrying on the writing activities essential to moving ahead in the area of learning. Such liaison between social studies and language arts strengthens learning in both areas.

At all levels teachers follow children's writing efforts with needed instruction or individual guidance. Generally speaking, the teacher does not interrupt a writing activity to insist on perfect sentence structure, punctuation, or spelling. He moves about quietly among the children, giving help where needed, spelling words for them, or suggesting a word or phrase that will move the writing forward. When children decide that some piece of writing—a poster, an invitation, a class summary for the reading table booklet, or a newspaper report—is to be shared with others, they begin the task of revision and polishing, drawing upon writing skills as the need for them arises.

Speaking and listening skills are equally important in the area of learning and are called into use almost constantly.[3] Because good speaking and good listening do not come about by chance, they are likely to be more highly motivated when pupils have something worthwhile to communicate and when someone wants to hear—in short, when exchanging ideas and information with other people will achieve some useful end. Because children vary greatly in their listening and speaking skills, the teacher has the responsibility for setting the stage for effective speaking and listening and for helping each child improve his skills. Note in the following example how an area of learning about newspapers provided the opportunity for development of useful skills.

Finding out how newspapers were made and how they help the community led one second grade into much purposeful speaking and listening. The teacher, realizing that each opportunity for cooperative planning emphasizes the need for effective use of skills in speaking and listening, helped children center their contributions carefully on the topics for discussion—how to answer the problems raised by the group, how to carry out the trip to the newspaper office, and how to make a newspaper in the classroom. The teacher then directed the attention of the pupils to careful evaluation of their discussions by asking such questions as these: Did everyone have an opportunity to speak? Did some boys and girls talk too much? Did each person listen carefully to those who were speaking? Were the decisions clearly understood by everyone? Interviews were thoroughly planned and practiced, too—what the newsboy would be asked, how to request old newspapers from the librarian, and how to interview businessmen about their use of newspapers. Children also considered ways of reporting back the information secured in the interview. Introductions for resource visitors were planned with attention to courtesy, intelligent questioning, and attentive listening. Opportunities like these help young children develop and practice useful skills in listening and speaking.

With maturity and practice, communication skills steadily improve. Intermediate-grade children often use these skills with great ease, writing letters and summaries, conducting interviews with confidence, making announcements about their activities to other groups, giving talks in assemblies for both adults and children, reporting on information and ideas, and introducing resource visitors to the classroom. Children who have many opportunities to practice communication skills in a variety of situations and in groups of varying kinds exercise these skills with poise and assurance.

Skills in the use of reference materials play a prominent role in the area

[3] Leland B. Jacobs, "Speaking and Listening," in Carpenter, *Skill Development in Social Studies*, pp. 131–147.

of learning. Upon facility in these skills depends the efficient and wise use of printed sources in solving problems and answering questions. Purposeful reading and successful search are impossible without effective control of skills involved in locating information, in reading critically, in selecting pertinent data, and in organizing information to be shared with other participants in the search. Conversely, the need to know is the best possible motivation for learning the skills of reference use.[4]

Location skills are obviously basic to the search for background information and for answers to questions. Skill in the use of index and table of contents facilitates the search for data in books and other printed materials. Children learn that although the table of contents lists only the titles of large divisions in the order in which they appear in the reading material, the index lists many topics in alphabetical order. The use of the index involves special skills in selecting key words to be searched for in the index, in locating words in alphabetical order, and in interpreting the information given, including, for older children, special symbols for illustrations and cross references. Using the index and the table of contents is a basic skill in the identification of useful materials.

Skills in locating information in references that arrange materials alphabetically must not be neglected. Children learn that the dictionary assists with the meaning, spelling, and pronunciation of new words. Skill in the use of the dictionary depends upon knowledge of the alphabet and ability to locate words listed in alphabetical order and upon skill in interpreting the various symbols, diacritical marks, and meanings. Children's encyclopedias are also arranged in alphabetical order, and pupils must learn the particular scheme each publisher uses to indicate the contents of the encyclopedia as well as the alphabetical arrangement of materials within the volume. Intermediate-grade children also learn to use the cumulative index that accompanies most encyclopedias. These indexes usually group together many references relating to a single topic and are useful to children who are making a thorough exploration of an area of content. Development of these special skills in locating information greatly improves pupils' use of alphabetized references.

Locating hard-to-find information in specialized references requires a knowledge of the special characteristics of each type of reference. Children become acquainted with almanacs, atlases, handbooks, government bulletins, newspapers, and magazines as need for them arises. Where can detailed map information be found? Using the atlas becomes practical when children know the arrangement of maps and tables and the symbols needed for their interpretation. What kinds of information are included in an almanac of

[4] Leo Fay, Thomas Horn, and Constance McCullough, *Improving Reading in Elementary Social Studies* (Washington, D.C.: National Council for the Social Studies, 1961), p. 43.

facts? Such volumes can be used successfully by intermediate-grade children after they have become familiar with the types of materials included, have learned how to use the detailed index, and have acquired the skills needed in reading the various tabular presentations. How can new books in the library be located? The card catalogue becomes the important tool in locating information, requiring not only a knowledge of alphabetical arrangement but also skills in locating books on the library shelves with the information supplied by the catalogue. Children may use many of these specialized references from time to time, each requiring skills that must be developed when the reference comes to the attention of the group. Since each reference has special characteristics, the teacher analyzes it carefully to make sure that pupils have the skills needed to use it.

Location skills include not only skills in selecting the appropriate reference but also skills in finding the exact information needed. Once the general location of references has been found, children must search out the specific details that will answer their questions. Finding this information involves skill in using headings and subheadings within a selection, followed by skill in skimming to locate pertinent details. Pupils and teachers together can discover the arrangement a particular author gives his material—how he uses titles to divide it, what special type is used for subtopics, or how to recognize the topic sentence of a paragraph. When children have clearly in mind the author's arrangement of his material and have located a likely portion for exploration, they are ready to skim from one topic sentence to another to find the paragraphs that must be read carefully.

Skill in reading with comprehension and speed is crucial to the search for information. Into service are now drawn the skills children have acquired in the developmental reading program, and the teacher facilitates their use by making sure that each child is reading at his ability level. He develops ahead of time new vocabulary that the pupils may meet in their reading and emphasizes the importance of reading pictures as well as words. He encourages children to read rapidly to get the general idea and then to reread for specific details if the material seems useful. To develop skills in comprehension, the teacher may provide study sheets that help pupils identify important information related to the problems or questions being studied.

Skill in critical evaluation of materials read to determine whether or not they are pertinent to the questions under consideration is essential in research. The teacher helps children to develop this skill by making sure that every pupil has clearly in mind the problem about which he is seeking information. He may say, "Before we begin our reading, let's make sure that we know about what we are going to read. Lowell, will you please read from the chart the questions that are checked? They are the ones we decided to try first. Will the rest of you please listen as Lowell reads?" When the questions are reviewed, the teacher may continue, "Which ones can you list, John, without looking at the chart? Who else can list them all? Close your eyes and say the questions over to yourself. If you can do this, then you are ready to start reading. You won't need to interrupt your study to refer to the chart again." With questions and problems in mind, pupils can read critically, accepting or rejecting information according to its relationship to these questions. Such skill prevents aimless and wasteful reading.

Skill in finding key sentences and summary statements contributes greatly to the development of comprehension. Many writers for children, keeping children's needs and abilities in mind when they write, put the main idea of each paragraph in a topic sentence at the beginning of the paragraph or in a summary statement at the end. Although paragraphs do not always follow this pattern, children can practice finding out whether or not the important ideas are given in either of these ways. When children find, however, that some writers depend on the reader's making his own summary statements, practice in reading and summarizing paragraphs from various kinds of materials can develop skill in extracting the main ideas. Furthermore, children may discover that paragraphs in a piece of writing serve different purposes; some are introductory, some informational, and some illustrative. Skill in identifying important ideas in the reading material is clearly useful in the research pupils do.

Skill in organizing information for later use becomes necessary as children read widely and begin to relate what they read to their problems and questions. It is usually economical for elementary school children to organize information in terms of the questions that motivate the reading. Information from several references should be brought together whenever possible. The teacher may assist by posting the questions where they can be plainly seen or by giving older children their own copies of the questions, with adequate space for notes. Teacher and children can then plan ways to organize information for the various types of questions. For example, if the question asks for a process—How is wheat made into flour?—the pupils will probably decide to list the steps in the process. If the question involves a choice—What kind of boat was the most useful for carrying freight on the Mississippi?—pupils may organize information in terms of the advantages and disadvantages of each alternative. If historical events make up the content of an answer—How was the airplane invented?—chronological order will be the appropriate approach to organization. If a community problem is under consideration, information may be given as a series of facts describing the present situation and emphasizing cause-and-effect relationships. Information to answer a question that implies a comparison or contrast—How did Plains Indians and other Indians differ in their ways of living?—will probably be organized in terms of similarities or differences. Most questions will suggest a useful organization. Knowing how to select and organize relevant information in terms of the question is an important skill that elementary school children should begin to acquire.[5]

Skill in taking notes to record significant information about a question or problem is also useful in all simple research in social studies. Very young children, of course, do not take extensive notes, but they can help the teacher record key words to remind them of the answers to questions when discussion time comes. Such note taking is often a cooperative undertaking in the early primary grades. Intermediate-grade children, however, can learn efficient and economical ways of recording information they will need when they share facts and information with each other. Through planned instruction children learn that note taking should come after careful study of a portion of the reading and not during the reading itself, that the purpose of the note is to recall the author's idea and not to record it in detail, that note taking is useful only when one plans to use the ideas later. Intermediate-grade boys and girls take their first notes by writing key words needed to recall ideas for later discussion. For example, to record how a log cabin was built the pupil learns to write the key points in as few words as possible—*logs cut, rolled to site, cut to length, notched, lifted into place.* To answer the question: How can we communicate across oceans? children list such words as *television, telephone, radio,* and *cable.* Efficient note taking of this kind facilitates ready recall of information and does not impede wide reading.

Skill in outlining helps pupils organize facts and information about a problem or question. Teachers usually help pupils recognize the values of this method of taking notes by encouraging them to organize their questions and problems in outline form and to complete the outline with words, phrases, or sentences that suggest the answers to the questions. For example,

I. Where is most of our steel produced?
   A. Pennsylvania.
   B.
   C.
II. Why is steel such a useful metal?
   A. It can be made into many shapes.
   B. It is very strong.
   C.
   D.

As children acquire skill in outlining, they can select and use key sentences from paragraphs as the topics of the outline and complete the outline of the paragraph by adding the significant details. This method of taking notes becomes increasingly useful as children read more extensively and feel the need for some record of their reading to assist in recall.

[5] Alice Eikenberry and Ruth Ellsworth, "Organizing and Evaluating Information," in Carpenter, *Skill Development in Social Studies,* pp. 77–80.

Skill in reading and interpreting maps facilitates the answering of many of the questions that are the objects of children's research in the area of learning. Skills in reading maps must be directly taught and are most successfully developed when maps are needed by children in their daily experiences.[6] Young children learn what a map is and how to interpret very simple symbols. Older children need skill in interpreting map symbols, in comparing maps of different locales, in seeing relationships between two or more maps, and in constructing maps of various kinds. Planned instruction in these skills is appropriate and essential when children's questions lead them to maps for information.

In the primary grades, development of a sense of direction—right, left, east, west, north, and south—is basic to finding direction later on a map. Recognition of the globe as a model of the earth and awareness that the places people talk about can be located on maps and globes are also important in the readiness program. Ability to portray with blocks and later with pictures on paper locational relationships and surface features of places in their environment is usually a natural outgrowth of block play and opportunities to illustrate where things happen. As pupils move into the middle grades, more formal attention is given to building map and globe skills. Here children are exposed to simple maps from which they can generalize about uses of various symbols; they begin to see relationships between maps and globes; they notice the east-west and north-south lines on maps and globes; they learn to find locations they are encountering in their experiences and to read maps in preparation for home and school trips.

Through the middle grades and in the upper grades, children's skill in using maps and globes is considerably extended. Not only do children expand their knowledge of map symbols; they also learn to use the map legend and to interpret map colors. Their knowledge of direction grows to include the in-between directions and direction in relation to the poles and the equator. They use grid systems for locating places and thus develop readiness for a later study of latitude and longitude. They are using outline maps more frequently and continuing to draw or construct maps of their own experiences or those needed in group or individual reports. Sixth-grade pupils carry on from there, learning to use the scale of miles to measure distance, exploring the meaning and use of latitude and longitude, tracing great-circle routes, and using maps increasingly for historical as well as geographical purposes. These boys and girls are usually able to compare maps showing related data, to explore types of map projection, and to make relief maps. And as children's skill in using maps and globes

[6] Lorrin Kennamer, "Developing a Sense of Place and Space," in Carpenter, *Skill Development in Social Studies*, pp. 148–170.

improves, their map vocabularies continue to grow and the meanings of geographical terms deepen.

Skill in the interpretation of graphic materials is a study skill that opens up many sources of data useful in problem solving, but it is important to remember that children do not naturally turn to graphs and charts as sources of information. They must be taught to use them and encouraged to do so.[7] Children need to ask several questions as they select graphs and charts to use in problem solving. Which of our questions or problems will this graph or diagram help us answer? What is the graph or diagram trying to show us? What is the meaning of each symbol or part of the drawing?

At this point pupils are ready to analyze critically the content of the graph, chart, or diagram tentatively chosen for use. Was the information prepared by a reliable individual or group? Can the information be confirmed by other sources? Is all the information related to our purpose? Is this information all we need in order to solve our problem?[8] The simplicity or complexity of the graphic aid as well as the children's maturity will determine what use can be made of the resource. Children will need planned instruction to help them interpret accurately information graphically presented.

Clearly, skills in using reference materials are an integral part of problem solving in social studies. Without them children are limited to the resources of a single textbook. Knowing how to locate and select useful information, how to read with comprehension, how to organize information, and how to use various graphic aids gives pupils confidence in their ability to carry out the search for answers to their questions.

SKILLS OF QUANTITATIVE THINKING

Pupils often need *skills of quantitative thinking* in the area of learning, especially those skills involved in using whole numbers, fractions, decimals, and in measuring, using money, and making graphic representations of data. In most schools, these skills, like communication skills, are developed systematically in periods especially set aside for them in the school day. It is through social studies and other areas of the curriculum, however, that mathematical ideas and processes can function as they do in real life. Skills in the use of numbers can be reinforced through the problem-solving activities of the area of learning.[9]

Skills in the use of whole numbers are called into use frequently in the development of the area of learning. Beginners make very simple uses

---

[7] Fay, Horn, and McCullough, p. 33.

[8] George H. McCune and Neville Pearson, "Interpreting Materials Presented in Graphic Form," in Carpenter, *Skill Development in Social Studies*, pp. 211–214.

[9] Lavone Hanna, Gladys L. Potter, and Neva Hagaman, *Unit Teaching in the Elementary School* (rev. ed.; New York: Holt, Rinehart and Winston, Inc., 1963), pp. 288–292.

of numbers in their school activities. Practical counting in a primary room was motivated by questions like these: How does a garden grow? How many pennies are in our garden fund? How many kinds of seeds shall we buy? How much will be spend for each kind? How many children will do the buying? How many hoes will be needed? How long is the garden plot? How many pumpkin seeds to each hill? In addition to needs for counting, there were numbers to be read and written—the price of the seeds, the directions for planting, the list of purchases made, the number of tools needed, and the schedule for work in the garden. There were simple computations, too, requiring the use of old knowledge whenever a new problem involved an unfamiliar process. Because they could not multiply, these young children added or counted to find the cost of several packages of seeds of like cost. Because they could not yet divide, they subtracted over and over to find out how many work groups of three there were in the room. They were discovering for themselves that skill in the use of whole numbers plays an important part in putting project plans into action.

Intermediate-grade children use skills with whole numbers in similar but more mature ways. They figure the costs of their projects, estimate the timing of a program, follow intricate directions for constructing and processing, read and interpret large numbers given in their social studies reading, and make financial arrangements for trips of various kinds. Because most children at this level have whole-number operations rather well in hand, continual use of these skills in social studies provides highly meaningful practice.

Skills in the use of fractions are often required in a variety of social studies activities. These experiences provide the setting and create the need for knowing more about fractions. Young children often make their first acquaintance with fractions in cooking activities—baking cookies for a tea party, churning butter, or mixing a fruit drink. Later they meet new needs for using fractions as they sew, build, illustrate, repair, and divide. Older pupils use both common and decimal fractions in comparing data, in making scale graphs, in making purchases, in measuring, and in developing a variety of construction and processing activities. Children use skills in fractions in many practical ways in problem solving.

Skills in handling money are reinforced by their use in a variety of social studies experiences. Many of the number experiences already described involve these skills. There are so many things to buy in carrying out projects to solve problems—seeds for the garden, a tree to plant in the schoolyard, food for the classroom pet, a booklet from the park conservatory, and films for the trip, as well as room supplies from the school bookstore. Primary-grade children soon learn that certain coins are equivalent to others, that some bigger coins are worth less than some smaller ones, and that it is important to handle money carefully. Older children manage room accounts with great confidence, relieving the teacher of unnecessary work and at the same time gaining valuable experiences in using money properly.

Skill in measurement is useful in almost all construction and processing experiences in social studies. Laying out maps, creating models and dioramas, building equipment, processing foods, and sewing require skill in measuring. Young children learn to use the ruler, the yardstick, and simple liquid measures as they measure the paper needed for a mural, the milk for a pudding, the roof for the playhouse, the oilcloth for a display table, or the distance between rows of vegetables in the garden. They begin to understand that measurement is an essential daily activity and that standard measures help them to build and construct accurately. As children mature, their use of measures is extended to more intricate operations, to building an accurate model of a log cabin, to drawing to scale a map of conservation projects, to following pioneer cooking recipes, to making a time line to show events in American history, or to keeping accurate temperature records. With every new situation children see more clearly the practical need for tables of measure and of measuring instruments and the importance of skill in using them.

Skill in representing numerical data graphically facilitates the organization of social studies information and requires a variety of number skills. Selecting the type of graph or chart appropriate to the data and to the purpose for which it is to be used is very important. Time lines are used to show historical events in sequence; circle graphs show percentages clearly; picture or bar graphs can show numerical comparisons and relationships effectively; tables are used to compare numerical data as well as other information. When the proper graphic form is chosen, children may convert the information they have collected to the form needed for the representation. Additional skills are called into use as pupils divide time lines into appropriate units of time, divide circles to show various portions to be allotted each item, select symbols or lines or bars to represent units on the graphs, or put into simple table or chart form various kinds of quantitative information. Such activities are almost certain to improve children's skill in thinking mathematically.[10]

Many skills of quantitative thinking are needed in the area of learning. The need for interpreting ideas of number and for computing, measuring, and handling money appears again and again. When children can use this knowledge of number to solve problems in social studies, they have valuable incentives for perfecting these mathematical skills.

GROUP PROCESS SKILLS IN THE AREA
OF LEARNING

Group process skills are those skills of working together that make possible the identification and cooperative solution of problems. Because

[10] Fay, Horn, and McCullough, p. 33.

the area of learning is centered on problems that are significant to children, the skills of group process are essential to its development. These skills permeate every aspect of children's study and exploration in social studies; and although they are given special consideration at this point, they are never practiced apart from a real problem-solving situation. The group process skills that characterize the vital area of learning are many—skills in cooperative planning, in group work, in reporting and discussion, and in evaluation.

Skills in cooperative planning are essential to good group process. The important role of cooperative planning in the area of learning has already been emphasized at length in an earlier part of this book. It is sufficient to say here that cooperative planning enables children to move purposefully from one experience to another in pursuit of their goals; and to emphasize that skills in cooperative planning—identifying problems and planning ways to solve them, considering and evaluating the methods that are proposed, and keeping records of plans and decisions—are learned only through participating in the planning experience. There is no other way to acquire these essential skills.

Skill in group work, an equally important feature of good group process, grows naturally out of children's experiences in cooperative planning. As children plan how they will answer questions and solve problems, they begin to think in terms of small-group responsibilities. Although many experiences in social studies are total-group experiences or individual projects, working in small groups develops some skills that cannot be achieved in any other way. Group work serves such important purposes in social studies that attention to essential skills cannot be overlooked.

Skills in group work can be developed only through group work experiences. Each committee needs to know how to organize itself for work, to choose leaders, to locate materials, and to find a place to work. Each committee member needs to understand fully the responsibilities of each member of his group, some of whom may have the special roles of chairman or secretary. When the group is ready to work, it first checks the agreed-upon plan and then embarks upon its execution. The teacher moves about from one group to another, helping where difficulties arise—smoothing out arguments, locating better information, suggesting a new technique, or helping an individual play his part adequately. Later evaluation of the process will help children to improve their group work skills.

Skills in reporting and discussion are also an integral part of group process. Children cannot function as a group unless they effectively share information, ideas, and experiences that will help them to make progress toward problem solving. When small groups or individuals complete tasks they have assumed for the larger class group or because of a special individual interest, they share the results of their efforts through discussion and reporting, relating their contribution to the work of the class group and subjecting it willingly to constructive evaluation. These sharing sessions are successful only when children control skills in reporting and discussion.[11]

Participation in group discussion involves a number of specific skills. Each participant must be able to hold in mind the question or topic being considered, to select information appropriate to it, and to stay on the subject. If he has organized his contribution well, he is ready with materials he may want to use in the discussion—quotations, maps, diagrams, or pictures. He is aware of other children in the group, recognizing their right to contribute also and listening to them. He knows how to disagree politely and how to state an opinion forcefully but tactfully. He is ready to prove a point with facts and to concede when others have proven theirs. Occasionally children need to analyze their discussion periods, testing them against such standards as these developed by a fifth-grade group:

CHARACTERISTICS OF A GOOD DISCUSSION

1. The purpose of the discussion is clear to everyone.
2. All group members have opportunities to take part.
3. Members support their contributions with evidence.
4. The ideas of all group members are considered.
5. When necessary, ideas are courteously challenged.
6. Contributions are evaluated in terms of the purpose of the discussion.
7. The discussion is summarized by the group.

The teacher, of course, plays a key role in helping pupils acquire skill in discussion. Because he often serves as leader he is alert to the direction the discussion is taking, and he encourages pupils to keep to the point and to be accurate and thorough in their contributions.[12]

Making committee reports, often an effective way of sharing information, requires further skills in organization and presentation. These committee reports may be given in several ways. Sometimes the chairman of the committee introduces a series of speakers, each of whom discusses one aspect of the problem; sometimes he serves as a moderator who keeps the free discussion moving from one committee member to another. Such reporting requires skills that are, of course, more appropriate for intermediate-grade than for primary-grade children, and must be painstakingly developed.

Among the skills most frequently needed in making individual or small-group reports are those that relate to organizing the report. Pupils need to develop skill in selecting the method of presentation most appropriate to the material to be presented, with special attention to selection of the

---

[11] Edith P. Merritt, *Working with Children in Social Studies* (Belmont, Calif.: Wadsworth Publishing Company, Inc., 1961), p. 191.

[12] James B. Burr, Lowry W. Harding, and Leland B. Jacobs, *Student Teaching in the Elementary School* (New York: Appleton-Century-Crofts, Inc., 1958), pp. 156–161.

most important ideas to be included. They need skill in the use of illustrations that will make the report more interesting or more easily understood. They need practice in planning the presentation so that each person involved will know what his role is to be. They need to develop a sense of timing so that what they plan to do will easily fit the period scheduled for reporting.

Children must also develop skill in the presentation of reports, for a well-organized report can be ruined by lack of skill in communicating it to others. The following check list, developed by a group of intermediate-grade boys and girls, identifies the several skills needed in oral reporting and can be adapted to both individual and group presentations.

CHECK LIST FOR EVALUATING ORAL REPORTS

1. Did the reporter speak clearly and distinctly?
2. Did he pronounce words correctly?
3. Did he speak without hesitating?
4. Did he look at his audience as he spoke?
5. Did he show an interest in his subject?
6. Did he make the purpose of the report clear?
7. Did the report seem to be well organized?
8. Did the report have an interesting beginning?
9. Did the report have an interesting close?
10. Were illustrations well chosen?
11. Was the audience attentive to the report?

The evaluation of oral reports by the class group usually results in improvement of skills in this facet of group process. Only practice will bring spontaneity and poise in this important phase of problem-solving activity.

Skill in evaluation makes it possible for children to appraise their success in achieving good group process. Such evaluation relies upon skills of critical analysis as pupils look at what they have done, asking certain pertinent questions. Were our purposes clear? Was our work plan effective? What problems did we encounter in working together? Can we improve our group work in some way? Skill in evaluation helps children apply group standards they have set and to anticipate problems that may arise in future group work. Skill in self-evaluation is also vital. It helps to improve individual contributions to the work of the group, enabling pupils seriously to appraise their ability to assume responsibility, to carry a task through to completion, and to use materials and equipment successfully.

Group process skills are of fundamental importance in the area of learning. Skills in cooperative planning, in group work, in discussion and reporting, and in evaluation make it possible for children to participate successfully in group activities and to practice democratic behavior. Because social studies purposes to help children learn the skills of democratic group living, practice in the use of group process skills assumes major importance in the elementary school social studies program.

SKILLS OF CRITICAL THINKING IN THE AREA
OF LEARNING

Skills of critical thinking are among the most crucial of all related skills, for critical thinking—that thinking which leads to discriminating and cautious judgment—is an integral part of the problem-solving process. In fact, problem solving depends for its success upon certain related skills in critical thinking, skills that can be identified, learned, and practiced.[13]

What does the critical thinker do? First of all, he evaluates the sources from which he secures the information he needs in problem solving. He tests it by asking certain evaluative questions. Did the writer or speaker have firsthand knowledge of his subject? Did he have the training necessary to make him an accurate observer? Is the information clearly presented? Is it free from bias or prejudice? Are there flagrant departures from obvious truth? Although skill in evaluating sources of information is difficult to acquire, continual practice in applying standards of accuracy and objectivity to selected materials helps children become more keenly aware of at least the more obvious violations.

From this accurate, acceptable information the critical thinker draws justifiable conclusions. Although children reach many conclusions in the course of their problem-solving experiences, the quality of those conclusions depends, of course, upon the nature and extent of the evidence from which they are derived. What is this skill of formulating reliable conclusions? It is the ability to judge the applicability of information to a major idea; it is the ability to see persistent relationships. As children gather data they sometimes try to fit fact to fact to see the pattern the facts make; this pattern, if it is continuing, may suggest some tentative conclusions. At other times, without conscious effort on the part of the learner, the facts begin to develop a pattern, a point of view, or a conclusion; at still other times, the teacher suggests some possible hypotheses to which children may try to relate the information they are gathering.

Once tentative conclusions are made, children and teacher review the information upon which conclusions are drawn, making sure that they have made the best possible use of available sources and that they have not drawn a more sweeping conclusion than the information warrants. With maturity children begin to recognize that conclusions are never final and that when tested in experience they may need drastic alteration or may be discarded altogether. Moreover, skill in drawing conclusions is improved and refined only when opportunity for its use is provided.

Skills of critical thinking are indispensable to the problem-solving process. Although critical thinking is vital at every stage of this process from

[13] Isidore Starr, "The Nature of Critical Thinking and Its Application in the Social Studies," in Carpenter, *Skill Development in Social Studies*, p. 35.

identification of the problem to decisions about its solution, the skills that require particular attention are those involving the critical analysis of information and those leading to the formulation of reliable conclusions based on that information. No effective resolution to a problem can be achieved without these special skills.[14]

Planning for the Development of Related Skills

Planning for the development of related skills is the teacher's responsibility, for he alone can sense the opportune moment when each skill becomes essential to the progress of the area of learning and to the problem-solving process. The teacher must be resourceful in identifying those skills that pupils need and in helping children reach the desired level of efficiency in their use.

IDENTIFYING NEEDED SKILLS

Skills needed in the area of learning are identified in several ways. Cooperative planning, for example, usually points up the need for a variety of related skills. When children are planning committee activities and responsibilities, the skills of group leadership and group membership must be identified and discussed. When they are planning to locate materials to answer questions and to solve problems, their own skills in simple research must be evaluated and if necessary extended and improved. As children look ahead to sharing and reporting information, they may find that they need help in preparing graphic materials or in writing notes from which they can speak to the group. Because both individual research and group work depend upon children's effective use of skills, every planning session must give some attention to skills needed and to ways in which new skills may be acquired. Every planning session considers not only what action is to be taken but also what skills are needed in order to carry it out.

Pupil achievement in a variety of situations clarifies needs for essential skills. In a school day that frees the teacher to observe children as they work in groups, as they make plans and carry them out, and as they participate in a variety of experiences, the teacher has many opportunities to study children's need for skills. While he moves about during the construction period, he notes that some children do not handle tools well enough to enjoy the work they are trying to do or that others are making serious errors in measurement that will ruin their models and dioramas. Another small group may be experiencing difficulties in following written directions or in locating information in the encyclopedia. The teacher notes

[14] Starr, pp. 40–42.

these inadequacies and makes plans to eliminate them. Through observation of pupils at work he can identify needs for skills, needs that otherwise might not be apparent.

Children themselves often make known to adults their needs for skills. "Let's ask Mr. Doyle in the shop how to fasten the corners of the rabbit cage," suggests Dick. "Miss Adams, I can't make the roof of this barn go back into my picture. What'll I do?" moans Shirley. "Too many words to spell," complains Harry. "I wish I could be a good group leader like Steven. Nobody will do what I say," wails Jack. Because ability to use skills will help children feel secure and successful in the group, they are usually alert to their own needs and ready to seek assistance. They want to do things properly. To know how is important at all ages. When teachers and other adults listen to children and observe them thoughtfully, they can readily discover pupils' needs for related skills.

DEVELOPING NEEDED SKILLS

When the need for related skills is revealed through discussion or pupil achievement or by individual pupils themselves, the teacher must help children make plans for developing the skills they cannot yet command. New skills may be developed in several ways. When the need that develops is a personal one or pertinent for only a small group, the teacher may assist those who need the skill to acquire it. When the need for a particular skill is widespread in the group, helping individuals may be unprofitable in terms of time and energy. If the group as a whole can learn a new skill or improve an old one with satisfying results, the teacher must decide whether to develop the skill at the exact moment the need for it arises or to postpone the teaching or practice for the sake of leaving unbroken the continuity of the social studies experience. The extent and urgency of the need will help the teacher decide how best to meet it.

Some skills are developed individually or with small groups as need arises. When the teacher does not think it wise to interrupt the entire class to teach a skill and to provide for its practice, he helps children who need a particular skill at that time to develop it. He may guide a small group in the construction of a circle graph, helping them develop principles they can later share with other children. A committee group that seems to be having difficulty assuming responsibilities can pause for a time to work out with the teacher better techniques for getting its work done. If the map reading an individual is doing is handicapped by lack of an understanding of the scale of miles, the teacher can give special help, always trying to make sure that the child has the ideas well enough in mind to practice effectively by himself. The boy or girl who recognizes that the spelling in his last written summary was unsatisfactory can discover correct spellings with the aid of the dictionary. The children who obviously have forgotten how to write a business letter can be directed to use their language arts textbook as a resource in locating and eliminating errors in form. Children who see a real need for a skill are usually eager to learn and to practice it.

Increasingly in the future programed learning may be of assistance in helping individual or small groups learn and practice skills in which they are deficient or for which the area of learning points up a need. Although the number of programs in social studies and related skills is not yet large, several interesting ones that intend to develop map-reading skills needed in the upper elementary grades are showing the direction in which this type of individual instruction is moving.[15] Of course, as more and more programs are developed in various skill areas, criteria for evaluating format and content will become imperative. Essentially teachers will need to be aware of authorship, accuracy, pattern of teaching, and, finally, the contribution a program can make to the improvement of particular skills.[16]

Some skills are developed as a part of the social studies experience. If the identified skill is essential to moving forward in the area of learning, then the group has no choice but to take time out to become proficient in it. For example, if a discussion about differences in climate between west coast and inland states requires the reading of rainfall and temperature maps, it does very little good to continue the discussion until skill in reading these maps has been acquired. "Children, perhaps we'd better stop here to find out more about using these maps that have been brought in by Janet's committee. What do we know already about maps? Yes, we know the directions on the map. We can recognize each of the states on this outline map. We know that the information in the corner is the legend. Good, we know some things about maps. What is new? Of course, the information in the legend is different from our wall maps. What does it tell us? How are these rainfall areas shown on the map? Who can find the states that have the heaviest rainfall in April and May? What kind of temperature do these states have at this same time of year?" And on the questioning goes, helping children learn by easy steps how to read these specialized maps and ultimately to see relationships between them. The comparison of regions the pupils are trying to make is pointless without the data that perhaps have been made available in no other way. The discussion cannot proceed without the development of this particular skill at the time it is needed.

Group process skills usually are developed as part of the social studies experience rather than at another time in the school day. "Before we begin our discussion of oil resources," the teacher begins, "do we need to think about our last discussion session and remember some of the problems we encountered? Yes, our biggest problem was staying on the subject, wasn't

---

[15] *Maps—How to Read Them* (315 frames, sixth grade); *Latitude and Longitude* (380 frames, sixth grade) (Chicago: Coronet Instructional Films).

[16] Leonard W. Ingraham, "Programed Instructional Materials in Social Studies: 1963," *Social Education* (January, 1964), pp. 15–16.

it? Who has a suggestion that may help us develop this important skill?"
The pupils propose these ideas for a wall chart:

FIRST AID FOR STAYING ON THE SUBJECT

1. Be sure you know what topic is being discussed.
2. If the topic is not clear, ask to have it repeated.
3. Listen to the contribution of each person.
4. Do not repeat what someone says unless you wish to challenge it or add to it.
5. Have pictures and materials you want to quote ready before the discussion begins.
6. Don't introduce another topic until the group decides to change the subject.

A follow-up discussion may serve as practice in observing these suggestions. Children may evaluate their own skill and that of others by stopping now and then during the period to ask, "How are we doing?" Then the list is referred to in later discussions until children have reached a level of skill commensurate with their maturity. This group process skill, like many others, can be developed best as a part of the area of learning.

Some skills are developed through special instruction in appropriate curriculum areas. If a needed skill is identified but is not immediately essential to the experience in progress, its development can be safely delayed to later language arts, mathematics, or crafts periods, as the case may be. Regular instructional periods are usually strengthened when they are used frequently to develop skills needed in social studies; in such lessons children can then see the close relationship between a skill and its functional use.

Quite often the regular reading period may be used to develop skill in reading social studies materials. The social studies textbook in the hands of each pupil in the group can be a useful tool as children practice using the index to find specific information about a given topic, skimming to find pertinent information on a particular page, or reading and summarizing the main idea of a paragraph. Learning to take notes became the objective of one group of children who found that lack of skill in this technique hindered effective sharing of information with others in the group. After the pupils decided on procedure—to read the paragraph carefully, to identify the important points, to reread to check the points once again, to select the important ideas, and to choose key words to recall these important ideas—they worked together practicing with one paragraph after another in the textbook. More practice periods later on helped children improve and maintain their skill.[17]

Following a series of community experiences, one group decided to write thank-you notes to several persons and groups. Because children had found adults friendly and helpful, they wanted to do more than to write a per-

[17] David L. Tavel, "The Textbook and Skill Development," *Social Education* (December, 1961), pp. 403–404.

functory note of thanks. They felt that those who had been gracious to them deserved something more. They asked, "How can we write a thank-you note that not only expresses our appreciation but also tells how we really feel about our excursions?" The language arts periods during the next few days seemed to be the logical time to examine samples of thank-you notes in textbooks, to suggest interesting content, to discuss kinds of expressions that would be appropriate, and to make sure of the mechanics of note writing. With real adults to communicate with, children's motivations and incentives were deepened and the results of their efforts sincere and charming.

As teachers of social studies become more and more aware of the importance of skills to the success of the problem-solving process, there is a definite trend toward planning for and implementing a comprehensive program for skill development—always within the framework of pupil needs in the area of learning. Such a planned program provides a vertical gradation of skills in their ascending difficulty and makes possible also the horizontal use of the skills throughout the school day.[18] It does not, however, negate the learning of skills as previously suggested here; it simply precludes the omission of important skills that may have escaped the notice of the teacher.

In all these ways, skills related to social studies are developed. Whether the skills are taught as a part of the area of learning and through instruction in appropriate curriculum areas or are taught to individuals and small groups only as needed, the process of development becomes a vital part of problem solving. Teachers cannot discount the fact that skills are learned most effectively in situations that call for their use; they are learned most efficiently when they are needed in the development of the area of learning.

QUESTIONS FOR DISCUSSION

As the focal point for discussion use the dialogue that introduces this chapter.

1. What related skills were being developed in this situation?
2. To what extent were these skills essential to the progress of the area of learning?
3. In what ways will these activities lead to new experiences with skills?

SUGGESTIONS FOR CONSTRUCTING
A RESOURCE UNIT

Analyze each of the problem-solving experiences you have planned and note the skills related to it. Identify and describe appropriate related experiences that will reinforce or develop these skills. Use the following questions as guides in describing each experience:

---

[18] Dorothy McClure Fraser and Eunice Johns, "Developing a Program for the Effective Learning of Skills," in Carpenter, *Skill Development in Social Studies*, pp. 296–309.

1. What skill or skills—reading, writing, speaking, listening, or quantitative thinking—does the related experience reinforce or develop?
2. What is the purpose of the experience; that is, how does it relate to the problem-solving experience it is designed to reinforce or develop?
3. By what procedure will the skill be reinforced or developed?
4. What materials or resources are needed to carry out the related experience?

See the resource unit in the appendix for an example of an arrangement of experiences that illustrates the relationship between problem-solving experiences and skill-developing experiences.

11

Culminating
an Area of Learning

MRS. JOHNSON: Several weeks have passed since we began to work on our problem about the effect of communication on community living. Now it's time for us to take stock of the information you've obtained through the searching activities we've carried on these past weeks. In other words, it's time to organize and summarize our information.

JACK: If you ask me, we've found out enough about communication to fill a book.

MRS. JOHNSON: Indeed, a book of our own that pulls together what we've found might be a very workable way to organize our information about communication and community living. Does anyone else have other suggestions?

BARBARA ANN: We could make a bulletin board display of the reports we wrote about the different kinds of communication.

JANET SUE: And we could illustrate our reports with pictures of the many kinds of communication there are.

MARTHA: Why stop with just a bulletin board? Why not a lot of displays —a whole exhibit?

MRS. JOHNSON: An exhibit of what, Martha?

MARTHA: What we've found out about communication. Janet Sue's pictures about the pony express. The telegraph set the boys made. We've a lot of things for an exhibit.

MRS. JOHNSON: So we have, but our problem today is to take stock of our information and to organize it. Let's start with communication devices used in a community. Patricia, can you start us off?

PATRICIA: We found out that there are many kinds and that each one is used for different purposes. Shall I name the kinds and their uses?

MRS. JOHNSON: You don't need to name them, now that you've reached a conclusion about them, do you?

JACK: Going back to the book idea. We could collect our notes about communication devices and the ways they are used and make them into a book or make a chapter in a book. The main idea would be to put together information that shows how many communication devices there are and how many ways they're used.

WAYNE: And another thing we found out was how the telephone brings people everywhere closer together.

MARY: Why not have imaginary telephone conversations between many kinds of people in different parts of the world to show that the telephone makes our world smaller because it makes it possible for people to communicate over long distances, and tape it. I have some good ideas for conversations.

BILL: So have I. How about my dad calling from a meeting on the East Coast to wish me a happy birthday? And how about the President calling the FBI in a big city to tell them personally he wants more action on the spy case they're working on?

ANDY: Let's not tape the conversations. Let's act them out. A doctor in another country could call one of our big drug companies to get a special drug sent by plane for someone with a rare disease.

JACK: A couple of big business tycoons could be talking about a million-dollar deal.

BILL: That sounds like you've been watching too much TV.

JACK: TV or not, businessmen are always calling someone faraway to talk business.

BARBARA ANN: I'll never forget the news item we read about the people in Alaska being the talkingest people in the world. I'll bet many people there feel they know each other by their voices even if they never meet.

MRS. JOHNSON: We can pursue Mary's suggestion about telephone conversations more fully later on. Let's use the remainder of our time this morning in trying to identify the understandings or big ideas to be derived from the information we've discovered about communication. We can then concentrate on ways to show the relationship between the understanding we have reached and the information we used to reach it. We've identified two big ideas. One, there are many kinds of communication devices used for different purposes. The other, improved methods of communication—you used the telephone as an example—have brought people everywhere closer together. What other big ideas can we draw from answers to our problems about communication?

RONNIE: There's the one about all of the communication workers.

MRS. JOHNSON: Can you state it as an understanding?

RONNIE: Hmm—I'll try. It takes many kinds of people doing many different kinds of work to keep our communication systems working.

MRS. JOHNSON: Very well said. Another?

JANET SUE: One about the early days of our country. Since there were only a few communication devices like mail when our country was first settled, it was difficult for people to communicate with each other.

MRS. JOHNSON: Good. And another important idea we want to remember has to do with the importance of science in communication. But it's time for recess so we'll have to postpone our discussion until tomorrow. In the meantime think ahead to the other understandings to be identified.

JACK: Before we stop, Mrs. Johnson, I'd like to say something. Couldn't we invite our parents to see what we have done? After we pull everything together, I mean.

MRS. JOHNSON: I should think so. At least we can give it serious thought. Recess time now!

.   .   .   .   .   .

JACK: We're glad you could come to our communication fair, Mr. Anderson. We're so proud of it that we want many people to see it. The numbers of all the exhibits are on this sheet here. We made a sheet for every visitor.

MR. ANDERSON: A guide to your exhibits! Now that's a good way to help us get around to see things.

JACK: Is there anything special about communication you'd like to see, Mr. Anderson? Or would you rather just look around? One of the guides will be glad to explain things to you.

MR. ANDERSON: Why don't I start here by the door? This chart about kinds of communication looks interesting. Quite a list. I didn't realize there were so many.

JACK: We made that chart when we began to study about communication. It helped us start on the things you see here today. We put it by the door because we thought it would give people an idea of what the fair is about. Here's Mr. Sweeney. You know Mr. Anderson, don't you, Mr. Sweeney?

MR. SWEENEY: How are you, Jim? Did you just get here? You want to be sure to see the children working on their newspaper. They'll probably corner you for an interview about what you think of this fair. They say they are writing a news story about it. Look at those girls signaling with flags! Some of the signals are ones we used on my ship during the war. Excuse me, I'm going to ask them some questions.

MR. ANDERSON: I'll be moving on, too. Some more people want to talk to Jack. What's this, Janet? Something about the pony express? Isn't that out of place here? Everything else looks pretty up-to-date.

JANET SUE: Don't you know how important the pony express was in settling our country? How brave the riders were and how many hardships they faced? They were the only means of communication people in those days had. Wait, I'll get a book from the book exhibit to show you.

MR. ANDERSON: I can see that you are somewhat of an authority about the pony express, aren't you, Janet Sue? Do you suppose Wayne and Bill and Andy know as much about telegraphy and radio? I see that Wayne has built some kind of intercom set. Does he know how it works?

MRS. JOHNSON: Yes, Mr. Anderson. He and the other boys have read everything they could get their hands on. Go over and talk to them. They have an interesting demonstration. So do the boys and girls in the telephone exhibit.

JANET SUE: Isn't this fun, Mrs. Johnson? Can you tell which exhibit people like best? Do you see how many people are stopping to look at the mural? It takes both Donald and Alice to explain about it. It's a good thing we could use the hall for some of our exhibits; we'd never get all the people in our room. When my mother comes, can Anne take my place here so I can show her everything?

MRS. JOHNSON: Of course, Janet Sue. Isn't that your mother at the door now? I'll go speak to her while you're finding Anne.

MRS. FISHER: Here I am at last. So many cars! I couldn't find a place to park.

MRS. JOHNSON: Janet Sue has been waiting to show you around, Mrs. Fisher. Would you like a cup of tea first?

MRS. FISHER: That would be wonderful. I had no idea this was such a large undertaking. Janet Sue has been talking about the fair morning, noon, and night. I just passed it off as another one of her enthusiasms. When did you and the children do all these things?

MRS. JOHNSON: Most everything was made or prepared in connection with a particular problem the children wanted to solve during their study of communication. Some things, like Janet Sue's pony express display, are the result of special interests.

MRS. FISHER: But just getting things together must have been an enormous job.

MRS. JOHNSON: Actually, it's a simple fair. A great deal of preliminary planning, of course. That's the key to the whole thing. Once our plans were settled, the rest wasn't difficult.

MRS. FISHER: You make it sound so easy, and I suppose it was. You probably had the plan well in mind ahead of time, didn't you?

MRS. JOHNSON: No. As a matter of fact, I didn't. That was for the children to decide. I did make sure that all the children would participate actively in the fair and that it would be a summary of what we have learned about communication. How successful I've been you can judge for yourself.

MR. BROWN: It's the children's fair all right. If you don't ask them questions about it, they'll ask you. That group at that map over there! They asked me to name the main kinds of communication in our community. I know now, if I didn't before.

MRS. JOHNSON: A special committee worked on that exhibit. I think it's given them a new understanding of the importance of communication in our community. If you'll excuse me now, I'll get people moving toward the auditorium. Here comes Janet Sue, Mrs. Fisher.

JANET SUE: Mother, it's about time to go to the auditorium to see our telecast. Hurry up and look at everything here first.

MRS. FISHER: Telecast? You mean the children's program is going on the air? Janet Sue didn't tell me that.

MRS. JOHNSON: Not today. This is just a program of the children's plays and the music they've created. The children's interests have gone in so many directions that we'll have difficulty in deciding what we want to study next. Maybe sound or electricity. Both have come up several times in connection with their problems on communication.

The culminating experience is the zenith in the ascending progression of experiences designed to help children solve problems and to develop desired understandings, attitudes, skills, and behaviors. Functioning through a variety of activities, it sorts, scrutinizes, organizes, and summarizes information acquired in an area of learning. Through it, relationships among facts are discovered, tentacles of association are thrust out, and closures of learning take place.[1]

Central to the idea of the culminating experience as an integral part of the area of learning are three basic premises postulated by Bruner. Premise 1: Unrelated facts are short-lived in memory; fragmentary bits of knowl-

---

[1] For other descriptions of the culminating experience see Lavone A. Hanna, Gladys L. Potter, and Neva Hagaman, *Unit Teaching in the Elementary School* (rev. ed.; New York: Holt, Rinehart and Winston, Inc., 1963), pp. 166–167; Wilhelmina Hill, *Unit Planning and Teaching in Elementary Social Studies* (Washington, D.C.: U.S. Department of Health, Education, and Welfare, 1963), pp. 48–49.

edge are quickly forgotten. Premise 2: The only known way to reduce the quick rate of loss of memory is to put details together and to organize them into logically associated units from which facts may be inferred. Premise 3: New and fertile patterns of thought often come from conceptual sorting of facts and the making of new combinations of these facts.[2]

Function
of the Culminating Experience

Reasons for the culminating experience are thus as telling as those for the initiation. Yet, if anything, there is even more confusion surrounding the culminating experience than surrounding the initiation. Certainly it is not widely used by teachers as a means of organizing and summarizing information that children acquire through problem-solving experiences. Why this is so is one of the paradoxes of teaching, for no other single experience, among the many that make up an area of learning, contributes so fundamentally to the achievement of the desired understandings, attitudes, behaviors, and skills.

No doubt some of this confusion stems from teachers' stereotyped ideas about the function of the culminating experience and their belief in the folklore that the culminating experience is primarily designed to display accomplishments. If these ideas are widely held, and there is every indication that they are, then effective use of the culminating experience lies in the direction of understanding the reasoning behind it. In other words, to achieve the purposes of the culminating experience to the fullest degree is to know, first, the reasons for organizing learning and, second, to know what makes the culminating experience uniquely effective as an organizing experience.

Paramount, of course, is the fact that organization systematizes, classifies, and transforms information into useful knowledge. It is a thread that ties learnings together; it is an instrument that culls the important from the unimportant and puts fragmentary facts into related clusters so they can be generalized. Without it, knowledge acquired in an area of learning is aimless and piecemeal. A feeling of organization is essential to the child who wants the satisfaction of accomplishment. A child who experiences satisfaction in learning always has it, and very strongly. Organization makes the difference between learning that fades from memory and learning that is usable in the future.[3]

---

[2] Jerome S. Bruner, *The Process of Education* (Cambridge, Mass.: Harvard University Press, 1960), pp. 17–32.
[3] Glenn Myers Blair, "How Learning Theory Is Related to Curriculum Organization," in Victor H. Noll and Rachel P. Noll, *Readings in Educational Psychology* (New York: The Macmillan Company, 1962), p. 209.

Moreover, the more complex the process of acquiring information is, the greater the need to organize it. To get at the crux of this problem, consider the factors that influence the degree and extent to which children achieve the desired knowledge in an area of learning.

First, the information that children amass from problem solving in an area of learning ranges from discrete facts—realities, phenomena, happenings, and events—to generalizations of broad applicability. Some of this information is of little consequence. But some of it is knowledge that is basic to the understandings evolving in the area of learning, and some of it is needed to illumine learnings in future areas of learning.

Second, the information is obtained through multiple and varied experiences—direct experiences, including educational media and community experiences, construction and processing experiences, reading and research; group experiences, such as committee activities and discussion, and individual experiences; related experiences in dramatization, art, music, and writing; and information gained by drawing on skills in other curriculum areas.

Third, individual differences of learners influence the rate at which children acquire information and the amount they acquire. There are slow learners, average learners, fast learners, and learners of varying interests. There are sex differences in learning, differences in the idiomatic meanings that individuals give to their experiences, and differences in the kinds and variety of experiences with which to interpret new learning.

Add up these complexities; include the numerous other variables that influence the acquisition of knowledge in an area of learning; look at them in terms of the understandings, attitudes, behaviors, and skills to be developed from this information; it is then possible to grasp to some degree, at least, what is involved in ensuring for every child a body of fundamental ideas, concepts, and generalizations that will serve as usable points of reference in the future. It should also be clear that failure to organize this miscellany of information not only negates many of the values to be derived from the area of learning but also raises a serious question about the amount of time and effort spent acquiring this information.

Contributions
of the Culminating Experience

Clearly, then, the primary contribution of the culminating experience is to the content goals of social studies. It provides needed opportunities for organizing bodies of information evolving from the area of learning and for summarizing important ideas, and it structures information in ways that enhance its usefulness and does so within the framework of individual children's interests and abilities.

But the contributions of the culminating experience are not limited to intellectual learnings. In addition, it furthers the development of socially useful meanings and nurtures the skills of democratic action, each intrinsically a social studies goal. Culminating activities are usually group enterprises planned by groups and executed by group action. They precipitate the need for group planning, their implementation requires the thinking and ideas of many individuals, their execution requires cooperative action. In short, a culminating experience is a mosaic of many ideas and many efforts.

Also, in assuming responsibilities coincident with the execution of culminating experiences, children learn, at firsthand, the meaning of such concepts as responsibility, dependability, and obligation. They learn consideration of various points of view, and they learn to seek counsel from others before taking action. Most important, they gain skill in the process of cooperative evaluation. Skills in this process, for example, emerge in a clearinghouse discussion in which children evaluate the knowledges they have acquired as a result of the area of learning. Implicit in planning a culminating experience is a recognition of this learning and an evaluation of its adequacy for the activity to be executed. Planning together for the activities that will comprise a culminating experience, whatever they are —a play, a bulletin board display, a puppet show, or scrapbooks—children must necessarily think together about the knowledge and skills they have for these activities. Necessarily they raise such questions as these: What are the important ideas we need to put in our play? Is there something else we need to know about the subject to write our play? Or, should the facts we are using for our bulletin board display be checked to be sure we have them right?

The backward look that children take of a culminating experience they have completed stimulates group evaluation also. Here they identify the weak spots of their learning as revealed by the culminating experience. Here they note what they do not know and what they should know about the content of the area. What is more, in doing so they evaluate the behaviors they exhibited throughout the culminating experience. Desired standards are reaffirmed, revisions suggested, and new goals of behavior identified. Thus, the culminating experience can be and should be a highly effective climate in which to nurture children's ability to evaluate their achievements *and* their behavior.

Moreover, the culminating experience contributes to the development of group process by providing children with opportunities to share their achievements and experiences with others. It is human nature to want to share with others those thoughts, those experiences, and those achievements that have elicited excitement, enjoyment, and encouragement. Children are no exceptions to this truth. Admittedly, the line between the act of sharing and that of "showing off" is a fine one, so thin, in fact, that it is easily broken. But the wise teacher will guard this line and will keep the act of sharing within its proper boundaries. For if he is successful in doing so, he not only provides his children with a socializing experience that is immensely satisfying, but he also sets up an infallible motivation for creating the most effective organizing, summarizing experience possible.

In addition to its contributions to the content and social goals of social studies, there are other values to be considered—its contribution to the other areas of the curriculum, for example. Not only does the culminating experience utilize, in a variety of situations, the skills and knowledges developed in other areas, it also creates a need for these knowledges and skills and thus demonstrates their usefulness and validates reasons for learning them.

Finally, the culminating experience helps children bring an area of learning to a close before beginning a new one. Certainly, this is a contribution not to be minimized in any way. From a psychological point of view alone, the need for bringing learning to a terminal point is important; children need the satisfaction of arriving at conclusions, even if they are only temporary conclusions (see Figure 11).

For a more illuminating treatment of the contributions of the culminating experience, consider the following accounts and excerpts drawn from a culminating experience carried on by a group of sixth-grade children. Consider, first, the following descriptive account of the experience narrated by a girl who engaged in it. Written in typical childlike language, it nonetheless conveys the children's emotional response to the experience and their understanding of its purpose. Note their apparent awareness of the organizing and summarizing task and their readiness to accept responsibility for this task. Note also the amount of pupil involvement this account reveals, and particularly note the evidence of interest and satisfaction that the culminating experience generated.

To tell you about our play, "It Depends on the Future," I think I should start at the beginning of the second semester.

We, my sixth-grade class and I [Tulle], were all groping around for an idea for a way to study countries and peoples of the world. We wanted an original idea. We discussed a lot and finally David Porter came up with a good idea, "Why not use the International Student Exchange?" Many of us did not know what this was, but after it was explained we were all for it! Mr. David, our teacher, talked to Dean Dowling. He thought it was a good idea. He said that as long as it did not interfere with their studies he would be glad to send exchange students over to talk about their countries.

Finally we came out with a schedule, for what successful things don't run on a schedule?

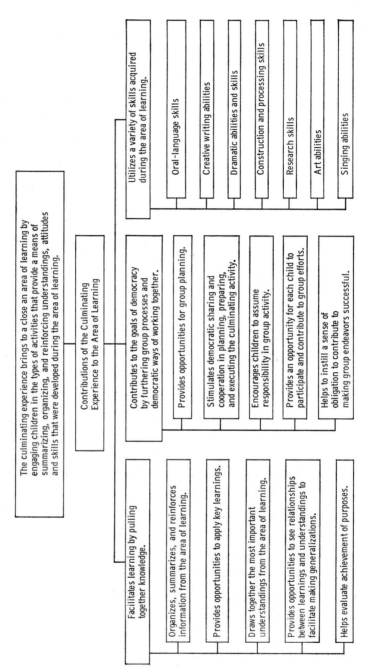

Functions of the Culminating Experience

The culminating experience brings to a close an area of learning by engaging children in the types of activities that provide a means of summarizing, organizing, and reinforcing understandings, attitudes and skills that were developed during the area of learning.

Contributions of the Culminating Experience to the Area of Learning

Facilitates learning by pulling together knowledge.

Organizes, summarizes, and reinforces information from the area of learning.

Provides opportunities to apply key learnings.

Draws together the most important understandings from the area of learning.

Provides opportunities to see relationships between learnings and understandings to facilitate making generalizations.

Helps evaluate achievement of purposes.

Contributes to the goals of democracy by furthering group processes and democratic ways of working together.

Provides opportunities for group planning.

Stimulates democratic sharing and cooperation in planning, preparing, and executing the culminating activity.

Encourages children to assume responsibility in group activity.

Provides an opportunity for each child to participate and contribute to group efforts.

Helps to instill a sense of obligation to contribute to making group endeavors successful.

Utilizes a variety of skills acquired during the area of learning.

Oral-language skills

Creative writing abilities

Dramatic abilities and skills

Construction and processing skills

Research skills

Art abilities

Singing abilities

Figure 11

The zenith of experiences in the area of learning is the culmination, designed to bring learnings into focus and structure them in ways that will enhance their usefulness.

MONDAY: Gather data.
TUESDAY: Gather data.
WEDNESDAY: Give our reports.
THURSDAY: Have a visitor come from the exchange.
FRIDAY: Analyze!

After analyzing, we would write down our conclusions and put them on the bulletin board devoted to "A Look at Life in Other Nations through the International Student Exchange!" (We shortened it to Llontise!!!) Then (still on Friday) we would decide what country we were going to study next week and divide into groups. The five prospective groups were Government, Education, Economy, Religion, and Side. The people on Side could study whatever they wanted as long as it pertained to that country and did not interfere very much with people's reports in other committees. There could not be over five people on a committee. Perhaps you think a week is a pretty short time to study a country, but it usually worked out pretty well! We studied thirteen countries in Llontise.

We thought our study was such a good idea and had worked out so well that we decided to let other people know about it. After considerable discussion we decided to have a play and a tea. First, we had to decide what the play was to be about and how we could put what we'd learned in a play. There were so many ideas and, and all at once—a grandfather telling his grandchildren about all the countries he had been to and some children finding something magic that could take them to different lands. Finally, I don't quite know how, we hit on the idea of Future who holds a peace conference on a small volcanic island in international waters. Meanwhile, we worked on the tea too. You can see how this turned out, and for this we had almost as many ideas as for the play. How we did it and the play too I don't know!

Then came writing the play. This wasn't as hard as it seems. Someone would go up to the blackboard and write what ideas we wanted to put in the play. Another person would copy what was on the board, at his seat. Mr. David would assign two people to write these ideas in the next part of the play at home. The next day their accomplishments were read to the class, and parts of one and parts of another were used. The class was also free to add anything they wanted. We worked on the play all day, except for spelling and occasional arithmetic. It was really much more difficult than the Three R's.

It's sort of hard to tell you what the play and wonderful experiences in Llontise meant to me and my class. The play helped us put together what we learned. It was something we were all in together, and we learned how important it is to work together. I'm sure we all felt pretty nervous when the curtain first went up, but it was a real comfort to have your companion with you and hoping for you to do real well when it was your turn to go out on stage. I can't say much more, because it meant so much it's hard to put it in mere words.

There are those who may question the value of a play as an organizing and summarizing activity. To be sure, it is a departure from the traditional practice of testing for this purpose. Yet most teachers would readily concede the shortcomings of tests—their low motivation value, for one. Not so a play. Evidence indicates that writing and dramatizing a play is one of children's most preferred social studies activities, whereas test activities and writing summaries are among the least liked.[4]

Because a play is an end product, the organizing and summarizing processes involved in writing and dramatizing it are not readily apparent. Even the learnings that derive from it are not always clearly obvious. Yet without the processes and learnings there would be no end product. In writing and dramatizing their play, these children utilized both critical thinking and creative thinking processes. According to their teacher, they spent several days laying the groundwork for the play. They reviewed the facts and ideas they had acquired in the area of learning. They evaluated the importance of these facts and ideas and ultimately selected from them the key ideas derived from the area of learning. They discussed relationships among these ideas, formulating them into general themes (understandings) to be integrated into the play. One, if the countries of the world are going to live in peace, people living in different countries must work hard to try to understand each other. Another, when people from different countries meet and talk together, they learn how others feel and think. Later, as described in Tulle's account, pupils set about the play-writing activity. Unfortunately, the play is too long to quote here. Perhaps, however, the following excerpt from it reflects, in some measure, the organizing and summarizing activities that undergird it.

IT ALL DEPENDS ON THE FUTURE

(*Narrator introduces the play. Curtain opens with only* FUTURE *on stage with mop and pail.*)

FUTURE: Oh! I wasn't expecting you so soon. I am Future, and you must excuse me as I am having some difficulties. Perhaps you are wondering where I am. Well, I am on a special island—a special island, indeed—and I will make it even more special. This is a newly risen volcanic island in international waters. I, Future, have chosen this island as a location to create a new era in international cooperation. For this reason, I have chosen this island in international waters so no one country can destroy my purpose for being here. Before I explain more about my purpose, please excuse me as I discard this mop and pail. Oh yes, it has just occurred to me that I have not explained what I am doing with this mop and pail. You see, this island is so new that it is partially below sea level when high tide comes in, and as a result of this I have almost worn out my mop trying to keep the water off this platform. (*Discards mop.*) As I started to say earlier, my purpose for being here is to promote world peace. You probably think this is impossible, but you forget that I'm a special person and I know the way to promote world peace. Look around me, up here, and I will show you how I expect to put my plan into operation. Through this viewer, I

[4] Harriet M. Foley, "Preferences of Sixth-Grade Children for Certain Social Studies Activities." Unpublished master's thesis, Boston University, 1951, as reported in W. Linwood Chase and Gilbert M. Wilson, "Preference Studies in Elementary School Social Studies," *Journal of Education* (April, 1958), p. 17.

can see all the countries I want. For example, if I wanted to know about the economy of Brazil, all I have to do is turn this knob and that knob. It's all very simple. With this viewer I have chosen delegates from thirteen countries *excluding* the United States and the Soviet Union. Without these two powers, the thirteen chosen countries will not be influenced by the political, economic, and military strength of these two countries. I invited the delegates by tuning into a political discussion in each country. As an example, I will show you how I did this by tuning in on a country. I will turn this knob to Canada and this one to economy. (*Canadian economy flashback.*)

FIRST CANADIAN: We are here today to talk about our economy.

SECOND: Let's talk about trade with the United States first.

. . . .

FUTURE: I have sent one of these men an invitation explaining my purpose. (*Turns off viewer.*) I am expecting this delegate and twelve others to attend this special meeting. These delegates should be arriving very shortly, but since they live in different directions they will arrive at different times. Well, I guess I'd better decide where to seat my guests. I'll divide them into three basic groups —socialists, neutralists, and capitalists. (*Places signs as he talks.*) The socialists will sit here. It will certainly be a pleasure to have these countries talk freely as long as the Soviet Union is not attending this meeting. I will seat the neutralists here. I'm afraid that there will not be many neutral countries. And here I will seat the capitalist bloc. I am also glad that the United States will not attend this meeting because its political policies would influence the other countries. Now, let's see, have I forgotten to tell you anything? Oh, yes, when each country's delegate comes in, I will tune in on a song from that country on my viewer. I think it will make him feel more at home.

(*Bell*)

(FUTURE *hears the bell and refers to a paper.*) It looks as though my first delegate is here. (*Looks at watch.*) Hmmmm, the delegate from Thailand. (*Tunes viewer to Thailand. Tunes in Thai music with low volume.* FUTURE *briefly listens to music and then turns up the volume. Volume still not too loud.* FUTURE *goes to door.*) You're not from Thailand!!

RUSSIAN: Of course not, I'm from Russia. (FUTURE *rushes back to turn off the viewer.*)

FUTURE: Did you say you were from *Russia?*

RUSSIAN: Yes, I am from the Soviet Union, and I do think I should be included since my country is a leader in promoting world peace. Now, show me my seat! (*He grabs* FUTURE *by the arm. The American struts in.*)

AMERICAN: Wait! Wait! If you seat him, where do I sit? My country does more to promote world peace than his country. (*The Russian looks up into the air.*)

FUTURE (*turns to Russian*):   What do you think you are doing?

RUSSIAN: Where is that U-2 plane flying? Or how else did that American know that we Russians were going to crash this meeting?

FUTURE: Oh, go ahead, be seated, but mind your own business. (*The two delegates set up their own name plates and switch the two signs around.*)

(*Bell*)

FUTURE: This should be the German delegate. (*Turns on viewer. German music is heard. Goes to door.*)

FUTURE: No, this can't be the German delegate. There are two people!

GERMANS: But we are the Germans!

FUTURE: Don't tell me we have another uninvited guest!

WEST: You see, since Germany is divided into two main sectors, communist and free, the authorities have sent two delegates. One is for the communists, and the other is for the free sector.

FUTURE: Oh, I see. (*Motions them toward the tables.*) The German from the communist sector will sit here. The German from the free sector can sit here. (*They sit down in proper places.*)

YUGOSLAV: Too bad Germany was split up.

RUSSIAN: It was Hitler's fault. He shouldn't have started the war. We couldn't help take the land that was rightfully ours after the war was over.

BRAZILIAN: Hitler sure did make a great mistake in starting such a bloody war.

ITALIAN: I wish Mussolini had not brought us into the war because the war created many problems. The German people have these problems also. Then the splitting of Germany has added to their difficulties.

THAI: I'd say splitting up the country didn't help them at all.

AMERICAN: I agree.

ITALIAN: Why couldn't we make all of Germany like the West?

RUSSIAN: I don't agree! (*Slams shoe.*)

AMERICAN: I knew you'd say that.

· · · · · · ·

(*Bell*)

FUTURE: Someone is earlier than I expected. Excuse me, I'll be back in a minute. (*As he walks to the door, he mumbles.*) You can't win them all. (*Goes on to door.*) You must be from Switzerland. What did you do, take a jet?

SWISS: I'm sorry I am early, but I just couldn't take the chance of being late.

FUTURE: I will be right with you as soon as I seat the delegate from France. (*Swiss remains standing by the door.*)

FRENCHMAN: (*He is approached by* FUTURE.) As I was saying, I wanted to tell you about our government. We have a president who is elected by the people. We have a parliament with two houses, and we have a constitution that somewhat limits the power of the president. Our main problem now is the Algerian situation, which was caused by Algerians' efforts for independence.

AMERICAN: Yes, you almost lost Algeria in a revolutionary riot.

FRENCHMAN: But—

YUGOSLAV: And what about your economy? It would not be quite as stable without Algeria.

FRENCHMAN: Our economy is very stable. Algeria only helps. We have very little unemployment and that is more than I can say for the United States, with its several million unemployed.

AMERICAN: Uhh—

FRENCHMAN: I have you cornered, don't I?

FUTURE: That proves my point. None of you, or the countries you represent, is perfect. That is why you need my plan for world peace. Please find a seat; I must talk to the delegate from Switzerland. (*Goes to door.*) Sorry I've kept you waiting. Oh, just a minute. (*Turns on viewer. Swiss music is heard.*) Won't you please be seated?

SWISS: Yes, thank you. (*Takes seat.*) I overheard your conversation with the French delegate, and I am prepared to tell you something about my country.

FUTURE: That will be very good. Then we can get on with the meeting.

SWISS: Well, seeing that all of the invited representatives are present, I feel that it would be most impolite to give a lengthy speech so I will only give a few facts. First of all, my country has been host to many peace conferences so in that way I feel right at home in this meeting. Perhaps one of the reasons these meetings are held in my country is because it is neutral. Through the years we have found that we can raise our standards by living in peace rather than wasting property and human lives by having wars.

GERMAN: Doesn't everyone know that Switzerland is neutral? This is just a waste of time.

CANADIAN: Yes, we've waited long enough. Let's get on with this peace conference.

GERMAN   (*points to* FUTURE): What about your plan?

RUSSIAN: Yes, we are all here. Tell us now.

JAPANESE: We have all told you about our countries, so why don't you tell us now about your plan? (*Delegates act as though they want an answer.*)

FUTURE   (*motions for silence*): Well (*gulp*)—how you do it is—well (*gulp, gulp*) all you have to do is—it's—it's all very simple, you see. (*Drums indicate a volcano is about to erupt.*) Run for your lives! The volcano is about to erupt. (*They hurry out; the Japanese lingers behind.*) You go on, I have to get my—my papers. (*Japanese leaves.*) Whew! That was too close for comfort. (*Gets mop and pail.*) I was afraid they would catch on to my scheme. I must admit that I am a fraud because I really do not have a plan for world peace. The way these delegates acted at times makes me think that the world is in as much trouble as this unstable island. Did you see how aggressive the Russian delegate was? And how the U.S. delegate would not even recognize the Cuban delegate? (*He pauses.*) But perhaps all wasn't bad—they learned about other countries, and they all seemed pleased with the music. You know, maybe we will have world peace someday. It depends on the

FUTURE

Kinds
of Culminating Experiences

Not all culminating experiences are as elaborate as this one, of course. Nor is such elaborateness always necessary. Indeed, in some instances it may even be undesirable.[5] In general, simple experiences that emphasize only a few learnings call for the simplest kind of culminating experience. More extensive and prolonged areas of learning, like the one above, usually

---

[5] Lucile Lindberg, *The Democratic Classroom* (New York: Bureau of Publications, Teachers College, Columbia University, 1954), pp. 55–56.

require more time and effort to organize and summarize the learnings that problem-solving experiences yield.

In other words, culminating experiences can be brief and simple or extended and elaborate. They can be a cluster of activities, each one organizing a specific set of learnings but all forming an integrated pattern that unifies these learnings. They can evolve slowly or explode dramatically, their development controlled by the number and pace of emergent learnings. They can be classroom activities only or activities that are shared with other groups of children and adults.

Various types of written records—summaries, logs, diaries, and scrapbooks—are simple organizing activities. Typically, in these activities children summarize in writing the key ideas and understandings pertaining to a special problem or area of content. Often these summaries are presented orally as reports. Often individual summaries are combined into scrapbooks or arranged as chapters of a book. Frequently they are illustrated with children's drawings and paintings. In some cases the special abilities of individual children are drawn upon. For example, printing captions for the bulletin board may be the responsibility of a child who is gifted in this art. Logs and diaries are an especially appealing way of organizing and summarizing learnings. Understandings about the problems pioneers faced as they moved westward in the settlement of the Great Plains take shape when children assume the roles of pioneer boys and girls and create a diary or a log of the hardships and hazards of these journeys. Or a diary that describes the devastation of the South during the Civil War is an effective way to organize essential understandings about this era in history. For young children, particularly, such culminating activities are effective ways to summarize learnings because they are relatively easy to execute.

Somewhat more difficult to execute is a second general type of culminating activity—the exhibit. Generally, this is an activity in which bulletin boards, murals, dioramas, and displays are used to organize and summarize learnings. The mural, "The Communication Story in Pictures," referred to earlier is an example of the exhibit type of culminating activity.

Still another kind of culminating activity—assemblies, fairs, or the open house—is well suited to the abilities of older children. The educational gains to be derived from these activities are many and varied. For one, they necessitate considerable recording and integration of knowledge. For another, they create multiple problem-solving situations. Moreover, they offer many opportunities to assume and carry out responsibility. The following anecdote is an example.

Miss Davis sat in the audience with the mothers of her fourth-grade pupils watching them present the play they had written for a culminating experience. Intermission was over. It was time for Tom to open the next scene with a read-

ing of his poem, "Little Alp, The Cave Boy." But to Miss Davis's astonish-
ment, Carole, not Tom, came into the room and went directly to the piano to
play a musical composition. Miss Davis fidgeted, "What has happened? Where
is Tom?" Before the applause died away, however, Tom, barefooted and dressed
in his ragged cave-boy costume, appeared in the doorway. He walked to the
center of the stage, announced the title of his poem, and then recited it in a
clear, unfaltering voice.

When the program was over, Miss Davis hurried back stage. "What went
wrong? Why didn't Tom come out when he was supposed to?"

"Nothing went wrong, Miss Davis. Tom's white underwear showed below
his cave costume. Cave boys didn't wear white underwear, so we had to find a
safety pin to pin it up."

Criteria
for Selecting Activities
in a Culminating Experience

Because the activities in a culminating experience are literally the
agents that organize and summarize children's accumulated information,
a critical analysis of these activities is a necessary prerequisite to their selection. Although many teachers are sufficiently well informed and experienced to make critical judgments about the activities they select, many
more are not. Where the problem lies for most teachers is in knowing what
the unique character of these activities should be to fulfill the functions
they are to perform in the culminating experience. Criteria for selecting
these activities are thus practical and helpful.

A criterion of first consideration is identified by this question: Does the
activity come about naturally as a follow-up of earlier activities? Central
here are the words *naturally* and *follow-up*. What they mean in this context
is simply that the activities selected for the culminating experience must
be intrinsically related to learnings developed in the area of learning and
a consequence of them. Examples of such activities are described in the
dialogue at the beginning of this chapter. Within the limitations set by
the dialogue, there are many indications that the culminating activities
were an intrinsic part of the area of learning. A girl's display of the pony
express is a case in point. Her display and her explanatory statements were
a summary of information obtained earlier from seeing a film, from reading
and taking notes, and from discussion. In every sense, it was the consequence of what she had learned and for her an undeniably satisfying
consequence.

The second question is a vital one for it gets at the outcome of the area
of learning: Does the activity draw together the most important understandings of the area of learning? In effect, the process of drawing under-

standings together parallels the periodic inventories that business enterprises take of their assets. Basically, it is a process of surveying stock to see what is on hand and then regrouping the specifics into related units to increase their usability. Again, the scrapbook referred to earlier is to the point.

To find reasons why man has settled along the rivers of the world, children in a sixth-grade class engaged in a variety of activities to obtain specific information about man's use of rivers. They searched for facts about river trade all over the world, they studied maps to find similarities in the geographic environment of river cities in numerous countries, they looked at films of cities located on rivers, and they recorded some of their information in individual notebooks. Some of it they shared in reports; some they recorded on a chart of cause-and-effect statements like the following:

1. Cities developed along rivers because they are a direct source of water to supply the needs of many people.
2. Cities developed along rivers because they offered a chance for trade.
3. Cities developed along rivers because of the rich soil in the river valleys.

Up to this point, however, there was no pattern to this information, no recognizable structure that could serve as a reference in the future. Therefore, it was time to sort, to analyze, and to draw together this miscellany of information about why man has settled along rivers. In short, it was time to climax the search with activities that would pinpoint the significant understandings to be derived from the accumulated information. Two kinds of culminating activities facilitated the identification of these understandings—class discussion and the making of a scrapbook.

Class discussion focused on the task of scrutinizing facts and ideas, sorting facts, and formulating several generalizations that reflected the understandings the teacher had identified as goals at the outset of the experience. For example, rivers have made it possible for a people to trade with others, have provided necessary water power for their industries, and have improved agriculture by supplying the water power needed for irrigation. The scrapbook was the second step in drawing understandings together. Using their generalizations as section headings in the scrapbook the children clustered their original stories, poems, and pictures into several units, each of which illumined a specific generalization.

To guide children in formulating generalizations about information they have acquired in an area of learning demands knowledge and skill. For this reason, many teachers never take their children beyond the stage of accumulating information. But if learnings are to be retained and their transfer is to be assured, they must be structured into principles or generalizations from which facts and concepts can be inferred. Moreover, the process of drawing understandings together must begin early in the primary grades.

A third criterion refers less directly to the main purpose of the culminating activity than to its secondary purposes: Does the activity call upon a variety of skills learned in the area of learning? In other words, in the process of organizing and summarizing the information, do children use and thus reinforce the skills—communication skills, number skills, and group process skills—that they acquired or perfected during the development of the area of learning?

The labels the skills bear are far less important than the function they perform, however. Often, in fact, children may use skills in a culminating activity but fail to recognize them as such. This was true of the sixth-grade girl who, in describing the play, "It All Depends on the Future," wrote, "It was really much more difficult than the Three R's." In reality, she and her classmates used a variety of skills commonly associated with the "three R's"—writing, certainly, in large amounts, speaking, listening, and reading for information. All these skills and many others made the play-writing experience possible and successful.

But labeled or not, skills are necessary implements with which to plan and execute culminating activities. Culminating activities in turn create valid reasons to use the skills children are learning in other areas of the curriculum.

The fourth criterion centers on the problem of self-direction: Can children develop the culminating activity with a minimum of teacher direction? To develop self-directive individuals is an ultimate goal of all social studies teaching. Culminating activities should further the achievement of this goal by creating a complex of problems to be solved, decisions to be reached, and ideas to be converted to realities. They should also encourage independent thinking and execution of ideas. It matters not that neither the end product is perfect nor the performance polished. The activities of the culminating experience should be simple enough for children to execute on their own but sufficiently challenging to precipitate the desired action.

The fifth and final criterion should need little elaboration: Is the activity appropriate for the children's maturity level? The purpose of the question is to remind teachers of the need to select activities that are within the ability of a particular age group to execute. Important here are the consideration of the probable duration of children's interest in the activity, their facility in manipulating materials and tools, the background of knowledge needed for the activity, and similar concerns. Also, this criterion serves to keep culminating activities within the boundaries of a learning experience and curbs a teacher's desire to make it a display piece for accomplishments. What first-grade teacher, for example, who gives serious thought to the maturity level of his children, can honestly justify the tedious effort that goes into a polished show of accomplishments?

Implementing
the Culminating Experience

Unlike the initiation, which in the main is teacher-planned and teacher-directed, the culminating experience is a cooperative enterprise. Whereas in the initiation the teacher selects and plans for the implementation of the initiation, in the culminating experience children participate actively in planning and decision making. This is not to say, however, that the teacher has no initial responsibility for planning the culminating experience. On the contrary, he pinpoints the learnings to be tied together and identifies the generalizations to be developed through the culminating experience. He surveys the activities by which the children have acquired many of their learnings and considers their usefulness in the culminating experience. Using criteria for selecting culminating activities, he weighs the relative values of types of culminating activities and considers possible problems. He is then ready to guide his children in making judicious decisions as they plan ways to culminate their area of learning.

COOPERATIVE PLANNING
OF THE CULMINATING EXPERIENCE

Planning for a culminating experience focuses on three specific problems, selecting the activity or activities, planning to carry out the activity, and organizing for work and delegating responsibility.

Selecting the activity, the first problem, is facilitated through these questions: What have we learned about the subject we have studied? What information is important to remember? What can we do to help us remember what we have learned? In other words, in selecting activities that will further the purposes of the culminating experience—namely, to organize and summarize learnings—children must first sort out and scrutinize the information they have acquired during the development of the area of learning. For example, a group of fourth-grade children spent several weeks in finding answers to this problem: Why do people in different places live in the houses that they do? Among the outcomes of the experience were two generalizations: One, shelter is important to people because it protects them from different elements and because it serves as a place where they can meet. Two, climate, materials available, discovery and invention, occupation, and financial status all have an influence on the type of house in which a person lives.

At the outset of their planning for the culminating experience, the children reviewed the miscellaneous information they had acquired about people's shelter. This information included facts about the materials people in different parts of the world use to build houses, the source of these materials, the different purposes that a house serves for different peoples, the changes in man's housing since the cave men's dwellings, the reasons for housing shortages in various parts of the world, and the problems created by these shortages.

Concrete evidences of learnings obtained from the area of learning were the models of typical houses to be found in the climate zones of the world, a picture collection of houses built in different periods of history, imaginative stories about the life of the people who lived in these houses, drawings of houses on the moon, experiments to demonstrate the weathering qualities of building materials, the report of an interview with the mayor of their city about an urban renewal project, and a map showing its location.

Having scrutinized their accumulation of information, the children's next point of concern was the preservation of this information. Specifically, how could they organize it so they would remember the important ideas? How could they tie everything together into a unified whole that would clearly show why people build the kinds of shelter they do? To answer these questions, the teacher and children discussed the advantages of various types of culminating activities. They discussed the possibility of writing a play about their study. But this idea was discarded as impractical. Printing a book of their findings was another idea suggested and rejected because of the problems it involved. Why not prepare an exhibit in which the model houses would be displayed with guides to explain the background of each, and why not present the history of housing by arranging the picture file and writing a commentary to go along with it? Thus, step by step, the children took stock of their learnings and achievements and ultimately decided on activities that they concluded were the most effective ways to organize and summarize these learnings.

The second problem, planning to carry out the individual activities of the culminating experience, is largely a matter of considering and deciding on the details of implementation. Chiefly, it consists of facing and making decisions about such concerns as these: How much time is to be spent in getting ready for the culminating experience? When will it take place? What materials will be needed to carry out the selected activities? Where can they be obtained? How much of the work will be done at school? how much at home? Is the culminating experience to be a shared experience? If so, how shall the sharing be arranged? with whom? when?

The third phase of planning for a culminating experience—organizing for work and delegating responsibility—is undoubtedly the most critical point in the culminating experience. What happens at this stage usually determines whether the culminating experience will fulfill its purpose or will instead be fruitless. Whether the task to be performed is small or large, important or unimportant, a clearly defined work plan is essential. Sometimes the plan is the result of class discussion; sometimes a small committee produces it; sometimes it is the teacher and one child sharing ideas who produce the plan. But planning is always a preliminary to action.

At this point, also, the basic principles of democratic action should operate at the highest level—planning for each child to share in the total effort, planning in which each child considers group welfare above self-interest, and planning in which every child is willing to settle problems by the will of the majority.

EVALUATING THE PROGRESS
OF THE CULMINATING EXPERIENCE

Any plan of action, no matter how detailed or meticulously conceived it may be, must be subjected to evaluation and revision and alteration. For it is not humanly possible to foresee all the complexities and problems that emerge as ideas are transformed into action. Generally, evaluation of the progress of a culminating experience is accomplished through observation of the activity or activities in progress, through group discussion, and through analyzing the effectiveness of the products in terms of their purpose.

Observing the activity in progress is a method of evaluation used by teachers and children alike. For the most part, it consists of sizing up what is accomplished and then reacting positively or negatively to the evidence. Commonly in this kind of evaluation, questions such as these are posed and answered: Is this bulletin board arrangement of our materials the best possible one to show off the information we want to present? Do these backdrops for our play create the proper setting for the action of the play? Should we make the box for our puppet play larger or smaller?

Discussing the problems related to the progress of a culminating experience is another effective way to evaluate progress. Through discussion, impediments to progress are aired and resolved as teacher and children consider the problem or problems, explore possible solutions, weigh suggestions, and decide on a solution that they then try out. The following illustration sheds light on the way discussion serves to evaluate the progress of a culminating experience.

Searching for a way to summarize their learnings about the early Egyptian civilization, a fourth-grade class wrote a play. The setting for the play was a museum display of Egyptian mummies. Two children visiting the museum express disinterest in the mummies because they believe them to be old and worthless. But the mummies hear what the children say and resent what they hear. Determined to prove its worth, each comes to life and tells the children about the people and activities during the period of Egypt's civilization.

To give the mummies a realistic appearance, the class decided each one should be encased in strips of sheeting wrapped around the body from neck to feet. Once they put their ideas into effect, however, they discovered that the mummies could not move. Faced with the problem of getting the mummies on stage without the advantage of a stage curtain, they discussed their dilemma. Should they give up the whole idea and start again? Was there any way to hang a curtain in the classroom? Maybe someone could carry the mummies on the stage as a caretaker might do in a museum. But, looking at pudgy Katherine, one of the girls chosen to be a mummy, the children quickly rejected this suggestion. Finally, someone asked, "Why doesn't Carol make up a piece that she could play while the mummies shuffle in from the hall to take their places?" In response to this suggestion, Carol wrote the following musical composition, and the problem was solved.

Analyzing the effectiveness of the products in terms of their purposes is a third and most important step in evaluating the culminating activity. For, to repeat an earlier point, the value of a culminating activity rests on the degree to which it fulfills its purpose. Regardless of type of activity, its products must be constantly analyzed to determine how effectively they achieve the purpose for which they were designed. As an example, a play that is written for the purpose of summarizing learnings must be judged in terms of this purpose, its other attributes notwithstanding. Undoubtedly, Mr. David, the sixth-grade teacher whose children wrote the play, "It All Depends on the Future," continually cautioned the playwriters about their need to include in it basic understandings about each country studied. No doubt, too, he asked the playwriters each day to analyze each new section of the completed script to determine how and to what extent they had incorporated these understandings in their writing.

To sum up, the culminating experience performs a twofold function in the area of learning. As a concluding experience, it serves to increase the usefulness of acquired knowledge. Through it children bring random facts and ideas into focus, relate and structure them into generalized forms, thus making them fuller and richer in meaning. As a social-living experience, the culminating experience offers multiple opportunities for learning and practicing the processes of democratic citizenship. It is therefore an experience that is both unique and functional in its purpose.

QUESTIONS FOR DISCUSSION

Use the dialogue at the beginning of this chapter to guide you in thinking about the following:

1. How did the culminating experience help the children summarize the learnings they acquired during the development of the area of learning?
2. In what ways would other culminating experiences have achieved this purpose?
3. How did this culminating experience further group processes?

SUGGESTIONS FOR CONSTRUCTING
A RESOURCE UNIT

Recall the understandings, attitudes, and skills you selected to develop in your area of learning. Review the content and experiences you included.

Identify and describe briefly the type of culminating experience you will use to summarize the area of learning. List, in order, the steps you and your pupils will follow in carrying out the culminating experience. Include teacher's planning, children's experiences in planning, development of the culmination, and materials.

Use the following questions to test your plan.

1. Does it draw upon many skills and knowledges acquired in this unit?
2. Does it give children opportunities to summarize important ideas?
3. Does it grow naturally out of the area of learning?
4. Does it provide further opportunities for sharing and working together?
5. Does it open the way to new areas of learning?

12

Evaluating
Children's Progress
toward Desirable Goals

MRS. JOHNSON: Let's all get comfortable and talk a little about what we have just been doing. Our trip to the television studio was interesting, wasn't it?

ROBERT: I think most of our questions about television were answered. Could we check to see? If we forgot any, Frank can ask his father tonight.

MRS. JOHNSON: All these ideas you brought back with you should help you to appreciate television more than ever. Were there any problems about taking the trip that we need to discuss?

ANNE: I think we should look at our standards again to see how well we followed them. I think I can read them.

MRS. JOHNSON: I'm sure you can. Read the chart for us, Anne.

ANNE: It says, "A good visitor stays with his group, avoids handling materials or equipment unless invited to do so, asks intelligent questions, speaks softly, and listens politely."

ANDY: One thing we learned from our trip to the greenhouse we remembered today. We didn't break a thing. I never will forget about that broken pot of violets. Maybe we were afraid to touch all that important looking equipment at the TV station, but anyway we didn't. We're just getting better, I think.

WAYNE: Yes, but some of us didn't stay with our group. Once when we were watching the monitors, two people went back into the studio. There was a program going on, too, and they could have ruined the whole thing.

MRS. JOHNSON: I agree that it seems hard for us not to wander around when we go visiting, especially when there are so many interesting things going on all at once, but we'll do it better next time. Any other suggestions? What about our voices? Were they as quiet as they could have been?

SUSAN: In the studio it seemed natural to whisper. But on the bus I couldn't hear myself think. We forgot all about the quiet games we were going to play on the way. And the first thing our guide at the station had to do was to remind us to keep our voices down.

MRS. JOHNSON: It does seem that there are some things we do well on a trip and some which we need to improve. Shall we put a check on our chart beside the items that still are a little troublesome? The checks will serve as good reminders the next time we go traveling.

* * * * * * *

MRS. JOHNSON: The reports on your projects have made one of the most interesting sharing periods we have had all year. Were there some things you especially liked about the reports?

FRANK: I think everybody liked the reports that had action in them, like demonstrating how to connect batteries and to print with a linoleum block. When you see something as well as hear about it, you remember it better.

MARY LOU: I liked the reports that told exactly how people communicated with the equipment that was made by the group! After all, that's why we did the work. Our group was going to do that, but we were so interested in showing how the batteries worked that we forgot the important part.

CHARLES: Bill and his group gave a good report because they told just how their telegraph keys were different from telegraph keys used by real operators. The block print committee did that, too. They showed how their printing is different from printing in a newspaper office. I think it's important because everybody knows we couldn't make things just exactly like those that are used by communication workers. And we ought to know the difference.

MRS. JOHNSON: You've made a good point, Charles. When something is real, we say it is authentic. Do you know that word? Ronnie's group made some fine signal flags and demonstrated them very well, but we all know that real signal flags are not made and do not look just like those Ronnie and the committee made for us. Any other good points about our reports? Any places for improvement?

PATRICIA: One is easy to see. We all use our papers too much when we give our talks. We hide behind them sometimes. Could we work on that, Mrs. Johnson?

PEGGY: I agree with Pat, Mrs. Johnson. And another thing. The same people always give the reports. Can we do something about that? Many of us need practice, but it's easier to let someone else do the work. Everybody ought to have a chance.

MRS. JOHNSON: Don't you think Wayne's group handled that problem nicely? Everybody talked a little, each one telling some special part about the intercom set. Perhaps other groups can try that idea.

BARBARA ANN: Mrs. Johnson, I think there is something in our language arts book about how to give good talks. Do you think it might help us? And when I was getting my part ready at home, my big sister said, "What you need is an outline." Could we find out about outlines?

* * * * * * *

MRS. JOHNSON: Everybody seems agreed that our fair was very successful. We were able to show our parents and friends many things we learned about communication. Can we forget about the whole subject for the rest of the year?

ROBERT: We might forget some of the information we learned, but we shouldn't forget how to communicate with other people. We'll be using communication for the rest of the year and for all our lives.

MRS. JOHNSON: How can we tell whether or not our experience with communication has taught us how to communicate with other people?

JACK: That's easy. When we write letters or use the telephone, we can find out how well we do.

ANDY: Or if we choose good TV programs at home.

RUTH: Or if we speak clearly or not.

MRS. JOHNSON: Would you like to help list the communication skills you think are most important? Then we can check on ourselves for the next few weeks until these skills become habits.

MARTHA: I'll start. Would it be "Speaks clearly and distinctly"?

MRS. JOHNSON: That would be a good one for the top of the list. Who knows why?

ALICE: I think it's because we communicate by speaking more than any other way.

SUSAN: How about "Writes clearly and correctly"? My father is always talking about some of the poor newspaper copy he has to read.

FRANK: Don't forget "Chooses good radio and television programs." That one always causes arguments at our house.

JANET SUE: Along with the one about writing correctly comes this one: "Chooses proper materials for writing."

BILL: And don't we want one about the telephone and telegraph? Of course we use the telephone the most. We could say, "Uses the telephone properly."

MRS. JOHNSON: This is going to be a helpful list. Shall I put it on a big wall chart arranged with your names? Then we can put a check after the skill when we are agreed that you have it pretty well in hand. The chart will be a good reminder, too. Let's finish the list, and I'll have the chart ready for tomorrow.

* * * * * * *

MRS. JOHNSON: In our study of communication there have been some very important ideas that we should not forget, and there have been some interesting facts that we may not remember very long because they are not important. I need to know how well you can recognize important ideas about communication.

MARTHA: Sounds like a puzzle. Is it?

MRS. JOHNSON: No, not really, Martha. This is a serious bit of business, but you may enjoy it just the same. It will be almost like being detectives.

WAYNE: Let's try it.

MRS. JOHNSON: This is how it goes. On the sheet of paper that Peggy is giving you are some sentences about communication. Some of these sentences are important ideas. Some of them are interesting facts. Your job is to put a check mark in front of each of the big ideas. Just a minute, Charles, let's not rush through!

ANDY: I see one that's not important.

MRS. JOHNSON: I think it might help everyone if we read each of the sentences aloud before we begin. Then each person can spend most of his time thinking about which sentences to check. Will you start, Anne?

ANNE: "Speaking is our most common form of communication."

MRS. JOHNSON: That sounds familiar, doesn't it?

RONNIE: It's one of the most important—oh, I forgot, Mrs. Johnson. May I read the next one? It says, "Modern communication has brought the world closer together."

MRS. JOHNSON: Now don't give it away by the look on your face, Ronnie. Can you do the next one, Wayne? It's a good one for you.

WAYNE: Sure. "The dot and dash are used in many different ways to make the Morse code." That's easy. Janet Sue has the next one ready.

JANET SUE: "People have not always communicated as we do today." This is my favorite topic of the whole study.

* * * * * * *

MRS. JOHNSON: Now no one will have any difficulty with reading the list. Andy, will you tell us again what we are to do?

ANDY: It's simple. We just read the sentence. If it's an important idea we ought to remember, we put a check in front of it. If it's only an interesting fact, we don't mark it.

MRS. JOHNSON: Is everyone sure about what to do? Alice? Yes, no doubt there'll be arguments. We'll settle those later. Now each person on his own, please.

* * * * * * *

MRS. JOHNSON: I'm so glad you came in this afternoon, Mrs. Sewall. Let's sit here by the window where we can be comfortable.

MRS. SEWALL: I really didn't come for any special reason, Mrs. Johnson, but I didn't have a chance during the fair to speak to you about Peggy's work. I was impressed with the fair and all that the children had done, but I had a hard time finding out just what part Peggy had played in it. How does she get along in her work—in social studies, for example?

MRS. JOHNSON: I think we can talk about it more easily if we use this folder of materials to help us. I keep one of these for each pupil. This one is Peggy's. This past month I have been noting especially the children's reactions to social studies. Any evidence I find I put here for just such an occasion as this. And, of course, the information is also useful in making out various kinds of records about Peggy. Let's see what we have here.

MRS. SEWALL: Oh, there's that drawing of her favorite television show. I wondered why she brought it back to school.

MRS. JOHNSON: Each of the children made one of these when we were discussing the merits of various television programs. Peggy's was quite revealing. Does she usually prefer adult programs?

MRS. SEWALL: Yes, but do you know—Peggy hasn't watched that program for several weeks. It was her favorite and most unsuitable, but now she doesn't look at it at all. Did you do that, Mrs. Johnson?

MRS. JOHNSON: No, not really. Group discussion and pressure often accomplish what parents and teachers cannot. You may want to watch for other changes in Peggy's listening habits. Do let me know what you observe. But, here is something else that's interesting. Do you remember the day Peggy brought in a whole armload of encyclopedias from home? With all the parts about communication marked? It was the first time she had done anything like that.

MRS. SEWALL: You're right. Many times I've suggested that she bring objects or materials to school to share, but I usually find them left behind. She wouldn't rest this time until we had gone through the whole set. My husband couldn't believe she was doing it willingly, but I managed to keep him from saying anything. I see you jotted down the whole list and just what she did with them at school.

MRS. JOHNSON: Yes, an occasion like that is worth remembering. Now, here is a copy of Peggy's newspaper report of the fair. If you read it, you can see that she really does have a good understanding of the importance of communication. The writing is correct and quite legible, too.

MRS. SEWALL: I'm surprised at the words she has used. Do you think these new communication words are really part of the children's vocabulary? They certainly used them well at the fair.

MRS. JOHNSON: We hope so. We'll continue to use them in many ways just to make sure. Some of them appeared in the tests we gave at the end of our communication study. Here are Peggy's papers. Yes, there's only one missed on the vocabulary section where she matched new words and their meanings. She did quite well, too, in recognizing the important ideas we have emphasized. And here is the paragraph that describes the part of the study she liked best. This kind of information is especially helpful in planning new experiences for the children.

MRS. SEWALL: Perhaps I shouldn't be, but I'm beginning to be a bit pleased with Peggy. And I shall certainly encourage her interest in your next social studies experience.

Does the problem-solving approach to social studies as embodied in the development of the area of learning bring lasting knowledge? Does it promote pupil progress toward acquisition of desirable understandings, attitudes, behaviors, and skills that will enrich children's living now and in the future? To answer these questions is the task of evaluation—a comprehensive and continuing process that functions through cooperative evaluation as it relates to everyday experiences in social studies, through teacher evaluation concerned with changes in pupil behavior, and through evaluation of the achievement of long-range objectives.

Role
of Cooperative Evaluation
in the Area of Learning

Cooperative evaluation is referred to often in the preceding chapters of this book. It is the process by which teacher and pupils critically examine their work together and make some judgments about its values and problems. It is a process that goes forward largely in terms of children's purposes—what they plan to do and what they want to achieve. It is a process that uses a variety of techniques and yet depends heavily upon discussion and exchange of ideas.

Cooperative evaluation differs from other kinds of evaluation in its frequency and timing. Although evaluation is usually associated with the end of a major project or topic of study, cooperative evaluation is continual, taking place in a variety of situations, occurring at strategic points in the development of the area of learning, and serving as a transition from past experiences to new ones.[1]

So much has already been said about cooperative evaluation in relation to pupils' problem-solving experiences that here it seems necessary only to summarize the important values of this essential facet of the area of learning. When pupils need to see their progress, cooperative evaluation provides the opportunity. When it is important to identify strengths and weaknesses, cooperative evaluation makes this identification possible. When children ask in what way improvement lies, the shared experiences in cooperative evaluation encourage them to be constructively critical of their own work.[2] And all these opportunities to analyze the progress of their work naturally point the direction to new experiences. Thinking about what to do next is the logical outcome of cooperative evaluation.

OPPORTUNITIES FOR COOPERATIVE EVALUATION

From the initiation on, through all the problem-solving experiences in which pupils engage, there are myriad opportunities for cooperative evaluation. These have been described at many appropriate points in this book. Continually, as children plan their experiences, they are called upon to evaluate the quality of their ideas and proposals. As research gets under way, the accuracy of reading materials and other resources must be assessed. In community experiences pupils must select critically the projects they will undertake and cooperatively evaluate the success of these undertakings in terms of their purposes. They must choose films and recordings with equal care, working cooperatively with the teacher, selecting, previewing, and sometimes rejecting. When construction and processing experiences are completed, children must look sharply at the products of their work and their ways of working together. In a word, cooperative evaluation is an ever-recurring experience in the problem-solving process.

RELATIONSHIP OF COOPERATIVE EVALUATION
TO TEACHER EVALUATION

Because cooperative evaluation and teacher evaluation are closely related, the two occur in part simultaneously. Although the teacher must take a somewhat broader view of evaluation than the children, he is alert to all aspects of children's behavior and learning as they are revealed in cooperative evaluation. Cooperative evaluation is an important source of data for the teacher who seeks to arrive at reliable judgments of children's achievements and needs. When, for example, cooperative evaluation re-

---

[1] Ernest W. Tiegs and Fay Adams, *Teaching the Social Studies* (Boston: Ginn & Company, 1959), pp. 321–324.

[2] Lavone A. Hanna, Gladys L. Potter, and Neva Hagaman, *Unit Teaching in the Elementary School* (rev. ed.; New York: Holt, Rinehart and Winston, Inc., 1963), pp. 323–324, 350–351.

veals children's successes and failures in planning and carrying out an activity, the teacher has an opportunity to evaluate pupils' ability to assess their strengths and weaknesses. When cooperative evaluation results in standards for improvement in some area of endeavor, the teacher can use these standards to measure the success of future undertakings. If cooperative evaluation brings about plans for a follow-up experience, the teacher has an opportunity to evaluate these plans in terms of objectives. Even the extent of the children's knowledge of important information is revealed to the teacher as children discuss in evaluation periods what they have seen or read, and relate it to the problems they have raised. In these and in similar situations, teacher evaluation is naturally associated with cooperative evaluation.

Importance
of Teacher Evaluation

The responsibility of finally evaluating children's achievement in social studies, however, rests with the teacher. He is the person best qualified to view the area of learning as a whole, evaluating all aspects of pupil progress and relating the findings to the future experiences of his pupils. One of the purposes of teacher evaluation is to assess children's growth toward certain worthwhile understandings, attitudes, behaviors, and skills. Although cooperative evaluation gives the teacher some evidence about children's progress, these impressions are likely to be general rather than specific. The techniques of teacher evaluation permit him to attend to the individual child's success in achieving each of the objectives selected for the area of learning. An anecdotal record of John's behavior, for example, reveals that he does not display in real life some of the understandings about playground safety that the teacher thought he had developed. An attitude check list indicates that some children do not yet accept readily those in their group who represent minorities in the population. The interview with William reinforces the teacher's belief that he needs additional practice in applying the skills of good group relationships. Through such teacher evaluation, attention can be focused directly upon the individual child's growth toward desirable understandings, attitudes, behaviors, and skills.

Teacher evaluation, revealing as it does the special needs of children in social studies, also serves as a guide to selecting further experiences. If the teacher finds that important concepts have not been fully or accurately developed in the current area of learning, future experiences to meet these needs must be planned. If the teacher's observation of children's discussion reveals that new and unexpected interests are developing, and if his evaluation of them in terms of children's needs is positive, then future study begins to take form. It evaluation shows that children need more opportunities to know their community better, these important aspects of school-community relationships must be strengthened in the experiences to come. If careful analysis of available evidence clearly exposes children's inability to use certain basic skills required in social studies, the teacher plans experiences that will promote the development and functional use of these skills. Because new experiences grow out of and are built upon previous experience, teacher evaluation gives direction to plans for future learning.

Teacher evaluation also reveals objective evidence that can be shared with parents in a variety of ways. Because evaluation is broader in scope than it was once conceived to be, teachers expect to do more than send to parents a mark to indicate the quality of a child's work in school.[3] In scheduled conferences teacher and parents together study test results, anecdotal records, check lists, and samples of a pupil's work to discover evidence of interests, initiative and creativity, problems, and needs. The teacher discusses the extent and quality of the child's knowledge of useful social studies information. He shares with the parents his analysis of the child's ability to use various skills needed in social studies—working with a group, doing simple research and reporting, and using arithmetic and language in functional ways. Particular problems that the pupil and the teacher have encountered are discussed as the teacher refers to notes he has taken during the progress of the area of learning. When the teacher can discuss with parents firsthand evidence of the child's performance and achievement in an area of learning, parents can be more objective in evaluating their child's growth and can acquire a keener insight into the objectives of social studies instruction.

When written reports are used to help parents understand their children's progress, the objective evidence gathered through teacher evaluation is equally essential and helpful. The teacher who relies only on general impressions in describing a pupil's behavior in social studies may generalize in a way that does not make clear the true level of the pupil's achievement or the direction of desirable improvement. But the teacher who has concrete evidence on which to base his report can be quite objective in describing a child's growth. To report, for example, that a child seems to like or dislike social studies does little to inform a parent of the child's development, needs, or interests. To suggest instead that the child's wide reading of library books at home can help to minimize his lack of success with the reference materials at his grade level is surely more meaningful to parents than a general statement would be. Such reports, supported by data gathered by the teacher, provide a realistic picture of present status and a blueprint of desirable emphases for the future.

Teacher evaluation, moreover, provides guidelines for developing the social studies curriculum as a whole. As evidence about children's behavior accumulates, the social studies curriculum can be critically evaluated. Are children developing the understandings considered to be important for them? Do these understandings represent a balance among various areas that are of concern to children and to the society in which they live? Are some of the important aspects of social living neglected? Are some included that now seem to be beyond the developmental level of the children or are far outside the range of their present or expected interests? Does the evaluation evidence reveal that children are developing attitudes that lead to actions appropriate to their maturity? Are the skills learned in social studies being put to use in life inside and outside the school? For example, evidence that a particular group does not have at its command the skills of group process emphasizes the need for more opportunities for teacher-pupil planning and for cooperatively planned group work. If playground accidents and illness arising from careless health habits persist in the school, this evidence should turn the attention of teachers and pupils to the problems of health and safety. When children fail to see how the skills they learn in language arts and mathematics operate in social studies, the need for more emphasis on the use of these skills in the area of learning is indicated. As the teacher takes a broad view of the results of the year's evaluation activities, he can focus upon the scope of the program, noting the extent to which children's needs have been met by the areas of learning that have been developed and the relationship of the social studies curriculum to the life of the community.

Thus, the importance of teacher evaluation in social studies must not be overlooked or minimized. It moves beyond teacher-pupil evaluation of the achievement of near-at-hand goals and extends to other important aspects of social studies—progress toward understandings, attitudes, behaviors, and skills; selection of further experiences to meet identified needs; accumulation of evaluative data to be shared with parents; and development of the social studies curriculum on a long-range basis.

Techniques for Evaluating Learnings

A variety of techniques provides for the teacher the evidence he needs to describe accurately the growth of children in social studies and to determine the effectiveness of the curriculum. Although tests have traditionally been the chief instruments of evaluation, more and more use is now being made of data drawn from interviews, anecdotal records, children's diaries of their experiences, and a variety of check lists and charts (see Figure 12). Some discussion of each of these may be useful in broadening the teacher's concept of evaluation and his understanding of ways of securing evaluative evidence.

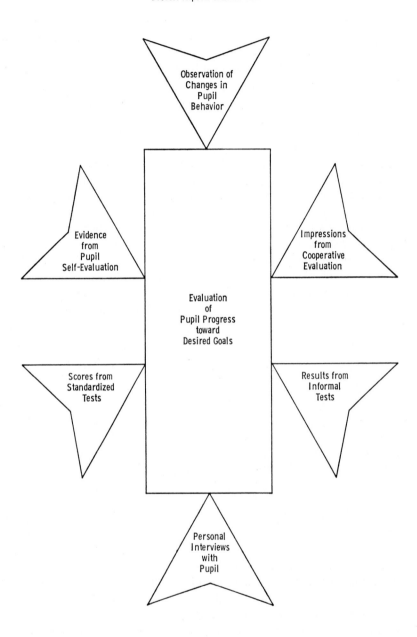

Figure 12

The function of evaluation is to assess the child's progress toward desired understandings, attitudes, skills, and behaviors.

EVALUATION THROUGH INFORMAL TESTING

Tests are among the most commonly used instruments of evaluation, although not necessarily the most important or the most useful. Informal, teacher-made tests in social studies have some values, providing evidence of children's development and their needs, data for reporting to parents, and guidance in planning future experiences. Tests make their special contribution in the evaluation of children's knowledge of background information and of their progress toward the understandings selected as important in learning.[4]

Informal tests in social studies must meet certain criteria, however, if the evidence they provide is to be truly useful in evaluation. The following questions may serve as guidelines for teachers and pupils who are constructing tests. Does the test have a real purpose? Are the kinds of items used appropriate to the purpose of the test? Is the language of the test easily understood? Are the directions simple and clear? Does the test emphasize important ideas rather than insignificant detail? Does the test encourage pupils to think critically?[5]

Informal tests utilize several kinds of items to test a variety of knowledges, understandings, attitudes, behaviors, and skills. The more objective types ask children to recall and supply definite information, to choose from among several possible responses, to recognize one of two alternatives, or to match one item with another. Older boys and girls can write responses to questions that call for discussion or opinion when the questions are clearly stated and the writing task is simple enough to encourage self-expression. The type of item, however, is important only to the extent that it facilitates evaluation for the purpose intended and to the extent that it is appropriate to the maturity level of the child.

In wide use are tests of background information that children have acquired in the area of learning. Because children need a body of facts that can function in problem solving and from which conclusions and generalizations can be drawn, testing for specific information can be justified. Good tests, however, emphasize significant facts while omitting detail that has little functional value. Furthermore, effective tests of information require children to see relationships among facts, to relate facts to important problems, to use facts to support ideas—in short, to use facts in the process of critical thinking about the area of study. Such tests are not easily con-

[4] J. Wayne Wrightstone, "Evaluation of Learning in the Social Studies," in John U. Michaelis (Ed.), *Social Studies in Elementary Schools* (Thirty-second Yearbook of the National Council for the Social Studies; Washington, D.C.: National Education Association, 1962), p. 315.

[5] R. Murray Thomas, *Evaluating Student Progress* (New York: David McKay Company, Inc., 1957), pp. 39–56.

structed, but they are far more valuable than conventional tests of isolated facts.

For example, a teacher-prepared test of factual information related to a significant problem is appropriate for these older children who are deep in a study of the industrial problems of their community. Note the provision for follow-up discussion.

> If we are to know and understand our community and its problems, we need correct information about its various activities. If the statement about industry in our community is true, mark it T; if it is false, mark it F. Be ready in class discussion to support all true statements with concrete evidence.
>
> _____ 1. Our factories manufacture more than one hundred different products.
> _____ 2. More than 5000 citizens work in our factories.
> _____ 3. The factories in our community contributed $50,000 last year to important community projects.
> _____ 4. Our factories pay much higher wages than do those in other large cities in our state.
> _____ 5. Most of the factories have pleasant working conditions for their employees.
> _____ 6. Factories in our community are asking for better water and power facilities than they have now.
> _____ 7. People of many groups come to our community to work in the factories.
> _____ 8. Various groups in our factories always get along well together.

Such tests of background information are especially useful when they require children to relate one aspect of their learning to another as they must do in the test that follows.

> On our camping trip we found many relationships between the natural environment and the ways in which primitive people lived. Choose the best answer for each question.
> 1. Why was the sassafras tree especially useful to early people?
>   a. It has a striking orange color that makes it easy to identify.
>   b. It grows thickly on banks of streams.
>   c. Its root can be stripped of its bark easily.
>   d. It has leaves of three different shapes.
> 2. Why were the rocks in the area made into paint?
>   a. They are a variety of shades of brown.
>   b. Sedimentary rocks are usually easily crushed.
>   c. The river washes many rocks down to the camp site.
>   d. Rocks were primitive people's best source of paint.
> 3. Why would primitive people not have chosen to live directly on the banks of the stream near our camp?
>   a. The water is not deep enough for fishing.
>   b. There are too many mosquitoes near the banks.
>   c. There is evidence that the river floods at each hard rain.
>   d. There are no bridges across the river to the other side

Tests of background information frequently emphasize children's knowledge of vocabulary and their understanding of concepts. Because successful achievement in every area of learning in social studies depends in part upon children's ability to understand and to use the special terms associated with the area, assessing their knowledge of key words and phrases is an important function of evaluation. Although every type of test item can be adapted to this purpose, various types of matching tests are very commonly used. Terms may be matched with appropriate ideas—for example, workmen and their special jobs, objects and their correct names or uses, machines and their functions, foods and their sources, or countries and their locations.

Pictures are often effective in testing concepts and vocabulary because the teacher can eliminate problems of reading that often affect the child's ability to make the correct response. For example, one fifth grade interested in the local air observation corps devised a test in which silhouettes of aircraft types were matched with their correct identification. Sketches of earth-moving machines observed at a building site helped another group test its use of the proper names for the machines as well as the particular kinds of work each could do. Second-grade pupils who were planning a garden tested their knowledge of harmful and helpful insects by attaching the appropriate name to a picture of each. Sixth-grade children's knowledge of terms applied to conservation practices was evaluated in part by asking them to name the techniques—strip farming, contour plowing, and the like —illustrated in a set of pictures. Vocabulary and concepts acquired in the area of learning often can be effectively tested in these ways.

Informal tests can provide also some evidence of children's knowledge of the important understandings of an area of learning. Although tests of basic understandings are much more difficult to construct than tests of information, it is possible to build tests that require pupils to identify important ideas, to organize data in some functional pattern, to apply principles to new situations, to interpret data, or to generalize on the basis of facts and information.[6]

Some of these tests, like the one given below, assess children's ability to recognize the basic understandings in an area of learning, distinguishing them from facts of lesser importance.

> In our study of television we have learned many interesting facts and some very important ideas. We may not remember all the facts, but we should remember the important ideas. Put an X before each of the sentences that you think everyone should remember.
> ———— 1. "Scanning" results in thirty separate pictures per second.
> ———— 2. Television performs valuable services for the community.
> ———— 3. In 1925 Vladimir Zworykin developed the iconoscope camera.

[6] Robert L. Thorndike and Elizabeth Hagan, *Measurement and Evaluation in Psychology and Education* (New York: John Wiley & Sons, Inc., 1961), p. 82.

———— 4. Television can be used to influence or persuade people.
———— 5. Coaxial cables are made of copper.
———— 6. Many workers are required to bring us a single television program.
———— 7. Some television programs are more worthwhile than others.
———— 8. Technical equipment used in television is very expensive.

In the following set of items children demonstrate their understanding of an essential community service by arranging in a logical order information about an important process.

The sentences below tell the story of the printing of a newspaper story. Can you number them in the correct order?
———— The mat is fitted into the press.
———— The reporter writes his story.
———— A metal plate is cast from the type.
———— A heavy paper mat is made from the metal plate.
———— The story is printed.
———— The reporter gathers the news.
———— The editor checks the reporter's story.
———— The mat is covered with ink.
———— The story is set in type.
———— The press begins to roll.

In this evaluation exercise, pictures supply the information from which children must generalize.

Here are pictures of three farms, one from prehistoric times, one from pioneer days, and one from today. Study them carefully and then put an X before each of the sentences in the list you think is a correct generalization about farming.
———— 1. Methods of farming have changed very little since early times.
———— 2. Hand labor is becoming more common on modern farms.
———— 3. Machinery helps modern farmers do more work with fewer helpers.
———— 4. Crops were better in early times because the soil was not worn out.
———— 5. Animals were used for farm work in early times.
———— 6. Good farmers today make many of their own farm tools.
———— 7. Scientific farming was unknown to primitive farmers.
———— 8. Many members of the primitive family helped with the farming.

Although informal tests function best for the kinds of evaluation just described, they can provide some limited evidence of the the attitudes and skills children have developed during the progress of an area of learning. Such tests may ask children's opinions about certain problems that have been discussed in the group; they may present situations in which children indicate the appropriate actions; they may identify children's attitudes toward certain important understandings developed in the study; they may call for children's opinions about various aspects of their recent study. It is clear, however, that tests of these kinds can produce only verbal expressions and cannot be accepted as final evidence of children's true feelings or probable behaviors. Only extensive observation of children can confirm the information revealed by tests of children's progress toward desirable attitudes, behaviors, and skills in the area of learning.[7]

Evaluation of attitudes through responses to a questionnaire was attempted in this simple test prepared for primary-grade children who had been thinking about ways in which members of the family work and play together. Note its potential and its limitations in terms of evaluating the pupil's true feelings.

> We have learned many things about our families. As I ask you these questions, please answer by writing *yes* or *no* on your paper. Say exactly what you feel is best.
>
> 1. Do you think Johnny's mother should expect him to care for his baby sister when he is interested in watching his favorite television show?
> 2. Do you think it would be a good idea for the families in your neighborhood to try to work together to keep their yards neat and clean?
> 3. Do you think that cooking, cleaning, and washing dishes are Mother's special job?
> 4. Do you think that it is necessary for the children in a family to help with family work?
> 5. Do you think the children in a family should choose the television programs for the family?
> 6. Do you think a family plan for work and play is a good idea?

Situation tests that describe some possible action to be taken can be used to evaluate children's attitudes and skills.[8] Although teachers recognize that such tests reveal only what children say they would do, nevertheless, the problem-situation approach has some merits. These samples attempt to test both attitudes and skills in several content areas. Again note their limitations if the teacher is concerned with children's actual behavior.

> Select the sentence that best tells what should be done in each situation.
>
> _____ Susan finds a box of matches on the walk outside her house. What should she do?
> a. She should strike each and blow it out so that other children will not try to use them.

---

[7] For further suggestions concerning the evaluation of attitudes, see J. Wayne Wrightstone, Joseph Justman, and Irving Robbins, *Evaluation in Modern Education* (New York: American Book Company, 1956), pp. 355–375.

[8] Hanna, Potter, and Hagaman, pp. 415–416.

     b. She should put them on the porch where her mother can get them later.

     c. She should put them in her book bag to take them to school the next day.

     d. She should take them to some adult who can put them safely away.

_____ Larry is a new boy in the school. He looks a bit different from the others and seems somewhat shy. What should other children do?

     a. Leave him alone for a few weeks until he stops being shy.

     b. Tell him he can stand on the sidelines and watch the ball teams play.

     c. Stay away from him until they know more about him.

     d. Show him around the school and invite him to play with them.

_____ Judy shares a room with her sister, but they cannot agree about who should keep the room clean. What should Judy do?

     a. Agree to take over the job of keeping the room clean.

     b. Refuse to do any cleaning in the room until her sister agrees to help.

     c. Ask her mother to help the two of them make a work plan that will be fair.

     d. Leave the room for her mother to clean.

The attitudes developed in an area of learning and some hint of children's probable behavior are suggested by items in which pupils are asked to indicate agreement or disagreement.[9] Items like the following are appropriate in a study of intercultural understanding.

Below are some statements about people. Place a check mark after each statement in the column that most nearly shows your feeling about the statement. Put a check under A if you agree, under D if you disagree, under the question mark if you are not sure.

A   D   ?

1. Some racial groups in our country are more intelligent than others.

2. It is important to know people well in order to understand them.

3. The American way of doing things should be taught to all peoples of the world.

4. People who are different from us are probably not as intelligent as we are.

5. People behave in certain ways because of custom and environment.

6. If people in other countries worked hard, they could have the things Americans have.

7. All children in our country have the right to an education.

[9] Wrightstone, pp. 320–321.

Informal tests that require written statements can be planned to reveal children's attitudes, skills, and interests. Although the teacher makes sure that the writing task is not too difficult for older children, he can secure the same kinds of information in interviews with younger children. The teacher may ask such revealing questions as the following:

1. Why do you think we studied about how to use fire?
2. What is the most important thing you learned about fire?
3. Are you afraid of fire? If you are, tell why.
4. What would you do if your dress or suit caught on fire?
5. What part of our study of fire did you like best?
6. What other questions about fire would you like to have answered?

It is clear that informal tests of understandings, attitudes, behaviors, and skills, as well as of background information and vocabulary, can provide some meaningful evidence about child growth in social studies if they emphasize significant ideas rather than insignificant ones and if they challenge children to think rather than merely to remember. The evidence gathered from these sources must, of course, be supplemented by many other kinds of information about the child's behavior in social studies.

CHECK LISTS, CHARTS, AND INTERVIEW RECORDS IN THE EVALUATION PROCESS

Although a well-constructed test facilitates the evaluation of children's knowledge of information and their ability to draw from facts the important understandings of the area of learning, other evidence must be used to throw additional light upon children's attitudes and behaviors in social studies. Some of these evidences come directly from experiences in cooperative evaluation, where teacher and children develop a variety of charts, check lists, and rating scales for use in assessing skills and attitudes. Similar devices constructed and employed by the teacher himself are further aids to more accurate observation of growth in social studies.[10]

Cooperatively-developed check lists and rating scales that grow out of teacher-pupil discussions are readily available sources of information for teacher evaluation. Note how a fifth-grade teacher uses a check list and rating scale developed by his pupils during a study of the meaning of democracy.

The boys and girls in this group have agreed upon standards they consider necessary for successful participation in group work:

A GOOD GROUP MEMBER

1. Listens carefully when others speak.
2. Considers the ideas of other people.

---

[10] For further examples, see John U. Michaelis, *Social Studies for Children in a Democracy: Recent Trends and Developments* (3d ed.; Englewood Cliffs, N.J.: Prentice-Hall, Inc., 1963), pp. 583–591.

3. Gives everyone a chance to participate.
4. Gets the facts before he disagrees.
5. Treats everyone in the group in a friendly way.

As pupils use these standards in discussing their skill as effective group members, their teacher observes closely, noting those who are more willing than others to evaluate themselves, those who are likely to dominate the discussion, those who show real concern about interpersonal relationships, and those who find group living difficult. Revelations like these, some new and some merely corroborative, help teachers realistically describe children's behavior.

When these pupils turn their attention to considering how democracy works in real life, they develop this rating scale for each person to use in evaluating his own participation in the life of the community.

DO I PRACTICE DEMOCRACY IN MY COMMUNITY?

1. Do I say unkind things about others in the community?
   Never___Sometimes___Often___
2. Do I let somebody else do a community job I should do?
   Never___Sometimes___Often___
3. Do I try to be friendly to the people in my neighborhood?
   Never___Sometimes___Often___
4. Do I follow safety rules on the street and in public places?
   Never___Sometimes___Often___
5. Do I do my part to keep parks and playgrounds clean?
   Never___Sometimes___Often___
6. Do I practice democracy in my scout troops and clubs?
   Never___Sometimes___Often___

The individual checking of the rating scale, as well as the group discussion that follows, makes available to the teacher information about pupils that might not be revealed in casual classroom contacts. The experiences children relate, the opinions they express, and the attitudes they reveal —Jack's comment about crossing the street with the red light, Sally's concern about an unfair election in her club, Robert's treatment of a newcomer in his neighborhood—all provide significant data for evaluations the teacher must make. Many other devices developed in cooperative evaluation have similar possibilities.

The teacher also devises similar records to aid in gathering accurate information about his pupils.[11] He may use a simple check list, such as the one given below, to record data about pupil growth in the skills of group participation. Such a check list, kept in a convenient but inconspicuous place on the teacher's desk, is easily available when the teacher has evi-

---

[11] For lists of behaviors to be evaluated in selected situations, see Hanna, Potter, and Hagaman, pp. 421–424.

dence that will justify giving a pupil credit for one of the skills being emphasized. He may choose to check each instance he observes or to check only when he feels the child has the habit or skill well in hand.

SKILLS IN GROUP PARTICIPATION

Evaluation Period_____	*Names of Children*							
WORK HABITS	HARRY	JOHN	SUSAN	HENRY				
1. Takes part in group planning								
2. Participates in discussion								
3. Considers the opinions and ideas of others								
4. Assumes leadership at appropriate times								
5. Participates in making group decisions								
6. Accepts and abides by group decisions								
7. Assumes responsibilities in carrying out group plans								
8. Participates in teacher-pupil evaluation of group experiences								

The teacher may prefer a separate check sheet for each pupil with space to record specific notes as supporting evidence. Such check lists, although time consuming, generally provide more objective information for teacher evaluation and for reporting to parents. The teacher may keep these record sheets alphabetized so that he can find quickly the appropriate page when he has a significant note to record.

A study of data recorded on these charts reveals the answers to many questions the teacher must ask as he evaluates children's progress in social studies. Which children are making successful growth in these skills and habits? Who has difficulty cooperating with others? Who has special skill in organizing a group for work? Who finishes independent work quickly and well? Who knows how to use many kinds of materials and equipment? The teacher's check lists provide in part answers for these and other questions and makes readily available evidence of children's progress toward the goals represented by the check lists or rating scales.

WORK HABITS

*Name of Pupil*_____*Evaluation Period*_____

DESIRABLE HABITS	STRENGTHS AND WEAKNESSES
1. Follows directions successfully.	
2. Works independently at assumed tasks.	
3. Uses materials and equipment properly.	
4. Returns materials to proper storage place after use.	
5. Finishes work promptly and in good form.	
6. Evaluates his work in terms of standards set up by his group.	

The teacher may supplement such knowledge of children with individual interviews that are planned to reveal children's attitudes toward the area of learning all have been pursuing. The teacher chooses carefully the questions he will ask, sometimes varying the questions to suit the particular pupil. He plans some way to record the responses on paper or on a tape recorder to make them available for later study. He may ask such questions as these:

1. What did you like about our study of the United Nations?
2. What was the most important thing you learned about the United Nations?
3. Why do you think we studied this problem?
4. What special contribution did you make to our study?
5. How are you going to use the ideas you gained from our study?

Although the interview questions will vary widely from one situation to another, the teacher can determine the child's general likes or dislikes in the study, his enthusiasm for putting into practice the skills he has learned, his interest in learning more about the subject, his feelings about the group activities that have been completed, his relationships with other children in the group, and his appreciation of the work that has been done. These kinds of information are more easily secured in personal interviews than in any other way.

The use the teacher makes of information drawn from check lists, rating scales, interview records, and the like, depends upon his concept of evaluation. The teacher who is interested in more than the acquisition of facts and information studies the notes he makes during cooperative evaluation and the records he has kept on his own, searching out the evidence of children's progress in acquiring certain skills and attitudes related to the area of learning. Are boys and girls putting into practice skill in using the telephone learned in their study of communication? skills of wise use of materials learned in their conservation study? skills of research learned in their investigation of the history of their community? From these records also may come evidences of the development of attitudes—respect for community service people visited, appreciation of the arts of a minority group, concern for refugee children in the community, or desire to improve the play area outside school. From these records, too, may come knowledge of children's work habits and study skills as well as knowledge of their ability to participate in cooperative activities.

EVALUATIVE DATA THROUGH ANECDOTAL RECORDS

Anecdotal records, the written description that the teacher keeps of pupil behavior, provide further useful information about children. Data for these records are secured only through careful observation of pupils throughout the problem-solving experience. Whenever a revealing situation arises, the teacher observes objectively the role the child is playing and records accurately significant information about his behavior.[12] He may make rough notes on a bit of paper kept at hand for that purpose and later transfer the data to more permanent form, or he may immediately employ some useful scheme he has devised. Some teachers keep an indexed notebook on the desk, ready for the date and a line or two about the incident. Others have a file of small cards with a current card for each pupil. Depending upon the needs of children and the ingenuity of the teacher, these anecdotal records take a variety of forms.

Some teachers prefer to keep a running account for a particular child who has special needs or problems. Steven, described below, is seeking his place in the group and beginning to show some interest in a social studies area of learning.

MONDAY: The children dashed in from recess to say that Steven was in the auditorium turning stage lights off and on. Later Steven interrupted noisily as he came in late.

TUESDAY: During morning planning Steven suggested that maybe we could do part of our social studies in the auditorium. He would work the lights for us. The children began to scold him for yesterday's escapade.

THURSDAY: Steven and his "gang" were late coming in from recess. They reported a surprise coming up in social studies. Some others started to tell but were rudely silenced!

MONDAY: The surprise Steven promised hasn't "jelled." He had a terrific word battle with some of his friends just before the class began to work on its problems about transportation.

[12] Thomas, pp. 182–197.

TUESDAY: Steven asked if his group could use the stage in the auditorium. We made arrangements, but plans exploded. No one is speaking to anyone right now.

THURSDAY: In planning period, someone asked Steven about his wonderful idea. They accused, "It was just a way to get to play with the stage lights some more, wasn't it?" Steven looked really miserable. Later in social studies class he said, "We could have done something good with this transportation problem if the others had cooperated."

What can a teacher learn by studying such a running account of a child's reactions to his classmates and to social studies? Evidence is far from complete, of course, but there are straws in the wind. Why is Steven having difficulty working with his friends? What is his real interest in the study of transportation? What will his "surprise" reveal to the teacher? What does Steven expect of his teacher in this situation?

Some anecdotal records include only the most significant happenings together with the teacher's questions and reactions. In this type of record, like the following one about Jack, the observer records briefly and objectively a situation or incident and may also record his immediate reaction. Both these notations are then available for later study.

Name	*Class*	*Grade*
DATE	SITUATION	TEACHER REACTION
1/2	Jack was chosen to be the pilot today; he agreed.	His first willing compliance with group suggestion.
1/7	Jack brought a book about airplanes from the library; he asked to have it read aloud.	A suggestion made to Jack's mother may be bringing results.
1/15	Jack and Philip had a big argument about how to assemble a model plane. Philip is really the expert, but Jack was persistent.	Does Jack feel inferior? He's poor in reading and in this activity, too.
1/16	Jack's father brought him to school today and commented in the boy's hearing that he didn't understand why Jack couldn't read his textbooks like other boys instead of just playing with model planes.	Has his father's concern made Jack more sensitive about his shortcomings?

What keys to Jack's problems in social studies are provided in this record? Has he made any recent gains in group status? What action should the teacher take in relieving home pressures? Is this airplane interest an opening wedge to improvement in reading reference materials? The teacher considers these questions, plans some action that may help Jack, and continues to record relevant events as they occur.

Some teachers encourage children to keep what are in a sense anecdotal records about their social studies experiences. Boys and girls are asked to record each day how they use their social studies time and to tell what they think of what they have done. Helen's diary, started during a study of family members and their responsibilities, is representative of this kind of anecdotal record.

MONDAY: My question WHAT IS A FAMILY got on our list. It's a good question.

TUESDAY: We took too long to organize our questions. I got tired. I read a book.

THURSDAY: During planning time, I said I could bring my baby sister to school and show how I take care of her. Teacher said WAIT. I didn't want to wait. So I read a book.

FRIDAY: I drew a picture of Cindy. That's my baby sister. The others talked about their jobs at home. I found another book to read. I'm still looking for one about how to be a baby sitter.

TUESDAY: Two of my friends are helping me fix a crib in the reading corner for Cindy when she comes to visit our room. My mother is going to bring her. The teacher says Cindy will be our first resource visitor. Sounds important.

Even though Helen is only nine, her writing shows clearly her reactions to social studies, her special interests, her vocabulary level, and the extent of her cooperation. How much could be learned from thirty such records!

Anecdotal records in themselves, however, expensive as they are in teacher time, do not evaluate children's progress in social studies.[13] If they are objectively compiled, they reveal simple evidences of children's behaviors: they tell what happens. It is the teacher's responsibility to study these records carefully to identify children's needs and problems and to search for evidences of growth in understanding, attitudes, behaviors, and skills. It is the anecdotal record that provides some of the most useful data about how children behave as a result of their social studies experiences.

RECORDS OF CHILDREN'S WORK AS AIDS TO EVALUATION

The records of their problem-solving experiences that children keep —progress charts, logs, summaries, bulletin boards, and the like—also play an important part in teacher evaluation. Although children have their own purposes for keeping these records—to list their questions and plans, to log an activity for later evaluation, to summarize important ideas for future

[13] Tiegs and Adams, p. 330.

use, or to show the problems they have been studying—teachers find them useful for other reasons.

The records children keep of their problems and plans for solving them provide clues for teacher evaluation. As teachers study the problems which children have raised, recall the individuals who were responsible for the problems, remember the discussion which the problems stimulated, and analyze the questions for significant content, they have some opportunities to evaluate children's attitudes and the quality of their thinking. What can the teacher learn about boys and girls from their questions and the work plans they organize? Consider these records made by pupils studying an important community agency.

ABOUT THE COMMUNITY SERVICE CENTER

1. Why do we have a Community Service Center?
2. Who is responsible for keeping the center open?
3. How does the center help our community?
4. Why is the center our responsibility?
5. What should a good citizen do for the center?
6. How can we help the center in its work?

OUR PLANS TO HELP

1. A committee will interview Mr. Severs to find out what work needs to be done at the center.
2. We will ask the fourth and sixth grades to help us in a Saturday paper drive for funds.
3. Each pupil will plan to spend one Saturday morning a month at the center to work.
4. The girls will begin collecting and repairing interesting story books.
5. The boys will ask Mr. Abel to help them repair toys and games for the center.

The logs children keep of their experiences also help teachers evaluate what the children have done. Logs are day-by-day accounts of the problem-solving activities in which the children engage, each day's entry added by an individual or a committee or dictated by the class group to the teacher. As he studies the log of experiences, the teacher considers problems encountered by the group, points of strength and weakness in group activity, special contributions of individuals, and changes that should be made in procedures. He is especially interested, however, in children's growth toward important understandings, attitudes, behaviors, and skills.

Note the following record kept by fourth-grade children as they raised silkworms from eggs to cocoon. Were the children who were keeping the log appreciating the great care that must be given to delicate creatures? Were they successfully following through on the steps of a useful process? Did they understand that great numbers of silkworms contribute to each tiny piece of silk they use? These excerpts from a daily log illustrate the opportunities for evaluation that exist in such records.

APRIL 24:   The silkworm eggs arrived today. They are black and no bigger than the point of a pin. We put them in the refrigerator until the mulberry leaves begin to come out.

MAY 8:   Peter brought the tiniest green leaves from his mulberry trees. We can start the silkworms.

MAY 20:   Janet, William, and Peter are the committee this week to feed the silkworms. Now that the eggs are hatched and the worms are growing, they had to cut holes in the netting so that the worms could crawl up through it and get to their food.

MAY 27:   The worms are ⅜ of an inch long now. We put one in a little tube of formaldehyde today to preserve it. We plan to do this at each stage of growth.

JUNE 3:   When we came today, we discovered that Andy had not come in over the weekend to feed the worms. They are alive, but they look limp.

JUNE 21:   The worms are quite large and beginning to look yellow. They move about very slowly and are not eating so much. Miss Wilson says some will begin to spin soon.

JUNE 26:   This morning we found a worm crawling across the floor, the first one that has left the table. Miss Wilson says he is looking for a place to spin his cocoon. We put him back with the others.

In a smiliar way the summaries of information written by individuals or groups offer opportunities for teacher evaluation. Group summaries of the results of problem solving are usually dictated to the teacher, with the children discussing and selecting the important ideas that should be recorded. What can be learned from studying the summaries children write? Are children including important understandings in the record they are making? Is their information correct? Are they making accurate generalizations? Are they using appropriate vocabulary? All these questions can be answered by studying the summary written by a third-grade group for a book about trains that they were making for younger children.

FREIGHT TRAINS

Freight trains carry very heavy loads. Our large freight trains are pulled by diesel engines. Freight trains have many different cars. The refrigerator car keeps things fresh. The tank car carries milk, vinegar, gas, oil, or other liquids. The box car carries food and goods that must be protected from the weather. The flat car carries machinery for farms and factories. The hopper car carries coal. The caboose is the last car on the train. The train is not a complete train until the caboose is fastened on and the lanterns are up.

Pictorial and graphic records such as bulletin board displays and murals are equally fruitful for evaluation purposes. The composition of such records reveals individual and group ability to select the most important facets of a problem to be illustrated, to show relationships among ideas in the presentation of a unified picture, and to visualize the various concepts encountered in the area of learning. In addition, such records reveal children's skill in using a variety of materials, in planning interesting presentations, and in working together. Such evidences of pupils' growth were easily observed in a bulletin board used by a first grade to record its trip to the local dairy. Illustrations in poster paint showed each stage of the trip from the time they entered the front door of the dairy to the end of the tour. Pictures placed in serpentine fashion signified the twists and turns inside the dairy, with pictures joined by cords from which hung small silhouettes of the children. Below each picture was its caption, dictated to the teacher and reproduced in manuscript by an adept pupil. Here was a record for others to enjoy, but for the teacher it was a source of evaluative data presented in the children's own style.

Thus the teacher who studies thoughtfully the records children make of their work—progress charts, logs and diaries, summaries, and pictorial records—can learn many things about his pupils as a group and some things about them as individuals. Evidence of group strengths and group needs as well as individual insights and skills are the rewards of a careful analysis of records that grow out of children's experiences in social studies.

THE STANDARDIZED TEST
AS AN EVALUATION DEVICE

The evidence about children's progress toward desirable goals gathered in all the ways previously described can be supplemented in most schools by a study of the scores pupils make on formal achievement tests.

In a social studies program that emphasizes problem solving, the selection of a standardized test appropriate to the nature of the curriculum is not a simple matter. An examination of existing tests in elementary school social studies reveals that few tests satisfactorily identify and measure the broader objectives of social studies; for the most part, the emphasis is upon specific content, with perhaps some attention to such study skills as reading maps and interpreting graphs. Even so, the usual standardized test can be useful, not for the purpose of testing accumulated knowledge for its own sake, but for determining whether or not pupils have an adequate reservoir of facts and information upon which to base conclusions and from which to formulate understandings and generalizations.[14]

Needless to say, however, the standardized test that concentrates on evaluation of understandings and problem-solving skills is more effective than the test that stresses only recall or recognition of facts. The test that asks the child to respond to a series of unrelated items like those given

[14] Harold G. Shane and E. T. McSwain, *Evaluation and the Elementary Curriculum* (rev. ed.; New York: Holt, Rinehart and Winston, Inc., 1958), p. 229.

below determines only his knowledge or lack of knowledge of specific facts. It is obvious that problem solving does not play a part in these test samples.

> A country with large jungles is
>   1. France   2. Holland   3. Brazil   4. Siberia
> The chief export of Brazil is
>   1. Coffee   2. Oil   3. Rice   4. Bananas

It is obvious that if teachers are concerned with children's ability to use facts in critical thinking and problem solving, they must search for and use tests that evaluate this ability.

A useful, cooperatively developed test represents the kind of standardized test that can effectively contribute to evaluation of the social studies curriculum. The test assumes there are certain skills and understandings basic to all good social studies curriculums despite variations in content from level to level as children progress through school. The test is built on the premise that what a pupil can do with his knowledge is as important as what he knows; hence each item of the test requires the application of a skill as well as the understanding of an important idea. The test is based upon the following understandings:

> The nature of social change and its effect on man's ways of living
> The profound effects of geographic environment on man's institutions and ways of living
> Control over the forces of nature as a major factor in accounting for the ways in which we live today
> The nature of a democratic society and the rights, privileges, and responsibilities of free men
> The means by which society directs and regulates the behavior of its members
> Man's economic wants and the ways of satisfying them
> The ways in which man attempts to understand and adjust to his environment and his place in the universe
> The interdependence among individuals, communities, societies, regions, and nations
> The sources of human nature and personality[15]

The test further requires the pupil to utilize certain skills in interpreting social studies materials and in seeing relationships among facts, concepts, and ideas learned. The test puts a premium on ability to do the following:

> Identify generalizations, main points, and central issues
> Identify, compare, and contrast underlying values, attitudes, assumptions, biases, and motives

[15] A *Brief*, Cooperative Sequential Tests of Educational Progress (Princeton, N.J.: Educational Testing Service, 1958), p. 18.

Distinguish fact from opinion; recognize propaganda
Assess adequacy of data with respect to relevancy, sufficiency, verifi-
ability, and consistency
Compare and contrast data
Apply appropriate outside information and criteria
Draw valid generalizations and conclusions

Moreover, this particular test is unique in that its various forms at several levels make it possible to evaluate children's growth through ten years of education—from the fourth through the fourteenth year.

Another excellent standardized test useful in social studies classes in which problem-solving and techniques of search are paramount goals is a test of work-study skills for pupils from grades 3 through 9.[16] This well-constructed test requires pupils to respond to items that evaluate their skill in using a variety of study techniques—map reading, selection and evaluation of reference materials, use of dictionary, interpretation of data, use of table of contents and index. A unique feature of this test is the recommendation that following the scoring of the test pupils analyze their scores and responses with a view to mapping plans for individual improvement in these important skills. In social studies groups in which flexible planning within a liberal framework of content removes the emphasis from memorizing and then reacting to a specific body of facts, such a test as this one gives the teacher concrete data about pupils' ability to work and study independently. In other words, it evaluates acquisition of many of the everyday techniques for "learning to learn."

Evaluating
the Problem-Solving Approach
to Learning

All evidence gathered through pupil self-evaluation, through cooperative evaluation, through teacher evaluation, and through the administration of standardized tests improves the teacher's judgment about the effectiveness of the problem-solving approach to learning. As the evidence makes clear, children's achievement of the knowledge goals of social studies and their progress toward the development of worthwhile understandings, attitudes, behaviors, and skills, continually supports the wisdom of emphasis upon problem solving.

Furthermore, several classic studies, which produced undeniable support for problem-solving methods of learning and teaching, strengthen the teacher's belief in the course he follows. These studies indicated clearly that

[16] *Iowa Every-Pupil Test of Basic Skills: Test B, Work-Study Skills* (Boston: Houghton Mifflin Company, 1965).

pupil involvement in the identification and solution of problems resulted in superior achievement in critical thinking, interpretation of data, and application of generalizations to new situations and in superior qualities of citizenship and good human relationships, with no attendant deficiencies in the acquisition of knowledge or basic skills.[17]

Such evidence from the past does not, however, excuse the teacher from critically observing the results of his pupils' experiences in problem solving. Even though he is completely satisfied with their achievement of the goals of the area of learning, he must be concerned about the methods children are using in their learning, concerned about the answers to several penetrating questions. How well are pupils identifying and clarifying problems? What evidence is there that they recognize the need for facts and information before trying to solve a problem? How effectively do pupils follow through on the plans they make for acquiring needed facts? How well do they use a variety of references? Are they alert to inconsistencies and inaccuracies in their reading and in the expressed ideas of others? How well do they organize the information on which conclusions are to be based? Do they withhold judgment until all the available facts are assembled? How fully do they put their conclusions into action? In what ways are they exhibiting democratic principles in their behavior? To what extent do they use problem-solving methods with problems that arise outside the social studies class?[18]

Although, as already concluded, there are few formal ways by which answers to these questions can be secured, the answers are nevertheless at the heart of social studies learning designed to produce individuals who can think critically and behave responsibly. Upon the teacher rests the tremendous task of identifying, observing, and recording for purposes of evaluation behaviors compatible with positive answers to these questions.

The crux of the matter is, of course, that true evaluation is necessarily closely related to objectives. It is purposeless to emphasize the achievement of objectives basic to living in democratic society and to evaluate the performance of boys and girls only in terms of facts and information learned. And, although it is much more difficult to measure achievement of understandings, attitudes, behaviors, and skills than it is to measure quantity

---

[17] F. A. Pistor, "Evaluating New School Practices by the Observational Method," in *Appraising the Elementary School Program* (Sixteenth Yearbook of the Department of Elementary School Principals; Washington, D.C.: National Education Association, 1937, pp. 377–389); J. Wayne Wrightstone, *Appraisal of Newer Elementary School Practices* (New York: Bureau of Publications, Teachers College, Columbia University, 1938); A. T. Jersild *et al.,* "An Evaluation of the Activity Program in New York City Public Elementary Schools," *Journal of Experimental Education* (December, 1939), pp. 166–207.

[18] Richard E. Gross, Raymond H. Muessig, and George L. Fersh, *The Problems Approach and the Social Studies* (Washington, D.C.: National Council for the Social Studies, 1960), p. 23.

of facts learned, there are promising developments that may make the task easier and the results more reliable. When children and teachers are actively involved in evaluation of pupil progress, many heretofore unused techniques and sources of information may be called into service.

QUESTIONS FOR DISCUSSION

Reread the dialogue at the beginning of the chapter as a basis for discussion.

1. How did the children's experiences create the need for evaluation?
2. How did the teacher make sure that the children would give continuing attention to skills developed in the area of learning?
3. How did group discussion function in the evaluation situations? Was there evidence of critical thinking? Were strengths and weaknesses being identified? Was there active participation among the children?
4. How did the teacher utilize in the parent conference the evaluative data gathered during the development of the area of learning?

SUGGESTIONS FOR CONSTRUCTING
A RESOURCE UNIT

Review the purposes of the area of learning. Select from the evaluation techniques suggested by your reading those that may be adapted to evaluation of children's growth toward these purposes.

Consider the opportunities for cooperative evaluation. List each of these opportunities and include the questions that will guide pupils in their review and evaluation of the experiences they have planned and implemented.

Consider the opportunities for teacher evaluation that arise during the progress of the area of learning. List these opportunities and include check lists and rating scales that will be used.

Consider and list the techniques the teacher will use at the close of the area of learning to assess pupil growth toward purposes as well as acquisition of essential information. Include interview guides and suggestions for observation of pupil behavior and skills.

Construct an informal test that utilizes various types of items designed to determine children's progress toward desired understandings, attitudes, skills, and behaviors. If items to test information are included, make sure that the expected responses represent facts and information essential to the development of significant understandings.

13

Resolving
Curriculum Issues

Children's voices, raised in friendly arguments, vibrated through the school corridors, quickening them to life. Doors slammed. Teachers, walking to their classrooms, exchanged morning greetings.

The school nurse, unlocking her office door, turned to remind a group of children, "Shots today. Don't forget."

A milkman clanked his bottles noisily on his way to the cafeteria. A blend of smells permeated the air—the smell of brewing coffee, the sharp clean smell of strong soap, the pungent odor of floor wax. In the principal's office, a telephone jangled loudly above the staccato sounds of a typewriter. Another day at McKinley Elementary School had begun.

In her classroom, Mrs. Johnson stood beside her desk, riffling through the pages of a book. She glanced at the wall clock. "It's nine o'clock, boys and girls. Time to begin our work. Donald, put your signal flags on the library table for now. We'll find a permanent place for them later. How nice to see you back, Susie. But where's Ronnie? He didn't seem ill yesterday."

"I'm here, Mrs. Johnson," Ronnie, his baseball cap askew, shouted from the doorway. "But Jimmy Walters almost isn't."

"Take your cap off and sit down, Ronnie. You're all out of breath. Have you been running? Why are you late? What do you mean, Jimmy Walters almost isn't here? Are you talking about Jim Walters in the fourth grade next door?"

"Me and him were riding our bikes peddling fast so we wouldn't be late."

"Not me and him, Ronnie," interrupted Mrs. Johnson. "Jim and I."

"Jim and I," Ronnie repeated. "We were almost here. The light was red and Jimmy yelled, 'Come on, we'll be late!' He ran the red light, and a car knocked him off his bike. It didn't hurt him much. Tore his pants. His chin's bleeding and his knee, too. He was lucky, that's all I got to say."

"Are you sure he is all right? I can't see why you boys and girls aren't more careful when you're riding your bicycles." Mrs. Johnson admonished her children as though they, too, had been involved in the accident. "We've talked and talked about safety rules, but you don't seem to pay any attention, and now somebody's hurt."

Half speaking to herself, she said, "I'm going to ask Mr. Teller to discuss this accident at our faculty meeting this afternoon. There must be some way to make children more safety-conscious."

At the faculty meeting that afternoon Mr. Teller, the principal, looked about the circle of teachers. "You recall that we decided last week to continue exploring the possibility of trying team teaching in some of our classrooms. Several of you have been reading about this kind of teaching and want to discuss it. But first we've another important matter to talk about today. Mrs. Leonard's Jimmy Walters was hit by a car this morning. He wasn't hurt but he was knocked off his bicycle, and it was just luck that he escaped serious injury. I know how you all keep after your children about observing safety rules and being careful. But obviously that's not enough. We're going to have to do something that will make every child safety-conscious."

Mrs. Leonard nodded her head emphatically. "We're going to make safety posters. Displaying them in the room and the halls should be a constant reminder to my boys and girls that they must be more careful."

"I don't think making safety posters is going to make children safety-conscious," Mrs. Rizak said. "Reading about safety, seeing films about it, listening to people talk about it are just as futile. Somehow, we've got to make our children understand the consequences of disobeying safety regulations and of being careless. They must understand the risks they are taking and act accordingly. But how to develop this understanding—that's the problem."

Mrs. Johnson mused, "I suppose we should go about it as we would any other problem."

"How's that?" Mrs. Kennedy asked. "Produce an imposing amount of information, enough information to convince them they can't ignore the facts, perhaps?"

"We've done that," Mrs. Adams protested. "We've given them facts and facts and facts."

"Yes, we have," agreed Mrs. Johnson. "But they aren't using them. I've thought a lot about this particular problem. The longer I work with children the more I'm convinced that they are influenced by the conclusions they themselves draw from the facts they know."

"Well, as your principal, I couldn't agree with you more," Mr. Teller said. "We are all reluctant to act on ideas until we've formed our own conclusions. Obviously there is concern about the success of our social studies program. I know some of you have been reading about new approaches to teaching this subject."

"Not just reading about them," declared Mr. Jacks. "I've been listening, too. During the past year I've heard half a dozen speakers tell us to stop trying to cover the subject matter of social studies. They're saying 'Teach children how to learn, to form generalizations and solve problems.' Mrs. Johnson, you've been using this approach with your boys and girls. You believe in it, don't you?"

"Indeed I do," Mrs. Johnson answered. "And I've felt for a long time that our social studies program needs more direction. Sometimes it seems to me that we're poles apart in our ideas about the ends and means of teaching social studies. I, for one, would like to see us develop a program that does what authorities are saying a social studies program should do—provide for cumulative learning, develop processes of inquiry, generalizing, and problem solving."

"Well, we can make a beginning," Mr. Teller said. "Next week we'll begin to do some planning. But it's getting late, and we've several other things to take care of this afternoon."

A Curriculum in Flux

From an almost exclusive emphasis on factual learning in history, civics, and geography to a problem-solving approach, the metamorphosis of social studies instruction has been slow, somewhat sporadic, and more evolutionary than revolutionary. To the point is Mayer's survey of instructional practices in the nation's schools in which he reports that facts, and where to find them, rather than explanations of how the facts came to be, are the almost exclusive focus of social studies instruction.[1] Yet for all the pedestrian pace of its curriculum changes, social studies is an area of the curriculum peculiarly in flux. Certainly of the many noteworthy attempts to improve it, only a few have been widely implemented.

Individually, perhaps the various efforts to improve social studies instruction that have been made during the past half century have little to contribute to the context of today's social studies curriculum. But looked at as a whole, one in relation to the other, these efforts clearly reflect an emerging concern for the child in the learning situation. And they indicate a changing point of view regarding the goals of social studies.

One of the earliest of these efforts attempted to capitalize on the natural correlation that exists among the social sciences. In this plan, children studying a geographic area—the New England states, for example—also studied the historical background of the region and the development of its government. For all its merit, however, this plan failed to win much support, probably because it was impractical to implement. But a related curriculum design, the fusion plan, was somewhat more widely adopted. In it, content from geography, history, and civics was merged in terms of problems, topics, or themes and was studied in relation to them. But selecting content to be taught created difficulties that were never satisfactorily resolved.

The next phase in the evolution of the social studies curriculum was a marked departure from these unproductive attempts at curriculum reform. Discouraged by the failure of previous approaches to curriculum change, some state and local curriculum makers proposed a plan using common social functions as the organizational framework. Basically functional in its approach to the goals of social studies, this plan was developed on the assumption that by studying the common activities in which cultural groups of the world have engaged for a long time, children will acquire the learnings they need for effective citizenship.[2]

For various reasons—its freshness, its feasibility, its logic, or for perhaps others—this plan garnered enough support to be incorporated into many curriculum guides. The first to publish a state course of study embodying this organization was Virginia. The social functions around which this course of study was developed are these: in the first grade, home and school

---

[1] Martin Mayer, The Schools (New York: Harper & Row, Publishers, 1961), pp. 215, 219–222.
[2] For a more detailed account of the history of the social studies curriculum see Henry J. Otto, Social Education in the Elementary Schools (New York: Holt, Rinehart and Winston, Inc., 1956), pp. 225–233.

life; in the second, community life; in the third and fourth, adaptation of life to varied natural environments and to advancing physical frontiers; in the fifth, effects of inventions and discoveries on daily life; and in the sixth, effects of machine production on living.[3] At this time, also, the concept of the functional unit as a vehicle for implementing this curriculum gained recognition and support.[4]

Originally serving as a model for other courses of study in which the social functions are used as the organizational framework, the Virginia Course of Study has undergone many modifications to fit local situations. But the majority of courses of study, both state and local, that have been designed since the publication of the Virginia Course of Study in 1934, perpetuate the concentric arrangement of learnings focused on social functions that this course of study pioneered. In other words, the widening-horizons approach to learning (as this approach is usually identified) is a deeply entrenched concept of curriculum organization.[5]

One exception to this approach is the curriculum, proposed by Stratemeyer and others, that is organized around the "persistent life situations" children face as they grow to adulthood. All-encompassing in character, this curriculum uses persistent life situations as the basis for both the scope and the sequence of the curriculum. Such persistent life situations as those involved in growth in individual capacities (health, intellectual powers, moral choice, esthetic expression and appreciation), growth in social participation (person-to-person relationships, group membership, intergroup relationships), and growth in dealing with environmental factors and forces (natural environment, industrial and technological forces) make up the scope of the curriculum. The changing aspects of these situations that the child encounters as he moves through successively higher levels of growth to maturity determine the sequence in which the learnings are to be introduced.[6]

Still another curriculum pattern is Miel and Brogan's "life space" curriculum. Designed to extend children's life space, it provides continuous orientation experiences through which children can explore what lies beyond the known—backward into the unknown as well as forward. Miel and Brogan cite illustrations of ways in which children's life space is extended through social studies. A kindergarten studies about the work that goes on in the world. A first grade prepares to understand newcomers to

[3] *Tentative Course of Study for Virginia Elementary Schools* (Richmond: Virginia State Board of Education, 1934).

[4] C. C. Trillingham, "Earmarks of a Functional Unit," *National Education Association Journal* (December, 1935), p. 282.

[5] Mayer, pp. 172, 178–179.

[6] Florence Stratemeyer, Hamden L. Forkner, Margaret G. McKim, and A. Harry Passow, *Developing a Curriculum for Modern Living* (rev. ed.; New York: Bureau of Publications, Teachers College, Columbia University, 1957).

the community. A second-grade group studies ways of getting to a metropolis. In a fourth grade children are finding out how people help a city to grow. Building respect for foreign backgrounds is the concern of pupils in a sixth grade. These and other examples suggest many possibilities for the extension of life space.[7]

More recently, Hanna has proposed a curriculum plan that has as its central theme the expanding communities of man. As in the widening-horizons curriculum design, the learning sequence in Hanna's proposal progresses from focus on the family unit to the perimeter of the wider world environment. But areas of study at each level are treated wholistically and relationships between the areas are stressed. Thus, children study the neighborhood in relation to the family's need to join in carrying on the activities of everyday living. At the next level children study the larger community, which has been formed to meet the needs the neighborhood cannot provide. And they study the state as a larger community in which the basic human activities inherent in smaller community units are carried on in more complex forms.

To Hanna, grade assignment of the community to be emphasized is relatively unimportant. What is important, however, is that children move sequentially from a study of a lesser community to the next larger one. He suggests the following sequence as one typically followed by schools adopting this pattern of curriculum organization: in the first grade, the child's family community and the child's school; in the second, the child's neighborhood community; in the third, the child's local communities—country, city, county, metropolis; in the fourth, the child's state community and the child's region of states community; in the fifth, the United States national community; and in the sixth, the United States and the Inter-American Community.[8]

A Curriculum Emerging

In a sense this chronology of divergent ideas about the social studies curriculum explains the current ferment of ideas about it. Indeed, in the face of this record it is to be expected that the social studies curriculum is currently a curriculum in flux. Yet there is more behind the current ferment in social studies than the processes of evolution. New forces and new catalysts are setting the mold for today's social studies curriculum, shaping it into the curriculum of the future.

Among these forces are the impressive gains made in recent years in the revision of mathematics and science programs—gains so impressive

[7] Alice Miel and Peggy Brogan, More Than Social Studies (Englewood Cliffs, N.J.: Prentice-Hall, Inc., 1957), pp. 217–258.
[8] Paul R. Hanna, "Revising the Social Studies: What Is Needed?" Social Education (April, 1963), pp. 190–196.

they are cracking the walls of complacency that have boxed in much of social studies instruction in the past. New curriculums in these areas are, in some cases, so bold in concept, so rich in the dimensions they add to children's learning, that they raise serious questions about social studies curriculums in operation.

Moreover, it is increasingly clear that some of the basic assumptions that undergird existing curriculum designs are no longer valid. There is a growing conviction, for example, that today's child, because of travel experiences and the impact of television, has a far wider range of interests, ideas, and concepts than was earlier thought to be true. Today's child, in other words, is ready for a more complex kind of intellectual stimulation than he has received in the past. In fact, Bruner's often-quoted hypothesis that any subject can be taught effectively in some intellectually honest form to any child at any age of development may prove to be more true than speculative.[9]

Take the findings of several recent studies that sought to discover whether or not young children are ready to deal with intricate and complex content and are capable of assimilating it. Smith and Cardinell have challenged the deeply entrenched expanding-environment theory with findings indicating that primary school children have well-defined interests in people and ideas that extend beyond their immediate environment.[10] Wann and his associates, after a long period of observation of nursery school and kindergarten children, concluded that even at this age today's child demonstrates readiness to engage in intellectual processes involving conceptualization.[11] Spodek's trial unit study of New York Harbor proved his hypothesis that kindergarten children not only can begin to develop history and geography concepts but can transfer their understandings to new situations.[12]

In addition, the dichotomy that has existed between elementary and secondary school social studies instruction is being attacked. Many who are concerned with instruction in social studies are raising questions about the logic of such a dichotomy. Are there real or contrived differences between the goals of elementary school social studies and those of the secondary school? And why, if learning is a developmental process, should

[9] Jerome Bruner, The Process of Education (Cambridge, Mass.: Harvard University Press, 1960), p. 33.
[10] Ronald O. Smith and Charles F. Cardinell, "Challenging the Expanding Environment Theory," Social Education (March, 1964), pp. 141–143.
[11] Kenneth D. Wann, Miriam S. Dorn, and Elizabeth Ann Liddle, Fostering Intellectual Development in Young Children (New York: Teachers College, Bureau of Publications, Columbia University, 1962).
[12] Bernard Spodek, "Developing Social Science Concepts in the Kindergarten," Social Education (May, 1963), pp. 253–256.

this process take a different direction midway up the escalator that transports the child to desired social studies understandings, attitudes, behaviors, and skills?

But of all the forces that impinge on the social studies curriculum none carries the impact of the knowledge explosion. Knowledge is basic to understanding. It is essential to insight. Without it there can be no perception, no conceptualization. Much knowledge to be taught is of recent origin, and knowledge will continue to explode at an accelerated rate. In fact, the realities of the knowledge explosion are such that only a more functional approach to learning can avoid complete disintegration of social studies as a significant area of the curriculum.

The reasoning involved in developing a functional social studies curriculum can be infinitely complex. However, the entry of some social scientists into the arena of social studies has produced a strand of ideas about this curriculum that are as logical as they are operational. As discussed in Chapter 1, the social scientists concerned with the teaching of their discipline to children have admonished teachers to abandon their unrealistic belief that they can "cover" a field of knowledge. They propose, instead, that children explore selected materials, materials that help them understand the important ideas of a discipline, the structure of a field. For example, they propose that children learn what history is by sampling key events that give them increasing understanding of historical processes.[13]

These social scientists also propose that the study of the structure of their discipline should be done through processes of inquiry appropriate to each field of study. At the base of this proposal is the premise that children who learn social science content through inquiry learn to study on their own, to verify data, and to become rational inquirers. They learn, in short, to use the tools of social science inquiry to open doors to the mysteries of human relationships.[14]

Perhaps these proposals conjure up visions of hundreds of classrooms with children intensively studying separate social science disciplines. Not so. Few social scientists expect, or even want, to make children specialists in their field of study. Rather, many of them, along with educators, believe that the prime emphasis in the elementary grades should be on problems that cut across the separate fields of study and often demand a synthesis from many fields. In other words, what appears to be emerging from the recent ferment of ideas about social studies in the elementary school is a curriculum that furthers two purposes. First, it affords children experience

[13] Fannie Shaftel, "Today's Social Studies," *The Instructor* (December, 1964), pp. 7, 94.
[14] *Ibid.*

with the real problems and tasks of modern society; and second, by the way it is implemented, it teaches the structure of the disciplines and the procedures of social science inquiry.[15]

- To date, this curriculum remains largely on the drawing board, but some groups are attempting to implement it, and a number of efforts to clarify it have appeared in print.[16] One explanation of this curriculum follows:

> The essential point in this curriculum is that the basic ideas from the social sciences would be so carefully and thoroughly analyzed that all instruction at all grade levels would point in the direction of achieving some one or more of important social science understandings.
>
> Under this arrangement actual topics selected for study would be allowed to vary since the major learnings which are the focus of concern transcend any specific topic. Fundamentally, topics selected for unit study should be considered as models, or exemplars, rather than being highly important in and of themselves. This seems to be absolutely essential since it is utterly impossible for the pupil to study all societies, past and present, even in several lifetimes, let alone the few years he has in school. The teacher must of necessity use selected topics to get across the basic learnings which can be widely applied in situations yet to be encountered by the pupil.[17]

Note a singular fact about the character of the currently emerging social studies curriculum. Unlike many of the earlier designs, this curriculum does not solidify content into prescribed specifics to be taught. In this approach, the particular facts chosen as the basis for communicating the generalization are not critical to the major learning involved. A number of factors may influence the choice of one content rather than another, factors such as the background and experience of the teacher, the nature of the community and cultural background of its members, the learning resources available, and, most important, the particular interest of the children in the classroom.[18]

[15] *Ibid.*

[16] Among the published attempts to convert the generalizing, problem-solving approach to learning in social studies into a curriculum guide is a two-part document edited by Clyde Inez Martin, *An Elementary School Social Studies Program*, Part I, "Components of the Program" (Austin: The University of Texas Press, 1963) and *Elementary School Social Studies*, Part II, "The Children's Program" (Austin: The University of Texas Press, 1964). Other social studies curriculum activities are being carried on at many institutions of higher education under Project Social Studies, an operation administered by the U.S. Office of Education. Another is a project initiated by the Educational Research Council of Greater Cleveland in 1961, a social studies program to be articulated in grades K–12 with the specific goals and objectives to be developed sequentially.

[17] Adapted from John Jarolomek, "Curriculum Content in the Elementary School," *Social Education* (February, 1962), p. 62.

[18] George W. Denemark, "Balancing Stability and Flexibility in Today's Curriculum," *The Indiana Social Studies Quarterly* (Muncie, Ind.: Ball State University, Autumn, 1963), pp. 45–51.

Obviously, however, it is one thing to theorize about the organizational structure of a curriculum and another to implement it. For many teachers the flexible character of this curriculum will be its greatest appeal. By the same token, however, what is a strength to one group of teachers may be an Achilles' heel to another. Many teachers like specifics. They give direction and provide security. Without them teachers often flounder, grow bewildered, and become discouraged in their attempts to implement a curriculum. But although there may be a certain security in teaching a prescribed set of specifics, there may be no justification for learning these specifics.

Briefly then, what these facts add up to is this: Whether or not the generalizing, problem-solving approach to social studies takes hold in the nation's schools depends to a large degree on the feelings of security a teacher has about implementing it. That the implementation of this curriculum should hinge on such a tenuous element may seem to be a non sequitur of the highest order. Yet few would argue to the contrary.

IMPLEMENTING THE PROBLEM-SOLVING APPROACH

On the theory, then, that there is security in knowledge, the way to assure the implementation of the problem-solving approach is to deepen teachers' understandings about it. To begin with, it may take an altered point of view to see as an educational task the perfecting of processes by which children can continue to grow into their culture.[19] An altered point of view may also be necessary to see the development of problem-solving abilities as facilitating children's growth into their culture. And basic to either consideration is an understanding of the problem-solving process.

In the very core of problem solving lies something more solid, more deeply dimensional than mere accumulation of information. To be sure, acquiring information is inherent in the problem-solving process. In the problem-solving process, however, information is accumulated not as an end in itself but as the means by which the process is furthered and completed. Information is subjected to analysis and interpretation. It is culled until only its essence remains. But this essence bears the stamp of logical, organized thinking and reflects an attitude of open-minded questioning and inquiry. It is possible, therefore, to use the conclusions or generalizations derived through such a process as principles from which to infer new facts. Important also is the fact that the conclusions are reached through discovery rather than through the method of assertion and proof. Hence, the probability of understanding the generalizations is increased.

[19] Lawrence K. Frank, "Four Ways to Look at Potentialities," in Alexander Frazier (Ed.), New Insights and the Curriculum (Yearbook of the Association for Supervision and Curriculum Development; Washington, D.C.: National Education Association, 1963), pp. 33–34.

Applied to social studies instruction, the problem-solving approach to learning provides a manageable, effective way to manipulate the extensive content of the social studies curriculum. It circumvents the more or less lockstep, "equal time" approach to knowledge of human relationships that many teachers use in their classrooms. Instead, selected areas of learning are probed in depth in attempts to find reasons, to discover cause–and–effect relationships, and to uncover logical explanations. The outcome of this concentrated study is a tentative conclusion based on the findings. This conclusion is then tested in less extensive areas of study that have elements in common with the initial area of learning. If validated, it is formulated as a working principle from which new facts about other areas may be inferred.

Essentially the problem-solving approach to learning in social studies is one of training children in the technique of discovery. It is more than learning the formalized procedures for the solution of problems, more than analytical thinking that characteristically proceeds a step at a time. It is also the development of effectiveness in intuitive thinking.[20] It is learning to utilize conceptually adequate modes of thought. It is learning the art of predictive reasoning, of manipulating knowledge to make it fit new tasks. It is, in short, developing a style of problem solving that will serve for most of the difficulties encountered in life. The hypothesis on which it is based is this: By generalizing what they have learned about the solving of intellectual problems in social studies, children can solve their problems of everyday living efficiently and effectively.

Thus, to reiterate what has been said before, teachers who would implement the problem-solving approach to learning in social studies must see clearly the objectives to be achieved. They must be sure of the generalizations toward which they expect to guide their pupils' learning. Teachers may arrive at these generalizations through their own knowledge and understanding of the various social science disciplines from which social studies draws its content, or they may decide to accept, or adapt to their purposes, statements of generalizations such as those appearing in the first chapter of this book. Whatever the source of the generalizations, they probably will be similar to or variations of the following:

People everywhere have certain basic needs and wants; how they meet these needs depends upon their environment and cultural level.

People depend upon each other for satisfaction of basic needs; the more complex these needs, the more interdependent people become.

The world in which we live is constantly changing; people must alter their ways of meeting needs and solving problems to meet changing conditions.

[20] The nature of intuitive thinking is explored by Bruner, pp. 55–68, and in his later book, *On Knowing (Essays for the Left Hand)* (Cambridge, Mass.: Belknap Press of Harvard University Press, 1962), pp. 102–105.

Ways in which people solve the problems of today and tomorrow are influenced by their cultural heritage; insight into the problems of the past gives direction to decision making for the future.

A peaceful world is based upon mutual respect and understanding; cooperation among individuals and groups is essential to the well-being of people everywhere.

These generalizations are the focal point of social studies; they center the attention of teachers upon the four basic concerns identified in the opening chapter of this book—man's essential needs; the interdependence of people and nations; the American heritage; and empathy with other cultures, peoples, races, and religions. At every grade level areas of learning must emphasize these central concerns and lead pupils surely to the generalizations that undergird all instruction in social studies.

The teacher's task, then, is one of making these generalizations operational in the classroom. What areas of learning will illumine these basic concerns and develop these generalizations? What kinds of problems can serve as the focus for areas of learning that achieve the objectives of social studies? It is possible to identify problems of varying levels of complexity for each area of concern. Pursuit of inquiry into such problems leads inevitably to important generalizations such as those identified above. Thoughtful consideration of problems like those that follow reveals clearly their relationship to basic concerns and resulting generalizations.

MAN'S ESSENTIAL NEEDS

Primary Level

Why is a family important?

Why do we go to school?

Why does our community provide many services for its people?

How do the needs of people for food, clothing, and shelter influence the work activities of the community?

Why is it important that people have many ways to move about and to communicate with each other?

Why are many communities different from ours?

Why do people live in different ways in different places?

Intermediate Level

Why must people continually struggle to control their environment?

Why is good health essential to individual and community welfare?

Why is education essential in a democracy?

Why is it necessary for the community to make regulations for the behavior of its members?

How does changing knowledge about the world affect the ways in which people meet their needs?

How does cooperative effort in the community make it a more pleasant and attractive place in which to live?

Why do the regions of our country vary in the ways people carry on their daily activities?

INTERDEPENDENCE OF PEOPLE AND NATIONS

Primary Level

Why must the workers of the community help each other in performing services?

How do people of a community depend on each other in times of emergency?

Why does our community get many of the things it needs from other communities?

Intermediate Level

Why is it impossible for our community to be self-sufficient?

Why is it necessary for our country to be concerned about the welfare of other people in the world?

Why do events and changes in one part of the world today affect the lives of people in other parts of the world?

Why is cooperative effort to solve problems becoming increasingly important?

THE AMERICAN HERITAGE

Primary Level

How have ways of living in our community changed since the days of the first inhabitants?

Why do we celebrate special days in our country's history?

How can we be democratic at home and school?

Intermediate Level

Why did democracy come into being and thrive in America?

How can we maintain and improve the democratic way of life?

Why is democracy still not a reality for many people in our country?

Why is democracy the best way of life for the American people?

Why do people depend on government for many of the services they once provided for themselves?

Why are some community and national problems the result of ways in which we solved problems in the past?

How do the lives of our national heroes help us to understand our country's history?

How has America's growth been influenced by the kinds of people who settled here?

EMPATHY WITH OTHER CULTURES, PEOPLES, RACES, AND RELIGIONS

Primary Level

Why do people in our community go to different churches?

How do the lives of famous people help us to understand the groups they represent?

Why should we help people of other groups who come to our community?

How are families everywhere alike?

Intermediate Level

Why do peoples of the world worship as they do?

How do the traditions and customs of a people influence their beliefs and behavior?

How does knowing about the culture of a people help us to understand them?

Why does a person's race sometimes make a difference in the way he is accepted?
How have the various cultural groups that live in the community influenced its growth and character?

These problems, which illustrate how children may find entrée into areas of learning focusing on the basic concerns and generalizations of social studies, are necessarily broad and general. The specific problem that triggers the area of learning in the classroom will necessarily reflect the local situation as well as the needs and interests of the children. The teacher is well aware that a variety of problems may lead children to a particular generalization; he is also aware that is is the generalization that is more constant and less variable, whereas it is the nature of the specific problem that is subject to alteration in a changing world.

Consider, for example, one of the general problems identified above: *Why do people live in different ways in different places?* Inherent in this general problem is a variety of problems, any one of which may be significant to pupils because of a real-life situation in which they are personally involved. Here are some of the possibilities:

Primary Level
Why do people eat the food they eat?
How does weather affect the way the people live?
Why have people built so many kinds of shelter?
How do people adjust their way of living to the place in which they live?
Why do people use different kinds of transportation throughout the world?
Why do the people in our community live in different ways?

Intermediate Level
How do natural resources help a region to grow?
How do scientific discoveries affect the use of natural resources?
Why are rivers and waterways important to the development of a region?
How does the geography of a region influence the industries that develop there?
Why is our region different from other regions in the United States?
Why have some regions developed more rapidly than others?
How are people in the developing countries changing their ways of living?

Clearly many areas of learning may contribute to the development of a given concept or generalization. Children in several schools in a community may be working on different phases of the same problem or on different problems, and yet all may be in the process of developing the same basic generalizations. Inherent in this approach to social studies is the flexibility and adaptability so essential to making sure that social studies is completely responsive to the current needs of the children in a particular community.

Fostering
Cumulative Learning

But there is more to the task of implementing the problem-solving approach to learning in social studies than engaging children in the processes of inquiry, problem solving, and generalizing. More fundamental, perhaps, is the task of assuring for every child the continuity of learnings acquired through these processes. Essentially this is the task of devising a strategy for linking children's immediate understandings about the subject matter of social studies to more abstract ways of thinking about it.

It is the task of designing a sequential arrangement of experiences that will produce a spiral of cumulative learning. In more specific terms, it is the task of creating problem-centered situations in which children in the lower primary grades begin to develop simple generalizations about man carrying on his everyday activities. Gradually as they progress through the elementary school they work with more and more difficult arrangements of information and as a result deepen and reshape the dimensions of their generalizations about these activities. Thus, by the time they complete high school, children refine the same generalization many times, using increasingly more abstract levels of thought at each higher echelon of learning. In short, it is the task of devising a strategy that fosters continuous, unbroken learning of the subject matter of social studies through the elementary and secondary schools, a strategy that will develop children's ability to think precisely, abstractly, and critically about the subject matter of social studies. As an illustration of continuous learning consider the following example:

Many second-grade children know that their community employs men and women to protect them. Reasons for employing these people, however, are not generally familiar. Thus the problem of why a community employs protectors is an important matter of inquiry for these children. To find the answer to it, they search for and discover a miscellany of information about protectors who work in their community—traffic policemen, fire watchmen, fire fighters, fire inspectors, public health officers, the school nurse, and others—information that leads them to the important generalization: When individuals cannot provide themselves with the kinds of protection they need, they cooperate with other people to arrange for it.

Later, these children deepen their understanding of this generalization when they discover that in their state and nation there are cooperatively organized agencies and services specifically devoted to the protection of citizens. As children mature they find that the United Nations Security Forces are set up for the same basic reasons that motivate people in the local, state, or national community to employ policemen and similar protectors. At an even higher level, consideration of treaties and military alliances—the North Atlantic Treaty Organization, for example—adds more depth and preciseness to the original generalization. In each instance the problems that set off the search for information are different, and each calls for a collection of different kinds of data, in different kinds of sequences. But the examination of data in each case establishes the same set of relationships. Hence, by drawing on previously formulated generalizations, children are able to interpret the relationships discovered at higher levels of learning, think in more abstract terms about them, and ultimately formulate generalizations of increasingly higher levels of thought (see Figure 13).

Identifying Relationships with Other Disciplines

The fact that the social sciences lose their individuality when they are distilled and blended into social studies content is a matter of concern to some social scientists. Indeed, there are teachers who contend that children fail to acquire important history or geography or other social science learnings when they concentrate on social studies problems. Admittedly, unless the teacher deliberately plans for these learnings, they may be neglected. But children's failure to acquire desired social science learnings is a teacher's failure. It cannot be attributed to the nature of social studies content. Residing in every social studies generalization are generalizations from other social science disciplines. Note the economics, geography, and history generalizations that exist in this social studies generalization: *People everywhere have certain basic needs; how they meet these needs depends on their environment and their cultural level.*

ECONOMICS

Trade between peoples begins when there is a scarcity of resources in one group and an abundance of the desired resources in another.

When there are not enough of the necessities of life, such as food, clothing, and shelter, to meet the demands for them, their cost to the individual increases.

When competition occurs without a system of checks and balances, people who lack adequate means to bargain may be deprived of needed goods and services.

Dividing the labor needed to produce essential goods and services increases efficiency in producing these goods and services, but it also increases interdependence among the producers.

GEOGRAPHY

There is a relationship between the climatic features of an area and the ways people in the area meet their basic needs.

Because men everywhere have certain basic needs that must be met, there are many similarities in the daily lives of people in all parts of the world.

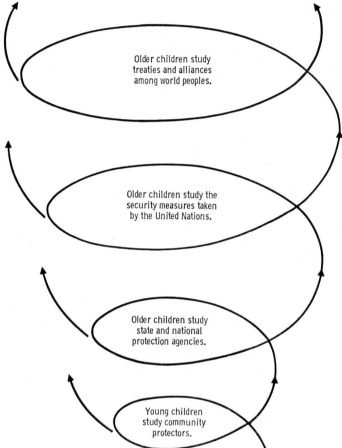

Children's Learning Is Cumulative

Generalization: When individuals cannot protect themselves with the kinds of protection they need, they cooperate with other people to arrange for this protection.

Older children study treaties and alliances among world peoples.

Older children study the security measures taken by the United Nations.

Older children study state and national protection agencies.

Young children study community protectors.

Figure 13

Through a sequential arrangement of experiences children examine new data that reinforce the relationships expressed in the generalization.

Generally, the more natural vegetation there is in an area where man lives, the easier it is for him to meet his need for food, clothing, and shelter.

Since mountainous areas create problems of living, they are, for the most part, less heavily populated than plateau and lowland areas.

HISTORY

Throughout time, man has sought to meet his needs for food, clothing, and shelter by exploring unknown areas of the world.

In general, the leaders of a particular period in history are the men whose ideas and inventions improved the welfare of the people among whom they lived.

Full assessment of a particular people's productivity in meeting their needs cannot be made without knowledge of their historical background.

Moreover, not only does social studies draw upon generalizations from the social sciences; it also draws into its orbit generalizations from the science disciplines. Educators agree that children and youth should sense the essential relationships between the advancements of science and their social implications. It seems logical, therefore, that science generalizations should play an increasingly important part in the study of human relationships explored in social studies. Consider the science generalizations inherent in the previously explored social studies generalization: *People everywhere have certain basic needs; how they meet these needs depends on their environment and their cultural level.*

SCIENCE

Whenever man creates an effective substitute for a natural resource or discovers new ways to use it more effectively, he reduces his dependence upon this resource.

Man's constant experimentation with ways to preserve and package foods is changing the eating habits of people everywhere.

The rate at which scientific inventions occur in an area directly influences the ways people in the area meet their basic needs.

In inventing machines that make it easier for him to meet his physical needs, man often creates new social problems that he must solve.

It remains for teachers to identify these generalizations and to do so with full knowledge of their relatedness.[21] For, as pointed out again and again in this book, the goals of the social studies curriculum at the elementary school level are not the mastery of discrete bodies of content from various social science disciplines or from the disciplines of science. To what end such mastery? Only as these disciplines mesh together to shed light on the goodnesses and problems of human living are they important. No single discipline can adequately shed this light.

---

[21] For basic consideration of the geographic concepts and learnings to be developed from kindergarten through the twelfth grade see Wilhemina Hill *et al.*, *Curriculum Guide for Geographic Education* (Normal, Ill.: National Council for Geographic Education Publications Center, 1963); for a guide to economic education within the framework of a social studies curriculum see Garney L. Darrin, "Economics in the Elementary School Curriculum." Unpublished doctoral dissertation, University of Maryland, 1959; for assistance in the identification and application of basic social science concepts at each grade level see *A Conceptual Framework for the Social Studies in Wisconsin Schools* (Madison, Wis.: State Superintendent of Public Instruction, 1964).

As teachers and children seek to draw on various disciplines to illumine the problems of human relationships, it follows that the problems children undertake to solve in the area of learning will naturally involve questions and problems that have implications for these disciplines. To the point are the specific problems children may identify in an area of learning based on the general problem: *Why are many communities different from ours?*

Some understanding of geography, both physical and cultural, naturally follows the pursuit of queries about the community: In what kind of place is our community located? How does the place in which our community is located influence the lives of its people? What kinds of work can be done by people who live in communities like ours? Why is it more difficult to live in some communities than in others? Why are communities in other latitudes sometimes different from ours? Certainly these problems make it clear that the geographic setting of the community must be considered an important condition affecting differences among communities. Study of the natural environment of the community and the use man makes of it leads even young children into some knowledge of physical and cultural geography.

Sociology, man's life in the social group, is reflected in other questions about the community: What groups of people live in our community? Why do communities have different kinds of people? How to people in the community help each other? Why is it necessary for people to work together to make their community better? How do various community agencies help communities? Why do some communities have more problems than others? These inquiries are merely indicative of concerns that involve concepts and generalizations from the field of sociology.

More mature children find that problems about differences in communities turn their attention to the historical development of their own communities and that of others. Has our community always been as it is now? What evidences are there in our community of events of the past? Does history help to explain why some communities are different from ours? How are some of the problems of the community related to things that happened in the past? Such problems as these represent the history concerns of social studies.

Government and citizenship are an appropriate part of any study of communities. What kind of government does our community have? Why do some communities have a different kind of government from ours? How does the community protect its citizens? Why are laws necessary? Why do some communities discriminate against some of their citizens? Problems like these lead directly to generalizations from the field of government.

Similarly, other social science disciplines are involved in exploring differences in communities. Considerations of economics are basic to the following problems: What kinds of work are done in the community? Why do communities specialize in different kinds of work? How are the natural resources of the community used? What can be done to improve living conditions in the community? Why are some communities poorer than others? When children begin to understand the implications of facts they gather from such inquiry, generalizations from economics become possible.

Understandings from anthropology are inherent in other questions about communities and the differences among them: Why do people of our community have different habits and customs? Why do the customs of some communities differ from ours? Do the things people believe make a difference in the way they behave? Although considerations that reflect the concerns of anthropology may seem mature for elementary school children, nevertheless the effective area of learning offers opportunities for children to explore elementary facets of anthropology.

Even philosophy has its place in the problem-solving experiences of social studies, represented not so much in the content as in the method of problem solving. Here it is that the principles of logic, the scientific method, and critical thinking operate to help children in their search for knowledge.

All this is not to say that the teacher must consciously attend to the several social sciences in each area of learning that is developed in the classroom; it is only to say that if the teacher intends that pupils will have experiences leading to important social science generalizations, he has ample opportunity to guide pupils in raising and solving problems that will help them formulate these fundamental ideas.

Those who are critical of social studies as an area of the curriculum might better turn their attention to the preparation of teachers than to attacks upon the subject itself. In teacher education the autonomy of the social sciences is important, for teachers must know each discipline, its unique contributions, and its key concepts and generalizations. Moreover, their knowledge should embrace the less traditional social science disciplines, such as anthropology and social psychology. Ideally, too, they should have had firsthand experience in living in cultures other than their own. They should avoid stagnation by reading widely from the vast repertoire of books pertaining to man's activities, past, present, and future, and they should be active participants in community life.[22]

Teachers thus prepared are teachers who can identify the range of social science learnings that are inherent in all social studies generalizations. What is more, they can teach in ways that enable children to acquire these learnings.

---

[22] Roy A. Price (Ed.), *Needed Research in the Teaching of the Social Studies; A Conference Report*, Research Bulletin No. 1 (Washington, D.C.: National Council for the Social Studies, 1964), p. 15.

Adapting Problems
to Individual Differences

To adapt instruction to the nuances of behavior that exist in a classroom is one of the teacher's greatest challenges. That no two children in a classroom are alike is a truism most teachers accept. In every classroom there are children of lesser abilities, children who plod along with mediocre successes, and children of talent whose gifts shine brightly. When teachers adapt their instruction to these differences, learning for all is a joyous, productive adventure. When they fail to do so, it is none of these. Instead, learning is anxiety. It is drudgery. It is boredom. And never in any case is it truly productive.

It takes many skills and much ingenuity to adapt classroom instruction to individual differences. And it takes all the resources at a teacher's command. One of these resources is the general problem that serves as the core of an area of learning. This problem, by its very nature, facilitates the task of individualizing instruction. It has a functional kind of potential, limited only by a teacher's insight into its possibilities.

Inherent in every general problem, around which the area of learning unfolds, is a series of subordinate or corollary problems that range in difficulty from the simplest to the most complex kinds of problems. Some of these problems contain only one or two familiar concepts. Others involve abstractions of the highest order. Some require a minimum amount of effort to solve. Others take many different kinds of and levels of operations to reach the solution. Note, for example, the range and variety of subproblems that are inherent in the problem: *How do people in a community communicate ideas and express feelings about the happenings around them?*

How do people in a community find out what is happening around them each day?
Why is some mail delivered by postmen whereas other mail must be called for at the post office?
Why are mail boxes and mail trucks painted red, white, and blue?
Why do some communities have television stations and others do not?
Why do we pay for news printed in newspapers but do not pay to hear broadcasts on television and radio?
Why does the United States government own the post office in our community and pay the people who work in it?
How does the size of a community affect the way people share ideas and opinions?
How did people share ideas and opinions before the invention of modern media of communication?
How has automation affected mail service in the United States?
Why is freedom of the press a cherished American ideal?

Why does the government set up controls for operating radio and television stations?

How will international television affect communication among peoples in a community?

Within this range of problems are problems that children of the most limited abilities can solve and problems that challenge the abilities of gifted children. The problem about why mail boxes are painted red, white, and blue is one that children who have reading difficulties can solve. Solving it is simply a matter of writing an easily constructed letter to the Post-master General or interviewing the local postmaster, whereas to solve the problem that asks why freedom of speech is one of America's most cherished ideals takes the abilities of exceptionally gifted children to carry on the research needed to solve it. And so with the other problems listed above. Taken as a whole they provide many opportunities for adapting instruction to individual differences.

Part of the teacher's task in planning ahead for an area of learning, therefore, is to look at the ramifications of the general problem to be solved, dissect it, and analyze it in terms of children's abilities. To dissect a problem in this manner, of course, requires knowledge of the content that sheds light on it. Without this knowledge there is little basis for identifying the components of the general problem. To subdivide general problems to meet the abilities of many children a teacher must be fully aware of these abilities and know, too, the interests of each child.

Utilizing
the Social Studies Textbook

Many teachers find themselves in the dilemma of being held accountable for the content contained in a particlar social studies textbook while they recognize that such a commitment circumscribes learning in the area. Unfortunately, for many this dilemma remains unresolved. To them the problem-solving approach and the textbook approach to learning in social studies seem too incompatible to be reconciled. The fact of the matter is, however, that it is both practical and feasible to adapt the textbook approach to a problem-solving approach.

Like most operations that involve change, moving from textbook teaching to unit organization and problem-solving experiences is a transitional process. To effect this transition a teacher first considers the generalizations to be developed through social studies instruction. He then analyzes the content of the social studies textbook in terms of these generalizations and rearranges discrete chapters in the textbook to bring them into a closer relationship to the generalizations. When the content is reorganized, he summarizes it into specific understandings that ultimately lead to the generalizations identified earlier. Finally, he identifies general problems that will serve as the stimulus for study and research. What emerges from this process are several sets of understandings and related problems, each of which may serve as the nucleus of an area of learning.

Still, such an adaptation must be recognized for what it is—a transitional way to bridge the gap between the two approaches.[23] Fundamental differences remain. In the textbook approach, content is limited in scope, motivation is necessarily artificial, and evaluation is circumscribed by the textbook. In contrast, content in the problem-solving approach is drawn from a variety of sources and includes many levels of difficulty. Motivation is problem-centered. Children, not the teacher, propose the problems to be solved. Evaluation is broadly conceived and involves many kinds of learnings and many behaviors.

Teachers cannot assume, therefore, that to modify their textbook teaching, as described above, is to use the problem-solving approach to learning in social studies. At the same time, however, having structured their teaching in a pattern that conforms more closely to teaching through problem solving, they undoubtedly will rely less on the textbook as their basic tool of learning and more on multiple sources of information. In fact, it is quite possible that the results achieved through even a limited modification of the textbook approach will encourage teachers to move toward full use of the problem-solving approach to learning in social studies.[24]

Planning a Time
for Social Studies

It is clear that the area of learning requires more than a short period of time in the daily schedule. Once children and teachers begin to plan together, unlimited resources of time appear to be desirable. On the other hand, the wise teacher knows that social studies alone cannot consume the whole school day. Planning so that problem solving can be effectively developed within reasonable time limits becomes of real concern to pupils and teacher.

As the teacher plans adequate time for social studies and yet maintains a balance with other experiences in the daily program, he is aware that the school day that is cut into many short periods, each of which confines within its boundaries a definite subject, is not well adapted to problem

[23] See Raymond H. Muessig, "Bridging the Gap between Textbook Teaching and Unit Teaching," *The Social Studies* (February, 1963), pp. 43–47, for a more detailed accounting of steps that facilitate the transition from textbook to unit teaching.
[24] Albert H. Shuster and Milton E. Ploghoft, *The Emerging Elementary Curriculum* (Columbus, Ohio: Charles E. Merrill Books, Inc., 1963), pp. 99–101.

solving in the area of learning. Although it is quite possible, of course, to give a textbook assignment that will conveniently utilize a specific time on the schedule, many of the experiences that grow out of cooperative planning to solve problems cannot be confined so successfully to small blocks of time. How impossible it would be to plan and take a field trip, to organize work groups to carry on a construction experience, to interview a resource visitor, or to visit the library for the purpose of research in the short time often assigned each day to social studies in the conventional school.

On the other hand, the daily schedule that provides large blocks of time not so specifically designated for particular subjects can be a boon to problem solving. Sometimes social studies and reading periods are combined; on other days arithmetic periods may become a part of social studies as children figure the cost of materials they need to buy or make financial arrangements for a field trip. Larger blocks of time make possible better use of the school day and avoid abrupt changes that break into children's problem-solving experiences.[25]

The need for these expanded periods of time also suggests that a flexible daily schedule is highly advantageous. There seems to be no particular reason why each day's schedule must be the same as every other, although many administrators and teachers adhere to this practice. True, certain routines of the school day probably should be regularly scheduled, but if children plan their day cooperatively, they are not disturbed by rearrangements in the daily program. For example, if the entire morning is required for the social studies field trip on one day, the following days, when only short periods are needed for a follow-up discussion or for planning a new activity, can be rearranged to give more time to other subjects. When a longer period for research becomes desirable, the flexible program provides for it. Such flexibility in the daily schedule is prerequisite to the social studies curriculum that utilizes to best advantage children's planning, capitalizes upon their interests and needs, and encourages true problem solving.

Interpreting Social Studies to Parents

The development of the problem-solving approach to social studies has important implications for relationships with parents and other persons in the community. To those unfamiliar with the modern school the de-

[25] G. Wesley Sowards and Mary Margaret Scobey, *The Changing Curriculum and the Elementary Teacher* (San Francisco: Wadsworth Publishing Company, Inc., 1961), p. 502.

velopment of areas of learning will be quite new. Parents and other adults may not see in the experiences of their children the old and familiar textbook study and recitation routines they knew when they were in the elementary school. They may be puzzled by the questions children ask and the research activities they undertake. They may misinterpret the purposes of the many community experiences in which pupils engage as they pursue solutions to problems.

On the other hand, parents have a variety of opportunities to know something of the experiences their children are having in cooperative planning and problem solving. Perhaps the most formal contact they have with the social studies curriculum comes through report cards and parent-teacher conferences. As pointed out earlier in the chapter on evaluation, the modern report card interprets the social studies curriculum through emphasis on the child's skill in problem solving as well as on his acquisition of important understandings and attitudes. In the evaluation conference teachers have further occasion to interpret social studies to parents and to answer their questions about their children's experiences.

Perhaps the most fruitful avenue for improving parent understanding of social studies comes through parent participation in the implementation of the area of learning. The problem-solving experiences of children inevitably involve parents and other members of the community. Often parents are participants in home projects that grow out of the area of learning pupils are developing—together parents and children look for foreign foods in the kitchen, record types of TV advertising, search for fire hazards around the home, take photographs of important events, or collect samples for a display in the classroom. Frequently parents or other adults are guides on class field trips and do their share of answering questions, interpreting information, or providing for group safety. In the classroom they share talents and hobbies or help with an activity in which they have special skill. Extensive participation of these kinds is characteristic of the problem-solving approach to social studies. Providing opportunity for parents to experience at firsthand what their children are learning is a most effective way to help them understand the social studies curriculum.

In some school communities parents also participate in curriculum improvement activities, serving as an advisory group on the needs of the community and representing parents' desires for their children. Although the task of curriculum construction is the responsibility of professional persons, parents and other lay members of the community can make useful contributions to the identification of goals to be achieved. Through these experiences parents acquire knowledge of the social studies curriculum that they can share with the community at large.

Engaging
in Curriculum Improvement

Teachers who believe in the problem-solving approach to social studies and want to implement it feel compelled to evaluate critically the social studies curriculum of their schools, asking whether or not it is centered in problems significant in the lives of the children, whether or not it is likely to develop important generalizations, and whether or not it gives impetus to critical thinking and problem solving. A variety of questions may set off the chain reaction that leads to curriculum change. Teachers who are truly concerned about their pupils' development in social studies begin to ask penetrating questions: Is the problem-solving approach more effective than textbook assignments? Are we teaching the social studies concepts and skills pupils actually need? Are social studies learnings functioning in the life outside school? Must we teach all the topics included in the course of study? Are field trips effective learning experiences? Are multiple texts better than a single textbook in social studies? Do parents understand the social studies curriculum of the school?

When teachers are truly concerned about such questions, they usually hypothesize. They have ideas about why the situation is as it is, or they have theories about how it may be altered. Occasionally a teacher gathers information to support his hypothesis or tries out an idea to prove a theory. When such action is planned thoughtfully, with reasonable attention to the control of influencing factors, the data that result can be of help in planning for the future. This kind of research—action research—has real significance because it is close to the concerns of teachers and affords them an opportunity to investigate a problem and to put the results immediately to work. Furthermore, action research inevitably involves teachers in curriculum problems and kindles their interest in curriculum improvement.

When the number and variety of questions that teachers are discussing or attempting to investigate through action research seem to point to the need for a thorough study of the social studies curriculum, an interested group of teachers may plan ways to identify the total range of problems in a somewhat more systematic way. At this stage all teachers may be surveyed through interviews, questionnaires, and study groups to find out the *status quo* in social studies and to discover various dissatisfactions and problems.

Teachers who would build a curriculum based on problem solving must first know the community they serve, for problems of significance for children emerge only from situations in which school and community are closely interwoven. What do teachers need to know about the community that sends its children to the school? What elements of the community must be understood by those who are planning the curriculum? There are at least three features of the community that must be explored—its geography, its population, and its communal setting.

From a study of the community's geographic environment come data about its weather and climate, topography, natural resources and location. An analysis of the population reveals social and racial groups, kinds of workers, housing conditions, patterns of family life, and needs and characteristics of children. Further study of the community emphasizes housing plans, health conditions, water supply, stores and industries, communication and transportation, and public services. But more important, the community survey reveals problems that exist in the community—conditions that need to be eradicated, rights that need to be protected, or facilities that call for improvement. Out of such information come the problems that vitalize social studies.

Against the background supplied by their study of the community, teachers must also study their pupils, their problems and needs. They must consider these children in the light of their knowledge of children in general, comparing and contrasting them with normal expectancies. School achievement, home backgrounds, psychological problems, retardations and accelerations—all are kinds of knowledge that paint the picture of the school population for which the curriculum is being planned. What kinds of problems do these children face at home? What are their needs and difficulties at school? Are they achieving as well as they should in social studies? Are health problems interfering with success in school? Are there marked social class differences among them? What skills will children need as adults in this community?

When initial surveys are completed, the task of building curriculum begins in earnest. Teachers realize that in the problem-solving approach social studies combines emphasis on real-life problems with emphasis on basic objectives of social studies. They must agree upon these objectives. How these are arrived at will vary from group to group; it is certain that study and discussion of the ideas of authorities in the field will be combined with careful analysis of the results of community and child surveys.

To bring objectives and problems together into a functional curriculum is then the task that remains to be accomplished. Teachers work in a variety of ways at this creative task. But whatever their work plan, the following principles, strictly adhered to, improve working relationships and final product.

Those who will put the curriculum into practice should participate in its development.

To avoid fragmentation and stratification, teachers should view the curriculum as a whole and participate in all major decisions made in relation to it.

Participation in the project should be voluntary, but all teachers who will be affected by the results should be fully informed of developments.

Definite but flexible plans for work should be devised and followed and the responsibilities of each work group clearly defined.

Consultants should help groups work successfully and serve as advisers on subject-matter content and procedures.

It would be misleading to suggest here that there is only one way to proceed in arriving at an improved social studies curriculum. But following agreement on objectives, the next obvious step is the exploration of problems that teachers believe to be appropriate for each grade level in terms of contributions to the improvement of community life and in terms of basic generalizations to be developed. These problems may be supplemented by intellectual problems that teachers believe to be essential to children's growth toward maturity and that will extend children's knowledge and understanding of the past and of the world beyond the local community.

Then work groups take over the process of curriculum planning. Usually these work groups cut across grade levels to ensure a smooth flow of experiences from grade to grade and to improve teachers' understanding of the importance of continuity in the curriculum. Ideally, skillful teachers are released from teaching to begin the construction of resource units for use in areas of learning. These resource units are illustrative and may or may not be used by a particular teacher. The resource units serve as a liberal framework within which teachers may build up resources for pupils to use and improve their own subject-matter background. And then the plans are put into usable form by competent writers and prepared for classroom tryouts. If many teachers have participated at various stages in the development of the curriculum, acceptance of the plans for classroom use and adaptation is usually assured. This continuing concern for the curriculum on the part of the teachers is essential to maintaining its flexibility and pertinence to the lives of children. Because the problem-solving approach to social studies is never static, the curriculum that fosters it must always be considered tentative and subject to change and to constant evaluation.

Foreseeing the Outcomes
of the Problem-Solving Approach

The true values of the problem-solving approach to social studies can finally be assessed only in the lives of those who participate in its vital, dynamic experiences. How will children growing into adulthood use problem solving as they face the challenges of the future? How will they solve the problems that hover on far horizons? Will skill in problem solving provide a method of attack upon the perplexing dilemmas of their adult years?

Only the future can answer these questions. But there is every reason to believe that better methods of problem solving cannot but improve man's relationships with other men and ultimately improve his ways of satisfying basic needs. It is crystal clear that approaches to social studies in vogue in many schools today—emphases upon fact-gathering and memorization—hold little hope for a future in which new facts render useless and even obliterate facts learned in childhood. Nor will authoritarian methods used by many teachers—highly directed textbook assignment and recitation—develop skill in democratic processes that children grown to adulthood can apply to problems great and small.

Generalizations clearly identified earlier as desirable goals of social studies become part of the intellectual equipment of the child who has experienced the problem-solving approach. These generalizations will deepen and broaden as adulthood provides opportunities for their continuing application to the current scene. Clearer understandings of basic human needs, richer appreciation of the cultural heritage, keener awareness of the interdependence of people, and deeper empathy toward people of all groups are the inevitable results of continuing application of generalizations developed through problem solving.

Of most importance, of course, are the actions that adults of the future will take because of their conviction that generalizations drawn from experiences in social studies have real meaning in everyday life. What will such adults do in the face of problems that arise in the life around them? Will they not make concerted effort to improve the well-being of all people, strive to right the wrongs of their society, apply the principles of democracy to decision making, protect and preserve the heritage of the past and its gifts to the present, and promote improved relationships among peoples and groups?

The methods they use to achieve these ends will be equally important. In an increasingly interdependent world—a world of exploding populations —cooperative planning, critical thinking, group action, and thoughtful evaluation of plans and outcomes will be essential to successful implementation of proposals for improvement of everyday living. Where will adults learn these methods of cooperative action if social studies fails to live up to its full potential? It is the problem-solving approach to social studies that gives the most promise to adequacy for a future that will make unforeseen demands upon its adults, demands for insightful problem solving and for human relationships of the highest quality. To prepare children for the years ahead is the twentieth century's challenge to the teacher of social studies.

Selected References

The titles in the following bibliography are selected and arranged to facilitate further exploration of topics of concern to teachers of social studies.

FOUNDATIONS OF SOCIAL STUDIES

American Council of Learned Societies and the National Council for the Social Studies, *The Social Studies and the Social Sciences*. New York: Harcourt, Brace & World, Inc., 1962.

Hanna, Lavone A., Gladys I. Potter, and Neva Hagaman, *Unit Teaching in the Elementary School*. Rev. ed. New York: Holt, Rinehart and Winston, Inc., 1963, Chapters 1, 2, and 3.

Hanna, Paul R. (Ed.), *Education, an Instrument of National Goals*. New York: McGraw-Hill, Inc., 1962.

Henry, V. Horatio, *New Social Studies Methodology*. Minneapolis: Burgess Publishing Co., 1958, Parts 1 and 2.

Hunnicutt, C. W. (Ed.), *Social Studies for the Middle Grades*. Washington, D.C.: National Council for the Social Studies, 1960, Chapters 1 and 3.

Jarolimek, John, *Social Studies in Elementary Education*. 2d ed. New York: The Macmillan Company, 1963, Chapter 1.

————, and Huber M. Walsh (Eds.), *Readings for Social Studies in Elementary Education*. New York: The Macmillan Company, 1965, Section 2.

Johnson, Earl S., *Theory and Practice of the Social Studies*. New York: The Macmillan Company, 1956, Chapters 5 and 6.

Larson, Arthur, *What We Are For*. New York: Harper & Row, Publishers, 1959.

Lee, John R., and Jonathon C. McLendon (Eds.), *Readings on Elementary Social Studies: Prologue to Change*. Boston: Allyn & Bacon, Inc., 1965, Parts B and C.

Massialas, Byron G., and Andreas M. Kazamias (Eds.), *Crucial Issues in the Teaching of Social Studies: A Book of Readings*. Englewood Cliffs, N. J.: Prentice-Hall, Inc., 1964, Chapters 1 and 3.

Michaelis, John U., *Social Studies for Children in a Democracy: Recent Trends and Developments*. 3d ed. Englewood Cliffs, N. J.: Prentice-Hall, Inc., 1963. Chapter 2.

———— (Ed.), *Social Studies in Elementary Schools*. Thirty-second Yearbook of the National Council for the Social Studies. Washington, D.C.: National Education Association, 1962, Chapter 1, pp. 17–25.

————, and A. Montgomery Johnston (Eds.), *The Social Sciences: Foundations of the Social Studies*. Boston: Allyn & Bacon, Inc., 1965.

Miel, Alice, and Peggy Brogan, *More Than Social Studies*. Englewood Cliffs, N. J.: Prentice-Hall, Inc., 1957, Chapters 1 and 2.

National Society for the Study of Education, *Social Studies in the Elementary School*. Fifty-sixth Yearbook, Part II. Chicago: University of Chicago Press, 1957, Chapter 2.

Noar, Gertrude, *Teaching and Learning the Democratic Way*. Englewood Cliffs, N. J.: Prentice-Hall, Inc., 1963.

Otto, Henry J., *Social Education in Elementary Schools*. New York: Holt, Rinehart and Winston, Inc., 1956, Chapters 2, 9, and 10.

President's Commission on National Goals, *Goals for Americans*. Administered by the American Assembly, Columbia University. Englewood Cliffs, N. J.: Prentice-Hall, Inc., 1960.

Preston, Ralph C., *Teaching Social Studies in the Elementary Schools*. Rev. ed. New York: Holt, Rinehart and Winston, Inc., 1958. Chapters 2 and 9.

Quillen, I. James, and Lavone A. Hanna, *Education for Social Competence*. Rev. ed. Chicago: Scott, Foresman and Company, 1961, Chapter 3.

Ragan, William B., and John D. McAulay, *Social Studies for Today's Children*. New York: Appleton-Century-Crofts, Inc., 1964, Chapters 1–4.

Smith, B. Othanel, William O. Stanley, and J. Harlan Shores, *Fundamentals of Curriculum Development*. Rev. ed. New York: Harcourt, Brace & World, Inc., 1957, Chapter 2.

Tiegs, Ernest W., and Fay Adams, *Teaching the Social Studies*. Boston: Ginn & Company, 1959, Chapters 1–3.

Wann, Kenneth D., Miriam Selchen Dorn, and Elizabeth Ann Liddle, *Fostering Intellectual Development in Young Children*. New York: Bureau of Publications, Teachers College, Columbia University, 1962, Chapter 1.

Willcockson, Mary (Ed.), *Social Education of Young Children*. Washington, D.C.: National Council for the Social Studies, 1956, Chapter 5.

Woelfel, Norman, *Educational Goals for America*. Washington, D.C.: Public Affairs Press, 1962.

CHILD DEVELOPMENT AND SOCIAL STUDIES

Hanna, Lavone A., Gladys I. Potter, and Neva Hagaman, *Unit Teaching in the Elementary School*. Rev. ed. New York: Holt, Rinehart and Winston, Inc., 1963, Chapter 2.

Hunnicutt, C. W. (Ed.), *Social Studies for the Middle Grades*. Washington, D.C.: National Council for the Social Studies, 1960, Chapter 2.

Leonard, Edith M., Dorothy D. VanDeman, and Lilliam E. Miles, *Foundations of Learning in Childhood Education*. Columbus, Ohio: Charles E. Merrill Books, Inc., 1963, Part 9.

Merritt, Edith P., *Working with Children in Social Studies*. San Francisco: Wadsworth Publishing Company, Inc., 1961, Chapter 2.

Michaelis, John U., *Social Studies for Children in a Democracy: Recent Trends and Developments*. 3d ed. Englewood Cliffs, N. J.: Prentice-Hall, Inc., 1963, Chapter 3.

———— (Ed.), *Social Studies in Elementary Schools*. Thirty-second Yearbook of the National Council for the Social Studies. Washington, D.C.: National Education Association, 1962, pp. 25–47.

Miel, Alice, and Peggy Brogan, *More Than Social Studies*. Englewood Cliffs, N. J.: Prentice-Hall, Inc., 1957, Chapter 3.

National Society for the Study of Education, *Social Studies in the Elementary School*. Fifty-sixth Yearbook, Part II. Chicago: University of Chicago Press, 1957, Chapter 4.

Preston, Ralph C., *Teaching Social Studies in the Elementary Schools*. Rev. ed. New York: Holt, Rinehart and Winston, Inc., 1958, Chapter 4.

Ragan, William B., and John D. McAulay, *Social Studies for Today's Children*. New York: Appleton-Century-Crofts, Inc., 1962, Chapter 2.

Tiegs, Ernest W., and Fay Adams, *Teaching the Social Studies*. Boston: Ginn & Company, 1959, Chapter 2.

Wann, Kenneth D., Miriam Selchen Dorn, and Elizabeth Ann Liddle, *Fostering Intellectual Development in Young Children*. New York: Bureau of Publications, Teachers College, Columbia University, 1962, Chapter 2.

Willcockson, Mary (Ed.), *Social Education of Young Children*. Washington, D.C.: National Council for the Social Studies, 1956, Chapters 3 and 4.

PROBLEM SOLVING

Anderson, Harold H. (Ed.), *Creativity and Its Cultivation*. New York: Harper & Row, Publishers, 1959, Chapter 11.

Bingham, Alma, *Improving Children's Facility in Problem Solving*. New York: Bureau of Publications, Teachers College, Columbia University, 1958.

Bruner, Jerome S., *The Process of Education*. Cambridge, Mass.: Harvard University Prass, 1960.

Burton, William H., Roland B. Kimball, and Richard L. Wing, *Education for Effective Thinking*. New York: Appleton-Century-Crofts, Inc., 1960, Chapters 2, 3, and 18.

Carpenter, Helen McCracken (Ed.), *Skills in the Social Studies*. Twenty-fourth Yearbook of the National Council for the Social Studies. Washington, D.C.: National Education Association, 1954, Chapter 3.

Educational Policies Commission, *The Central Purpose of American Education*. Washington, D.C.: National Education Association, 1961.

Fleming, Robert S. (Ed.), *Curriculum for Today's Boys and Girls*. Columbus, Ohio: Charles E. Merrill Books, Inc., 1963, Chapter 8.

Gross, Richard, Raymond H. Muessig, and George L. Fersh (Eds.), *The Problems Approach and the Social Studies*. Washington, D.C.: National Council for the Social Studies, 1960, Chapters 1–3.

Hanna, Lavone A., Gladys I. Potter, and Neva Hagaman, *Unit Teaching in the Elementary School*. Rev. ed. New York: Holt, Rinehart and Winston, Inc., 1963, Chapter 8.

Jarolimek, John, and Huber M. Walsh (Eds.),*Readings for Social Studies in Elementary Education*. New York: The Macmillan Company, 1965, pp. 176–216, 322–333.

Merritt, Edith P., *Working with Children in Social Studies*. San Francisco: Wadsworth Publishing Company, Inc., 1961, pp. 112–124.

Michaelis, John U., *Social Studies for Children in a Democracy: Recent Trends and Developments*. 3d ed. Englewood Cliffs, N. J.: Prentice-Hall, Inc., 1963, Chapter 4.

——— (Ed.), *Social Studies in Elementary Schools*. Thirty-second Yearbook of the National Council for the Social Studies. Washington, D.C.: National Education Association, 1962, pp. 47–61, 150–175.

Miel, Alice, and Peggy Brogan, *More Than Social Studies*. Englewood Cliffs, N. J.: Prentice-Hall, Inc., 1957, Chapter 10.

Quillen, I. James, and Lavone A. Hanna, *Education for Social Competence.* Chicago: Scott, Foresman and Company, 1961, Chapter 10.

Russell, David, *Children's Thinking.* Boston: Ginn & Company, 1956, Chapters 9–10.

Thorndike, Robert L., "How Children Learn the Principles and Techniques of Problem-Solving," in *Learning and Instruction.* Forty-ninth Yearbook of the National Society for the Study of Education, Part I. Chicago: University of Chicago Press, 1950, Chapter 8.

Tiegs, Ernest W., and Fay Adams, *Teaching the Social Studies.* Boston: Ginn & Company, 1959, Chapter 9.

Wellington, C. Burleigh, and Jean Wellington, *Teaching for Critical Thinking.* New York: McGraw-Hill, Inc., 1960, Chapter 2.

Wrightstone, J. Wayne, Joseph Justman, and Irving Robbins, *Evaluation in Modern Education.* New York: American Book Company, 1956, Chapter 20.

DEVELOPMENT OF CONCEPTS AND GENERALIZATIONS

Carpenter, Helen McCracken (Ed.), *Skills in the Social Studies.* Twenty-fourth Yearbook of the National Council for the Social Studies. Washington, D.C.: National Education Association, 1954, Chapter 10.

Hanna, Lavone A., Gladys I. Potter, and Neva Hagaman, *Unit Teaching in the Elementary School.* Rev. ed. New York: Holt, Rinehart and Winston, Inc., 1963, Chapter 7.

Hunnicutt, C. W. (Ed.), *Social Studies for the Middle Grades.* Washington, D.C.: National Council for the Social Studies, 1960, Chapter 8.

James, Preston (Ed.), *New Viewpoints in Geography.* Twenty-ninth Yearbook of the National Council for the Social Studies. Washington, D. C.: National Education Association, 1959, Chapter 8.

Jarolimek, John, and Huber M. Walsh (Eds.), *Readings for Social Studies in Elementary Education.* New York: The Macmillan Company, 1965, pp. 146–151, 231–236, 257–266, 283–289.

Johnson, Earl S., *Theory and Practice of the Social Studies.* New York: The Macmillan Company, 1956, Chapters 10 and 20.

Michaelis, John U., *Social Studies for Children in a Democracy: Recent Trends and Developments.* 3d ed. Englewood Cliffs, N. J.: Prentice-Hall, Inc., 1963, Chapter 4.

———— (Ed.), *Social Studies in Elementary Schools.* Thirty-second Yearbook of the National Council for the Social Studies. Washington, D.C.: National Education Association, 1962, pp. 62–93.

National Society for the Study of Education, *Learning and Instruction.* Forty-ninth Yearbook, Part I. Chicago: University of Chicago Press, 1950, Chapter 4.

————, *Social Studies in the Elementary School.* Fifty-sixth Yearbook, Part II. Chicago: University of Chicago Press, 1957, Chapter 2.

Otto, Henry J., *Social Education in Elementary Schools.* New York: Holt, Rinehart and Winston, Inc., 1956, pp. 377–391.

Tiegs, Ernest W., and Fay Adams, *Teaching the Social Studies.* Boston: Ginn & Company, 1959, Chapter 7.

Wann, Kenneth D., Miriam Selchen Dorn, and Elizabeth Ann Liddle, *Fostering Intellectual Development in Young Children.* New York: Bureau of Publications, Teachers College, Columbia University, 1962, Chapter 3.

THE UNIT OF WORK

Burton, William H., *The Guidance of Learning Activities*. 3d ed. New York: Appleton-Century-Crofts, Inc., 1962, Chapters 13–15.

Burr, James B., Lowry W. Harding, and Leland B. Jacobs, *Student Teaching in the Elementary School*. 2d ed. New York: Appleton-Century-Crofts, Inc., 1958, Chapter 6.

Daniher, E. L., and Clifford R. Dunphy, *Teaching the Social Studies*. Don Mills, Ont.: J. M. Dent & Sons (Canada), Ltd., 1961, Chapter 10.

Darrow, Helen Fisher, *Social Studies for Understanding*. New York: Bureau of Publications, Teachers College, Columbia University, 1964, Chapter 4.

Hanna, Lavone A., Gladys I. Potter, and Neva Hagaman, *Unit Teaching in the Elementary School*. Rev. ed. New York: Holt, Rinehart and Winston, Inc., 1963, Chapters 5, 6, and 16.

Henry, V. Horatio, *New Social Studies Methodology*. Minneapolis: Burgess Publishing Co., 1958, Part 4.

Hill, Wilhelmina (Ed.), *Selected Resource Units: Elementary Social Studies*. Washington, D.C.: National Council for the Social Studies, 1960.

———, *Social Studies in the Elementary School Program*. Bulletin 1960, No. 5. Washington, D.C.: Office of Education, U.S. Department of Health, Education, and Welfare, 1960, Chapter 5.

———, *Unit Planning and Teaching in Elementary Social Studies*. Bulletin 1963, No. 23. Washington, D.C.: Office of Education, U.S. Department of Health, Education, and Welfare, 1963.

Hunnicutt, C. W. (Ed.), *Social Studies for the Middle Grades*. Washington, D.C.: National Council for the Social Studies, 1960, Chapter 6.

Jarolimek, John, *Social Studies in Elementary Education*. 2d ed. New York: The Macmillan Company, 1963, Chapter 3.

Lee, John R., and Jonathon C. McLendon (Eds.), *Readings on Elementary Social Studies: Prologue to Change*. Boston, Allyn & Bacon, Inc., 1965, pp. 316–345.

Merritt, Edith P., *Working with Children in Social Studies*. San Francisco: Wadsworth Publishing Company, Inc., 1961, Chapter 4.

Michaelis, John U., *Social Studies for Children in a Democracy: Recent Trends and Developments*. 3d ed. Englewood Cliffs, N. J.: Prentice-Hall, Inc., 1963, Chapter 7.

——— (Ed.), *Social Studies in Elementary Schools*. Thirty-second Yearbook of the National Council for the Social Studies. Washington, D.C.: National Education Association, 1962, pp. 262–292.

Miel, Alice, and Peggy Brogan, *More Than Social Studies*. Englewood Cliffs, N. J.: Prentice-Hall, Inc., 1957, Chapters 5, 9, and 14.

Noar, Gertrude, *Teaching and Learning the Democratic Way*. Englewood Cliffs, N. J.: Prentice-Hall, Inc., 1963.

Preston, Ralph C., *Teaching Social Studies in the Elementary Schools*. Rev. ed. New York: Holt, Rinehart and Winston, Inc., 1958, Chapter 5.

Ragan, William B., and John D. McAulay, *Social Studies for Today's Children*. New York: Appleton-Century-Crofts, Inc., 1964, Chapter 9.

Thralls, Zoe A., *The Teaching of Geography*. New York: Appleton-Century-Crofts, Inc., 1958, Chapter 9.

Tiegs, Ernest W., and Fay Adams, *Teaching the Social Studies*. Boston: Ginn & Company, 1959, Chapters 5 and 6.

Warner, Ruby H., *The Child and His Elementary School World*. Englewood Cliffs, N. J.: Prentice-Hall, Inc., 1957, Chapter 4.

Willcockson, Mary (Ed.), *Social Education of Young Children*. Washington, D.C.: National Council for the Social Studies, 1956, Chapter 7.

EXPERIENCES IN SOCIAL STUDIES

Experiences in Cooperative Planning

Association for Childhood Education International, *Social Studies for Children*. Washington, D.C.: The Association, 1956, pp. 37–39.

Burr, James B., Lowry W. Harding, and Leland B. Jacobs, *Student Teaching in the Elementary School*. 2d ed. New York: Appleton-Century-Crofts, Inc., 1958, pp. 107–110.

Burton, William H., *The Guidance of Learning Activities*. 3d ed. New York: Appleton-Century-Crofts, Inc., 1963, pp. 357–362.

Darrow, Helen Fisher, *Social Studies for Understanding*. New York: Bureau of Publications, Teachers College, Columbia University, 1964, pp. 35–39.

Hilliard, Pauline, *Improving Social Learnings in the Elementary School*. New York: Bureau of Publications, Teachers College, Columbia University, 1955 Chapter 4.

Michaelis, John U., and Enoch Dumas, *The Student Teacher in the Elementary School*. 2d ed. Englewood Cliffs, N. J.: Prentice-Hall, Inc., 1960, pp. 62–65.

Parrish, Louise, and Yvonne Waskin, *Teacher-Pupil Planning*. New York: Harper & Row, Publishers, 1958.

Preston, Ralph C., *Teaching Social Studies in the Elementary Schools*. Rev. ed. New York: Holt, Rinehart and Winston, Inc., 1958, pp. 81–85.

Ragan, William B., and John D. McAulay, *Social Studies for Today's Children*. New York: Appleton-Century-Crofts, Inc., 1964, pp. 98–103.

Tiegs, Ernest W., and Fay Adams, *Teaching the Social Studies*. Boston: Ginn & Company, 1959, pp. 108–114.

Wiles, Kimball, *Teaching for Better Schools*. 2d ed. Englewood Cliffs, N. J.: Prentice-Hall, Inc., 1959, Chapters 6 and 7.

Group Work Experiences

Burr, James B., Lowry W. Harding, and Leland B. Jacobs, *Student Teaching in the Elementary School*. 2d ed. New York: Appleton-Century-Crofts, Inc., 1958, Chapter 7.

Hanna, Lavone A., Gladys I. Potter, and Neva Hagaman, *Unit Teaching in the Elementary School*. Rev. ed. New York: Holt, Rinehart and Winston, Inc., 1963, Chapter 14.

Jarolimek, John, *Social Studies in Elementary Education*. 2d ed. New York: The Macmillan Company, 1963, Chapter 7.

Merritt, Edith P., *Working with Children in Social Studies*. San Francisco: Wadsworth Publishing Company, Inc., 1961, pp. 124–136.

Michaelis, John U., *Social Studies for Children in a Democracy: Recent Trends and Developments*. 3d ed. Englewood Cliffs, N. J.: Prentice-Hall, Inc., 1963, Chapter 8.

Noar, Gertrude, *Teaching and Learning the Democratic Way*. Englewood Cliffs, N. J.: Prentice-Hall, Inc., 1963, Chapter 7.

Ragan, William B., and John D. McAulay, *Social Studies for Today's Children*. New York: Appleton-Century-Crofts, Inc., 1964. Chapter 8.

Wiles, Kimball, *Teaching for Better Schools*. 2d ed. Englewood Cliffs, N. J.: Prentice-Hall, Inc., 1959, Chapters 5–7.

Reading Experiences

Fay, Leo, Thomas Horn, and Constance McCullough, *Improving Reading in the Elementary Social Studies*. Washington, D.C.: National Council for the Social Studies, 1961.

Huus, Helen, *Children's Books to Enrich the Social Studies*. Washington, D.C.: National Council for the Social Studies, 1961.

Jarolimek, John, *Social Studies in Elementary Education*. 2d ed. New York: The MacMillan Company, 1963, Chapter 6.

———, and Huber M. Walsh (Eds.), *Readings for Social Studies in Elementary Education*. New York: The Macmillan Company, 1964, pp. 289–322.

Merritt, Edith P., *Working with Children in Social Studies*. San Francisco: Wadsworth Publishing Company, Inc., 1961, Chapter 7.

Michaelis, John U., *Social Studies for Children in a Democracy: Recent Trends and Developments*. 3d ed. Englewood Cliffs, N. J.: Prentice-Hall, Inc., 1963, Chapter 10.

National Society for the Study of Education, *Social Studies in the Elementary School*. Fifty-sixth Yearbook, Part II. Chicago: University of Chicago Press, 1957, Chapter 8.

Preston, Ralph C., *Teaching Social Studies in the Elementary Schools*. Rev. ed. New York: Holt, Rinehart and Winston, Inc., 1958, Chapter 10.

Ragan, William B., and John D. McAulay, *Social Studies for Today's Children*. New York: Appleton-Century-Crofts, Inc., 1964, Chapter 11.

Thralls, Zoe A., *The Teaching of Geography*. New York: Appleton-Century-Crofts, Inc., 1958, Chapter 7; pp. 222–235.

Tiegs, Ernest W., and Fay Adams, *Teaching the Social Studies*. Boston: Ginn & Company, 1959, Chapter 13.

Community Experiences

Henry, V. Horatio, *New Social Studies Methodology*. Minneapolis: Burgess Publishing Co., 1958, Part 5.

Johnson, Earl S., *Theory and Practice of the Social Studies*. New York: The Macmillan Company, 1956, Chapter 27.

Kohn, Clyde F., *Geographic Approaches to Social Education*. Nineteenth Yearbook of the National Council for the Social Studies. Washington, D.C.: National Education Association, 1948, Chapter 16.

Michaelis, John U., *Social Studies for Children in a Democracy: Recent Trends and Developments*. 3d ed. Englewood Cliffs, N. J.: Prentice-Hall, Inc., 1963, Chapter 16.

Preston, Ralph C., *Teaching Social Studies in the Elementary Schools*. Rev. ed. New York: Holt, Rinehart and Winston, Inc., 1958, Chapter 6.

Ragan, William B., and John D. McAulay, *Social Studies for Today's Children*. New York: Appleton-Century-Crofts, Inc., 1964, pp. 290–294.

Thralls, Zoe A., *The Teaching of Geography*. New York: Appleton-Century-Crofts, Inc., 1958, Chapter 5.

Tiegs, Ernest W., and Fay Adams, *Teaching the Social Studies*. Boston: Ginn & Company, 1959, Chapter 16.

Willcockson, Mary (Ed.), *Social Education of Young Children*. Washington, D.C.: National Council for the Social Studies, 1956, Chapter 23.

Construction and Processing Experiences

Association for Childhood Education International, *Children Can Make It!* Reprint Service Bulletin No. 28. Washington, D.C.: The Association, 1955.

Hanna, Lavone A., Gladys I. Potter, and Neva Hagaman, *Unit Teaching in the Elementary Schools.* Rev. ed. New York: Holt, Rinehart and Winston, Inc., 1963, Chapter 12.

Michaelis, John U., *Social Studies for Children in a Democracy: Recent Trends and Developments.* 3d ed. Englewood Cliffs, N. J.: Prentice-Hall, Inc., 1963, pp. 558–569.

——— (Ed.), *Social Studies in Elementary Schools.* Thirty-second Yearbook of the National Council for the Social Studies. Washington, D.C.: National Education Association, 1962, pp. 212–218.

National Society for the Study of Education, *Social Studies in the Elementary School.* Fifty-sixth Yearbook, Part II. Chicago: University of Chicago Press, 1957, pp. 212–218.

Thomas, R. Murray, and Sherwin G. Swartout, *Integrated Teaching Materials.* New York: David McKay Company, Inc., 1960, Chapters 19–20.

Experiences with Maps and Globes

Carpenter, Helen McCracken (Ed.), *Skill Development in Social Studies.* Thirty-third Yearbook of the National Council for the Social Studies. Washington, D.C.: National Education Association, 1963, Chapter 9.

———, *Skills in the Social Studies.* Twenty-fourth Yearbook of the National Council for the Social Studies. Washington, D.C.: National Education Association, 1954, Chapter 8.

Davies, Gordon F., *Map Skills and Understandings in Intermediate School.* Hayward, Calif.: Gordon Davies, 1962.

Harris, Ruby M., *The Rand McNally Book of Map and Globe Usage.* New York: Rand McNally & Company, 1959.

Jarolimek, John, *Social Studies in Elementary Education.* 2d ed. New York: The Macmillan Company, 1963, Chapter 10.

———, and Huber M. Walsh (Eds.), *Readings for Social Studies in Elementary Education.* New York: The Macmillan Company, 1965, pp. 237–256.

Kohn, Clyde F., *Geographic Approaches to Social Education.* Nineteenth Yearbook of the National Council for the Social Studies. Washington, D.C.: National Education Association, 1948, Chapters 11–12.

Lee, John R., and Jonathon C. McLendon (Eds.), *Readings on Elementary Social Studies: Prologue to Change.* Boston: Allyn & Bacon, Inc., 1965, pp. 404–419.

Merritt, Edith P., *Working with Children in Social Studies.* San Francisco: Wadsworth Publishing Company, Inc., 1961, Chapter 10.

Michaelis, John U., *Social Studies for Children in a Democracy: Recent Trends and Developments.* 3d ed. Englewood Cliffs, N. J.: Prentice-Hall, Inc., 1963, Chapter 14.

——— (Ed.), *Social Studies in Elementary Schools.* Thirty-second Yearbook of the National Council for the Social Studies. Washington, D.C.: National Education Association, 1962, pp. 196–205.

Preston, Ralph C., *Teaching Social Studies in the Elementary Schools.* Rev. ed. New York: Holt, Rinehart and Winston, Inc., 1958, Chapter 11.

Ragan, William B., and John D. McAulay, *Social Studies for Today's Children.* New York: Appleton-Century-Crofts, Inc., 1964, pp. 234–247.

Thomas, R. Murray, and Sherwin G. Swartout, *Integrated Teaching Materials*. New York: David McKay Company, Inc., 1960, Chapter 19.

Thralls, Zoe A., *The Teaching of Geography*. New York: Appleton-Century-Crofts, Inc., 1958, Chapter 2.

Tiegs, Ernest W., and Fay Adams, *Teaching the Social Studies*. Boston: Ginn & Company, 1959, Chapter 11.

Experiences with Other Educational Media

Brown, James W., Richard B. Lewis, and Fred F. Harcleroad, *A-V Instruction*. New York: McGraw-Hill, Inc., 1959.

Dale, Edgar, *Audio-Visual Methods in Teaching*. Rev. ed. New York: Holt, Rinehart and Winston, Inc., 1954.

Daniher, E. L., and Clifford R. Dunphy, *Teaching the Social Studies*. Don Mills, Ont.: J. M. Dent & Sons (Canada), Ltd., 1961, Chapters 20, 25–27.

Jarolimek, John, *Social Studies in Elementary Education*. 2d ed. New York: The Macmillan Company, 1963, Chapters 4 and 9.

Kohn, Clyde F., *Geographic Approaches to Social Education*. Nineteenth Yearbook of the National Council for the Social Studies. Washington, D.C.: National Education Association, 1948, Chapters 13–14.

Lee, John R., and Jonathon C. McLendon (Eds.), *Readings on Elementary Social Studies: Prologue to Change*. Boston: Allyn & Bacon, Inc., 1965, pp. 376–403.

Merritt, Edith P., *Working with Children in Social Studies*. San Francisco: Wadsworth Publishing Company, Inc., 1961, pp. 154–162.

Michaelis, John U., *Social Studies for Children in a Democracy: Recent Trends and Developments*. 3d ed. Englewood Cliffs, N. J.: Prentice-Hall, Inc., 1963, Chapters 12 and 15.

Preston, Ralph C., *Teaching Social Studies in the Elementary Schools*. Rev. ed. New York: Holt, Rinehart and Winston, Inc., 1958, Chapter 13.

Ragan, William B., and John D. McAulay (Eds.), *Social Studies for Today's Children*. New York: Appleton-Century-Crofts, Inc., 1964, pp. 281–287.

Thomas, R. Murray, and Sherwin G. Swartout, *Integrated Teaching Materials*. New York: David McKay Company, Inc., 1960.

Thralls, Zoe A., *The Teaching of Geography*. New York: Appleton-Century-Crofts, Inc., 1958, Chapters 3 and 4.

Tiegs, Ernest W., and Fay Adams, *Teaching the Social Studies*. Boston: Ginn & Company, 1959, Chapter 15.

Willcockson, Mary (Ed.), *Social Education of Young Children*. Washington, D.C.: National Council for the Social Studies, 1956, Chapter 25.

RELATED EXPERIENCES

Skill Development

Association for Childhood Education International, *Social Studies for Children*. Washington, D.C.: The Association, 1956, pp. 26–32.

Carpenter, Helen McCracken (Ed.), *Skill Development in Social Studies*. Thirty-third Yearbook of the National Council for the Social Studies. Washington, D.C.: National Education Association, 1963.

——— (Ed.), *Skills in the Social Studies*. Twenty-fourth Yearbook of the National Council for the Social Studies. Washington, D.C.: National Education Association, 1954.

Hanna, Lavone A., Gladys I. Potter, and Neva Hagaman, *Unit Teaching in the*

Elementary School. Rev. ed. New York: Holt, Rinehart and Winston, Inc., 1963, Chapters 9–10, and 14.

Jarolimek, John, *Social Studies in Elementary Education.* 2d ed. New York: The Macmillan Company, 1963, Chapter 7.

Johnson, Earl S., *Theory and Practice of the Social Studies.* New York: The Macmillan Company, 1956, Chapter 19.

Merritt, Edith P., *Working with Children in Social Studies.* San Francisco: Wadsworth Publishing Company, Inc., 1961, pp. 189–198.

Michaelis, John U., *Social Studies for Children in a Democracy: Recent Trends and Developments.* Englewood Cliffs, N. J.: Prentice-Hall, Inc., 1963, Chapters 8, 10–11.

———— (Ed.), *Social Studies in Elementary Schools.* Thirty-second Yearbook of the National Council for the Social Studies. Washington, D.C.: National Education Association, 1962, pp. 176–196.

Miel, Alice, and Peggy Brogan, *More Than Social Studies.* Englewood Cliffs, N. J.: Prentice-Hall, Inc., 1957, pp. 305–312.

National Society for the Study of Education, *Social Studies in the Elementary School.* Fifty-sixth Yearbook, Part II. Chicago: University of Chicago Press, 1957, Chapter 8.

Otto, Henry J., *Social Education in Elementary Schools.* New York: Holt, Rinehart and Winston, Inc., 1956, pp. 398–401.

Preston, Ralph C., *Teaching Study Habits and Skills.* New York: Holt, Rinehart and Winston, Inc., 1959, Chapter 3.

Ragan, William B., and John D. McAulay, *Social Studies for Today's Children.* New York: Appleton-Century-Crofts, Inc., 1964, Chapter 10.

Tiegs, Ernest W., and Fay Adams, *Teaching the Social Studies.* Boston: Ginn & Company, 1959, Chapter 10; pp. 407–409.

Creative Activities

Daniher, E. L., and Clifford R. Dunphy, *Teaching the Social Studies.* Don Mills, Ont.: J. M. Dent & Sons (Canada), Ltd., 1961, Chapter 5.

Hanna, Lavone A., Gladys I. Potter, and Neva Hagaman, *Unit Teaching in the Elementary School.* Rev. ed. New York: Holt, Rinehart and Winston, Inc., 1963, Chapters 11 and 13.

Jarolimek, John, *Social Studies in Elementary Education,* 2d ed. New York: The Macmillan Company, 1963, Chapter 8.

Marksberry, Mary Lee, *Foundation of Creativity.* New York: Harper & Row, Publishers, 1963.

Merritt, Edith P., *Working with Children in Social Studies.* San Francisco: Wadsworth Publishing Company, Inc., 1961, pp. 199 214; Chapter 9.

Michaelis, John U. (Ed.), *Social Studies in Elementary Schools.* Thirty-second Yearbook of the National Council for the Social Studies. Washington, D.C.: National Education Association, 1962, pp. 205–212.

Nichols, Hildred, and Lois Williams, *Learning about Role-Playing for Children and Teachers.* Bulletin No. 66. Washington, D.C.: Association for Childhood Education, 1960.

Preston, Ralph C., *Teaching Social Studies in the Elementary Schools.* Rev. ed. New York: Holt, Rinehart and Winston, Inc., 1958, Chapter 12.

Shaftel, George, and Fannie R. Shaftel, *Role Playing the Problem Story.* New York: The National Conference of Christians and Jews, 1952.

Siks, Geraldine Brain, *Creative Dramatics.* New York: Harper & Row, Publishers, 1958.

Tiegs, Ernest W., and Fay Adams, *Teaching the Social Studies*. Boston: Ginn & Company, 1959, pp. 391–398.

Tooze, Ruth, and Beatrice Perham Krone, *Literature and Music as Resources for Social Studies*. Englewood Cliffs, N. J.: Prentice-Hall, Inc., 1955.

Ward, Winifred, *Playmaking with Children*. 2d ed. New York: Appleton-Century-Crofts, Inc., 1957.

Wilt, Miriam E., *Creativity in the Elementary School*. New York: Appleton-Century-Crofts, Inc., 1959.

EVALUATION

Berg, Harry D. (Ed.), *Evaluation in Social Studies*. Thirty-fifth Yearbook of the National Council for the Social Studies. Washington, D.C.: National Education Association, 1965.

Burton, William H., *The Guidance of Learning Activities*. 3d ed. New York: Appleton-Century-Crofts, Inc., 1963, Chapter 20.

Carpenter, Helen McCracken (Ed.), *Skill Development in Social Studies*. Thirty-third Yearbook of the National Council for the Social Studies. Washington, D.C.: National Education Association, 1964, Chapter 14.

Green, John A., *Teacher-Made Tests*. New York: Harper & Row, Publishers, 1963.

Hanna, Lavone A., Gladys I. Potter, and Neva Hagaman, *Unit Teaching in the Elementary School*. Rev. ed. New York: Holt, Rinehart and Winston, Inc., 1963, Chapter 15.

Hill, Wilhelmina, *Social Studies in the Elementary School Program*. Bulletin No. 5. Washington, D.C.: Office of Education, U.S. Department of Health, Education, and Welfare, 1960, Chapter 6.

Hunnicutt, C. W. (Ed.), *Social Studies for the Middle Grades*. Washington, D.C.: National Council for the Social Studies, 1960, Chapter 13.

Jarolimek, John, *Social Studies in Elementary Education*. 2d ed. New York: The Macmillan Company, 1963, Chapter 16.

————, and Huber M. Walsh (Eds.), *Readings for Social Studies in Elementary Education*. New York: The Macmillan Company, 1965, Section 6.

Johnson, Earl S., *Theory and Practice of the Social Studies*. New York: The Macmillan Company, 1956, Chapter 17.

Lee, John R., and Jonathon C. McLendon (Eds.), *Readings on Elementary Social Studies: Prologue to Change*. Boston: Allyn & Bacon, Inc., 1965, pp. 345–362.

Merritt, Edith P., *Working with Children in Social Studies*. San Francisco: Wadsworth Publishing Company, Inc., 1961, Chapter 11.

Michaelis, John U., *Social Studies for Children in a Democracy: Recent Trends and Developments*. 3d ed. Englewood Cliffs, N. J.: Prentice-Hall, Inc., 1963, Chapter 18.

———— (Ed.), *Social Studies in Elementary Schools*. Thirty-second Yearbook of the National Council for the Social Studies. Washington, D.C.: National Education Association, 1962, Chapter 10.

Miel, Alice, and Peggy Brogan, *More Than Social Studies*. Englewood Cliffs, N. J.: Prentice-Hall, Inc., 1957, Chapter 13.

National Society for the Study of Education, *Social Studies in the Elementary School*. Fifty-sixth Yearbook, Part II. Chicago: University of Chicago Press, 1957, Chapter 11.

Otto, Henry J., *Social Education in Elementary Schools*. New York: Holt, Rinehart and Winston, Inc., 1956, Chapter 14.

Preston, Ralph C., *Teaching Social Studies in the Elementary Schools*. Rev. ed. New York: Holt, Rinehart and Winston, Inc., 1958, Chapter 14.

Ragan, William B., and John D. McAulay, *Social Studies for Today's Children*. New York: Appleton-Century-Crofts, Inc., 1964, Chapters 14–15.

Shane, Harold G., and E. T. McSwain, *Evaluation and the Elementary Curriculum*. Rev. ed. New York: Holt, Rinehart and Winston, Inc., 1958, Chapter 11.

Thomas, R. Murray, *Judging Student Progress*. 2d ed. New York: David McKay Company, Inc., 1960.

Tiegs, Ernest W., and Fay Adams, *Teaching the Social Studies*. Boston: Ginn & Company, 1959, Chapter 12.

Willcockson, Mary (Ed.), *Social Education of Young Children*. Washington, D.C.: National Council for the Social Studies, 1956, Chapter 15.

Wrightstone, J. Wayne, Joseph Justman, and Irving Robbins, *Evaluation in Modern Education*. New York: American Book Company, 1956.

SOCIAL STUDIES IN THE CURRICULUM

Association for Childhood Education International, *Social Studies for Children*. Washington, D.C.: The Association, 1956.

Darrow, Helen Fisher, *Social Studies for Understanding*. New York: Bureau of Publications, Teachers College, Columbia University, 1964, Chapters 1–2.

Ellsworth, Ruth, and Ole Sands (Eds.), *Improving the Social Studies Curriculum*. Twenty-sixth Yearbook of the National Council for the Social Studies. Washington, D.C.: National Education Association, 1955.

Fraser, Dorothy M., *Deciding What to Teach*. Washington, D.C.: National Education Association, 1964.

Hanna, Lavone A., Gladys I. Potter, and Neva Hagaman, *Unit Teaching in the Elementary School*. Rev. ed. New York: Holt, Rinehart and Winston, Inc., 1963, Chapter 4.

Hill, Wilhelmina, *Curriculum Guide for Geographic Education*. Normal, Ill.: National Council for Geographic Education, 1963.

———, *Social Studies in the Elementary School Program*. Bulletin No. 5. Washington, D.C.: Office of Education, U.S. Department of Health, Education, and Welfare, 1960, Chapters 2 and 4.

Jarolimek, John, *Social Studies in Elementary Education*. 2d ed. New York: The Macmillan Company, 1963, Chapters 1–2, 11–13.

———, and Huber M. Walsh (Eds.), *Readings for Social Studies in Elementary Education*. New York: The Macmillan Company, 1965, Section 1.

Kohn, Clyde F., *Geographic Approaches to Social Education*. Nineteenth Yearbook of the National Council for the Social Studies. Washington, D.C.: National Education Association, 1948, Chapter 18.

Lee, John R., and Jonathon C. McLendon (Eds.), *Readings on Elementary Social Studies: Prologue to Change*. Boston: Allyn & Bacon, Inc., 1965, Parts A and G.

Massialas, Byron G., and Andreas M. Kazamias (Eds.), *Crucial Issues in the Teaching of Social Studies: A Book of Readings*. Englewood Cliffs, N. J.: Prentice-Hall, Inc., 1964, Chapters 2–3.

Massialas, Byron G., and Frederick R. Smith (Eds.), *Current Research in Social Studies*. Bloomington, Ind.: Bureau of Educational Studies and Testing, School of Education, Indiana University, 1964.

McPhie, Walter E. (Ed.), *Dissertations in Social Studies Education: A Com-*

prehensive Guide. Research Bulletin No. 2. Washington, D.C.: National Council for the Social Studies, 1964.

Merritt, Edith P., *Working with Children in Social Studies*. San Francisco: Wadsworth Publishing Company, Inc., 1961, Chapters 1 and 3.

Michaelis, John U., *Social Studies for Children in a Democracy: Recent Trends and Developments*. 3d ed. Englewood Cliffs, N. J.: Prentice-Hall, Inc., 1963, Chapter 5.

————— (Ed.), *Social Studies in Elementary Schools*. Thirty-second Yearbook of the National Council for the Social Studies. Washington, D.C.: National Education Association, 1962, pp. 93–106; Chapter 4.

Miel, Alice, and Peggy Brogan, *More Than Social Studies*. Englewood Cliffs, N.J.: Prentice-Hall, Inc., 1957, Chapter 5.

National Council for the Social Studies, *A Guide to Content in the Social Studies*. Washington, D.C.: National Education Association, n.d.

National Society for the Study of Education, *Social Studies in the Elementary School*. Fifty-sixth Yearbook, Part II. Chicago: University of Chicago Press, 1957, Chapters 1, 3, 5–6.

Preston, Ralph C., *Teaching Social Studies in the Elementary Schools*. Rev. ed. New York: Holt, Rinehart and Winston, Inc., 1958, Chapters 1, 3, 7–9.

Price, Roy A. (Ed.), *Needed Research in the Teaching of the Social Studies*, Research Bulletin No. 1. Washington, D.C.: National Council for the Social Studies, 1964.

—————, *New Viewpoints in the Social Sciences*. Twenty-eighth Yearbook of the National Council for the Social Studies. Washington, D.C.: National Education Association, 1958.

Ragan, William B., and John D. McAulay, *Social Studies for Today's Children*. New York: Appleton-Century-Crofts, Inc., 1964, Chapters 5–7.

Shaplin, Judson T., and Henry F. Olds, Jr. (Eds.), *Team Teaching*. New York: Harper & Row, Publishers, 1964, Chapter 5.

Sowards, G. Wesley (Ed.), *The Social Studies: Curriculum Proposals for the Future*. Chicago: Scott, Foresman and Company, 1963.

Thralls, Zoe A., *The Teaching of Geography*. New York: Appleton-Century-Crofts, Inc., 1958, Chapter 1.

Tiegs, Ernest W., and Fay Adams, *Teaching the Social Studies*. Boston: Ginn & Company, 1959, Chapter 4.

Wann, Kenneth D., Miriam Selchen Dorn, and Elizabeth Ann Liddle, *Fostering Intellectual Development in Young Children*. New York: Bureau of Publications, Teachers College, Columbia University, 1962, pp. 108–112.

Willcockson, Mary (Ed.), *Social Education of Young Children*. Washington, D.C.: National Council for the Social Studies, 1956, Chapters 11–13, 16–20.

A Resource Unit:
How Does
Communication Affect
Community Living?

JUSTIFICATION

There is perhaps no basic human activity that pervades daily life more persistently than communication. The community, state, and nation depend upon communication as a unifying force; home, school, and community would soon collapse without the exchange which communication makes possible; the peace of the world depends upon the interaction made possible through communication; democracy itself could not survive without the give-and-take that communication facilitates.

Although no one would argue the important role of communication in daily life, too often it is taken for granted and attended to very little. In a day of rapid expansion of communication facilities, when people of the world are finding it possible to know almost instantly what transpires in another part of the earth, it is appropriate to direct the attention of elementary school pupils to this important basic human activity and to explore how man meets his need to communicate with those around him.

An area of learning developed around problems of communication can be justified on many grounds.

First, the area of learning in communication is a natural outgrowth of any one of a number of real-life situations. An emergency in the community may make it necessary to establish communication with large groups of people. News of a world event may touch children and their families in a personal way or involve them in television viewing, radio listening, and discussion. An important campaign in the community may require communication with many individuals. A breakdown in communication may cause some serious difficulties in the home, school, or community; or a new development in communication, such as Telestar, may capture the interest of the children. These or similar circumstances develop in most communities at one time or another and serve as useful initiations for the area of learning. Furthermore, children no doubt have had innumerable contacts with communication in its various forms—they have sent and received letters, used the telephone, and seen newspapers daily in the home; and they are continual consumers of television as well as avid movie attendants. All these communication facilities children accept quite casually.

Second, the area of learning in communication opens up significant problems. Such problems as these may be identified or implied from the questions children ask: Why is communication important in our community? Why do we need many different kinds of communication? What happens in our lives when communication breaks down? Why are so many people needed in communication operations? Why do some countries not have freedom of communication? Why is freedom of speech essential to democratic process? It is clear that these problems are not trivial nor to be answered perfunctorily.

Third, the area of learning has potential for helping children move toward some of the important generalizations that undergird social studies. It has a contribution to make to developing some aspects of each of the following:

1. People everywhere have certain basic needs and wants; how they meet them depends upon their environment and cultural level.
2. The world in which we live is constantly changing; people must alter their ways of meeting needs and solving problems to meet changing conditions.
3. A peaceful world is based upon mutual respect and understanding; cooperation among individuals and groups is essential to the well-being of people everywhere.

Fourth, the area of learning can satisfy many present needs and interests of pupils—the desire to imitate adults, curiosity about how mechanical things work, interest in manipulation and experimentation, eagerness to communicate with others in a variety of ways, need to know how to deliver and receive messages, need to know how to select appropriate means of communication for various purposes, and a lively interest in all that goes on in the community. Furthermore, the area of learning in communication is broad enough to be easily adapted to various grade levels of instruction and to individuals of varying interest and ability levels. It can be developed also to meet the needs of a particular group of children in a particular community.

In addition, certain new interests quite possibly will develop from a study of communication. Science interests are a likely extension: What makes sound? How does light travel? What is electricity? Foreign languages as a way of communicating with people who do not speak English certainly may attract the children's attention. Other social studies interests can be anticipated: How do people communicate with number? How has man made records of his activities? How are books made? What means of communication will be used twenty years from now? How do people communicate through music and art?

Not only are interests in new content a potential extension of the area of learning; equally important are the interests that may grow out of the experiences children have in exploring the community, constructing useful objects, dramatizing, and experimenting. They may discover that many of these are delightful ways to use leisure time both at home and at school and may continue to enjoy them long after the area of learning about communication is concluded.

Fifth, the area of learning is well suited to the nature of elementary school children, for there is ample opportunity for them to practice skills they are seeking to perfect—to work well with others, to handle materials skillfully, to refine muscle coordination, to meet adults on common ground, and to carry tasks to completion; and to engage in activities for which they have a natural bent—dramatic play, field trips, experimenting, construction, interviewing, and the like.

And finally, the area of learning in communication is practical from several other points of view. It has content that is normally considered in elementary school social studies. There are abundant opportunities in the community to explore communication facilities. Resource materials are quite adequate.

For all these reasons communication as the focus for an area of learning appears to be a justifiable selection.

OBJECTIVES

1. Understanding: Because the activities of everyday living in the community require person-to-person communication, speaking and writing clearly and correctly are important to every individual.

   Attitudes: Desire to write and speak clearly and correctly.
   Appreciation of the usefulness of speaking and writing in everyday life.
   Desire to communicate with persons of other groups.
   Awareness of the development of language.

   Skills and Behaviors: Speaks and writes his native language correctly and clearly.
   Demonstrates facility and judgment in the use of writing tools and materials.
   Speaks and writes properly in various situations.
   Reads intelligently the written communications of others.
   Communicates easily and freely with persons of other groups.

2. Understanding: Efficient means of communication have overcome the barriers of distance; consequently, people everywhere can communicate with each other.

   Attitudes: Awareness of the role played by communication in community life.
   Respect for and admiration of those who make the communication system work.
   Awareness of the role of communication in fostering progress and improving understanding among people.
   Appreciation of the unique functions of various types of communication.

   Skills and Behaviors: Uses the telephone properly.
   Uses the facilities of the postal services effectively.
   Selects the means of communication appropriate to his purpose.
   Cooperates with communication workers in appropriate ways.

3. Understanding: Through the development of mass media, large groups of people can become aware of and react to ideas, information, and events that may be significant to them.

   Attitudes: Appreciation of knowledge and pleasures made possible by mass media.
   Awareness of great technical skill involved in these operations.

Appreciation of their impact upon our way of living.

Respect for mass communication of high quality.

Awareness of the importance of mass media in bringing peoples of the world closer together.

Skills and Behaviors: Selects and views television and motion pictures with discrimination.

Reports emergencies properly.

Uses communication devices correctly.

Reads newspapers at his level.

4. Understanding: Since democracy depends upon interaction among well-informed citizens, the development of communication greatly facilitates the democratic process.

Attitudes: Desire to influence individuals and groups toward cooperative action.

Belief in the right of freedom of speech.

Awareness of responsibilities in use of free speech.

Recognition of the importance of dissemination of complete accurate information about current problems.

Skills and Behaviors: Uses language to promote good human relationships.

Speaks forcefully to defend individual rights.

Uses communication to win others to support worthy causes.

Uses communication to influence others to move in desirable directions.

Uses communication skills to give pleasure to others.

Communicates freely with people of other groups and cultures.

Seeks information in order to be well-informed.

INITIATION

The purpose of an initiation for an area of learning centered on the relationship between communication and community living is to assure children's interest in this area of learning and motivate them to engage in it. Several types of initiation serve this purpose, but a teacher selects the initiation he will use in relation to conditions that exist at the time the area of learning is launched. Among possible ways to initiate this area of learning are the following:

1. Engaging in a dramatic play enactment of the communication forces that operate during a community emergency.[1]
2. Engaging in a dramatic play enactment of the use of communication media in planning and executing a community event.
3. Engaging in a dramatic play enactment of the communication of national and world happenings that affect citizens of a community.
4. Making a tour of a community's communication centers.
5. Making a tour of selected business enterprises to study their use of communication media.
6. Drawing on resource persons from communication centers and others engaged in communication activities.
7. Arranging for the viewing of films that provide information about communication in relation to community living.

---

[1] This type of initiation is described in the dialogue that introduces Chapter 2.

8. Arranging an environment of realia, artifacts, and other sources of information about communication in the past, present, and future.

Planning that includes attention to details and to certain basic considerations is the key to an effective initiation. At the heart of all planning is this important consideration: All materials selected for display, procedures to be used, and possible problems should reflect the understandings to be developed in the area of learning.

Typical materials that a teacher might select and display in an arranged environment to create the desired readiness for a study of communication are as follows:

1. Bulletin board displays
   a. Pictures showing the progress of mail delivery service in the United States
   b. Pictures showing the delivery of mail in foreign countries, particularly in remote areas of the world
   c. Pictures of modern communication devices
   d. Pictures of devices primitive peoples used to communicate—Indian smoke signals, African drums, picture writing
   e. Maps showing pony express routes
   f. Maps showing the location of television stations in the United States
2. Realia
   a. Samples of community publications—newspapers, handbills, church bulletins, service organization bulletins, school papers
   b. Samples of newspapers and magazines published in foreign countries
   c. Samples of letters written in foreign languages
   d. Samples of various types of wireless messages—telegrams, cablegrams, and night letters
   e. Slides and tape recordings of nonverbal means of communication—traffic signals, pictorial road signs, fire sirens, police whistles, automobile drivers' signals, ships' foghorns
   f. Newspaper clippings about policemen directing traffic from the air and about communication centers in freight and truck terminals
   g. Lists of space-age vocabulary and vocabulary copied from early New England newspapers
   h. Radios, both electric and transistor, and other procurable communication devices
3. Models that demonstrate how science functions in communication
4. Books, periodicals, and newspapers pertaining to various aspects of communication

The teacher prepares captions and labels for these materials that will arouse children's curiosity and stimulate thought-provoking questions about communication.

Because the successful arranged environment initiation is one that invites children to discover and explore the materials displayed in it, a teacher opens the way for them to do so by arranging for the necessary time in the schedule. As the children explore the environment, the teacher observes and records their comments and questions about it. Later he guides the discussion of their reactions to the environment, helping them to identify problems and questions worthy of their study.

As noted earlier, problems that the teacher and children identify as a result of their discussion should coincide with the understandings originally identified as the desired goals for the area of learning. Moreover, the problems identified must be thought provoking in nature.

The process of identifying significant problems is one that exacts much skill on the teacher's part. It is a process of maintaining a delicate balance between children's curiosity about details pertaining to communication and the need to identify problems of significant scope to yield generalized information about it. Following is a list of secondary problems that children may identify as they consider the effect communication has on community living:

1. Why do people in communities have different ways of speaking to one another?
2. Why are speaking and writing the most common means of communication among individuals?
3. Why is communication necessary at home, at school, and in the community?
4. How other than by speaking and writing can individuals communicate?
5. How has spoken and written communication changed?
6. Why should users of communication devices know about their use?
7. How do mass media help large groups of people communicate?
8. How do mass media help people carry on political business and social activities?
9. How do many workers contribute to making communication with large groups possible?
10. Why is communication through mass media especially important to a community in time of emergency?
11. How do the telephone, telegraph, and mail service help people communicate with each other over distance?
12. How does increasing communication among people everywhere bring them closer together in time and space?
13. How are methods of communicating over distance changing and improving?
14. Why are many and varied service people needed to keep communication systems working efficiently?
15. How does the wise use of communication keep citizens in a democracy well informed?
16. How do good human relationships depend upon communication?
17. How does communication make the free exchange of ideas among groups and individuals possible?
18. Why is free communication among peoples essential to the democratic process?
19. How does communication influence people's behavior?

When teacher and children have recorded the problems they wish to solve, the initiation has served its primary purpose. The first stage of the development of the area of learning pertaining to communication is finished, and the children and teacher are ready to move ahead into their search in depth for information about it.

CONTENT OUTLINE

The content outline includes the specific learnings and related facts essential to the development of each understanding. For example, following is an outline of the content from which a selected understanding is derived.

Understanding: Efficient means of communication have overcome the barriers of distance; consequently, people everywhere can communicate with each other.

I. The telephone, telegraph, and mail service serve important purposes in the life of the community.
  A. Living together in a community requires frequent communication.
    1. The promotion of business depends on communication.
    2. Planning for and running the community require the use of communication facilities.
    3. Many kinds of social arrangements are made by telephone and letter.
    4. Home life runs more smoothly when communication over distance is easy.
    5. Friendships are extended and cooperative action is encouraged by efficient communication services.
    6. Reporting emergencies and securing aid depend on instant communication.
  B. Each type of communication service serves special purposes.
    1. The telephone is useful when a person wishes to speak with someone who is not present.
    2. The telegraph is used when there is need for rapid communication with someone not available by telephone.
    3. Mail service is useful when it is not possible or necessary to reach a person by telephone or telegraph.
  C. Each type has special advantages and disadvantages.
    1. Letters are inexpensive and the length of message is unlimited; receiving an answer often takes time.
    2. Telephoning is the speediest method of communicating over distance with another individual; it is relatively expensive; the response is immediate.
    3. The telegram serves as a permanent record of a message or transaction; the message is generally limited in length and relatively expensive; the response is reasonably rapid but not instantaneous.
II. As people find ways to communicate with each other, the distances between them seem to become smaller.
  A. Communication by telephone, telegraph, and mail helps individuals and groups exchange ideas and resolve their differences.
  B. Modern communication helps various parts of a country to be almost as close as next-door neighbors.
  C. Since it is possible to talk with someone in a distant land in a matter of minutes, the world seems quite small.
  D. Communication with people of other countries broadens horizons and leads to better understanding.
  E. Because communication has made the world seem smaller, it is more and more important that people understand the ideas and problems of their neighbors.
  F. Improved communication has made it possible for communities and countries to cooperate more easily.
III. Methods of communicating over distance are changing and improving in many ways.
  A. Long-distance communication in the past was not always fast or efficient.
    1. Early mail service was carried on by runner or on horseback.
    2. Carrier pigeons served in both ancient and modern times.

3. Messages in early times did not always involve speaking or writing.
   a. Sounds carried messages—drums, bells.
   b. Smoke signals were used by primitive peoples.
   c. Beacon lights were used to send messages.
   d. Special objects passed from sender to receiver conveyed special messages.
B. Faster means of transportation improved the delivery of mail.
C. Electricity made instant communication possible.
D. Many persons, some whose names are unknown, contributed to the improvement of communication facilities.
   1. Our postal service began in colonial times.
   2. Samuel Morse invented the telegraph in 1837; Thomas Edison also contributed to its improvement.
   3. Alexander Graham Bell invented the telephone in 1876.
   4. Others have helped to further develop and perfect these facilities.
E. Telephone service is continually improving.
   1. It extends to almost all parts of the world; many messages can be transmitted at one time.
   2. Direct dialing of all phones will be possible in the future.
   3. Mobile telephones, private line services, and teletypewriters are new developments.
   4. The televisionfone, or picture-phone, will help speakers see each other.
F. Telegraph service has become increasingly effective.
   1. The variety of messages that can be sent by telegraph has increased.
   2. The teleprinter, which sends signals over the line to another teleprinter, is used in many business offices.
   3. Private wire telegraph systems are available to business and industry.
   4. Special services, such as sending flowers and money by wire, are now possible.
   5. Radio beam systems, which are replacing the pole line, make possible transmission of many messages simultaneously.
G. Mail service has become more and more dependable.
   1. Sending letters and things by mail is a very safe and efficient way to transmit them.
   2. Trains, buses, ships, and planes help to transport mail.
   3. Registry of letters, money orders, special delivery, and special attention to stamp collectors are some of the special services of the postal department.
   4. Mail delivery is now possible for almost every householder in our country.
   5. Canceling machines, stamp-vending machines, zip codes, and mailing meters have helped to speed up the mail service.
IV. Many communication workers are required to maintain and operate the telephone, telegraph, and postal services.
A. We meet many communication workers during the course of a day.
B. There are many unseen workers who help to maintain these services.
C. All these workers have special skills to help them do their jobs efficiently.
D. All these services are becoming more and more automated; new machines are performing many jobs once done by individual workers.
E. Each communication worker depends upon other community workers in carrying out his job.

F. Many workers in all kinds of businesses and community activities are concerned with reports, bills, letters, and advertising that contain information to be communicated to others.

V. Proper use of communication devices assures speed and accuracy in sending and receiving messages and helps to maintain the efficiency of the equipment.

   A. There are specific instructions for sending telegraph messages of various types.

   B. There are rules of courtesy to be observed in using the telephone.

   C. There are rules for the preparation and sending of letters.

   D. When users observe these procedures, they help communication workers function more efficiently.

   E. Reporting inefficient service or defective equipment to the proper authorities helps to keep the services operating well.

EXPERIENCES

Experiences are arranged in chart form to show clearly relationships between specific learnings, secondary problems, and basic understandings; between purposes and experiences; and between experiences that solve problems and experiences that reinforce and enrich learning.

Charts of experiences that develop specific learnings and secondary problems related to a selected understanding appear on pages 360–369.

CULMINATING EXPERIENCES

The culminating experience functions to organize, summarize, and pull together knowledge gained from activities and experiences, and synthesizes facts and information to form generalizations about the area of learning.

In the culminating experience, the group works together in planning and presenting whatever it decides to do. Thus it also furthers children's experience in planning cooperatively, in assuming responsibility, and in fulfilling obligations. The area of learning may be brought to a close in a variety of ways. The following are examples of possible summarizing and culminating experiences.

1. Writing and enacting a series of episodes depicting the evolution of communication from the days of the caveman to the present.

2. Assembling in book form with illustrations information about communication as it relates to community life.

3. Creating a large wall mural that highlights the role of communication in community living.

4. Dramatic play enactments of a variety of situations in which communication is vitally important.

5. Writing a script and producing a mock television program on the subject, "Communication, Past, Present, and Future."

6. Presenting an open house to exhibit what pupils have accomplished in the area of learning.

Among many possible ways to summarize learnings and further sociocivic behavior, the open house offers many opportunities for all to see how and what the children have learned about communication and its effects on community living. Following are steps in development of this type of culminating experience.

1. In the teacher's preliminary planning he thinks about his children's progress from the beginning to the terminal point of the area of learning. He reviews

papers they have written, surveys the projects they have completed, evaluates their research and the charts, murals, diagrams, and displays they have constructed, and decides that an open house would serve his purposes.

2. Acting on his decision to use the open house as a culminating experience, he engages children in a discussion about the need to summarize learnings, explores with them ways to do so, and lays the groundwork for the experience.

   a. He guides them toward identifying basic understandings about communication to be derived from the potpourri of information acquired.
   b. He discusses with them ways to summarize and organize this information.
   c. He helps them identify gaps in information and set up plans for experiences that will yield the desired information.
   d. He helps them select key committees, such as the tour guide committee, exhibit committee, program committee, refreshment committee, and publicity committee; draw up a plan for the open house; list needed materials; and choose a general chairman to pull details together.

3. The children decide on the best way to publicize their open house. They may put posters throughout the school and publish a special issue of their class newspaper. Feature articles in the paper may tell about the various times of tours, displays, and refreshments. Enough copies may be printed for the children's friends and parents and one for each of the school's bulletin boards. Each person in charge of a certain aspect of the open house may be responsible for an article about his committee's area; there may be other reporters also. Copies of this paper should be distributed several days in advance, and, to be sure that parents receive the papers, the children may send them through the mail, with a responsible group taking the papers to the post office.

4. The children plan the activities of the open house. Following are examples of these activities.

   a. The guests will be greeted at the door by tour guides, who will direct the people around the open house.
   b. Every half hour, in a corner of the room or in an adjoining room, some students will dramatize a play called "From Then to Now," written by several of the children and chosen from the best papers written on that subject. Through a series of short sketches the play will portray what communication was like before the telephone and how people communicated without modern conveniences. The dramatization will show children's understanding of how ways to communicate have developed and changed.
   c. An exhibit of communication devices with explanation by the children will show their understanding of the various devices and their uses.
   d. A display of scrapbooks containing pictures of communication workers performing their jobs will be explained by children in relation to two understandings: Communication provides a livelihood for many people. It takes many people working together to keep communication devices operating.
   e. After the tour visitors will be free to browse among the exhibits; the children and teacher will answer questions asked by guests.

This open house ties together the learning the children have acquired and enables them to see in an inclusive way what and how much they have learned through their search for information about the way communication affects community living.

UNDERSTANDING: EFFICIENT MEANS OF COMMUNICATION HAVE OVERCOME THE BARRIERS OF DISTANCE; CONSEQUENTLY, PEOPLE EVERYWHERE CAN COMMUNICATE WITH EACH OTHER.

SECONDARY PROBLEM: HOW DO THE TELEPHONE, TELEGRAPH, AND MAIL SERVICE HELP PEOPLE COMMUNICATE WITH EACH OTHER OVER DISTANCE?

SPECIFIC LEARNING: THE TELEPHONE, TELEGRAPH, AND MAIL SERVICE EACH SERVES IMPORTANT PURPOSES IN THE LIFE OF THE COMMUNITY.

Experiences That Solve Problems		Experiences That Reinforce and Enrich Learnings	
READING	DIRECT EXPERIENCES	RELATED SKILLS	CREATIVE ACTIVITIES
Pupils select from a variety of books about communication displayed on the reading table. The teacher assists each to find content appropriate to his reading level. In the follow-up discussion pupils identify ways in which people may communicate over distance and list advantages and disadvantages of each. Purpose: To build background information about various means of interpersonal communication over distance.		Pupils review their knowledge of the use of index and table of contents to locate reading material about communication. Pupils begin a dictionary of communication terms they encounter in their reading.	

Pupils organize in committees to survey home, school, and business uses of the telephone, telegraph, and mail service. They compile the information in chart form. Purpose: To clarify the role of communication in the community.

Pupils review and practice skills in interviewing.

As a result of their survey of uses of communication in the community, pupils may try to imagine a day without the telephone, telegraph, or postal service from the point of view of various persons in the community—the doctor, the teacher, the police, etc. The resulting complications make interesting stories or dramatizations.

Pupils use their skill in mathematics to determine costs of various types of communication as a factor in determining usefulness for various purposes.

361

UNDERSTANDING: EFFICIENT MEANS OF COMMUNICATION HAVE OVERCOME THE BARRIERS OF DISTANCE; CONSEQUENTLY, PEOPLE EVERYWHERE CAN COMMUNICATE WITH EACH OTHER.

SECONDARY PROBLEM: HOW DOES INCREASING COMMUNICATION AMONG PEOPLE EVERYWHERE BRING THEM CLOSER TOGETHER IN TIME AND SPACE?

SPECIFIC LEARNING: AS PEOPLE FIND WAYS TO COMMUNICATE WITH EACH OTHER, THE DISTANCES BETWEEN THEM SEEM TO BECOME SMALLER.

Experiences That Solve Problems		Experiences That Reinforce and Enrich Learnings	
READING	DIRECT EXPERIENCES	RELATED SKILLS	CREATIVE ACTIVITIES
Pupils work in interest groups, each group selecting a device important in world-wide communication and doing simple library research to prepare its report. Purpose: To secure specific information about international communication systems.	Pupils invite foreign guests to discuss communication facilities in their countries. Purpose: To gather firsthand information to answer questions.	Pupils review group work skills and plan study groups. Pupils practice skills needed in giving interesting reports. Pupils learn how to use a simple library card catalogue.	

Pupils undertake a correspondence project with foreign children. Purpose: To demonstrate how communication over distance can build understanding among people.

Pupils review ways in which friendly letters can be interesting and informative.

Pupils may develop art work to use in communicating ideas and information to their foreign correspondents.

Pupils collect stamps from around the world and display them on a world map. Purpose: To show the spread of international mail service.

Pupils use map skills in arranging their display.

Pupils may become interested in the stories, myths, and historical events represented by stamp issues from various countries.

Pupils organize facts and devise a bar graph to show how increased speed of communication has reduced the "distance" between places. Purpose: To visualize a difficult concept.

Pupils use mathematical skills in converting verbal data to numerical data in constructing the bar graph.

UNDERSTANDING: EFFICIENT MEANS OF COMMUNICATION HAVE OVERCOME THE BARRIERS OF DISTANCE; CONSEQUENTLY, PEOPLE EVERYWHERE CAN COMMUNICATE WITH EACH OTHER.

SECONDARY PROBLEM: How are methods of communicating over distance changing and improving?

SPECIFIC LEARNING: Methods of communicating over distance are changing and improving in many ways.

Experiences That Solve Problems		Experiences That Reinforce and Enrich Learnings	
READING	DIRECT EXPERIENCES	RELATED SKILLS	CREATIVE ACTIVITIES
Pupils work in groups with a variety of materials at their reading levels. Slower readers use *We Look Around Us*, pp. 173–192, and *You and the Community*, pp. 105–117. Superior readers choose from encyclopedias and biographies of important inventors; others use *The Story of Our Country*, pp. 389–402, and *Your Country and Mine*, pp. 344–359. Purpose: To record steps in the development of communication over distance.	Pupils invite a resource visitor from the telephone office. Purpose: To secure up-to-date information about future developments in telephone service. Pupils assemble information from their reading for the construction of a time line. Purpose: To show the progress of communication in modern times. Pupils see two films, *Pony Express* (Barr) and *Communication—Story of Its Development* (Coronet) as sources of information for their "then and now" mural. Purpose: To emphasize the contrast between early and modern means of communication.	Pupils review skills in caring for guests courteously. Pupils use skills in mathematics to set up their time line.	Pupils may develop a mural portraying the old and new in person-to-person communication over distance. Pupils may enjoy dramatizing portions of such books as *Alexander Graham Bell—Man of Sound* by Montgomery or *Thomas Alva Edison* by Clark.

Pupils show pony express route and modern airmail routes on an outline map. Purpose: To make graphic increased facilities for delivery of mail.

Pupils determine symbols and locations needed to show mail routes on a map.

Pupils construct a simple telegraph key and disassemble an old-style telephone. Purpose: To compare these devices with modern telephone and telegraph equipment.

Pupils practice skills in following directions for the construction of the telegraph key.

UNDERSTANDING: EFFICIENT MEANS OF COMMUNICATION HAVE OVERCOME THE BARRIERS OF DISTANCE; CONSEQUENTLY, PEOPLE EVERYWHERE CAN COMMUNICATE WITH EACH OTHER.

SECONDARY PROBLEM: WHY ARE MANY AND VARIED SERVICE PEOPLE NEEDED TO KEEP COMMUNICATION SYSTEMS WORKING EFFICIENTLY?

SPECIFIC LEARNING: MANY COMMUNICATION WORKERS ARE REQUIRED TO MAINTAIN AND OPERATE THE TELEPHONE, TELEGRAPH, AND POSTAL SYSTEMS.

Experiences That Solve Problems		*Experiences That Reinforce and Enrich Learnings*	
READING	DIRECT EXPERIENCES	RELATED SKILLS	CREATIVE ACTIVITIES
	Small groups with parent sponsors visit telephone, telegraph, and post offices and report to the class the answers to questions previously identified by pupils. Purpose: To see communication workers at their jobs and to secure firsthand information from them.	Pupils make use of group planning skills in setting up the field trips. Pupils review letter writing skills in preparation for making arrangements for the trips. Pupils use skills in mathematics in organizing groups for trips and in planning for lunch and transportation expenses.	Pupils carry sketching materials with them on field trips in order to capture ideas for a mural they may wish to create later.

Pupils arrange pictures on bulletin board to show how communication workers depend upon each other and upon other workers to do their jobs. Purpose: To avoid seeing each job as an isolated task.

Pupils use filmstrips such as *Our Post Office* (EBF) and *Telephones for the Community* (EBF) and put into chart form the steps in each process of communication. Purpose: To reinforce learnings or substitute for field trips.

Pupils consider attractive arrangement of bulletin board and prepare necessary captions for the display.

Pupils may be encouraged to interpret with rhythm instruments the sounds they experienced on their visits to communication services.

Pupils enjoy and perhaps dramatize the story *Owney, the Postal Dog* (*Postal Service News*, Vol. 1, No. 4 [April, 1955], p. 10).

UNDERSTANDING: EFFICIENT MEANS OF COMMUNICATION HAVE OVERCOME THE BARRIERS OF DISTANCE; CONSEQUENTLY, PEOPLE EVERYWHERE CAN COMMUNICATE WITH EACH OTHER.

SECONDARY PROBLEM: WHY SHOULD USERS OF COMMUNICATION DEVICES KNOW ABOUT THEIR USE?

SPECIFIC LEARNING: PROPER USE OF COMMUNICATION DEVICES ASSURES SPEED AND ACCURACY IN SENDING AND RECEIVING MESSAGES AND HELPS TO MAINTAIN THE EFFICIENCY OF THE DEVICES.

Experiences That Solve Problems		*Experiences That Reinforce and Enrich Learnings*	
READING	DIRECT EXPERIENCES	RELATED SKILLS	CREATIVE ACTIVITIES
	During study trips pupils ask for special information about maintenance of communication devices and request demonstrations by persons in charge. Purpose: To gather official information to answer questions about care and use of equipment.	Pupils discuss and decide upon ways to take notes during their study trips.	Pupils may be interested in dramatizing correct and incorrect ways of using communication devices; creative efforts may be stimulated by suggesting that pupils write a story as told by a misused telephone or the adventures of an improperly addressed letter.
		Pupils use letter writing skills in sending notes of appreciation to those who have helped them.	
Pupils use telephone directory and blank forms for telegrams to find information relative to the use of these services. Purpose: To read and interpret special sources of information.	Pupils use model telephone, complete telegram forms, and address and mail letters according to information given them. Purpose: To follow proper directions for use of equipment and materials.	Pupils practice skills in speaking clearly over the telephone.	
		Pupils learn writing techniques needed in composing telegrams.	

Pupils review information relative to writing letters and addressing envelopes correctly.

Pupils use number skills in weighing mail and computing postage and in determining the costs of various types of telegraphic messages.

EVALUATION

Evaluation techniques should be specifically related to the purposes, content, and experiences of the area of learning. Pupils' knowledge of content and their progress toward important understandings, attitudes, behaviors, and skills may be evaluated in a variety of ways. For example, following are suggestions for evaluation related to a selected understanding.

Understanding: Efficient means of communication have overcome the barriers of distance; consequently, people everywhere can communicate with each other.

Teacher and pupils share many evaluation experiences like those in this list.

1. Following the community survey, pupils assemble and organize their data, discussing the effectiveness of the techniques they used, the validity of the information gathered, and the usefulness of the survey idea.
2. Following the visit of resource persons from foreign countries, pupils compare information learned with what they have read in books, identify still unanswered questions, and evaluate their skill in this social situation.
3. Pupils evaluate their time lines and graphs by checking carefully to make sure the information is correct and clear. They may suggest ways to improve such projects.
4. Pupils identify questions to be used in viewing a film and evaluate the film's usefulness in terms of its appropriateness to their purpose and how adequately it answers their questions.
5. The field trip to see various communication workers in action is followed by discussion of the values of the trip, of information obtained, of appropriate methods to preserve information, and of ways to improve the management of the experience.
6. Pupils evaluate their bulletin board display with attention to its arrangement and its effectiveness in clarifying an idea.
7. Pupils evaluate their construction activities by recalling the purpose of each and discussing their success in achieving it.

When the teacher needs more structured responses upon which to base evaluation, he may use some of the following:

1. Pupils put into proper sequence important events in the development of communication which the teacher has listed in random order.
2. Pupils list the important means of communication over distance and give the purposes for which each is used, or match means of communication with the most important purpose for each.
3. Pupils state the advantages and disadvantages of each means of communication.
4. Pupils list ways in which selected community businesses and services make use of telephone, telegram, and postal service.
5. Pupils match names of communication workers with descriptions of their jobs.
6. Pupils compare communication before 1837 with that after 1837.
7. Pupils show in some graphic way how a communication worker depends upon other workers in order to do his job.
8. Pupils put in order a random list of steps in the process of communication by mail.
9. Pupils match new vocabulary words—teleprinter, cable, pony express, and so on—with appropriate meanings.

10. From a list prepared by the teacher of sentences that include both generalizations and simple facts, pupils select the ideas that are important for all of them to remember.
11. Pupils study a group of related facts about communication and formulate the generalizations that may be drawn from the facts given.
12. The teacher draws information about pupil attitudes from their casual conversation and from class discussions about communication.
13. The teacher notes children's relationships with communication workers and foreign guests.
14. The teacher describes some problem situations concerning the proper use of telephone, telegraph, and postal service and asks pupils to select from among some possible solutions or asks pupils to tell what they would do.
15. Pupils demonstrate the following: using the telephone directory, using the telephone, preparing a telegram, addressing an envelope correctly, getting a money order, and so on.
16. The teacher observes children's use of communication devices at school and may ask for a report from parents about home use of the telephone and mail service.
17. Pupils answer such questions as these: What did you like best about this part of our study about communication? What were the most important things you learned about communication? Why do you think we chose communication as the subject for our study?

BIBLIOGRAPHY

References for Teachers

Berlo, David Kenneth, *The Process of Communication*. New York: Holt, Rinehart and Winston, Inc., 1960. Describes the scope and purpose of communication, the factors involved in the process, and the role of language in human behavior.

Doblhofer, Ernst, *Voices in Stone*. New York: The Viking Press, Inc., 1961. Traces the history of written language.

Dunlap, O. E., Jr., *Communications in Space*. New York: Harper & Row, Publishers, 1962. Contains information about use of satellites in communication.

Floherty, John J., *Man Against Distance, The Story of Communication*. Philadelphia: J. B. Lippincott Company, 1954. Describes how man has overcome barriers of distance through the invention of various communication devices.

Hogben, Lancelot, *The Wonderful World of Communication*. New York: Doubleday & Company, Inc., 1959. Traces the development of communication from earliest times.

Lacy, Dan M., *Freedom and Communications*. Urbana: University of Illinois Press, 1961. Emphasizes the importance of communication in a free world.

Schramm, Wilbur, *Mass Communication*. Urbana: University of Illinois Press, 1960. Surveys mass communication, emphasizing how these media may be used effectively.

Trade Books for Children

Anderson, Dorothy, *Junior Science Book of Sound*. Champaign, Ill.: Garrard Press, 1962. Contains many interesting experiments with sound.

Buehr, Walter, *Sending the Word*. New York: G. P. Putnam's Sons, 1959. Presents, with interesting illustrations, facts about communication.

Clark, G. Glenwood, *Thomas Alva Edison*. New York: Aladdin Books, 1950. Gives an interesting account of the inventor's life.

Cooke, David Coxe, *Behind the Scenes in Television*. New York: Dodd, Mead & Company, Inc., 1958. Describes the process of making books.

Cooke, David Coxe, *How Books Are Made*. New York: Dodd, Mead & Company, Inc., 1963. Describes the process of making books.

Epstein, Sam, and Beryl Epstein, *The First Book of Codes and Ciphers*. New York: Franklin Watts, Inc., 1956. Describes the use of many kinds of codes and ciphers in business, military, and diplomatic communications.

Everson, William K., *The American Movie*. New York: Atheneum Publishers, 1963. Tells the story of the development of motion pictures.

Folsom, Franklin, *The Language Book*. New York: Grosset & Dunlap, Inc., 1963. Tells the story of the development of language.

Foster, Joanna, *Pages, Pictures, and Print: A Book in the Making*. New York: Harcourt, Brace & World, Inc., 1958. Describes clearly and with illustrations how a book is created.

Gould, Jack, *All About Radio and Television*. New York: Random House, Inc., 1958. Gives the principles of transmission by radio and television with explanations in simple language and diagrams.

Greene, Carla, *I Want to Be a News Reporter*. Chicago: Children's Press, Inc., 1958. Describes the work of a reporter as it is observed by a boy on an assignment with his uncle.

Greene, Carla, *I Want to Be a Telephone Operator*. Chicago: Children's Press, Inc., 1958. Tells what the telephone operator does and emphasizes the many people involved in transmitting a message by telephone.

Miner, O. Irene, *The True Book of Communication*. Chicago: Children's Press, Inc., 1960. Describes the many different ways in which messages are sent and received.

Miner, O. Irene, *The True Book of Our Post Office and Its Helpers*. Chicago: Children's Press, Inc., 1955. Describes what happens to mail from the time it is sent until it is received.

Montgomery, Elizabeth, *Alexander Graham Bell*. Champaign, Ill.: Garrard Press, 1963. Tells the story of the inventor in simple language.

Nathan, Adele Gutman, *The First Transatlantic Cable*. New York: Random House, Inc., 1959. Brings out the vision and courage of those who planned and built the cable.

Neurath, Marie, *Around the World in a Flash*. New York: Lothrop, Lee & Shepard Co., Inc., 1954. Emphasizes the ease with which messages can be transmitted around the world.

Osmond, Edward, *From Drumbeat to Tickertape*. New York: Criterion Books, Inc., 1960. Tells the story of communication from early forms of writing to modern printing, radio, and television.

Posin, Daniel Q., *What Is Electronic Communication?* Chicago: Benefic Press, 1961. Explains electron flow and the use of electronics in radio and television.

Shapp, Martha, *Let's Find Out What the Signs Say*. New York: Franklin Watts, Inc., 1959. Calls attention to the many ways in which signs communicate messages.

Sterne, Emma, *Watchtowers and Drums*. New York: Aladdin Books, 1953. Shows how communication was used by the pioneers moving west.

Textbooks for Children

Barker, Eugene C., Marie Alsager, and Walter P. Webb, *The Story of Our Country* (Grade 5). New York: Harper & Row, Publishers, Inc., 1956, pp. 389–405. Gives historical information about the development of communication in the United States.

Brown, Gertrude Stephens, *Your Country and Mine* (Grade 5). Boston: Ginn & Company, 1960, pp. 344–359. Describes communication from colonial times to the present.

Eibling, Harold H., Fred M. King, and James Harlow, *Our Country's Story* (Grade 4). River Forest, Ill.: Laidlaw Brothers, Publishers, 1958, pp. 298–304. Gives a brief history of communication in the United States.

Hanna, Paul R., and Genevieve A. Hoyt, *In the Neighborhood* (Grade 2). Chicago: Scott, Foresman and Company, 1958, pp. 42–49, 124–135. Contains simply written material about the newspaper and mail service.

Hunnicutt, C. W., and Jean D. Grambs, *We Look Around Us* (Grade 3). Syracuse, N. Y.: The L. W. Singer Company, Inc., 1963, pp. 173–192. Discusses the uses of communication with special attention to television.

Samford, Clarence, Edith McCall, and Ruth Gue, *You and the Neighborhood* (Grade 2). Chicago: Benefic Press, 1963, pp. 92–103. Gives simply written information about a variety of means of communication.

Samford, Clarence, Edith McCall, and Ruth Gue, *You and the Community* (Grade 3). Chicago: Benefic Press, 1963, pp. 105–137. Stresses the importance of communication in the community.

Films

Communication and Our Town. 10 minutes, sound, black and white. Vocational Guidance Films. Intermediate grades. Shows many types of communication found in the average town.

Communication—Story of Its Development. 11 minutes, sound, black and white. Coronet. Upper grades. Gives information about the development of communications from primitive man to present-day techniques.

Letter to Grandmother. 19 minutes, sound, color or black and white. Coronet Films. Primary grades. Shows the journey of a letter from sender to receiver.

Newspaper Story. 17 minutes, sound, black and white. Encyclopaedia Britannica Films. Intermediate grades. Follows the newspaper story of a little girl rescued by boy scouts.

Pony Express. 12 minutes, sound, color or black and white. Arthur Barr Films. Intermediate grades. Pictures the activities of the pony express, the equipment used, the work of the riders, and the stopping places along route.

Television in Your Community. 11 minutes, sound, color or black and white. Coronet Films. Intermediate grades. Demonstrates the operation of a television station, showing various kinds of equipment in use.

Filmstrips

Covering the News. 33 frames, color. Vis-Ta Films. Elementary grades. Shows how the news is gathered by following the coverage of a single story.

Mailman. 70 frames, black and white. Encyclopaedia Brittanica Films. Primary grades. Develops appreciation of the work of the mail carrier.

Our Post Office. 48 frames, color. Encyclopaedia Brittanica Films. Primary grades. Pictures real people at work in the post office; uses captions that pupils can read.

Preparation of Live Television. 30 frames, color. Vis-Ta Films. Elementary grades. Shows how a television show is put on the air.

Telephones for the Community. 52 frames, color. Encyclopaedia Brittanica Films. Intermediate grades. Shows how the community depends upon telephone service.

INDEX

A

Adams, Fay, 107n, 140n, 156n, 167n, 284n, 299n
Alexander, Marthann, 163n
Ambrose, Edna, 85n
American heritage, 9, 25, 320
Anderson, Harold H., 207n
Andrews, Gladys, 205n, 207n
Anthropology, 15, 16, 74, 327
Area of learning, 22
    cooperative planning in, 50–59
    creative activities and, 211–222
    criteria for selecting problems for, 23–24
    culmination of, 259ff
    evaluation in, 23, 283–304
    initiation of, 29ff
    problem solving in, 56–58
    related skills in, role of, 232–234
    role of experience in, 74ff
    role of reading in, 98–104
    selection of, 24–25
Arnsdorf, V. E., 107n
Arts and crafts, 217–219
Attitudes, defined, 84
    development of, 84–86
    informal tests of, 292–295
    leading to action, 85
    as objectives of area of learning, 84–86, 352–353
    positive, 86

Audio-visual resources, 88, 181ff
    charts, diagrams, graphs, 191–193
    films, filmstrips, slides, 184–185
    pictures, 185–186
    radio and television, 187–188
    recordings, 186–187
    realia, 189–191
Automation, 7–8

B

Barnes, Fred P., 180n
Barron, Frank, 224n
Bathurst, Effie G., 128n
Behaviors, through experiences, 86–87
    informal tests of, 292–295
    as objectives of area of learning, 86–87, 352–353
Berry, Frances M., 168n, 170n
Bingham, Alma, 24n
Blair, Glenn Myers, 260n
Bonser, Frederick Gordon, 163n
Brogan, Peggy, 312, 313n
Brown, James, 160n
Brown, Ralph Adams, 108n
Bruner, Herbert B., 129n
Bruner, Jerome, 20, 260n, 314n, 318n
Burr, James B., 247n
Burrows, Alvina Treut, 104n, 108n, 111n

C